SPANISH STILL LIFE
from Velázquez to Goya

Sponsored by **Glaxo**

SPANISH STILL LIFE
from Velázquez to Goya

William B. Jordan and Peter Cherry

National Gallery Publications, London
Distributed by Yale University Press

The authors dedicate this work to the memory of
William Bryan Jordan (1896–1965) and Dixie Owen Jordan (1908–87)
and to the memory of S.D. Cherry (1933–93)

This book was published to accompany an exhibition at
The National Gallery, London
22 February–21 May 1995

First published in Great Britain in 1995 by
National Gallery Publications Limited
5/6 Pall Mall East, London SW1Y 5BA

NGPL ISBN 1 85709 063 2 hardback
525190
NGPL ISBN 1 85709 064 0 paperback
525191

British Library Cataloguing-in-Publication Data.
A catalogue record is available from the British Library.

Library of Congress Catalog Card Number: 94–73938

Editors: Felicity Luard and Halina Sand
Designed by Andrew Shoolbred

Index by Indexing Specialists, Hove

Printed and bound in Great Britain by
Butler and Tanner, Frome and London

Front cover: Juan Sánchez Cotán, *Still Life with Quince, Cabbage, Melon
and Cucumber* (cat. 1, detail).
Back cover (hardback): Luis Meléndez, *Still Life with Oranges and Walnuts*
(cat. 58).
Frontispiece: Juan de Arellano, *Basket of Flowers* (cat. 51, detail).

Acknowledgements

We are grateful to Neil MacGregor and the staff of the National Gallery, most especially to Gabriele Finaldi, Curator of Later Italian and Spanish Painting, who directed the exhibition project from its inception with intelligence, skill and unfailing enthusiasm. The exhibition could not have been realised without the smooth coordination provided by Christopher Brown, Michael Wilson, and their colleagues in the exhibitions, design and registrar's departments, press office and photographic department; nor could the catalogue have been completed without the patient and thorough oversight of Felicity Luard, and professional contribution of the production and publishing departments of National Gallery Publications Limited. We would also like to thank Andrew Shoolbred for his excellent book design. For the Spanish edition of the catalogue we are extremely grateful to Santiago Saavedra and Lola Gómez de Aranda of Ediciones El Viso, Madrid.

The friends and colleagues who have helped us are so numerous that space does not permit us to cite the specific contribution of each. But above all, we wish to express our gratitude to Manuela B. Mena Marqués, Deputy Director of the Museo del Prado, for her unstinting generosity in supporting our research and for supervising the museum's conservation staff, who cleaned all the paintings lent from the Prado for this exhibition. Alfonso E. Pérez Sánchez has been a generous friend over the years, and without his previous work in the field, ours would have been seriously handicapped.

Numerous museum colleagues have helped us in our work and have, in a real sense, contributed to this exhibition and its catalogue. We especially wish to thank: Trinidad de Antonio, Claire Barry, Marina Cano Cuesta, Keith Christiansen, María Margarita Cuyàs, Adela Espinós Díaz, María Concepción García Saíz, María del Carmen Garrido, Sam Heath, Reino Liefkes, Susana López, Darin Marshall, Juan Martínez, Jane Munroe, Mercedes Orihuela Maeso, Enrique Pareja López, Wolfgang Prohaska, Elena Ramírez-Montesinos, Claudie Ressort, Andrea Rothe, María Encarnación Sánchez Torrente, George Shackelford, Chia-Chun Shih, Jack Soultanian, Yvonne Szafran, Allen Townsend, Malcolm Warner, Martha Wolf, the staff of the Prado Conservation Department.

Many other friends and scholars have also provided valuable aid and information: Juan Ramón Aparicio, Teresa Baratech, José Luis Barrio Moya, Bill Blass, Jonathan Brown, Jésus Cantera Montenegro, Anne Crookshank, Victor Dixon, Jennifer Fletcher, Maria Gilbert, Nigel Glendinning, Amador Grinyó Andrés, Enriqueta Harris Frankfort, Duncan Kinkead, Alastair Laing, Dámaso de Lario, Rosa López Torrijos, Cristina Marsans, Melvina McKendrick, Edward McParland, Rosemarie Mulcahy, Priscilla Muller, Leslie Anne Nelson, Aisling O'Donoghue, César Palomino Tossas, Alan Paterson, John Richardson, Antonio Sánchez Barriga, Sarah Schroth, Tracy Schuster, Natacha Seseña, Juan Miguel Serrera, Robert Shepherd, Edward Sullivan, Carol Togneri Dowd, Juliet Wilson Bareau.

Scholars are often indebted to the assistance of picture dealers who are able to direct them to works they have sold or of whose existence they are aware in private collections. We wish to acknowledge the contributions of the following: Raimon Maragall, Xavier Vila, Barcelona; Christopher Gibbs, Derek Johns, Richard Knight, Patrick Matthiesen, Rodney Merrington, Peter Mitchell, Stephen Rich, Rafael Valls, London; Paloma Fernández Gortázar, Casilda Fernández-Villaverde, José Antonio Giménez-Arnau, Christopher González-Aller, Miguel Granados, Enrique Gutiérrez de Calderón, Guillermo de Osma, Edmund Peel, Rafael Pérez Hernando, José I. Saldaña Suances, José Antonio de Urbina, Juan Várez, Richard de Willermin, Madrid; Etienne Breton, Paris; Kurt von Schuschnigg, Adam Williams, New York; David H. Koester, Zurich.

With special gratitude for their loyal friendship and personal support, we wish to thank Maria Redpath, Jo Beech, John Bennett, Catherine Marshall, Seán Mulcahy and Robert Brownlee.

WBJ, PC

Map of Spain showing towns mentioned in the text.

Contents

Sponsor's Preface

Glaxo is proud to sponsor this exhibition comprising some of the finest Spanish still-life paintings from collections around the world. This display, the first of its kind to be staged in Britain, reveals the richness and diversity of the still-life tradition in Spain, and presents to the British public works of great beauty. The National Gallery is to be congratulated on bringing a collection of such quality to London.

This is Glaxo's first major association with the Gallery. As one of Britain's leading companies, we take our commitment to the visual and performing arts seriously, not only here, but in the many communities around the world in which our subsidiary companies operate.

Glaxo has a significant pharmaceutical research, manufacturing and marketing presence in Spain, reflecting a healthy exchange of scientific and medical expertise. I hope that this exhibition will contribute to an even stronger link between Britain and Spain in terms of wider appreciation of an important but little-known aspect of the Spanish artistic heritage.

Sir Richard Sykes
Deputy Chairman and Chief Executive
Glaxo plc

Foreword

This exhibition, which gathers together pictures from all over Europe and America, is about a tradition which flourished for over two hundred years in Spain, was practised by most of the leading Spanish artists of the seventeenth and eighteenth centuries, and was patronised by kings and cardinals. It produced some supremely accomplished and moving paintings. Yet it is hardly to be glimpsed in public collections in this country. True, some of the highest achievements of Velázquez in this field are indeed here: the eggs cooking slowly in the National Gallery in Edinburgh must surely be the greatest fried eggs in European art; and no visitor to the Wellington Museum in Apsley House forgets the huge water-seller's bottle, matt with condensation, one of those rare objects in painting of which you know the temperature as well as the texture. But now, for the first time in Britain, this exhibition makes it possible to look at these works in context.

And a complex context it is. It is a striking fact of art history that, for reasons which are far from clear, still life, as a subject in itself, emerges quite suddenly at the end of the sixteenth century in northern Italy, the Low Countries and Spain – all three areas effectively dominated by the Spanish crown. In Spain, it evolves amid a dense web of associations, at times alluding to the lost still lifes celebrated by the authors of classical antiquity, at others suggesting the essential vanity of all human existence. Part of the game is obviously to make us marvel at the technical virtuosity of the artist. Yet underlying many of the paintings is a spiritual intensity that compels us to consider the meaning and the point of the – often very ordinary – things represented.

In these pictures, in fact, we confront one of the key purposes of all painting. The objects shown are usually of little inherent value, and the paints used have no great worth. There is no story, often not even a symbolic significance. Yet the paintings make us slow down, look carefully at a walnut, a jug or a parsnip, make us realise that we had never truly looked at one before, and acknowledge how astonishing they are. After looking at Zurbarán, a jug will never be the same again, after Sánchez Cotán, no cabbage can seem ordinary. At their best, these paintings imbue the everyday with the miraculous, they allow us to keep recovering that miracle, and they change the way we look at the world.

This phenomenon is charted here, in the fullest study of Spanish still-life painting yet to appear in English, by two of the greatest authorities on it: Dr William B. Jordan, who organised the major exhibition, *Spanish Still Life in the Golden Age*, at the Kimbell Art Museum, Fort Worth, Texas, in 1985; and Dr Peter Cherry, the author of an important study on Spanish still life and genre painting in the first half of the seventeenth century.

This exhibition is possible only because of the great generosity of lenders, institutional and private, who entrusted their pictures to our care. To all of them we owe a debt of gratitude, but special mention must be made of our colleagues at the Prado, who were, as so often, prompt and open-hearted in their willingness to help and unstinting in their loans.

Our greatest debt is to Glaxo plc, who have supported the venture from the beginning, and who have enabled us to present to the British public for the first time this important part of the European tradition; Glaxo, S.A., supported the publication of the Spanish edition of the catalogue. On behalf of all at the National Gallery, and all who will see the exhibition, I should like to say thank you.

Neil MacGregor
Director of The National Gallery, London

Introduction

Towards the end of the sixteenth century certain painters throughout Europe began visually to explore the objects around them in a kind of picture that had not been painted since classical antiquity. The still life has become so integral a part of the pictorial tradition that it would be arbitrary to treat its origins as some kind of isolated phenomenon. Born as it was of forces that moulded the general culture of its time, the still life has continued to evolve as those forces have changed. The fact that it has continued to thrive among painters throughout the twentieth century means that we must look upon that initial episode of fertile creativity as a turning point in the history of art. Fascination with the impulse that lay behind the creative leap has led some of the great art historians of our century – among them Roberto Longhi, Charles Sterling and E.H. Gombrich – to seek to cast light upon it.

The development of still-life painting since 1600 has usually been studied within the larger context of the national school whose characteristics it shared. The development of the still life in Spain, the subject of this exhibition and its catalogue, has also been treated in this way. The national context, however, is unusual, owing to Spain's peculiar position in the world throughout its modern history. Isolated in a corner of Europe but tied by politics, diplomacy, commerce and ideas to far-flung cultures, it has proved at times remarkably resistant and at others remarkably receptive to developments from outside its borders. The picture collections of Madrid in the seventeenth century were incomparable for the catholicity of taste that informed them and for the rapidity with which major developments abroad were reflected in them. The best Spanish painters, despite their insularity, reached singular heights of originality, and when responding to the creativity of foreigners, they did so with exceptional vigour.

With the fewer than seventy paintings which comprise this exhibition, we cannot hope to illustrate every nuance in the development of a national school of still-life painting as rich and complex as that of Spain from 1600 to the early nineteenth century. But in this catalogue we have endeavoured to give an overview of that development which will help to enrich the reader's enjoyment and understanding of the pictures. In doing so, we are following in a tradition established over half a century ago in Spain itself.

All writers on Spanish still-life painting owe a fundamental debt to the pioneering research of Julio Cavestany, Marqués de Moret. His monumental exhibition *Floreros y bodegones en la pintura española*, held in Madrid in 1935, comprised 179 paintings from the seventeenth to the nineteenth centuries and was commemorated by a sumptuous illustrated catalogue which appeared in 1940. Not only was this the first scholarly monograph on Spanish still life, it was one of the first, and finest, to treat still-life painting from any European school. Its thoughtful discussion of the subject, documentary appendices and artists' biographies, based on original archival investigation, make it still an indispensable reference work for all interested in this field.

In 1983, Professor Alfonso E. Pérez Sánchez organised for the Museo del Prado an exhibition of similar scope, *Pintura española de bodegones y floreros de 1600 a Goya*, which included among its 190 paintings many works not shown in Cavestany's exhibition. This was accompanied by a lucid scholarly catalogue which exploited the most recent research to attain a deeper and more comprehensive picture of individual artists' activities and overall developments of still-life and flower painting in Spain than had hitherto been possible. A classic of its kind, this catalogue was updated and republished in book form in a French edition (1987) and was adapted to a recent exhibition in Tokyo (1992).

The present exhibition and its catalogue are the results of an intense and rewarding collaboration between the authors, a collaboration that occurred at the suggestion of the National Gallery. Each of us has worked and published independently in this field for many years. The opportunity to combine our different perspectives and to share accumulated information has led to insights which neither of us might have had independently.

In this catalogue we have tried to take advantage of and to acknowledge the contributions of all those who have advanced the scholarship of Spanish still-life painting, while at the same time presenting the results of our own research. Occasionally we have departed from the traditional attributions of certain paintings and where we did not know for certain we have tried to leave such questions open. It is our hope that this exhibition catalogue will encourage further work on the subject and that it will be succeeded by yet others which may answer some of the questions we have been unable to resolve.

William B. Jordan
Peter Cherry

The Still Life in Spain
Origins and Themes

Fig. 1 Unknown artist, *Comport of Pears*, 1590s. Oil on canvas, 27.5 x 27.5 cm. Madrid, Fundación Santamarca.

Fig. 2 Ambrogio Figino, *Still Life with Peaches on a Plate*, c.1595. Oil on panel, 21 x 30 cm. Bergamo, Lorenzelli collection.

Towards the end of the sixteenth century, artists in different parts of Europe began painting independent still lifes. Naturalistic still-life details had long been included in figural compositions, but the emergence of this new genre simultaneously in Italy, Flanders and Spain in the 1590s is not easy to explain.[1] It is a phenomenon integrally related to profound changes in the roles of art and artists in society which occurred at the end of the Renaissance. In Spain, the Toledan artist Blas de Prado (c.1546–1600) was painting fruit still lifes before 1593, and was followed by his pupil Juan Sánchez Cotán (1560–1627), whose earliest dated picture is from 1602 (cat. 3). The Sevillian painter and writer Francisco Pacheco (1564–1644) recalled in his *Arte de la pintura* (1649) that Blas de Prado had shown him some canvases of fruit (*lienzos de frutas*) which were 'very well painted'.[2] Prado had stayed in Seville while on his way to Morocco in May 1593 to serve the Jerife, or Moorish ruler, and the pictures were perhaps intended as gifts, souvenirs of Prado's native land that were more appropriate than figural works for a Muslim patron.[3]

No still-life paintings by Blas de Prado have yet come to light, although his name has been tentatively associated with three small, unsigned still lifes of fruit (fig. 1).[4] These Spanish paintings are similar in type to examples by early Lombard still-life painters such as Ambrogio Figino (1550–c.1608) and Fede Galizia (1578–1630), whose works may have been collected by members of the Spanish administration of

13

Milan (fig. 2).[5] Early Spanish still-life painting was not, however, dependent on the innovations of Italian artists, or, indeed, of Netherlandish artists such as Floris van Dijck (1575–1651) or Jan Brueghel the Elder (1568–1625). Developments in Spain were contemporaneous with those in other countries, and Sánchez Cotán's still lifes are highly original and quite unlike anything else produced at the time.

Still Life and the Challenge of Antiquity

A prerequisite for the appearance of the first still-life paintings was the *idea* of the pure still life. The still life had existed in classical antiquity, and modern sixteenth–century examples may be seen in the context of the Renaissance revival of this ancient genre.[6] Educated viewers in Spain, as elsewhere in Europe, were used to making comparisons between the ancient and modern worlds, usually in favour of the latter.[7] No Greek or Roman easel paintings had survived; but viewers were familiar with descriptions of the still lifes of classical artists such as Zeuxis, Parrhasius and Peiraikos, from ancient texts, principally Pliny the Elder's *Natural History*, which contains the only surviving history of ancient art, and the Elder Philostratus' *Imagines*, an account of an imaginary picture gallery in Naples. Spanish artists could read Pliny in Spanish translations published at the time Sánchez Cotán was painting his still lifes.[8] Rivalry with the fabled works of art of the past was a motivating force for artists, and the imitation of the ancients constituted for them a corollary of the imitation of nature. This relationship between antiquity and observation is unusually close in El Greco's early *Boy blowing on an Ember* (fig. 3), which is at once a study of naturalistic light effects and a recreation of an ancient prototype by Antiphilus of Alexandria.[9]

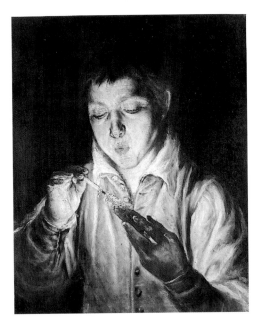

Fig. 3 El Greco, *Boy blowing on an Ember*, *c.*1570–5. Oil on canvas, 59 x 51 cm. Naples, Museo e Gallerie Nazionale di Capodimonte.

An important characteristic of the hyperbolic descriptions in the ancient texts is the high premium set on *mimesis*, or the imitation of the natural world.[10] Pliny, for example, praises Possis who modelled fruit and grapes in clay so naturalistically that nobody could tell them from the real thing.[11] The story of Zeuxis' grapes is a *topos* that is constantly repeated in the context of still–life painting: his fruit was so well painted that birds flew down and tried to peck at it.[12] Sixteenth-century painters' mastery of representational skills, combined with the challenge offered by the naturalism of antique precedents, led modern artists to paint their subject matter with emphatic verisimilitude.

Zeuxis' grapes may have fooled birds, but a rival picture by Parrhasius, which depicted a curtain partly covering a painting of a subject from the Trojan War, deceived Zeuxis himself, who tried to draw the curtain.[13] Thus the artist who makes paintings that appear to rational human beings to be the real thing wins the highest esteem. In the literature of art of the Renaissance, it was a commonplace to praise most highly art that was considered to look like nature itself.[14] It was certainly in response to these classical values that Caravaggio, Sánchez Cotán and other artists painted still lifes with a high degree of illusionism. In Caravaggio's *Basket of Fruit* of about 1595 (fig. 4), the realistic representation of the life-sized fruit set against a neutral background, combined with the placement of the basket so that it projects beyond the ledge, makes the painting a convincing *trompe l'oeil*. Sánchez Cotán aimed for similar effects; in his pictures the canvas both depicts and becomes a fictive window frame, and life-sized, realistically painted objects are situated within and in front of it, giving the illusion of a real physical presence (cats 1–3).[15]

Grotesque Painting and the Origins of Still Life

In his account of still-life painting in Spain, Francisco Pacheco linked the origins of the genre to the painting of grotesques. It was the discovery, in the early sixteenth

Fig. 4 Michelangelo Merisi da Caravaggio, *Basket of Fruit*, *c.*1595. Oil on canvas, 31 x 47 cm. Milan, Pinacoteca Ambrosiana.

Fig. 5 Giovanni da Udine, *Festoon with Bread, Flowers and Fruit*, *c.*1518. Fresco. Rome, Vatican Loggie.

century, of the ancient fresco decoration in the 'grottoes' on the site of the Emperor Nero's Golden House on the Esquiline Hill in Rome that led to the modern revival of the style, which became known as 'grotesque' painting. It rapidly became fashionable all over Europe.[16] The famous grotesques painted by Raphael's assistant Giovanni da Udine (1487–1564) in the Vatican Loggie (1518) include festoons and swags of naturalistically painted fruit, flowers and birds on the lunettes and pilasters (fig. 5).[17] Pablo de Céspedes (1538–1608), the Cordoban painter-priest who lived in Rome from 1570 to 1577, admired this contemporary work more than the surviving antique frescoes which had inspired it.[18] The beautiful festoons of fruit, flowers and vegetables that Céspedes painted between the Evangelists on the ceiling of the chapel of the Annunciation in Santa Trinità dei Monti in Rome are a direct response to the work of Giovanni da Udine. The festoons and garlands in easel pictures of the seventeenth century, which were quickly adopted by Spanish artists (cats 49, 53, 54), are derived from this kind of painting.[19]

For Pacheco, a learned artist and close friend of Pablo de Céspedes, there was no conceptual difference between the painting of fruit and flowers as ornament, the inclusion of still-life details in figural works, and the painting of fruit and flowers in independent still lifes. The factor that linked them was the common enterprise of imitating natural motifs, and the accuracy achieved was a measure of the artist's mimetic skills. As precedents for Spanish still-life painting, Pacheco cited the grotesques of Julio de Aquiles and Alejandro Mayner in Charles V's palace in the Alhambra in Granada, and in the palace of the emperor's secretary, Francisco de los Cobos, at Úbeda.[20] Although the frescoed grotesques on the walls of the *Salas de Frutas* in the Alhambra are lost or have been covered over, the gilded *artesonado* ceilings (*c.*1535–7), inset with octagonal panel paintings, have survived. These depict fruit, vegetables and bouquets of flowers set against a dark background (fig. 6).[21] This dark setting and the realistic rendering of detail are particularly significant for later developments in still-life painting in Spain. Aquiles, an Italian, and Mayner, probably a Fleming or German, had worked in the studio of Giovanni da Udine and imitated his manner. The poet Luis de Góngora recognised their work as painted in the 'antique style', and in his encomium of Granada, *Ilustre ciudad famosa*, of 1586, he rhetorically described it as superior to the achievement of the ancient painters Apelles and Timanthes.[22]

The Andalusian painter Antonio Mohedano (*c*.1561–1626), who specialised in grotesque decoration, was a pupil of Pablo de Céspedes.[23] According to Pacheco, Mohedano was inspired by the art of Aquiles and Mayner (as were Pedro Raxis, Blas de Ledesma and Antonio de Arfián).[24] Significantly, both Mohedano and Blas de Ledesma (doc. 1602–14), who was active in Granada, also painted independent still-life pictures (fig. 7). In 1637, a set of fourteen paintings of baskets of fruit by Mohedano was listed in the collection of the 3rd Duque de Alcalá in Seville, where it had probably been since before 1610.[25] Mohedano has been suggested as the painter of the grotesque borders with fruit and birds, thought to have been commissioned about 1604, which separate the figural paintings on the ceiling of the Prelate's Gallery in the Archbishop's Palace in Seville (fig. 8 and see fig. 10).[26] Bands of fantastic grotesque decoration, painted to look as if carved, enclose painted *quadri riportati*, fictive pictures of fruit and vegetables, which are painted in a naturalistic manner that is pointedly at odds with the surrounding decorative motifs. While these images are related to the work of Aquiles and Mayner in the Alhambra, they are more overtly classicising in intention.[27] In a clear allusion to the story of Zeuxis' painting of grapes, the artist has depicted birds, perched in niches, hungrily eyeing the fruit shown in the adjacent panels; other birds are shown actually eating it.

Given this classical context, it is not surprising that so many early still lifes in Spain and Italy depict fruit, often with birds present, or that grape still lifes came into vogue in Spain in the 1630s (see *Madrid: Barrera, Ponce, Labrador*). The Latin sig-

Fig. 6 Attributed to Julio de Aquiles and Alejandro Mayner, *Pears*, *c*.1535–7. Octagonal panel set in the ceiling of the *Sala de Frutas*, Palace of Charles V, Alhambra, Granada.

Fig. 7 Blas de Ledesma, *Still Life with Cherries and Flowers*, *c*.1610–15. Oil on canvas, 56.2 x 78.4 cm. Atlanta High Museum of Art.

Fig. 8 Unknown artist, *Pears and Grapes*, *c*.1604. 39 x 221 cm. Grotesque decoration from the Prelate's Gallery, Archbishop's Palace, Seville.

natures on some Spanish still-life and genre paintings are perhaps oblique references to classical precedents (see cat. 32). Caravaggio himself was no doubt making a witty reference to the Zeuxis story in his *Basket of Fruit* (fig. 4) when he included bunches of grapes from which two grapes have already been eaten.

Francisco Pacheco and the Imitation of Nature

Both Pacheco and Vicencte Carducho (*c*.1578–1638), court painter and author of the *Diálogos de la pintura* (1633), upheld the anthropocentric values of Italian art theory, which defined painting as an intellectual activity and laid great emphasis on drawing, proportion and anatomy, artistic skills based on reason, which were most fully demonstrated in the representation of the human figure. Thus it was figural painting that was most highly regarded, and more particularly religious painting, which helped to lead men towards salvation.

Pacheco praised *Lazarus and the Rich Man* by his fellow Sevillian, Alonso Vázquez (*c*.1565–1608), because he considered the figures to be as well painted as the still-life objects (fig. 9).[28] His remarks referred implicitly to another story of a painting by Zeuxis that depicted a boy carrying a basket of grapes; although the naturalistically painted grapes attracted hungry birds, the figure of the boy was deemed poorly painted, because it did not scare them off.[29] The story touched on the idea of relative skill: the easy imitation of inanimate objects versus the difficult painting of

Fig. 9 Alonso Vázquez, *Lazarus and the Rich Man*, *c*.1600. Oil on canvas. Location unknown.

the human form.[30] According to Pacheco, Vázquez succeeded in holding both in balance. In Vázquez's painting the rich trappings of the banquet are appropriate to the subject represented; but Pacheco cautioned against the easy appeal of the still-life detail in history painting which could distract attention from the more edifying figural passages of the picture.[31]

Pacheco reported the annoyance of Juan van der Hamen (1596–1631) at being regarded as a still-life specialist, which in the public eye overshadowed the figural work that he himself regarded as more important.[32] Pacheco construed still life as an elementary, unchallenging genre, a diversion from serious painting. For him the genre depended on the artist's mere copying of inanimate things, whose motionlessness facilitated retouching in oil until complete accuracy (*verdadera imitación*) was attained.[33] Pacheco's theoretical assumptions accord with the developing academic doctrine of the hierarchy of the genres, which relegated still-life painting to the lowest level, but are at odds with the sophistication and richness of the paintings themselves. In theoretical writings the 'imitation of nature' remained the rationale of the genre, despite the fact that this was a gross oversimplification. In fact, few paintings are the result of a first-hand encounter with objects posed in front of the artist; still lifes are often skilful and varied combinations of observed, borrowed and invented motifs, in which intuitively painted cast shadows create the impression of coherent spatial relationships. In this academic theoretical context, Caravaggio's remark (reported by Vincenzo Giustiniani) that it was as much work (*manifattura*) to make a good flowerpiece as a figure painting, sounded subversive.[34] Although it came from a painter for whom still life was almost an emblem of his naturalistic approach to art, the remark may well have echoed the feeling of many artists who practised the genre. Indeed, even Pacheco betrayed a slightly ambivalent attitude when he stated that still-life painting was nothing more than a diversion, but added that it allowed artists to exercise their *ingenio*, or the faculty of creative imagination.[35]

The World of Nature
In Spain, as elsewhere, the collector's cabinet, or *kunstkammer*, was a repository of artefacts and *naturalia*, things that were rare, beautiful and marvellous.[36] The sixteenth century saw the growth of empirical science based on the observation and study of natural phenomena, and the spirit of enquiry that informs the works of early Northern still-life painters has been called 'scientific naturalism'.[37] Artists such as Jan Breughel the Elder and Jan van Kessel (1626–79) depicted rare and expensive flowers, shells, insects and reptiles, and their paintings were regarded as precious and unusual in themselves; it was perhaps for this reason that in 1610 the Spanish Conde de Benavente had hung his single fruit still life on panel in his *camarín*, along with valuable and extraordinary objects.[38]

In Spain the botanical dimension of early still-life painting was not as highly developed as in Northern Europe, although Philip II is known to have had an interest in botanical illustrations, and had a collection of pictures of South American animals, birds and fruit trees.[39] Sánchez Cotán did, however, bring a remarkable intensity of observation and meticulous attention to detail to bear on common foodstuffs, and Antonio de Pereda's *Walnuts* of 1634 (cat. 25) provides as comprehensive a visual description of its subject as any naturalist might demand. An explicit botanical interest appears to be reflected in Sánchez Cotán's depiction of South American foods, such as the Mexican chayote fruit in *Still Life with Game Fowl* (cat. 2) and an unidentified variety of cereal in *Still Life with Hamper of Cherries and Basket of Apricots* (fig. 20). Such accurate botanical observation must have excited the curiosity of educated viewers, and falls within the tradition of the study of natural history in Spain, which focused almost exclusively on the flora and fauna of the New World.[40]

Food for Thought: the Symbolic Dimension of Still Life

The Christian belief in God as the beneficent Creator of heaven and earth, 'of all things, visible and invisible' (as the Creed puts it), predicates that nature has been sanctified by God, and that all natural phenomena, no matter how humble, are a manifestation of his wisdom and goodness. This belief informed the views of Cardinal Federico Borromeo (1564–1631), Archbishop of Milan, on still-life, flower and landscape painting, and was an important motivating factor in his collecting of examples of these genres. Caravaggio's *Basket of Fruit*, which Borromeo owned and possibly commissioned, was seen in this light.[41] Perhaps the Spanish ecclesiastics who were among the earliest collectors of still lifes shared this perception of the genre. The saintly Archbishop of Valencia who was canonised as San Juan de Ribera (1532–1611) owned a still life of 'kitchen articles',[42] and two archbishops of Toledo, Pedro García de Loaysa (d. 1599) and his successor Bernardo de Sandoval y Rojas (1546–1618), owned still lifes by Sánchez Cotán (see cat. 1).

The decorative elements of the ceiling of the Prelate's Gallery in the Archbishop's Palace in Seville are only one part of a complex scheme, whose larger meaning has relevance here. The anonymous figural paintings in the ceiling comprise the *Four Elements*, the *Four Seasons*, four scenes from the story of Noah based on works by one of the Bassanos, and a *Kitchen Scene* which reflects the style of the Cremonese artist Vincenzo Campi (1535/40?–1591), as well as elements familiar from the paintings of the Amsterdam artist Pieter Aertsen (1508–75) and his followers (fig. 10). The

Fig. 10 Unknown artist, *Kitchen Scene*, c.1600. Oil on canvas. Seville, Archbishop's Palace, Prelate's Gallery.

story of humankind's redeemed ancestor Noah is the key to interpreting this ensemble of works, which depicts the elemental forces and cycles of nature. God chose Noah to replenish the world after its destruction in the Great Flood, and established a covenant granting humankind dominion over every created living thing (Genesis 8:22 and 9:1–17). On the ceiling, therefore, the food which is shown being prepared in a contemporary kitchen is a reference to God's pledge that: 'Every moving thing that liveth shall be food to you; as the green herb have I given you all' (Genesis 9:3). The fundamental idea underlying the decorative scheme is that the natural world was created by a loving and generous God for the benefit of man.

Still-life details with symbolic meaning that were traditionally included in religious pictures were most effectively deployed by Francisco de Zurbarán (1598–1664). A small independent still life by Zurbarán depicts a cup of water with a rose (fig. 79). The same motif appears in two early religious paintings by Zurbarán, where it presumably has a symbolic function, denoting, in one of these, the Virgin's purity (fig. 75). When the motif appears in *Still Life with Basket of Oranges* of 1633 (fig. 74), does it retain its symbolic value? Is this painting indeed, as many critics have thought, a 'mystical' still life, with symbolic objects arranged like votive offerings on an altar?[43] The painting has lent itself to a lucid symbolic interpretation as a homage to the Virgin, with citrons emblematic of faithfulness, the oranges and blossom of virginity and fecundity, respectively, the vessel of water symbolic of purity and the rose of divine love.[44] Perhaps this beautiful conceit was intended for those with eyes to see, and was readily perceived by a Sevillian audience whose devotion to the Virgin was proverbial.

Pacheco's account of still-life painting did not acknowledge any transcendent function of the genre, perhaps because the Christian aspect was considered self-evident. In Spain the rich lore of popular proverbs was not generally translated into visual images as it was in the Netherlands, and it is difficult to see any connection between Spanish still lifes and the emblematic tradition of the Iberian peninsula. Allegories of the Five Senses were common in Flemish still lifes, but no Spanish examples have so far been identified. In literature, mundane things could be invested with religious significance; but 'hidden symbolism' is not, generally speaking, a characteristic of still-life painting in Spain. It is surely going too far to interpret Sánchez Cotán's *Still Life with Cardoon and Carrots* (fig. 11) as symbolising the instruments of Christ's Passion, the flail of the Flagellation and the four nails of the Crucifixion, as has been proposed.[45] However, in the case of this particular work, given that it was painted after the artist had professed as a lay brother in the Charterhouse of Granada, it may be legitimate to evaluate the relation of the subject matter to Carthusian life. The spare composition of vegetables may in fact be intended to evoke the vegetarian rule of the order, which is celebrated in Zurbarán's *Miracle of Saint Bruno* (Seville, Museo de Bellas Artes).[46] It may have been intended as a 'Lenten' still life (*bodegón de cuaresma*), since contrasting pairs of still lifes of foods appropriate to Carnival and Lent are documented in the seventeenth century.[47] Pairs of pictures depicting meat and fish (figs 71 and 72), are more common still. When both kinds of edibles appear in a single picture, there is often a marked separation between them, which perhaps reflects the custom of dividing the week into meat days and fish (fast) days. Some commentators have mistakenly seen Sánchez Cotán's earlier still lifes painted in Toledo (e.g. cats 1–3) as epitomising monastic austerity, but these pictures in fact display copious amounts of food and some include meat. There is no evidence that Spanish still lifes were moralising in promoting moderation and abstinence, or that they set out to show the dangers of gluttony.[48]

Fig. 11 Juan Sánchez Cotán, *Still Life with Cardoon and Carrots*, after 1603. Oil on canvas, 63 x 85 cm. Granada, Museo de Bellas Artes.

about 24 x 32

The Spanish still lifes that most conspicuously celebrate the pleasures of food are the many examples that represent produce associated with a particular month or season (cat. 18 and fig. 46). Compared with Flemish paintings, however, Spanish still lifes are reticent regarding the pleasures of the table, and do not usually depict complete meals, nor do they overtly celebrate the act of eating. They do, however, appeal to the senses and most evoke a world of plenty in a society where hunger and poverty were endemic. Cooked and prepared foods are sometimes represented alongside others in the raw state, the ingredients of meals that are to be imagined by the viewer. But still lifes of the seventeenth and eighteenth centuries are not a reliable index to the range of foods eaten in Spain of that period, which are detailed in the popular cookbooks of the time.[49] It is also surprising how often some foodstuffs are repeated; the cardoon, depicted in many paintings, topped, tailed and washed, is commonly eaten in Castile through the winter months, usually as an ingredient of stews, or served in a salad sweetened with orange. While Sánchez Cotán may have been fond of eating cardoon, the vegetable also held a strong visual appeal for him, and he exaggerated its pink coloration and its elegantly curved shape. It is also a vegetable that keeps well, as do root vegetables, such as carrots, parsnips, onions, and garlic, as well as hanging game; all of these allowed artists time to represent them in meticulous detail. Where decay is represented on the foodstuffs, such details may have provoked viewers to think about change, transience and the brevity of life.

The *Vanitas* Still Life

A painting in Berlin by an anonymous Spanish painter (cat. 28) shows three well-used books, letters, an ink-well and quill, and an hour-glass on a rose-coloured cloth. This small, allusive painting contains a profound message. The hour-glass marks the passing of time and symbolises the brevity of life. The quill and anonymous books, evidently much used, signify human knowledge; the worn and damaged condition of the latter alludes to the transcience of learning and intellectual achievement.[50] Such a painting would have appealed to a university graduate (*letrado*) in the court administration; or it may have been owned by one of the great literary figures of the Spanish Golden Age, who wished to be reminded of the ultimate futility of human enterprises.

In seventeenth-century Spain, such pictures were known by the generic name of *Desengaño del Mundo* (Disillusionment of the World) and are today called *Vanitas*, a title deriving from the pessimistic sentiment of Ecclesiastes 1:2: 'Vanity of vanities, all is vanity'.[51] These admonitory images exposed the illusory and fallacious nature of worldly achievements, pursuits and possessions before the Four Last Things – Death, Judgement, Heaven and Hell – and were intended to urge their viewers to be mindful the salvation of their souls. The ideas which underlie the *Vanitas* were fundamental to Christian culture in the seventeenth century, and the paintings rely on a widely understood symbolic language.

The depiction of three skulls and a pocket-watch in a small painting by Pereda (fig. 12) is enough to convey the idea of earthly time and the inevitability of death. The human skull being the most obvious *memento mori*, the presence of three skulls drives home the message. Jesuit preachers used a cross and human skull in sermons on the *Vanitas* theme, these objects speaking more eloquently than words. One Franciscan preacher adorned the skull he used in his sermons with headgear appropriate to his subject or his audience, using a doctor's wig, a judge's cap, a knight's helmet or a crown as occasion demanded.[52] Skulls were also familiar attributes in paintings of penitent saints, most commonly Mary Magdalene and Saint Jerome, and mere emblems of hope and redemption, which recalled the hill of Golgotha, the site

Fig. 12 Antonio de Pereda, *Vanitas*, 1640s. Oil on canvas, 31 x 37 cm. Zaragoza, Museo de Bellas Artes.

Fig. 13 José Antolínez, *The Christian Soul between Sacred and Profane Love*, 1660s. Oil on canvas, 74 x 94 cm. Murcia, Museo de Bellas Artes.

of Adam's tomb and Christ's crucifixion for the salvation of humankind.[53]

In the famous *Dream of the Knight* (cat. 27), an angel with unfurled wings and fluttering drapery is entering a room where a young gentleman is sleeping; he bears a banner marked with the arrow of death and the sobering inscription: AETERNE PUNG[I]T CITO VOLAT ET OCCIDIT (It pierces perpetually, flies quickly and kills). In the sleep, which prefigures the knight's death, the angel shows him the heaped-up symbols of earthly glory, wealth and pleasure, an encyclopaedic array of traditional *Vanitas* objects, including skulls, a snuffed-out candle and a clock. A bouquet of roses in a fragile glass vase is an emblem of youth and beauty, which quickly fade and die; symbols of temporal and ecclesiastical power – crown, papal tiara, bishop's mitre and pieces of armour lie beside a globe. Earthly riches, gold, silver and jewellery count for nothing in death, and the pleasures of culture, literature and music are enjoyed in this life alone. The laurel crown has slipped from the skull that is placed on an old book, subverting the traditional emblem of the permanence of intellectual achievements.[54] Some of the objects also suggest sins and vices; coins, for example, may signify avarice or dissipated wealth, and coins near playing cards suggest gambling and the depravity associated with it. The sleeping youth's fine clothes, the mirror, the miniature of a woman and the box of jewellery suggest the sin of vanity. In an allegorical painting of the *Christian Soul between Sacred and Profane Love* by José Antolínez (1635–75), Profane Love offers a basket of jewels (fig. 13). Such sins are grave impediments to the salvation of the soul. The form of repentance advocated was familiar from images of saints rejecting worldly luxuries: for instance, Mary Magdalene casting off her jewels and finery and, more appropriately in this case, the repentance of the Prodigal Son. The *Vanitas* theme in this painting is analogous to insistence on the ultimate insubstantiality and transience of worldly things in Calderón de la Barca's *auto sacramental* (religious play), *La vida es sueño* (Life is a Dream), first performed in 1637.

Valdés Leal's epic *Vanitas* paintings for the church of the Hospital of Charity (the Caridad) in Seville were called 'Hieroglyphs of the Four Last Things' (figs 14 and 15), and formed part of a decorative programme designed to make the wealthy and aristocratic members of the Hospital's confraternity contemplate their own deaths and devote themselves to charitable works.[55] *In Ictu Oculi* (In the Twinkling of an Eye) shows the candle of life being extinguished by Death, a menacing skeleton who bears a scythe and coffin and tramples underfoot a globe and a other symbols of wordly pursuits. *Finis Gloriae Mundi* (The End of Worldly Glory) depicts, in gruesome detail, the rotting, maggot-infested corpses of a bishop and a knight. Above is the hand of Christ holding a pair of scales: nothing more (*ni mas*) than the seven deadly sins – signified by the animals in one scale – is required for perdition, whereas nothing less (*ni menos*) than prayer and repentance – symbolised by instruments of penance and devotion piled up in the other scale – is needed for salvation.

Artists' materials and attributes of the liberal status of painting appear in Valdés Leal's *Allegory of Vanity* (cat. 45): a chalk holder, compasses, a rule and square, as well as books on art, perspective, anatomy and architecture. The putto directs bubbles at Vicente Carducho's opened treatise, *Diálogos de la pintura*, and Valdés Leal has signed his name on plate 6 of this book, which depicts a *tabula rasa*, signifying both the power and the scope of the artist's imagination. Pliny's *Natural History* is one of the books that appears at the lower left of *In Ictu Oculi* (fig. 14). The ambitious artist and admiring patrons could become ensnared by the sin of vanity; and *Vanitas* pictures themselves fell under the rubric of vanities, since they were valuable works of art, sought after by connoisseurs. It was inevitable that *Vanitas* should,

ironically, be turned against art, since painting was itself a fiction, an *engaño*, and was, like the image of the dream, a common metaphor for the illusory nature of worldly life.[56]

The Taste for Still Life in Spain
The earliest documentary reference to still lifes in a Spanish collection is in the 1599 inventory of the Madrid residence of Cardinal García de Loaysa (1534–99).[57] Loaysa was a canon of Toledo Cathedral in the 1570s, and from 1594 acted as governor of the archdiocese. He died shortly before he was to take up his appointment as Archbishop of Toledo. One of Loaysa's still lifes is described as 'another picture in which are painted fruits, a melon, quince, pomegranate, carrot and cardoon'.[58] The listing of the subject matter of this still life, perhaps read from left to right with the cardoon framing the composition, as it does in at least four of Sánchez Cotán's still lifes, strongly suggests that it was a work by Sánchez Cotán.

Loaysa's successor as Archbishop of Toledo was Cardinal Bernardo de Sandoval y Rojas (1546–1618).[59] He appears to have owned many more still lifes than Loaysa.[60] Perhaps some of these decorated Buenavista, his rural retreat on the outskirts of Toledo.[61] The subject matter of fruit and game still lifes and genre paintings made them suitable decoration for rural villas used for hunting and country pursuits.[62] In 1619, five still lifes which had been bought the previous year from the estate of Sandoval, which may have been works by Sánchez Cotán, were installed as overdoors in the south gallery of the royal hunting palace of El Pardo.[63] Van der Hamen was commissioned to paint a sixth picture of fruit and game to complete the series. These pictures were still in the palace in 1701, when the inventory of the royal collection following the death of Charles II identified at least one element of the subject matter of each. The correspondence between these descriptions and those in the inventory of Sánchez Cotán's studio in 1603 suggests that the still lifes, or at least some of them, were by this artist.[64]

Fig. 14 Juan de Valdés Leal, *In Ictu Oculi*, 1670–2. Oil on canvas, 220 x 216 cm. Seville, Hospital de la Santa Caridad.

Fig. 15 Juan de Valdés Leal, *Finis Gloriae Mundi*, 1670–2. Oil on canvas, 220 x 216 cm. Seville, Hospital de la Santa Caridad.

Imported genre paintings were more popular than still lifes among aristocratic collectors at the court of Philip III (reigned 1598–1621).[65] The Duque de Lerma, the king's first minister, who was one of the more sophisticated connoisseurs of painting at court, did acquire several still lifes,[66] and in 1608 the collection of the Condestable de Castilla included two fruit still lifes on panel and a pair of still-life pictures contrasting game and fish.[67] From an early date the genre also appealed to educated individuals of lesser means, the *letrados* mentioned above, who were well able to appreciate the antique pedigree of still-life painting, in addition to enjoying the pure visual appeal of these novel works.[68]

It is interesting that Philip IV (reigned 1621–65), one of the century's most discerning connoisseurs, did not collect Spanish still lifes to any great extent. True to the traditional Habsburg predilection for art from Italy and Flanders, Philip preferred the valuable and exquisite flower paintings of Jan Brueghel the Elder and the Jesuit painter Daniel Seghers (1590–1661), and the still lifes and hunts of Frans Snyders, Paul de Vos and Rubens. Large, flamboyant Flemish still lifes were extremely expensive in Madrid, and some Spanish artists made a trade in copies.

The sheer numbers of still lifes listed in inventories of Madrid houses during the period testify to the rapid growth of the genre's popularity. Still lifes were often hung beside landscapes, bringing nature into town houses. Little logic governed the decor of most houses, but by the middle of the century still lifes were considered appropriate for dining rooms. The custom of grouping still lifes together was quickly established and the horizontal format of many of them suggests that they were intended as overdoors and overwindows. Only a few paintings, however, take the low viewpoint of these locations into account in their compositions.

Still lifes were sometimes commissioned from artists, but they were more usually sold ready painted from shops (*obradores públicos*), the best known of which were those of Francisco Barrera (1595–after 1657) and Juan de Arellano (1614–76) in Madrid. Van der Hamen offered for sale works that ranged from autograph originals at the top end of the price range down to much cheaper studio products, which bore his signature like a trade mark. Easy to sell, still life was also a suitable genre for young artists who did not yet enjoy an established reputation and regular patrons, such as Burgos Mantilla (1609/12–72), Francisco Palacios (1622/5–52) and Juan de Zurbarán (1620–49). It was probably the ready market for still lifes that led an artist such as Antonio de Pereda to paint them throughout his career. The popular demand caused picture dealers to employ hack artists to mass-produce still lifes for piece rates.[69] The standardised formats, cursory handling and repeated motifs made it possible to turn out large numbers of works, but these were far from being thoughtful imitations of nature. This mediocre art, called *pintura ordinaria,* was destined for the least exacting clients, and was exported to the provincial markets and South American colonies.

But it is not *pintura ordinaria* that primarily concerns us here, but rather those works, by great artists as well as minor ones, in which the confrontation between the painter and what was before his eyes resulted in compelling images that awaken the senses and engage the mind. From its inception at the end of the sixteenth century, the still life has remained an integral part of the painter's repertory, and it challanged the imagination of most of the masters of Spain's Golden Age, whether they were specialists or not. As a genre whose appeal is mostly visual, it has never lost its allure or its ability to be redefined according to the priorities of each succeeding generation.

Sánchez Cotán and Still-Life Painting in Toledo around 1600

1 Juan Sánchez Cotán, 1560–1627
*Still Life with Quince, Cabbage, Melon
and Cucumber*
*c.*1600. Signed lower centre: *Juº Sāchez Cotan F.*
Oil on canvas, 69.2 x 85.1 cm
San Diego Museum of Art. Gift of Anne R. and
Amy Putnam

Described in the inventory of the artist's studio
in 1603 as 'A canvas on which there are a
quince, a melon and a cabbage', this painting is
among the earliest of all European still lifes. Its
irresistible visual impact results in part from the
ingenious composition, seemingly based in
mathematics. As remarked by Pérez Sánchez
(Madrid 1983), it reminds one of the Neo-
Pythagorean preoccupations evident in the
severe geometry of the Escorial monastery.

This painting was probably one of five still
lifes bought in 1618 by King Philip III from the
estate of Cardinal Bernardo de Sandoval y
Rojas, Archbishop of Toledo. For nearly two
centuries these works formed part of the decoration of the south gallery of the country palace
of El Pardo, outside Madrid, where in 1701 it
was described as: 'A small fruit still life with a
black-and-gold frame and an open melon in the
centre'. In 1813, it seems, King Joseph
Bonaparte took the picture, along with many
others pillaged from the royal collections, into
his American exile. Going by the name of
Comte de Survilliers, Bonaparte lent freely from
his collection to the Pennsylvania Academy of
Fine Arts, where this still life was first exhibited
to the American public in 1818.

The still lifes of Juan Sánchez Cotán (1560–1627) stand out as unique phenomena in the history of art. They have become part of the consciousness of art lovers only in the past fifty years, and they still astonish today as they must have done around 1600. Such is the impact of their illusionism that historians and the public alike still feel challenged to explain it. When rediscovered in 1945, *Still Life with Quince, Cabbage, Melon and Cucumber* (cat. 1) seemed to be unrelated to anything, except perhaps to the art of Caravaggio, whose works Sánchez Cotán could not have known and which, in any case, do not really antedate his own.[1] In recent years, however, we have come to see that a rich context of ideas and precedents had been accruing and that these spectacular images were a logical outgrowth of it.

In 1603, at the age of forty-three, Sánchez Cotán abandoned a successful practice as a painter in Toledo for the Andalusian city of Granada, in order to profess as a lay brother (*lego*) of the Carthusian order.[2] This fact, together with the artist's saintly reputation (as recorded by his eighteenth-century biographers), have coloured the way in which his still lifes, which were mostly painted before his religious profession, have been perceived in modern times: as austere, quasi-religious works, epitomising a 'humble and mystical' way of life.[3] The more deeply the aesthetic attitudes prevalent in sixteenth-century Spain are probed, however, the more it seems that these extraordinary pictures have other dimensions, which have not been fully explored.

Sánchez Cotán was baptised in the small town of Orgaz in the environs of Toledo on 25 June 1560.[4] Nothing certain is known of his early training, but the artist and writer Francisco Pacheco (1649) calls him a disciple of Blas de Prado (d. 1600), and documents confirm the friendship and collaboration of the two artists. To judge by his figural works alone, his training must have taken place within the stylistic orbit of the painters working at the Escorial monastery in the last quarter of the sixteenth century, with a certain Venetian orientation not far from Navarrete 'El Mudo' (*c.*1538–79). Thus formed in Castile, his style evolved little after his move to Andalucía. Critics have always noted the pronounced stylistic dualism between Sánchez Cotán's naturalistic still lifes and his comparatively bland figurative works. His most beautiful religious painting, the *Rest on the Flight into Egypt*, in the lay brothers' choir of the Carthusian monastery at Granada (fig. 16), reveals his figurative style at its best. Its carefully balanced construction and exquisite tenderness constitute a clear and poetic response to the dictates of the reformist theology favoured by Philip II and the church authorities during the years of Sánchez Cotán's formation. The treatment of the figures and of the landscape is uniformly idealising. Nevertheless, contrasting sharply with this is the naturalistic still-life detail of bread and cheese in the foreground and the glass which the Christ Child takes from the hand of the Virgin. Like other artists of this transition period, Sánchez Cotán could not resist the challenge to his descriptive skills when it came to painting incidental objects in religious works. Yet in its overall impact the picture is gentle and untheatrical, completely lacking in the great visual drama of still lifes such as *Quince, Cabbage, Melon and Cucumber*.

Pacheco says that before he became a friar, Sánchez Cotán was already famous for his fruit still lifes (*lienzos de frutas*) and that he followed Blas de Prado in this respect.[5] It can be assumed that Sánchez Cotán, according to the practice of the time, had completed his apprenticeship and was an independent artist by about 1585. We have no documentary knowledge of these years, but there are documents relating to the end of his Toledan period, perhaps the most important of which is one showing that El Greco owed him a considerable amount of money.[6] The nature of the debt is unspecified, but it is significant that the two artists knew each other. El Greco had lived in Italy and was steeped in naturalistic Venetian art, and he had experienced the classical ambience of the circle of Cardinal Alessandro Farnese in Rome; El Greco was probably a key figure in helping to mould artists' attitudes in Toledo through his ideas and conversation, and through the example of his naturalistic portraits and 'ekphrastic' genre images (paintings which recreate lost antique works, following classical descriptions), such as *Boy blowing on an Ember* (fig. 3).[7] Indeed, the singular distinction of Sánchez Cotán's career before he took vows was his production of still lifes, which were surely appreciated by his circle as having antique precedents of their own, not unlike El Greco's work.

Sánchez Cotán's career as a painter had lasted for almost twenty years when, on 10 August 1603, as a precaution before his journey to Granada and as a consequence of his retirement from the world, he signed his last will and testament on the eve of his departure from Toledo.[8] This unusually informative document, and the inventory of his belongings made three days later, reflect the artist's conventional piety and his considerable financial competence. Indeed, whereas most artists' testaments of the time reveal large accumulated debts, Sánchez Cotán had none. On the contrary, he was prosperous and lent money to, or was owed it by, many people.[9] His house was more than just comfortably furnished, he played music and was literate, although he does not appear to have owned many books.[10] In his testament he ordered that all money owed to him be collected and all his property be sold at auction. Contrary to the nearly universal misunderstanding arising from the incomplete publication of this document, he did not order that all or any of his assets be given 'to the Virgin'.[11] In the parts of his testament omitted from the published transcript he set up trust funds benefiting his niece and his sister, and gave property he owned in Orgaz to his brother and sister.[12]

Sánchez Cotán's studio inventory listed sixty unvalued paintings: half were religious subjects (mostly devotional images of the Virgin and saints); eleven were portraits (including some of sundry aristocrats and one of a bearded woman, Doña Brígida del Río [fig. 17]); two were erotic mythologies; and twelve were either finished still lifes and studies related to them, or unfinished still lifes.[13] As in the case of most other artists' inventories of the time, several of the pictures were identified as copies after such artists as Bassano, Titian and Cambiaso, which Sánchez Cotán had obviously made to sell. He also owned two original works by El Greco.

Sánchez Cotán's will names over thirty of his clients, associates and friends, and the document shows that he counted among his patrons important ecclesiastics, including the dean of Toledo Cathedral, as well as members of the aristocracy and the professions. These individuals, however, are not mentioned in connection with his still lifes.[14] Some were distinguished connoisseurs of painting, including Pedro Salazar de Mendoza, who was a close friend and patron of El Greco but who appears to have had no interest in still life.[15] As mentioned in the previous chapter, however, it would appear that the two most significant collectors of Sánchez Cotán's still lifes, prior to and just after his departure from Toledo, were two successive archbishops of the city, Pedro García de Loaysa and

Fig. 16 Juan Sánchez Cotán, *Rest on the Flight into Egypt*. Oil on canvas, 278 x 186 cm. Granada, Charterhouse.

Fig. 17 Juan Sánchez Cotán, *The Bearded Woman of Peñaranda (Brígida del Río)*, 1590. Oil on canvas, 102 x 61 cm. Madrid, Museo del Prado.

Bernardo de Sandoval y Rojas. Both these men evidently shared the interest in still-life painting of their Milanese counterpart Cardinal Federico Borromeo, whose activities as a collector around the same time were decisive for the development of the genre in Italy. While Sánchez Cotán must have sold still lifes to men like these before his retirement, one does not get the impression that the examples recorded in the inventory were the unsold leftovers of his production. On the contrary, he may possibly have kept the pictures to serve as a focus for discussions with other artists and connoisseurs.

In *Still Life with Quince, Cabbage, Melon and Cucumber* (cat. 1), as in all his still lifes, Sánchez Cotán arranged the products of nature within and in front of a framing space that appears to be a niche or window. This architectural setting allowed him to achieve a powerful sensation of real space, through its precise perspectival construction and the strong modelling of forms in light and shadow. Both the visual evidence of the paintings and the entries in the inventory of his studio confirm that he painted the window first, then added the fruits and vegetables.[16] He connected this space to the viewer's by arranging certain objects so that they overlap the front edge of the window and protrude sharply into the space in front of it. A sense of great depth is also given by the dark background against which the objects are silhouetted. It emerged during the recent restoration of this painting that this background was originally intended to be extremely black and rich, as it still appears in the Prado's *Still Life with Game Fowl, Fruit and Vegetables* (cat. 3).[17]

The framing space, or window, in Sánchez Cotán's still lifes would probably have been recognised by contemporaries as a *cantarero*, or primitive larder.[18] The hanging of fruits and vegetables from strings attached somewhere above was an allusion to actual practice that helped to keep them from spoiling. None of the compositions suggests the random disorder of a larder shelf, however, so it would be a mistake to forget that these are artfully arranged compositions. Indeed, the pure hyperbolic curve which serves to organise the composition seems so studied that it suggests some basis in mathematics.[19] It is the kind of invention that Pacheco must surely have had in mind when he wrote that still lifes gave artists the opportunity to display their *ingenio*, or inventiveness, in the arrangement of objects. Having arrested our attention by the artifice of setting and composition, Sánchez Cotán then proceeds to enthrall us with the mesmerising copiousness of the detail which his eye and hand have managed to see and describe. So much so that we find it difficult to take our eyes off the picture; our sense of vision is heightened and left expectant.[20] Working from painted studies, Sánchez Cotán could achieve the same conviction of painting from life even when he reused a motif, such as the hyperbolic arrangement of fruits and vegetables, which reappears in the Chicago still life (cat. 2). The way in which the Chicago picture is referred to in the artist's inventory of 1603 further reinforces this point.[21] The first item in the inventory refers to 'A duck on panel' (Una [sic] ánade en tabla). This was probably a study of a duck to be used in making still lifes. The Chicago painting is described a few entries further on as 'A picture of fruits with the duck and three other birds which belongs to Diego de Valdivieso' (Un lienzo de frutas adonde está el ánade y otros tres pájaros ques [de] Diego de Valdivieso). The reference to *the* duck makes it clear that the one in that picture was taken from the study.[22]

One of Sánchez Cotán's favourite motifs was the cardoon, which in his Toledo years he cast into a form that must have become linked with his name. His inventory described two still lifes with cardoons and implies, as happens to be the case, that both were painted according to the same design.[23] In the well-preserved painting in the Museo del Prado (cat. 3), the rangy thistle leans against the right side of the niche and protrudes forcefully into our space. Every thorn and crevice and unruly shoot is described with great precision. Sánchez Cotán painted the very same cardoon in a similar position in the beautiful but

2 Juan Sánchez Cotán, 1560–1627
Still Life with Game Fowl
*c.*1600. Oil on canvas, 67.8 x 88.7 cm
The Art Institute of Chicago. Gift of Mr and Mrs Leigh B. Block

Discovered only in 1955, when it was acquired by the Art Institute of Chicago, this still life at first inspired scepticism on the part of some scholars, because its composition repeats the hyperbola of the San Diego still life (cat. 1). All but Orozco Díaz, who never saw the painting before his death, have come to accept it, however, and to understand that such reuse of his own motifs was an integral part of Sánchez Cotán's working method. Somewhat altering the placement of the melon in relation to the edge of the niche, he has added a duck and three other hanging birds, which fill in the void in the San Diego work. It is important to note that the duck hangs very much in front of the window and casts a shadow across its corner, so that the whole group of birds does not hang in the same plane but seems to curve out into the viewer's space. To counterbalance the strong vertical of the magnificent duck, the artist has added at the left a plump, green squash-like fruit that overhangs the edge of the niche (as does the cucumber on the right). This fruit was a novelty in another respect as well; it is a chayote, a variety of cucurbit (*Sechium edule*) native to Latin America. It represents, therefore, one of the earliest instances of a New World fruit being represented in a European still life.

3 **Juan Sánchez Cotán**, 1560–1627
Still Life with Game Fowl, Fruit and Vegetables
Signed and dated, lower centre: *Juº sanchez cotan. f./1602*
Oil on canvas, 68 x 89 cm
Madrid, Museo del Prado

It is very likely that this is the still life described in Sánchez Cotán's studio in 1603 as 'Another picture of the cardoon with the partridges, which is the original of the rest and belongs to Juan de Salazar'. The brief entry informs us that the artist had either given or sold the painting to Juan de Salazar, manuscript illuminator and executor of his testament, and also indicates that copies of the painting or elements of it were made in the studio. The subtle play with visual elements in this picture is remarkable. In the simple window setting customarily used by the artist, the forms are silhouetted against a profound blackness, in this case very well preserved. The play of light and half-shadow on the carefully observed fruits and vegetables and the heavy shadows they cast on the planes of the niche create a clear and precise sense of space that heightens the illusion of reality. The known copies of the painting lack its perfect balance.

fragmentary *Still Life with Cardoon and Francolin* in the Piasecka Johnson collection (fig. 18).[24] There is no qualitative difference between the two images, each being depicted, strongly lit against the black backdrop, as though observed for the first time.[25]

The still lifes which Sánchez Cotán left behind in Toledo were no doubt acquired by various collectors. Most, as we have said, may have been bought by Cardinal Sandoval and, on the collector's death, entered the royal collection, where they remained for nearly two hundred years. In his later years as a lay Carthusian, the artist devoted most of his activity as a painter to illustrating the history of his order in an important series of works in the Charterhouse of Granada.[26] Both there and in the Charterhouse at El Paular, near Segovia, where he lived for an unknown period of time, he also painted scenes from the standard repertory of sacred subjects. His activity as a still-life painter, although much diminished, did not, however, cease entirely. The magnificent *Still Life with Cardoon and Carrots* (fig. 11), one of his masterpieces, was discovered in the Charterhouse of Granada, following the suppression of the monasteries in the 1830s. Being away from the examples of his own work he had left behind in Toledo, Sanchéz Cotán began anew with a different cardoon and arrived at a form quite distinct from the one he had used in 1602. He placed the cardoon and parsnips in the same kind of window setting he had habitually used, and followed the type of composition employed in *Quince, Cabbage, Melon and Cucumber*, with its gentle hyperbolic curve and a vast expanse of empty space above the vegetables. Although painted with a slightly more pastose and less fluid technique, the forms are observed with the same intensity as before. The light, however, is somewhat warmer, perhaps reflecting the gentler climate of the south. Significantly, while there are numerous pastiches and copies of the still lifes from the Toledo period, there are none reflecting this painting from the Granada period, save for several modern fakes that have periodically turned up on the art market. It seems, therefore, that the picture was done

Fig. 18 Juan Sánchez Cotán, *Still Life with Cardoon and Francolin*, c.1600. Oil on canvas, 66 x 62.2 cm. Princeton, Barbara Piasecka Johnson.

Fig. 19 Unknown artist, *Still Life with Basket of Fruit and a Thistle*, c.1615–25. Oil on canvas, 66 x 82 cm. Madrid, Private collection.

4 Unknown artist
Still Life with Hanging Fish and Baskets of Fruit
*c.*1615–25. Oil on canvas, 66.3 x 84 cm
Washington, Collection of Mrs H. John Heinz III

Although this exceptional painting, formerly in the collection of Sir William Stirling-Maxwell of Kier, bears witness to the powerful influence of Sánchez Cotán, we do not know the name of its author. The artist was an able draughtsman with a strong feeling for the tactile quality of things, but his illusionism is less compelling than Sánchez Cotán's. The still life, once attributed to the Seville School and more recently to Alejandro de Loarte, resembles no known signed work. We can, nevertheless, identify a body of the artist's works, which were probably executed in Toledo or Madrid during the first third of the seventeenth century (see discussion in text).

Fig. 20 Sánchez Cotán (copy), *Still Life with Hamper of Cherries and Basket of Apricots*, c.1600. Oil on canvas. Madrid, Private collection.

Fig. 21 Unknown artist, *Still Life with Hamper of Cherries, Basket of Apricots and a Melon*, c.1615–25. Oil on canvas, 49.5 x 106.6 cm. Madrid, Private collection.

for the artist's own satisfaction, and was unrelated to any extensive renewal of his activity as a still-life painter.

The impact of Sánchez Cotán's still lifes on painting in Castile was profound. The most creative examples are to be found in the work of Juan van der Hamen y León in the 1620s, as well as in that of Alejandro de Loarte. But other significant instances can also be pointed to, although we cannot always put an artist's name on them.[27]

The extremely good *Still Life with Hanging Fish and Baskets of Fruit* (cat. 4) is perhaps the best of these anonymous works.[28] The artist has employed symmetry as an organising principle of his composition, as would become common among Castilian artists, but he has followed Sánchez Cotán in the use of the window setting. A canvas of nearly identical dimensions in a Madrid private collection (fig. 19) must be the pendant to this picture.[29] The modelling of the fruit, particularly of the grapes and their leaves, is identical to that in *Still Life with Hanging Fish and Baskets of Fruit*. The artist has depicted at the right, rising up from behind the window frame, the flowering top of a cardoon (cut off in the trimmed examples depicted in Sánchez Cotán's known still lifes). This device for defining the space behind the window was used by Sánchez Cotán in a composition, known only in copies (fig. 20), which was recorded in his inventory of 1603 and which was probably one of those bought from Cardinal Sandoval's estate by Philip III.[30]

In one of three other still lifes possibly by the same hand (fig. 21), painted in the oblong format of overdoors, we can see that the artist has drawn from Sánchez Cotán's original the motifs of the hanging hamper of cherries and the small basket of apricots, and has used the same hanging melon as in fig. 19.[31] These are among the best works that show that in the period between 1603 and the early 1620s a considerable amount of activity was generated by the still lifes which Sánchez Cotán left behind in Castile. Whether most of this activity was going on in Toledo or Madrid is difficult to say, since we cannot be certain whether the artist's still lifes were taken to Cardinal Sandoval's Madrid palace before they were acquired by the king.

The most spectacular instance of Sánchez Cotán's influence on another painter is to be found in the beautiful *Still Life with Cardoon, Francolin, Grapes and Irises*, signed and dated by Felipe Ramírez in 1628 (cat. 5).[32] We know almost nothing about this artist, not even where he lived.[33] The fact that he copied a minor religious painting in Toledo Cathedral and his obvious connection with the works of Sánchez Cotán have led to the assumption that he was Toledan; but since we cannot be certain of the location of Sánchez Cotán's still lifes after 1603, even that is open to question. What is certain is that even twenty-five years after Sánchez Cotán left Castile, his still lifes could inspire the most eloquent homage.

5 Felipe Ramírez, doc. 1628–31
Still Life with Cardoon, Francolin, Grapes and Irises
Signed and dated in the background, upper right: *Philipe Ramírez/fa. 1628*
Oil on canvas, 71 x 92 cm
Madrid, Museo del Prado

This famous still life by Ramírez, long recognised as among the most beautiful in Spanish art, testifies to the enduring influence of Sánchez Cotán in the reign of Philip IV (1621–65). Despite its confident technique, it is in fact a copy or variant of one painted a quarter century earlier by the older artist. Both the cardoon and the francolin appear in the fragmentary still life by Sánchez Cotán in the Piasecka Johnson collection (fig. 18), from which perhaps ten inches have been excised in the centre of the composition. Although we cannot know what is missing from Sánchez Cotán's work, X-ray evidence confirms that it was not the vase of irises and the hanging grapes which appear in this work. Ramírez may, therefore, have been elaborating on Sánchez Cotán's painting, or copying a lost variant by the older artist, who is known to have reused elements of his own compositions. He did this, of course, in the case of the cardoon in the Piasecka Johnson work, which he included in the Prado still life (cat. 3). Another case in point would be the elaboration of the Chicago still life (cat. 2) from the essential elements of the San Diego picture (cat. 1).

Velázquez and the Bodegón

Between the ages of about sixteen and twenty-four, the young Diego Velázquez (1599–1660) painted a number of genre paintings in Seville, the best of which have never been surpassed. These remarkable works of the artist's youth depict the people and things in his immediate surroundings, and were perceived as novelties when they were first painted. By the time he had completed his education in 1617, it was obvious to those who knew him best that he was quite exceptionally talented. 'After five years of education and training, impressed by his virtue, integrity and excellent qualities, and also by the promise of his great natural genius, I gave him my daughter in marriage,' wrote Francisco Pacheco of his pupil.[1]

Pacheco referred to Velázquez's genre paintings as *bodegones*, the Spanish term already in use to denote imported genre pictures with figures and foodstuffs, which derived from *bodegón*, a humble public eating place.[2] So as to underpin the legitimacy and highlight the ingenuity of his son-in-law's early paintings, Pacheco cited from Pliny the precedent of the ancient Greek Dionysius, who painted 'ordinary and comic things', and that of Peiraikos, who painted 'humble things like barber-shops, stalls, meals and similar things...; these paintings caused great delight and by them the artist achieved the greatest glory'.[3] Pacheco then commented specifically on the *bodegones* of the young Velázquez in the spirit of the belief that 'modern times' offered equal, if not superior, talents and achievements to those of antiquity:

> Well, then, are *bodegones* not worthy of esteem? Of course they are, when
> they are painted as my son-in-law paints them, rising in this field so as to
> yield to no one; then they are deserving of the highest esteem. From these
> beginnings and in his portraits...he hit upon the true imitation of nature,
> thereby stimulating the spirits of many artists with his powerful example.[4]

Ancient precedents or not, more conservative painters, like Vicente Carducho (*c*.1578–1638) in Madrid, still disparaged such works as lowly and unworthy of the serious artist.[5] Pacheco, to prove his open-mindedness on the matter, went on to say that he himself had followed Velázquez's example in painting a *bodegón* in 1625; and he confessed that it made the rest of his works look merely 'painted'.[6]

Velázquez's *bodegones* are highly individual and creative responses to images and ideas that the young artist must have imbibed in the cultivated circle of Pacheco. The source of their strength derives from an attitude towards art – the *idea* of imitating nature – that had been charged with new energy in the early years of the seventeenth century. Certainly there were few visual exemplars among the works of the religious painters of Seville to inspire him: it was no doubt images from abroad that stimulated his imagination. And these were not hard to find. The growing interest of sixteenth-century collectors in profane subject matter had been met by the extensive importation of paintings in which everyday activities, foodstuffs and animals featured

Fig. 22 Vincenzo Campi, *Kitchen Scene*, *c*.1590. Oil on canvas, 125 x 168 cm. Málaga, Museo Provincial de Bellas Artes.

Fig. 23 Jacob Matham, after Pieter Aertsen, *Kitchen Scene with Christ at the Supper at Emmaus*. Engraving. London, British Museum.

prominently.[7] Italian genre paintings by such artists as Vincenzo Campi (*c*.1530–93) (fig. 22) were imported into Spain, where they were known as *bodegones de Italia*, and were imitated by Spanish artists.[8] One of these (see fig. 10) was placed on the ceiling of the Prelate's Gallery of the Archbishop's Palace in Seville and remains *in situ*. At the turn of the seventeenth century there was also considerable interest in the works of such Northern painters as Pieter Aertsen (1508–75) and Joachim Beuckelaer (*c*.1530–*c*.1573). Pacheco certainly knew at least one work by the former and he was familiar with their biographies in Karel van Mander's *Het Schilder Boeck* (1604).[9] Prints after their genre paintings were widely broadcast at this time (fig. 23), and original paintings and copies of their works were known in Spain. For example, the collection of the most important Sevillian nobleman, Don Fernando Enríquez de Ribera, 3rd Duque de Alcalá, an inventory of which was drawn up on his death in 1637, contained a number of genre paintings which he could have acquired in Italy or at court between 1597 and 1598; they included several that were reminiscent of the works of Campi and, most importantly, a large fish painting by Pieter Aertsen.[10]

The community of Flemish merchants in Seville also owned genre paintings from their native land, which could have included such works as the *Kitchen Maid* by the young Frans Snyders (1579–1657) (fig. 24). A picture such as this, which antedates Velázquez's *Kitchen Scene with Christ in the House of Martha and Mary* (cat. 6) by about eight years, relates closely to his work in the relative scale of the figure to the overall image.[11]

In his biography of Velázquez, Palomino (1724) portrays a rebellious young artist, whom he casts as a 'second Caravaggio' who rejects the elevated subject matter and ideal style exemplified by Raphael, saying that he 'would rather be first in coarseness than second in delicacy'.[12] But Velázquez's *bodegones* do not look like works by Caravaggio (1571–1610). It is unlikely that he knew any genre paintings by or after this artist, but – what is more important – he certainly did know of Caravaggio's reputation as a painter who worked directly from the life. He knew this either from friends and colleagues who had been to Rome or, more likely, from Karel van Mander's biography of Caravaggio, published in 1604.[13] The fact that Velázquez creatively explored the *idea* of imitating nature, relating it to his own experience by painting his *bodegones* from the life, likens this aspect of his work to the efforts of

Fig. 24 Frans Snyders, *Kitchen Maid*, *c.*1610.
Oil on canvas, 88.5 x 120 cm. Cologne,
Wallraf-Richartz-Museum.

6 Diego Velázquez, 1599–1660
Kitchen Scene with Christ in the House of Martha and Mary
Inscribed at right with fragmentary date: *1618*
Oil on canvas, 60 x 103.5 cm
London, The National Gallery

At first glance, the work appears to be a contemporary genre painting in which the young artist has worked hard at defining the physical reality of the two kitchen maids at the left and the makings of a meal on the table. But through a serving window at the right we see the Gospel scene of Mary sitting listening at the feet of Christ, while her sister Martha pauses momentarily in her chores to complain that Mary is not helping her (Luke 10: 38–42). To this Christ replies, 'Mary hath chosen that good part, which shall not be taken away from her'. According to the exegetical writings of Saint Augustine, Martha's concern about her work in preparing a meal for the Lord establishes her as the 'type' of the active life, while Mary's wish to sit at the feet of the Lord and listen to his words establishes her as the 'type' of the contemplative life: two poles that were seen not as bad and good, but rather as good and best. Thus this story became one of the key biblical texts in the Christian controversy over whether 'faith' or 'good works' is more efficacious in the salvation of the human soul. Neither of the two women in the foreground of Velázquez's painting is Martha or Mary; they are rather two contemporary women about whose daily lives we are encouraged to think in terms of biblical example. The young maid, whose sullen face is brilliantly characterised, seems to resent her chores, while the old woman – certainly not her sister, but just another, wiser woman in the kitchen – looks out at the viewer and points with her finger towards the biblical lesson.

early still-life painters in Castile, who were motivated not so much by examples they had seen as by the *idea* of such works.

Three of Velázquez's earliest *bodegones* are set in a tavern (*bodegón*). Two are the kind of scenes known as 'merry companies', or *pinturas de risa*, as pictures of drinking and music-making were called in Spain in the first third of the seventeenth century.[14] The earliest of them is the so-called *Three Musicians* in Berlin (fig. 26), probably a work from the artist's apprentice years (it is usually dated *c*.1616–17). We can see in it several of the preoccupations of which Pacheco wrote in describing his protégé's development: the striving after lively facial expressions, each one studied to the point of being psychologically isolated from the rest, and the strong contour of each form, which contributes to an emphatic sense of volume, and which Pacheco had insisted was essential to a lifelike image.[15] Significantly, these and other awkwardnesses that keep the image from holding together coherently did not inhibit the demand for copies of it, and these testify to the novelty of the subject in Sevillian circles.[16]

The St Petersburg *Two Men and a Boy at Table* (fig. 27), of which there are no fewer than five old copies,[17] shows a considerable advance in Velázquez's ability to integrate the various components into a coherent scene. The principal advance is in the handling of light, which defines the forms much more subtly – especially the still-life objects on the table and the cloth itself – and seems to unify the composition. The central figure of a smiling boy serving wine would have reminded viewers of the archetypal urchin (*pícaro*), the protagonist of Spanish picaresque novels, the earliest of whom was Lazarillo from *Lazarillo de Tormes* (1554).[18] None of Velázquez's *bodegones*, however, depicts specific episodes from literature.[19] The picture has an air of bacchic merriment appropriate to the tavern setting. The spread of humble foodstuffs – including mussels, a proverbial food of the poor all over Europe – is in keeping with the mood of picaresque novels, in which hunger and wretched food are the source of crude humour. The incongruous sight of an old man about to eat a raw tuber may well have amused prosperous contemporaries, who probably avoided eating in real Sevillian *bodegones*.

Velázquez's tavern scenes have been seen as examples of *pitture ridicole*, a term

Fig. 25 Pieter Aertsen, *Christ in the House of Martha and Mary*, 1552. Oil on canvas, 60 x 101.5 cm. Vienna, Kunsthistorisches Museum.

Fig. 26 Diego Velázquez, *Three Musicians*, c.1616–17. Oil on canvas, 87 x 110 cm. Berlin, Gemäldegalerie.

Fig. 27 Diego Velázquez, *Two Men and a Boy at Table*, c.1617. Oil on canvas, 107 x 101 cm. St Petersburg, State Hermitage Museum.

first used in 1582 by the Italian theorist Cardinal Gabriele Paleotti to denote comic genre paintings depicting morally reprehensible lower-class figures governed by their bodily appetites – eating, drinking and behaving libidinously (fig. 22).[20] While some of Velázquez's *bodegones* do seem to satirise plebeian vices, the ridicule is comparatively subtle.[21] And, although such pictures as the Budapest *A Girl and Two Men at Table* might be read as sexually suggestive, Velázquez's innuendo is never of the gross variety often seen in Italian paintings of a similar nature.[22]

Velázquez's two genre paintings with religious scenes (cat. 6 and *Kitchen Scene with the Supper at Emmaus*, National Gallery of Ireland) must be read on a more serious level and have justly been called 'moralised *bodegones*'.[23] They depict biblical events in the background, as though witnessed from within a contemporary kitchen, thus inverting the convention of religious narrative painting, in which the biblical story always takes precedence over still-life details. This ingenious format, which was originally an outgrowth of Erasmian humanism in that it conformed to Erasmus' belief that complex concepts should be made understandable by means of familiar things, was the inspired invention of Aertsen (fig. 25) and Beuckelaer.[24] It is not surprising that Velázquez knew of this convention, but it was perhaps daring of him to try it himself in the climate of Counter-Reformation orthodoxy that prevailed in Seville.[25] Be that as it may, these paintings are subtle and allusive, and they clearly reveal the extent to which Velázquez used the *bodegón* as a vehicle for experiment, as a challenge to his creative imagination (*ingenio*) and his mimetic powers as a painter.

The relative seriousness of Velázquez's greatest *bodegones* dissociates them from the tradition of comic genre, whose levity would threaten to trivialise the work of art. His *Old Woman cooking Eggs* (cat. 7) was painted in 1618, the year in which he was accepted into the Guild of Saint Luke and also married Juana Pacheco. In its imaginative departure from the tavern-scene genre of his earlier efforts, and in its increased mastery with the brush, it was his most ambitious *bodegón* to date. Still there are awkward spatial inconsistencies, such as the exaggerated tilt of the table-top and

7 **Diego Velázquez**, 1599–1660
An Old Woman cooking Eggs
Inscribed with the date: *1618*
Oil on canvas, 100.5 x 119.5 cm
Edinburgh, The National Gallery of Scotland

One of the great works of Velázquez's youth, *Old Woman cooking Eggs* shows how the nineteen-year-old artist took stock, as Pacheco (1649) said he did, of the individuals and objects in his immediate surroundings to create an image of vibrant immediacy. The model for the old woman, as noted by Harris (1982), is that used in the same year for the figure on the far left in *Kitchen Scene with Christ in the House of Martha and Mary* (cat. 6), and the boy who posed in this picture was portrayed again some two years later in the *Waterseller of Seville* (cat. 8). A parallel has been drawn with a scene in *Guzmán de Alfarache* (1599), the most widely read of picaresque novels, but there is nothing specifically anecdotal in the picture, and the encounter depicted by Velázquez is quite different from that in the novel. The carefully arranged objects have been captured with extraordinary virtuosity. Indeed, we cannot escape the impression that the prime motivation for painting the picture was to hone those skills. Before the end of the seventeenth century, the picture had been acquired by Murillo's most important private patron, the sophisticated Flemish merchant Nicolas Omazur, in whose inventory of 1698 it was described: 'An old woman frying a couple of eggs, and a boy with a melon in his hand'.

brazier. This permits us to see all the better how skilfully Velázquez could paint such things as the eggs coalescing in hot oil and the fall of light on a great variety of surfaces, but it also demonstrates the experimental nature of these works, in which the young artist was still perfecting his skills.

In Velázquez's *Waterseller of Seville* (cat. 8) such defects have been ironed out. This is not even a *bodegón* in the strictest sense and resists the conventional categorisation of the time. Northern genre paintings sometimes depicted lower-class figures with great dignity, but this was something new in Spain. Velázquez's waterseller has a gravity, a dignity more like that of a figure in a religious history painting. By avoiding the portrayal of any psychological interaction between the figures (something that has always been noted about the posed arrangements of his later *bodegones*), the artist was perhaps consciously endeavouring to lift them above the level of the anecdotal – the level at which he began his exploration of the imitation of nature.

Velázquez painted these scenes from daily life with a plain palette of earth tones, which emphasises the effects of volume, and this distinguishes the young Sevillian's *bodegones* from highly coloured Northern examples.[26] He may have been aware of the example of ancient painters such as Apelles and Nichomachus, who were praised by Pliny for their skilful creation of works of beauty and value from only four colours: white, ochre, red earth and black.[27] The *Waterseller* was surely conceived as a display of virtuosity, in which Velázquez seems bent on demonstrating, for himself and for others, the illusionistic possibilities of art. In this, the crowning work of his youth, he achieved a balance between eye, mind and brush that signalled his full preparation for what lay ahead.

It is not surprising that Velázquez's *bodegones* were owned by educated connoisseurs (*entendidos de la pintura*) who loved painting and were unconcerned with the received conventions of artistic doctrine: collectors such as Juan de Fonseca, the Duque de Alcalá, Philip IV and Nicolás Omazur. Even Pacheco's own *bodegón*, painted in Madrid in 1625, was in the collection of his 'learned friend' Francisco de Rioja, librarian of the Conde-Duque de Olivares.[28] Juan de Fonseca, the first owner of Velázquez's *Waterseller*, was an early admirer of the artist; he was himself an amateur painter, who wrote a treatise on ancient painting which is unfortunately now lost.[29]

In October 1623, as a result of his extraordinary skill in portraiture, which he had cultivated in Seville along with the *bodegón*, Velázquez was appointed painter to King Philip IV in Madrid, the first of many honours and titles that the monarch would bestow upon him throughout their long working friendship. From then on, portraiture predominated in Velázquez's oeuvre. The *bodegón*, which had played such a vital role in his early development, was not a feature of his mature work.

8 **Diego Velázquez, 1599–1660**
The Waterseller of Seville
c.1620. Oil on canvas, 106.7 x 81 cm (including a 4 cm strip added at the top)
London, Apsley House, The Wellington Museum

This work has traditionally been viewed as a straightforward genre scene related to the world of the picaresque novels of the early seventeenth century. Recently some scholars (e.g. Gállego, Moffitt, Wind) have tended to look for symbolic or emblematic meanings in this, the greatest of Velázquez's youthful works. Part of the painting's potency, of course, is that it resists 'difficult' interpretation. No matter on which level one chooses to read the picture, in the end its enduring allure is largely visual and derives from the fact that the artist was not very specific, except when it came to what he saw. Working with props and models in his studio, he 'stage-managed' a situation that closely approximated to something one might have seen on the streets of Seville. People did sell drinks of water, though probably not in elegant glass goblets with decorative blue glass bubbles in the bottom (Ramírez-Montesinos). The image is arresting for the force with which Velázquez has captured its physical reality, exploring further than he had ever done before the perception of objects and human figures of different ages (posed frontally, in profile and three-quarter view) in shadowy space; the power of the image, then, rests in the probity of the artist's eye and the skill of his brush. And that, probably more than anything, is the true meaning of this work, which Velázquez took with him to Madrid in 1623 and which became ineradicably identified with his name.

Van der Hamen and Still-Life Painting in Castile

Three years older than Velázquez, Juan van der Hamen y León (1596–1631) was one of the most famous painters of his generation; he was already well established at the court in Madrid when Velázquez arrived there in 1623. Van der Hamen's art inspired praise from some of the greatest writers of the Spanish Golden Age, including Lope de Vega, Luis de Góngora, Gabriel Bocángel and Juan Pérez de Montalbán.[1] The artist celebrated his friendship with his literary peers in a series of portraits, and he himself wrote verses touching on the relationship of painting and poetry (*Ut pictura poesis*) which earned him a place in Pérez de Montalbán's *Indice de los ingenios de Madrid* (1632), a kind of *Who's Who* of court intellectuals.[2] A pair of large allegories with spectacular displays of fruits and flowers (figs 28 and 29) reflect Van der Hamen's poetic cast of mind, and function as visual poetry, paralleling the imagery of his literary peers.[3] His fruit and flower paintings were themselves the subject of two sonnets by the playwright Lope de Vega, in one of which Jupiter commands Nature herself to copy the painted fruits of the 'New Apelles'.[4]

Van der Hamen was descended from a long line of Flemish nobles. He was named after his father, Jehan van der Hammen (sic), who had emigrated from Brussels to Spain before 1586. His mother, Dorotea Whitman Gómez de León, was half-Spanish/half-Flemish and was herself of noble lineage on both sides, being descended from two distinguished military families.[5] Like his father, Van der Hamen became a member of the Flemish royal Guard of Archers (*Archeros del Rey*), whose duty it was to guard the king's person. In fact, the Guard's role was part of the intricately choreographed ritual of pageantry surrounding the monarch. The distinction of this office should not be underestimated, as it made manifest the artist's patrician status and gave him regular access to the Palacio Real (Royal Palace) and the court. The captain of the Archers, the Comte de Solre, was one of his most distinguished patrons (cats 9 and 10, figs 28 and 29).[6]

Like all ambitious artists in Madrid, Van der Hamen hankered after royal recognition of his considerable talents. He was one of the twelve painters who petitioned for the vacant post of salaried painter to the king, following the death in 1627 of the royal portrait painter Bartolomé González.[7] The fact that he was not even short-listed has sometimes been construed as evidence that his reputation as a still-life painter obscured his work as a figurative artist[8] (Pacheco recorded the artist's annoyance at this narrow perception of his abilities).[9] But it has also been suggested that, in the context of art politics at the court, with its innate rivalries and jealousies, his greatest disadvantage in this competition (in which Velázquez was one of the judges) may simply have been that he was too talented.[10]

In fact, Van der Hamen was an admirable portraitist, a fact demonstrated by his *Portrait of a Dwarf* (fig. 30). On his visit to Madrid in 1626, the famous Roman anti-

Fig. 28 Juan van der Hamen y León, *Vertumnus and Pomona*, 1626. Oil on canvas, 229 x 149 cm. Madrid, Banco de España.

Fig. 29 Juan van der Hamen y León, *Offering to Flora*, 1627. Oil on canvas, 216 x 140 cm. Madrid, Museo del Prado.

quarian and connoisseur Cassiano dal Pozzo even preferred Van der Hamen's portrait of the Papal Legate, Cardinal Francesco Barberini, to one by Velázquez.[11] Van der Hamen also had an active career as a painter of religious subjects. Few such pictures are known today, however, except for those he painted in 1625 for the cloister of the convent of the Encarnación, a commission in which the royal family certainly had an interest, because the convent stood close to and was connected to the Palacio Real.[12]

Van der Hamen was a practising artist by 1615.[13] He acquired a reputation for still life early in his career, and in 1619 was commissioned to paint a still life with fruit and game (unknown today), which was to hang as an overdoor, with five similar pictures, in the south gallery of the recently reconstructed hunting palace of El Pardo.[14] The five pictures had been bought from the collection of the Archbishop of Toledo, Bernardo de Sandoval y Rojas, and, as we have seen earlier, there is reason to believe that they were by Sánchez Cotán. The experience of matching his work to Sánchez Cotán's must have been a formative one for Van der Hamen, for his early paintings

9 **Juan van der Hamen y León,**
1596–1631
Dessert Still Life with a Vase of Flowers,
a Clock and a Dog
*c.*1625–30. Oil on canvas, 228 x 95 cm

10 *Dessert Still Life with a Vase of*
Flowers and a Puppy
*c.*1625–30. Oil on canvas, 228 x 95 cm
Madrid, Museo del Prado

Peter Cherry recently discovered that this
unique and imposing pair of still lifes was first
owned by one of Van der Hamen's most important patrons, Jean de Croy, Comte de Solre and
captain of the royal Guard of Archers, of which
the artist himself was a member. In Solre's
house in the Calle de Alcalá the paintings were
hung flanking a doorway, which suggests that
they may have been commissioned for that spot
and may have served a *trompe l'oeil* function,
continuing the pattern of the room's reticulated
floor. Their depiction of sweets and liquid
refreshment on tables covered with green cut
velvet suggests the theme of hospitality. After
Solre's death in Madrid in 1638, the paintings
were bought by Philip IV for 330 *reales* each,
and in 1666 they were listed in the Alcázar
inventory in 'the room where His Majesty
dined'. In the appraisal of Solre's collection, the
paintings were said to depict, among other
things, 'two vases of flowers from Flanders',
suggesting that not only flowers such as tulips,
but probably also paintings of bouquets like
these, were associated with Flanders. Indeed,
while the paintings are in Van der Hamen's
own distinctive style, it is the bouquets of
Daniel Seghers that the appraiser may have had
in mind. The dog and puppy portrayed in the
pictures were perhaps owned by the patron.

Fig. 30 Juan van der Hamen y León,
*Portrait of a Dwarf, c.*1625. Oil on canvas,
122 x 87 cm. Madrid, Museo del Prado.

Fig. 31 Juan van der Hamen y León, *Still*
Life with Cardoon and Basket of Apples,
1622. Oil on canvas, 75 x 109 cm. Mexico,
Private collection.

follow the window-frame format and strive for a lucid portrayal of space. A painting
such as *Still Life with Cardoon and Basket of Apples* of 1622 (fig. 31), shows, however, significant differences in style: the cardoon and fruit are rather more generalised
in their detail and modelling. The effect is one of a very emphatic plasticity. A characteristic tendency to distil, conceptualise and order forms is also evident in Van der
Hamen's treatment of compositional types deriving from Flemish painting, such as
the handsome *Serving Table* (fig. 34).

Fig. 32 Juan van der Hamen y León, *Still Life with Fruit and Birds*, 1621. Oil on panel, 56 x 74 cm. El Escorial, Patrimonio Nacional.

Fig. 33 Frans Snyders, *Still Life with Fruit and Birds*, c.1615–20. Oil on panel, 46 x 64 cm. Paris art market, 1985.

Fig. 34 Juan van der Hamen y León, *Serving Table*, c.1622. Oil on canvas, 62 x 122 cm. Private collection.

While the supposed Flemish origins of Van der Hamen's style are no longer tenable, it is true that throughout his career he responded to the taste for Flemish art in Madrid.[15] In a painting of 1621 (fig. 32), he openly adapted the composition of a recently painted fruit still life by Frans Snyders (fig. 33), copying the Fleming's lusciously painted fruit bowl, but enriching his version with a red damask tablecloth, extra birds and fruit and an illusionistic fly on the pear.[16] Despite his overt homage to Snyders, this is not at all the work of an imitative artist: if anything, Van der Hamen's tendency to bring architectural clarity to his still lifes strengthens the composition. In the following year, he reused this arrangement of fruit in a 'Spanish' context (fig. 35), this time depicting a straw basket and hanging fruit in a symmetrical composition within a window frame.

Three fruit paintings commissioned from Van der Hamen by the king in 1629, and unknown today, appear to have been responses to Flemish works in the royal collection.[17] Philip IV's preference for copious and flamboyant Flemish still lifes and hunting scenes by artists such as Frans Snyders and Paul de Vos is exemplified by his

Fig. 35 Juan van der Hamen y León, *Still Life with Basket of Fruit*, 1622. Oil on canvas, 67 x 100 cm. Private collection.

11 Juan van der Hamen y León, 1596–1631
Still Life with Fruit Bowl and Hanging Grapes
Signed and dated, lower left: *Ju⁰ Vander Hamen/de Leon a.1622*
Oil on canvas, 59 x 93.3 cm
Spain, Juan Abello collection

Van der Hamen, like Sánchez Cotán and most early still-life specialists in Europe, maintained a repertory of motifs which he used over and over again in varying combinations throughout his career. This painting, with its monumental green-glazed and ormolu fruit bowl, is a case in point: this impressive object, which must have belonged to the artist, is the single most often depicted thing in his oeuvre. Here as in most cases, however, he has created a unique composition, filling the bowl with a succulent abundance of pears and grapes and framing it symmetrically with hanging branches of white and red grapes. The open pomegranate at the left is another motif that Van der Hamen used more than once. But here, as always, his image of it is charged with the conviction of something observed for the first time.

12 Juan van der Hamen y León, 1596–1631
Still Life with Sweets and Glassware
Signed and dated, lower left: *Ju⁰ Vanderhamen/... faᵗ 1622*
Oil on canvas, 52 x 88 cm
Madrid, Museo del Prado

Painted as an overdoor (*sobrepuerta*), this still life is identified in the inventories of the royal collection from 1702 on. The painting exemplifies a compositional type created by Van der Hamen that had a profound effect on later Spanish still-life painting, particularly that of Zurbarán (e.g. cat. 38). On a narrow stone ledge, the artist has arranged his objects in a zigzag that fills the shallow depth. A footed plate of dark green glass is piled with pastries and candied figs. Beside the dish, a roll of wafers, or *barquillos*, overhangs the edge of the shelf, establishing with clarity the pictorial space. Behind this is a glazed terracotta honey pot. At each end of the composition are Venetian-style crystals rendered with consummate skill, especially the two at the left, which rest on a scalloped ceramic dish. The flask at the right contains *aloja*, an aromatic infusion composed of honeyed water with such spices as cinnamon, clove and ginger, often scented with the essence of jasmine or roses. The flies depicted on the flask call attention to the sweetness of its contents. The fashion for drinking such infusions and eating expensive sweets had swept the upper levels of Madrid society in the early years of the seventeenth century, and such delicacies were usually served at the *merienda*, or tea time.

decoration of the summer dining-room of the Royal Palace. In 1636 this room was hung with thirty pictures broadly related to the room's function, including Snyders's beautiful *Table with Fruit* (Madrid, Prado), a gift from the Marqués de Leganés.[18] Two of Van der Hamen's pictures were painted specifically for this room.[19] One of them depicted a narrow vertical festoon of fruit and flowers held by three putti. What must have been the third painting from the 1629 commission, almost identical in its description to the latter, was hung in the adjacent royal bedroom and was juxtaposed with Rubens's and Snyders's very similar festoon, now in the Prado (fig. 36).[20]

Van der Hamen made a speciality of still lifes that appealed to the courtly taste of affluent private collectors.[21] Luxurious objects of silver-gilt and ormolu (cat. 11), imported porcelain (cat. 14) and expensive Venetian glassware (cat. 12) were favourite motifs. Venetian glass was avidly collected in wealthier households, and its depiction afforded Van der Hamen the opportunity to show off his painterly skills. He was the first artist to depict the imported Mexican and Portuguese pottery which it became fashionable for the nobility of Madrid to collect and display (cat. 13).[22] He was most famous for his still lifes with sweetmeats, the consumption of which was such a feature of life at all European courts. In one early painting (fig. 37), Van der Hamen teases the viewer by depicting a silver spoon alongside closed wooden boxes of jelly, a jar of preserved cherries and a pot of honey. Other paintings (cat. 13) represent mouth-watering piles of cakes and candied fruits.

The demand for Van der Hamen's still lifes from all sorts of collectors in Madrid meant that, like Sánchez Cotán, but to a much greater extent, he maintained a repertory of still-life motifs that he reused in different pictures.[23] The uneven quality of paintings bearing his signature indicates that the degree of his own participation in them might vary from case to case, depending on whether they were destined merely for sale on the open market or for the gallery of some grandee.

Van der Hamen made the most creative innovations in still life after Sánchez Cotán. He was the first documented Spanish still-life painter to vary the shape of his pictures, painting works on round and octagonal supports.[24] More importantly, while continuing to paint symmetrical window-frame still lifes, from 1626 he developed a new asymmetrical compositional format in which objects are displayed on an arrangement of stepped ledges (cats 13, 14 and 15).[25] This is the most inventive alternative to the symmetrical mode of composition within a window frame, on a table-top or on a simple ledge. The different levels obviated the need for suspended motifs

Fig. 37 Juan van der Hamen y León, *Still Life with Sweets*, 1621. Oil on canvas, 37.5 x 49 cm. Granada, Museo de Bellas Artes.

Fig. 36 Peter Paul Rubens and Frans Snyders, *Festoon with Putti*. Oil on canvas, 174 x 56 cm. Madrid, Museo del Prado.

13 Juan van der Hamen y León, 1596–1631
Still Life with Sweets and Pottery
Signed and dated on ledge at right: *Ju vanderHamen i Leon/faᵗ 1627*
Oil on canvas, 84.2 x 112.8 cm
Washington, DC, National Gallery of Art. Samuel H. Kress Collection

This great still life, one of Van der Hamen's masterpieces, reveals more clearly than any other the sophistication of his visual thinking. Composed along crossing diagonals, it is a play of circles, cylinders and spheres against the rectilinear severity of the stone ledges. But the painting's ingenious geometry only serves as the underpinning of a virtuoso performance with the brush. The artist has skilfully noted such effects as the powdery surface of doughnuts and the crinkled, glistening skin of candied figs, in contrast to the dull sheen of a silver plate. As in many still lifes painted for the upper classes, this one depicts objects of diverse provenance. The red stoneware bottle with a hole in it has been identified as a product of the Rhineland, while the terracotta bottle and one of the bowls on the lower shelf are of the type imported from the town of Tonelá in the province of Guadalajara, in New Spain (Mexico). Perhaps the greatest *tour de force* is the painting of the glass finger-bowl filled with water, with its cast shadow and fall of refracted light on to the stone ledge. The interplay of intellect and the senses is characteristic of Van der Hamen's works in general, but reaches perhaps its most satisfying expression in this work.

14 Juan van der Hamen y León, 1596–1631
Still Life with Artichokes and Vases of Flowers
Signed and dated, lower right: *Ju⁰ vanderHammen faᵗ,/1627*
Oil on canvas, 81.5 x 110.5 cm
Madrid, Naseiro collection

Like the Washington Van der Hamen, this extraordinary and never-before published still life belonged originally to the greatest private collection formed during the reign of Philip IV, that of the 1st Marqués de Leganés, who had served the crown in both Flanders and Italy before returning to Madrid. He died there in 1655, leaving his heirs over 1,300 pictures by some of the greatest artists of Europe. Among them were over twenty paintings by Van der Hamen.

The stepped-plinth format, seen in this and Van der Hamen's other still lifes after 1626, enabled him to develop to the fullest his penchant for evoking a lucid pictorial space. In contrast to the unadorned planes of the grey stone ledges, his precisely drawn and keenly observed subject matter takes on a heightened presence. The Venetian-style glassware, Chinese export porcelain, fruit and flowers are situated so as to provide the maximum articulation of the space. But it is the handling of the light, reminiscent of the Roman followers of Caravaggio, and the subtle use of shadow, for example, around the base of the green glass pitcher in the foreground, that are perhaps the most sophisticated components of Van der Hamen's mature style.

15 Juan van der Hamen y León, 1596–1631
Still Life with Flowers and Fruit
Signed and dated, lower right: *Ju⁰ vanderHamen faᵗ, 1629*
Oil on canvas, 84 x 131 cm
Collection of Lila and Herman Shickman

Extremely colourful in its portrayal of nature's abundance, this large still life may have been intended as an evocation of spring. Most of the flowers and fruit depicted are the products of those months, but artists were often cavalier about accuracy in such matters, even when they wrote the name of the month or season on the painting. What inclines us to credit such an hypothesis in this case is the picture's relationship to another still life by Van der Hamen, of nearly the same size and also painted in 1629, which belongs to the Williams College Museum of Art, in Williamstown, Massachusetts. The two paintings are particularly complementary of one another and could have been part of a series. The brighter coloration of the Shickman picture stands in marked contrast to the decidedly warmer character of the Williams picture, in which grapes, peaches and pomegranates, fruits of the summer months, are depicted.

Fig. 38 Juan van der Hamen y León, *Landscape with Garland of Flowers*, 1628. Oil on canvas, 85 x 107 cm. Hanover, New Hampshire, Dartmouth College Museum of Art.

and were exploited by the artist to enhance the spatial interplay within individual pictures and between pendant works. These large, expansive paintings seem also to have inspired the artist to display an even greater mastery of representational skills.

Both Lope de Vega and Pacheco single out Van der Hamen for singular praise as a flower painter, and there is no doubt that in the 1620s he was pre-eminent among Spaniards in this genre.[26] He frequently depicted flowers in his still lifes of fruits and sweets (cats 9, 10, and 14, 15) but also painted independent flowerpieces. None of these is known today, but most of them were octagonal,[27] a format that was later adopted by Bartolomé Pérez. Van der Hamen also pioneered in Spain the painting of garlands of flowers surrounding sacred images and landscapes (fig. 38), a practice adapted from Flemish as well as Italian models. The artist's most spectacular painting with flowers is, however, the beautiful *Offering to Flora* (fig. 29), which, with its pendant, *Vertumnus and Pomona* (fig. 28), belonged to one of Van der Hamen's important patrons the Comte de Solre (see above).[28] The artist's profound sense for the underlying structure of things, which in general tended to lend strength to his forms and order to his compositions, resulted in brightly coloured, highly studied blossoms, lacking, perhaps, in the suppleness of Brueghel or Seghers, but pleasing and elegant within the context of his style. In his garlands, however, we see a freer, more natural treatment of flowers. When Van der Hamen died unexpectedly at the age of thirty-five, Juan Pérez de Montalbán lamented – with hyperbole reflecting his sorrow in losing a close personal friend – that 'if he were living, he would be the greatest Spaniard his art had ever known'.[29]

Alejandro de Loarte (*c*.1600–26), although not as talented as Van der Hamen, nevertheless achieved a distinctive style during his apparently short life. He was prob-

Fig. 39 Alejandro de Loarte, *Miracle of the Loaves and Fishes*, 1622. Oil on canvas, 275 x 412 cm. Madrid art market, 1992.

Fig. 40 Alejandro de Loarte, *Still Life with Fruit*, 1624. Oil on canvas, 81.5 x 108 cm. Madrid, Plácido Arango collection.

ably a practising painter in Madrid by the time of his marriage in 1619.[30] He may have moved to Toledo by 1622, the date on the *Miracle of the Loaves and Fishes* (fig. 39), his most accomplished figural painting, which was recorded in the refectory of the Minims at the turn of the nineteenth century.[31] He is certainly documented in Toledo in February 1624.[32] He died in there in December 1626.[33]

Loarte enjoyed an active career in Toledo and won significant commissions for religious paintings in the city and provinces.[34] In general, his figural work reveals an artist of limited talent, who may have benefited from the relative lack of competition in Toledo compared to the court, but his few known still lifes, dated between 1623 and 1626, are accomplished and very appealing. Judging by the individuals mentioned in his last will and testament, Loarte's private clients were mostly professionals and well-off artisans, who bought figure paintings and still lifes. The extent of his practice as a still-life painter is evident from his studio inventory, which listed thirty-three finished still lifes and seven paintings of vases of flowers.

The window-frame format that Loarte used was a common feature of Castilian still life by the 1620s, when he seems to have reached maturity as an artist, and does not necessarily imply a specific debt to his great Toledan predecessor Sánchez Cotán. Paintings by Van der Hamen appear to have been of greater significance for Loarte, and his *Still Life with Fruit* of 1624 (fig. 40) is similar in type to paintings by the Madrid master (fig. 35). This painting may be typical of the *lienzos de frutas* (still lifes of fruit) listed in Loarte's studio inventory, some of which formed sets. The generalised representation of the fruit and the less careful execution suggest that these had a more decorative function than Loarte's other still lifes, and were perhaps intended to hang in less conspicuous locations, such as over a door or window, according to the custom of the time. In other works, such as *Still Life with Game and Fruit* (cat. 16), Loarte seems better able to capture the tactile qualities of things.

One of the still lifes in Loarte's estate was called a *despensa* (larder).[35] This term could be relevant to a pair of paintings attributed to the artist, formerly in the Casa Torres collection, that depict, respectively, fowl and fish hanging from rails in the foreground, with kitchen vignettes containing small figures in the background (fig. 41).[36] These well-preserved pictures appear to derive in a general way from Flemish prototypes, and their attribution to Loarte is tenable on the basis of the close similarity in execution between the hanging chicken in the centre of this picture and the one in the signed *Kitchen Still Life* of 1625 (fig. 43), in the Várez Fisa collection, Madrid. The two hanging chickens in the ex-Casa Torres picture are exactly the same in design and execution as those that appear at the left of the extremely good, unsigned *Still Life with Meat, Fowl and Tavern Scene*, which has never before been published (fig. 42).[37] The painting of the leg of lamb is a real *tour de force*. In realistically depicting the rail from which the meats are suspended, Loarte makes a more specific reference to the real-life context of his subject matter than Sánchez Cotán had done, and he carries this even further by opening up the background to show us the interior of a real *bodegón*, in which men and women are boisterously eating and being served, while children play. The painting also illustrates Loarte's painterly approach, which, when his pictures have not been flattened or overcleaned, still appears fresh and fluid.

Alejandro de Loarte's *Poultry Vendor* (fig. 44), painted in 1626, is his only known genre composition. It is a large, ambitious work which demonstrates his talents in the depiction of domestic and game birds, as well as human figures.[38] An autograph replica of the painting is known; both are signed with the emblem of a skull crowned with laurel, probably added after the artist's premature death and perhaps implying that

Fig. 41 Alejandro de Loarte, *Still Life with Fowl and Kitchen Scene*, *c*.1623–5. Oil on canvas. Madrid, formerly Casa Torres collection.

Fig. 42 Alejandro de Loarte, *Still Life with Meat, Fowl and Tavern Scene*, *c*.1623–5. Oil on canvas, 49.5 x 70 cm. Private collection.

Fig. 43 Alejandro de Loarte, *Kitchen Still Life*, 1625. Oil on canvas, 81 x 108 cm. Madrid, Várez Fisa collection.

his posthumous fame will rest on this composition.[39] One of these paintings may have been the picture of 'a poultry vendor signed with my name' mentioned in Loarte's will as having been bought by Antonio Martínez de Heredia, who was an important patron of his still lifes.[40]

Loarte may have been aware of Pliny's mention of the stalls painted by the ancient artist Peiraikos, and might have known foreign paintings of female poultry vendors. However, his painting is one of entirely local reference and is set in the main square of Toledo, the Plaza de Zocodover. The posed situation, in which the boy pays for a

16 Alejandro de Loarte, *c*.1600–26
Still Life with Game and Fruit
Signed and dated, lower left: *Alexandro de Loarte, fat. 1623*
Oil on canvas, 84 x 105 cm
Madrid, Fundación Santamarca

Art historians have noted, without being able to explain it, the similarity between the still lifes of Loarte and those painted at more or less the same time by the older Tuscan artist Jacopo Chimenti, called Empoli (1551–1640). The basis of that comparison is the game and meat hanging from meat-hooks along the top of some of Loarte's compositions, as seen here in his best-known still life. Apart from the use of this device, which may reflect little more than a common practice in Italian and Spanish daily life, there are more differences than similarities in the styles of the two painters. In the Santamarca still life, Loarte shows himself much more interested than his Italian counterpart in the description of textures and the creation of a coherent space through the use of light and shadow (note especially the plumage of the pigeons hanging near the left edge of the picture). He also knits his composition into a structural unity with a pronounced but subtly nuanced use of symmetry, a formal recourse he shared with many of his Spanish contemporaries.

Fig. 44 Alejandro de Loarte, *Poultry Vendor*, 1626. Oil on canvas, 162 x 130 cm. Madrid, Private collection.

live hen, simulates an everyday transaction. A joke may be implied in that the boy is incongruously dressed in full hunting gear. However, the dour expressions would seem to contradict this; they also dampen any lewd connotations the action might have.[41]

The painter Juan Bautista de Espinosa (*c*.1585–1640) who signed the *Still Life with Silver-Gilt Salvers* in 1624 (cat. 17) is probably to be identified with the Juan de Espinosa documented at the Valladolid court between 1603 and 1606.[42] He is certainly the artist documented in Madrid between 1611 and 1614, where he was in the employ of the Duque del Infantado, possibly as portrait painter.[43] He was resident in Toledo by 1616, where he enjoyed a conventional career as an approved painter of the archdiocese, mostly painting altarpieces for provincial churches until his death.[44] It is not certain where Espinosa painted his one known, signed and dated still life,

17 Juan Bautista de Espinosa, *c*.1585–1640
Still Life with Silver-Gilt Salvers
Signed and dated on shelves above: *Joannes Bap^{ta} Despinossa faciebat anno D, 1624*
Oil on canvas, 98 x 118 cm
Spain, Masaveu collection

The severe elegance of upper-class domestic life in the reign of Philip IV is evoked by this spectacular still life, which Eric Young went so far as to call 'the one most rigidly symmetrical composition that we know'. Indeed, its calculated but subtly varied symmetry and rich but restrained colour contrasts of red and white, black and gold are characteristic features of many Spanish still lifes of the early seventeenth century. The painting's opulence reminds us that the artist was once in the employ of the powerful Duque del Infantado and must have been familiar with the accoutrements of the courtly table. All of the objects in the picture – the glassware, the silver-gilt tableware, the terracotta bowls – are probably of Spanish manufacture. The red bowls probably contain *hipocrás*, a popular alcoholic concoction composed of good wine, sugar, cinnamon, ambergris and musk. A cone of cinnamon sticks rests on the table-top beside one of the bowls. It is in the artist's manipulation of all these elements, as we look beyond the obvious symmetrical premise of the composition, that one can observe an ingenuous but likeable sense of visual play at work: one of the two glass flasks of liquid flanking the central salver is filled with water, the other with white wine; of the two oranges at the front edge of the table, the one on the left is placed with its navel pointing up, the one on the right with its navel pointing straight out of the picture.

Fig. 45 Juan Bautista de Espinosa, *Still Life with Vases of Flowers and Basket of Fruit*, c.1625. Oil on canvas, 63 x 85 cm. Location unknown.

since he divided his time between Toledo and Madrid, where he is again documented in 1619 and 1629.[45]

Older than either Van der Hamen or Loarte, Espinosa appears to have been born in 1585.[46] He was probably a conventionally trained artist, who took up still-life painting late in his career as a consequence of the genre's rise in popularity. *Vases of Flowers and Basket of Fruit* (fig. 45), said to be signed by the artist, was exhibited in Madrid in 1935, when it was paired with another unsigned still life of a basket of grapes.[47] The jasper and gilt-bronze urns in the signed painting, which is now known only from a photograph, strike a courtly, affluent note, which is fully apparent in Espinosa's splendid still life of 1624 (cat. 17). A degree of refinement, bordering on preciousness, is evident in the description of details, and the depiction of the open-weave basket anticipates the later works of Tomás Hiepes in Valencia (fig. 91). In Espinosa's case, the dignified ordering of objects on a table-top or *aparador* (sideboard) may reflect actual practice. Such rigorous symmetry in the arrangement of motifs is also found in still lifes by Van der Hamen and Loarte. It should not be considered a naive quality of the pictures, but rather a reflection of a taste for highly formalised display, which characterised much of court and public life in seventeenth-century Spain.

Madrid: Barrera, Ponce, Labrador

Philip IV and certain grandees at the Spanish court set a fashion for collecting pictures that swept through the middle and upper levels of Spanish society in the 1630s.[1] This no doubt benefited the many artists in the capital who sought a livelihood from painting, and it probably encouraged the taste for still lifes among middle-class collectors. It is clear from documentary records, however, that there were certain collectors who had a particular predilection for still life. The informative inventories of the collections of Domingo de Soria Arteaga (1644), a royal accountant, and Francisco Merchant de la Cerda (1662), reveal their enthusiasm.[2] Although these inventories are unusual in that many pictures have attributions, there are many others that list large numbers of unattributed still lifes, suggesting the degree to which the genre had become a significant sideline of a host of minor painters. Francisco Barrera, Antonio Ponce and Juan de Espinosa perhaps typify this sort of artist, not considered important enough to have merited a biography in any of the old sources, but recognised in their time for paintings whose quality lifted their oeuvre above the level of the mass-produced painting (*pintura ordinaria*) that appears to have been the norm.[3]

Francisco Barrera (1595–after 1657) was an enterprising artist and an activist member of the Madrid Guild of Saint Luke, who in 1639 orchestrated a lawsuit on its behalf against a sales tax.[4] He headed a successful practice and sold paintings from two shops on a prime site in the centre of Madrid, opposite the church of San Felipe, near the spot where Juan de Arellano later opened his own shop (*obrador público*).[5] Vicente Carducho, the prime defender of the status of painting as a Liberal Art, regarded such outlets as demeaning to the profession.[6] It was here in 1644 that an Inquisitor denounced six unorthodox paintings of archangels that were hanging outside Barrera's door.[7] In 1633 Velázquez and Carducho headed a royal commission appointed for the purpose of curbing the spread of badly painted, improper or otherwise 'unofficial' royal portraits made for sale on the open market. Portraits by Barrera and Ponce were among those collected for review, but we do not know if these were among the few allowed to pass without revision or, indeed, destruction.[8] As a further indication of his enterprise, in the later 1630s Barrera led a team of artists, including Ponce, who were employed as contract workers (gilders and decorators) at the Buen Retiro Palace.[9]

Barrera's large output of still lifes varies in quality, but the best is appealing in its earthy informality. He made something of a speciality of seasonal still lifes; the most ambitious and best-known set of these, painted in 1638, comprises four large-scale works with emblematic figures and landscape vistas (fig. 46).[10] The format and scale of these works allow for spectacular displays of foodstuffs. One of Barrera's more ambitious projects was the painting of a set of large still lifes representing the Twelve Months (cat. 18). The production of works in series obviously satisfied a market for

18 Francisco Barrera, 1595–after 1657
Still Life with Meat, Fruit and Vegetables (the Month of April)
c.1640s. Fragmentary signature, lower right
Oil on canvas, 101.5 x 156 cm
Private collection

This painting by Barrera is one of several now known which comprised a larger series of the Twelve Months. The best preserved of the group, it tells us a good deal about his style. Here, as in the other works in the series, the artist has spread out a profusion of agricultural products on a stepped arena, presumably the corner of a kitchen or larder, giving onto a landscape. The seasonal foods include baskets of apples and oranges, a butchered mutton, a spring lamb, a ham, a brace of game fowl, bunches of leeks and radishes. Complementing this fare is a spray of apple blossoms, a pottery jug and a glass bowl of water, a salt cellar and a paper of peppercorns. The arrangement of objects is natural, even haphazard. While Barrera's draughtsmanship is not the equal of Van der Hamen's (the architectural setting, in particular, lacks the spatial clarity and perspectival precision normally achieved by the latter), the artist has successfully defined the earthy textures of what he depicted. He succeeded particularly well in the glistening quarter of mutton in the foreground, something of a painterly *tour de force*.

Fig. 46 Francisco Barrera, *Summer*, 1638. Oil on canvas, 166 x 250 cm. Seville, Museo de Bellas Artes.

19 Antonio Ponce, 1608–77
Still Life with Artichokes and a Talavera Vase of Flowers
c.1650s. Signed, lower left: *A. Ponze fecit*
Oil on canvas, 72 x 94 cm
Spain, Juan Abello collection

Although he began as a close follower of Van der Hamen, his uncle by marriage, Ponce reveals in this mature work a Baroque exuberance not found in his master's highly structured still lifes of fruit and flowers. Already by the 1640s, Ponce's use of a light background distinguished his practice from Van der Hamen's. Thus the backlit contours of leaves and blossoms stand out in vivid contrast. In this work, which probably dates from the following decade, there is a delicacy in the modelling of the flowers that may respond in a general way to the subtle style of Juan Fernández, El Labrador, but its ultimate roots lie not in the Caravaggesque tradition that motivated the latter but rather in the Flemish mode that inspired Van der Hamen.

Fig. 47 Francisco Barrera, *Hunting Still Life with Game Fowl*, c.1640s. Oil on canvas, 81 x 106 cm. Spain, Private collection.

still lifes as decoration, and ensured the sale of more pictures.[11] But Barrera also produced individual still lifes, such as the handsome *Hunting Still Life with Game Fowl* (fig. 47), which evokes one of the favourite pleasures of the leisured class.[12]

Antonio Ponce (1608–77) was apprenticed to his uncle Juan van der Hamen in 1624 and became an independent master three years later.[13] He is likely to have assisted in his master's studio and was an adept imitator of his style. Like Barrera, Ponce painted at least one series of large still lifes representing the Months of the Year.[14] In each of them he copied at least one motif used in the still lifes of Van der Hamen. A flowerpiece in Strasbourg, dated 1650 and one of five similar ones known, shows that Ponce perpetuated Van der Hamen's style with little change until the middle of the century.[15]

Ponce's generally tight and lacklustre handling, which remained essentially unchanged throughout his career, suggests that he was not able to adapt and update his style in response to works by his more progressive contemporaries.[16] His *Kitchen Still Life* (fig. 48) is an accomplished painting, but its uniform handling distances it from works by gifted contemporaries such as Antonio de Pereda (cat. 29). Ponce's fruit still lifes are among his best and are characterised by the novel feature of light backgrounds, against which the contours of grape leaves, for example, stand out in lively relief (fig. 49). These surely reflect the influence of Caravaggesque still-life painting. His grapes lack the translucency obviously valued in the works of El Labrador and Juan de Espinosa (cat. 20 and fig. 51). However, the best of his flower paintings and garlands (figs 50 and 102) are works of considerable refinement, in which the precision of his draughtsmanship and the delicacy of his modelling function together to best advantage. *Still Life with Artichokes and a Talavera Vase of Flowers* (cat. 19) is perhaps his most beautiful work.

Juan de Espinosa (documented 1628–59) was a contemporary of Ponce and was likewise married in 1628.[17] Until 1659 he is mentioned in documents in Madrid along with artist colleagues, including the painter Francisco de Burgos Mantilla.[18] In Espinosa's still lifes, fruit is often combined with exotic articles, such as seashells and imported, fanciful terracotta pottery; his works were sometimes sought after by discerning collectors.[19] He seems to have exploited his forte for painting grapes, which

Fig. 48 Antonio Ponce, *Kitchen Still Life*, c.1650s. Oil on canvas, 56 x 94 cm. Segovia, Lafora collection.

Fig. 49 Antonio Ponce, *Still Life with Grapes and Pomegranates*, 1651. Oil on canvas, 62 x 83 cm. Barcelona, Private collection.

Fig. 50 Antonio Ponce, *Flowerpiece*, c.1650s. Oil on canvas, 42.3 x 25.3 cm. Madrid, Private collection.

Fig. 51 Juan de Espinosa, *Still Life with Grapes, Apples and Plums*, c.1645–55. Oil on canvas, 76 x 59 cm. Madrid, Museo del Prado.

20 Juan de Espinosa, doc. 1628–59
Still Life with Grapes, Fruit and a Terracotta Jar
Signed and dated on ledge at left: *Juº despinosa/1646*
Oil on canvas, octagonal, 67.5 x 68 cm
Madrid, Naseiro collection

When this painting appeared in a London saleroom in 1992, it was masquerading as a nearly square canvas, with the corners filled in and the ledge at the bottom extended to the new edges. Cleaned and restored to its original shape, it is one of the few Spanish still lifes in the octagonal format to survive. Octagonal *fruteros* had been painted in Italy by Luca Forte, whose still lifes were already known in Madrid by this time. And two '*fruteros ochavados*' were catalogued in the collection of the Conde de Monterrey in 1653 (as number 141 in the inventory).

All of Espinosa's known still lifes, and most of those cited in old inventories, depict grapes. As can be seen here, he was particularly adept at rendering the translucency of the fruit. Responding to a *horror vacuui* that characterises all of his pictures, Espinosa has entirely filled up the pictorial space, yet no form, other than the thin cords at the top, touches the edge of the canvas. The stepped stone ledges interact beautifully with the octagonal shape, enlivening the shallow depth of the space.

appear in all of his known still lifes, but the quality of his works is variable. In some, such as *Still Life with Grapes, Flowers and Shells* in the Louvre, the relief of the grapes was arrived at quickly in a single process of modelling, resulting in a certain opacity. In others, such as the Prado's *Still Life with Grapes, Apples and Plums* (fig. 51), the forms have been realised through the application of several transparent glazes, resulting in an extraordinary inner translucency, an iridescent bloom on the grapes and plums, and a nuanced modelling of the apples that were virtually unrivalled at the time.[20] Clearly, Espinosa, like many of the other still-life painters treated here, could excel when he wanted to, but was often content to work on a routine level.[21] One of his most beautiful and ambitious paintings is the octagonal *Still Life with Grapes, Fruit and a Terracotta Jar* (cat. 20), in which the grapes have the glassy translucency often seen in his works.

In specialising in the depiction of grapes, Espinosa must have been addressing himself to the fashion for such pictures that was generated in the 1630s by the activity of his much more famous contemporary Juan Fernández, El Labrador, one of the few Spanish still-life painters to achieve international fame in the seventeenth century. El Labrador (The Rustic) lived outside Madrid – we do not know where – and only occasionally came to court, where those who had ordered his pictures awaited him.[22] Palomino's statement (1724) that Labrador was from the province of Extremadura is unproven; he remains, to some extent, an enigma.[23] Recent scholarship has rediscovered his real name, Juan Fernández, has documented the efforts of his English patrons to obtain his works, and has assembled a small corpus of still lifes.[24] But the majority of his pictures, which once graced the best collections of Madrid, remain unrecognised today.

Labrador made a speciality of still lifes and flowerpieces, from which his fame derived, but landscapes and religious pictures by him are also documented.[25] For the collectors and patrons at court, who eagerly awaited his infrequent visits, his paintings may have reflected his intimate contact with nature and epitomised an idealised view of country life familiar to them from the literature and theatre of the time.[26] Although Labrador's paintings are anything but naïve, it may be that he responded to this construction of his personality at court. That a rural painter of this description should have been pursued, as he was, by monarchs, aristocrats and wealthy collectors from the capital was indeed something of a phenomenon.

One of Labrador's most significant patrons was the Roman nobleman and architect Giovanni Battista Crescenzi, Marqués de la Torre (1577–1635). Crescenzi came to the Spanish court in 1617, bringing with him the Caravaggesque painter Bartolomeo Cavarozzi.[27] He enjoyed a reputation as a connoisseur of painting and was himself an amateur artist; on arriving in Spain, he presented one of his own still lifes to Philip III, a fact that became part of the lore of Spanish art history.[28] Crescenzi's interest in still-life painting was long-standing, and before he left Italy, he encouraged the painting of such pictures in a sort of 'academy' of artists which met in his Roman palace and included the young Pietro Paolo Bonzi.[29] After arriving in Spain, he continued to protect young artists.

In 1630 Crescenzi offered to sell a number of paintings from his collection to King Charles I of England; included among them were four landscapes by Labrador.[30] And among the still lifes in Crescenzi's collection at the time of his death in 1635, only one was attributed: 'a small painting of a plate of grapes by El Labrador'.[31] The Caravaggesque style of Labrador's still lifes may have been developed under the encouragement of Crescenzi,[32] who perhaps also encouraged the artist to pursue his speciality in painting grapes. Crescenzi's Roman protégé Pietro Paolo Bonzi excelled

Fig. 52 Pietro Paolo Bonzi, *Still Life with Grapes, Melons, Pears and Plums*, c.1610s. Oil on canvas, 97 x 130 cm. Formerly Spoleto, Galleria Paolo Sapori.

in painting grapes, and some of his pictures (fig. 52) are comparable to still lifes by Labrador (fig. 54). A painting of grapes by Bonzi was paired with one by Labrador in the remarkable collection of still lifes belonging to the royal accountant Domingo de Soria Arteaga, mentioned above (page 64). The collection also included four other grape still lifes by Labrador.[33]

Many of Labrador's paintings of grapes listed in early inventories were quite small and were simply described as 'a bunch of grapes'.[34] Reading these documents in the light of existing paintings long attributed to the artist, we can assume that some of the entries referred to pictures representing nothing more than a bunch of grapes hanging by a cord against a dark background. Two such paintings in the Cerralbo Museum in Madrid have long been known.[35] Another pair with identical qualities, now in separate collections, has recently come to light (cat. 21 and fig. 53). These are important visual documents for understanding the early development of the still life in Spain: eschewing the artifice of *trompe l'oeil*, the artist has confronted the fabled subject matter of Zeuxis with a directness bordering on ingenuousness. In one of the pictures, he has depicted a few desiccated grapes among the ripe ones; in the other, he has gone to great pains to depict, with microscopic accuracy, a fly alighting on one of the grapes. Thus we see in these works a corollary to the very earliest still lifes, in which the 'imitation of nature' was tried in its purest form.

The popularity of paintings of grapes generated by the activity of Labrador and his imitators has occasionally resulted in modern times in confused attributions. The beautiful but severely cropped *Still Life with Grapes and Apples* in the Prado (fig. 54) has been attributed to Espinosa since 1872, but is more probably by Labrador.[36] A contemporary copy of the painting (fig. 55) reveals its original proportions; in this copy, the black grapes (painted in a different technique from Labrador's) have not lost their definition, as they have done in the original (a consequence of Labrador's

Fig. 53 Juan Fernández, El Labrador, *Still Life with Hanging White Grapes*, c.1620s. Oil on canvas, 29.5 x 38 cm. Madrid, Private collection.

21 Juan Fernández, El Labrador, doc. 1630s
Still Life with Hanging White Grapes
*c.*1620s. Oil on canvas, 29.5 x 38 cm
Madrid, Naseiro collection

This small picture and its pendant (fig. 53), both published here for the first time, are identical in style and technique to another pair of even smaller canvases representing hanging white grapes in the Museo Cerralbo in Madrid, which have traditionally been attributed to Labrador. There is no reason to doubt the attribution. It is possible that all these works date from the time of the artist's early encounters with Giovanni Battista Crescenzi in the 1620s. The delicate modelling of the stems and grapes, some of which are bruised or withered, is consistent with what can be observed in the Hampton Court still life (cat. 23). In this case, however, the underpainting of the forms is comprised largely of lead white, which has not sunk into the ground and has allowed the glazes which give subtlety to the forms to function as intended. In the pendant still life, a microscopically detailed fly rests on one of the grapes. Such tiny and straightforward examples of Labrador's naturalism must have held a great appeal for collectors, since many of his works cited in seventeenth-century inventories were paintings of grapes no larger than this.

Fig. 54 Juan Fernández, El Labrador, *Still Life with Grapes and Apples, c.*1630s. Oil on canvas, 50 x 39 cm. Madrid, Museo del Prado.

Fig. 55 Juan Fernández, El Labrador (copy), *Still Life with Grapes and Apples.* Oil on canvas. Madrid, Private collection.

Fig. 56 Unknown artist, *Portrait of Sir Arthur Hopton and an Attendant*, 1641. Oil on canvas, 186.6 x 115.8 cm. Dallas, Southern Methodist University, Meadows Museum, Algur H. Meadows Collection.

practice of modelling grapes and foliage with thin glazes of colour directly on to a dark absorbent ground with no lead white underpainting, see note 44). On the back of the copy is a seventeenth-century inscription that reads: '*Orig. de Juan Fenz/Labrador*', which, in spite of the picture being merely a copy, is a more reliable guide to the attribution of the original than a nineteenth-century attribution. Moreover, the Prado painting, which comes from the Spanish royal collection, is probably the work referred to in an entry from the 1772 inventory of the Buen Retiro Palace: 'A bunch of grapes hanging on its stem, three-quarters high, two-thirds wide, by Juan Labrador'. This could be one of the thirteen still lifes sold by Crescenzi to Philip IV in 1634 as decoration for the Buen Retiro.[37]

Many still lifes were attributed to Labrador with conviction in nineteenth-century inventories, and some of them, such as cat. 22, are of exceptional quality. Our still limited knowledge of the artist's style, however, makes it difficult today to evaluate some of those attributions decisively.

Crescenzi, it seems, promoted Labrador's paintings among collectors at court. From 1629 Labrador was closely associated with the Englishmen Sir Francis Cottington (later Lord Cottington) and his secretary Arthur Hopton (fig. 56), English diplomats at the Spanish court who became great admirers of the artist's still lifes.[38] Writing from England at the end of 1631, Cottington was trying to obtain for Charles I a still life of 'painted grapes'. Between 1632 and 1633, Hopton sent five Labrador still lifes to England for Cottington's wife and for the king, apparently acquiring them from the artist himself. Among these was the *Still Life with Apples, Grapes, Chestnuts and Acorns* (cat. 23), described in the 1639 inventory of Charles I's collection as: 'The picture of several sorts of fruits in a white earthen vessel; grapes, apples, chesnuts [sic], and the like, painted upon the right light. Done by the Spanish Labrador; given to the King by my Lord Cottington'.[39] The style of the picture betrays the influence on the artist of Caravaggesque painting, but Labrador adopted none of the compositional conventions used in still lifes by Caravaggio's Roman or Neapolitan imitators. What seems likely is that Crescenzi discovered the talented rustic, who had already embarked on his own exploration of the 'imitation of nature',

22 Attributed to Juan Fernández, El Labrador?, doc. 1630s
Still Life with Bunches of Hanging Grapes
1630s–40s. Oil on canvas, 44 x 61 cm
Madrid, Naseiro collection

This imposing image of grapes is a powerful example of one of the most sought-after types of subject matter among Spanish still lifes of the seventeenth century. Never published or exhibited before, it has been attributed to Labrador since at least 1850. Nevertheless, because of the obvious popularity of still lifes of grapes and our limited knowledge of Labrador's style, it seems prudent to hold reservations as to its authorship.

   The painting provides a contrast to the style of Juan de Espinosa, whose grapes usually have a glass-like quality (see cat. 20). The rather free modelling of the curly leaves and the intense light and strong shadow that define their forms are more dramatic than in Espinosa's still lifes of grapes. Yet the modelling of the leaves is not as subtle as one expects from Labrador. This exceptional painting, coupled with the enormous number of inventory descriptions of such still lifes, some of them with attributions to known artists, is perhaps a lesson in how much we have yet to learn about this subject, and about Labrador himself.

23 **Juan Fernández, El Labrador,** doc. 1630s
Still Life with Apples, Grapes, Chestnuts and Acorns
c.1632. Oil on canvas, 83 x 68.4 cm
Hampton Court Palace, Her Majesty The Queen

First catalogued in the collection of King Charles I in 1639, this picture was probably among those sent by Arthur Hopton from Madrid to Lord Cottington in November 1632. On 22 January 1633, Lord Cottington wrote to Hopton in Madrid of the king's reaction to Labrador's works: 'The paintings are extremely liked'.

The composition of the painting represents the very antithesis of the studied artificiality of Van der Hamen's still lifes, in which symmetry, perspective and the interrelation of geometric shapes play such an important role. Labrador seems deliberately to have avoided the impression that artifice intervened at all. In the true spirit of Caravaggio, he seems to have caught nature just as it is, heightening the perception of detail through his use of a satiny chiaroscuro (perhaps exaggerated by chemical changes in the pigments over time). His style represents a personal, even eccentric, adaptation of the general features of Caravaggio's style, of the kind that could understandably have developed far from the master's coterie in Rome, perhaps under the encouragement of Labrador's Roman patron, Giovanni Battista Crescenzi, who seems to have taken the artist under his wing in the 1620s and early 1630s.

Fig. 57 Juan Fernández, El Labrador, *Vase of Flowers*, 1636. Oil on panel, 41 cm diameter. Private collection.

and opened his eyes to new artistic possibilities through conversation and through the example of works (not necessarily only still lifes) in his own collection.

In 1635, Arthur Hopton wrote that he had persuaded Labrador to 'try his hand at flowers', a further indication that the artist was guided by his patrons to expand his talents.[40] One of the results was the beautiful roundel dated in the following year (fig. 57), which is one of the most extraordinary flowerpieces of the whole seventeenth century.[41] Its idiosyncratic composition and satin-smooth chiaroscuro correspond to nothing done earlier in Spain. Labrador has filled the tondo with blooms, none of which is cropped by the edge of the panel; as a receptacle, he painted a rustic earthenware pot, to which the gradations of light and shadow lend an emphatic volume. The radial bouquet fans out in an unstudied way across the picture plane, and a moth hovers about the pink rose. The flowers the artist chose to paint (roses, narcissi, Spanish broom, foxglove, marigold and blue iris) could, except for the iris, have been grown in any country garden, and stand in marked contrast to the cultivated blooms, especially the tulips, that Van der Hamen arranged in fancy vases (cat. 9). Avoiding strong local colour, the picture's subtly graded chromatic harmony has been only slightly disturbed by loss of colour in the central iris, whose blue was painted with the fugitive smalt. The bouquet, illuminated as though by a blaze of daylight through the open window of a darkened room, takes on a haunting presence.

24 Juan Fernández, El Labrador, doc.
1630s
Vase of Flowers
1630s. Oil on canvas (fragment), 44 x 34 cm
Madrid, Museo del Prado

Long misattributed to Zurbarán, this important
little picture was finally recognised as the work
of Labrador in 1978, following the discovery
several years earlier of a signed flowerpiece by
the artist (fig. 57). The inherent problems of
Labrador's technique have resulted in a darkening of the pigments over time, so that the
faïence vase and foliage no longer have the visual presence they once had. Barely visible on the
table-top at the left is a fragmentary bunch of
grapes, which, like those in the Hampton Court
still life, have mostly lost their formal definition.
This indicates that the painting is a fragment,
and it may possibly be part of a larger still life
that was described in the 1651 inventory of the
collection of the Marqués de Eliche in Madrid:
'A canvas by Labrador with an earthenware jar
of roses, carnations and lilies with other flowers
and some bunches of grapes and open pomegranates, one and a quarter *varas* wide and one
in height with its black frame'.

In the 1640s, some of the great noble collectors of the court, who probably had
no personal dealings with Labrador, nevertheless managed to acquire some of his
works. The most distinguished of these collectors were the Marqués de Eliche and
Marqués de Leganés.[42] The former probably owned the beautiful *Vase of Flowers* in
the Prado (cat. 24), which seems to be a fragment of a larger work described in his
inventory of 1651.[43] The vase of flowers in this painting may have been cut out because
the rest had deteriorated. Labrador's technique, particularly when he painted on canvas, was unorthodox and may have resulted from deficient formal training.[44]

Madrid: Pereda to Deleito

Giovanni Battista Crescenzi's influence as a patron of painters, and of the still life, did not stop with Labrador; he was also responsible for encouraging, indeed launching, the most gifted young artist of his generation. While still in the workshop of his master, Pedro de las Cuevas, Antonio de Pereda (1611–78) was discovered by his first benefactor, Don Francisco Tejada, an important collector and lawyer on the Council of Castile, who took the young artist under his protection, 'desiring to help him to learn'.[1] On seeing Pereda's paintings, however, Crescenzi took him under his own wing and lodged him in his palace, where, 'under his guidance by the age of eighteen he was so excellent a painter that the first of his works to appear seemed to be by very experienced artists'.[2] Such was Crescenzi's pride in his protégé that in 1629, when Pereda was indeed only eighteen years old, Crescenzi sent an *Immaculate Conception* by the artist to Rome, to his brother Cardinal Pietro Paolo Crescenzi. This painting, when first shown in Madrid, 'made a lot of noise at court and aroused great jealousy'.[3] Crescenzi was also responsible for obtaining for Pereda his first commission for an altarpiece, in the Madrid church of San Miguel, and promoted him at court;[4] it was probably thanks to Crescenzi that Pereda secured in 1634 the commission for a battle painting for the Hall of Realms of the Buen Retiro Palace. He was the youngest artist to participate in this project, where he was pitted against painters of the calibre and reputation of Carducho, Velázquez and Zurbarán.[5] Pereda's début was the *Relief of Genoa* (fig. 58), whose warm, sensuous style, lively portraits and spectacular display of virtuosity in the naturalistic depiction of stuffs and detail made it recognisably one of the best of the series.[6] Pereda's promising court career was, however, abruptly cut short on Crescenzi's death in March 1635. The artist may have been the victim of the emnity of the king's favourite, the Conde-Duque de Olivares, towards Crescenzi and his circle, and it is possible that Velázquez was also jealous of his talents. Be that as it may, after such an auspicious beginning he never again painted for the king and was forced to build his career, like most other painters, on commissions from religious institutions and private collectors. Pereda never forgot his debt of gratitude to Crescenzi, however. On his deathbed forty-three years later, he ordered in his last will and testament the funding of masses for the soul of 'the Marqués, my Lord'.[7]

The earliest dated still life by Pereda that has come down to us was painted in 1634, the year before Crescenzi's death. In the tiny roundel *Still Life with Walnuts* (cat. 25), the twenty-three-year-old painter's genius is revealed with extraordinary force. At about the same time, according to Díaz del Valle (writing in 1656–9), he painted his first great masterpiece, the painting known today simply as *Vanitas*, which at the time was called *El desengaño del mundo* (The Disillusionment of the World) (cat. 26).[8]

Fig. 58 Antonio de Pereda, *Relief of Genoa*, 1634. Oil on canvas, 290 x 370 cm. Madrid, Museo del Prado.

It has been argued elsewhere, and can now be stated with virtual certainty, that the first owner of Pereda's youthful masterpiece was Philip IV's principal major-domo, Juan Alfonso Enríquez de Cabrera (1600–47), 9th Almirante de Castilla, 5th Duque de Medina de Rioseco.[9] It was very probably Crescenzi who obtained this commission for his young protégé. In 1634 the picture must have astonished the artistic community of Madrid, such was its confident technical mastery, the eloquence of its symbolic imagery and the ease with which it assimilated the best from foreign schools. The Almirante was already by then a prestigious collector, meriting Carducho's praise in 1633;[10] by 1638 he was one of three collectors in the capital, besides the king, singled out by Arthur Hopton for being 'more affectioned unto the Art of Painting...than the world imagines'.[11] On his death in 1647, the Almirante's collection numbered 938 paintings, in addition to a wealth of other *objets d'art* from all over the world.[12] The inventory made by the painter Antonio Arias listed, among the Old Master paintings, works by Dürer, Raphael, Leonardo, Titian, Sebastiano del Piombo and Giovanni Bellini; and, among contemporary masters, paintings by Brueghel, Rubens, Van Dyck, Caravaggio, Guido Reni, Guercino and Domenichino. There were fifteen canvases by Ribera alone. As was common at that time in the inventories of great collections taken in Madrid, few of the Spanish pictures (other than those by Ribera) were attributed: in fact, only two. One was a small fruit still life by Pereda.[13] The other, valued quite highly at 4000 *reales*, seems to be Pereda's *Disillusionment of the World*, but the entry is vague.[14] The matter is clarified, however, by the extremely detailed description of the picture – unpublished until now – when it was again inventoried a generation later, on the death of Juan Alfonso Enríquez de Cabrera's son, the 10th Almirante de Castilla (1625–91). The painting was at that time exactly where Palomino (1724) said it had been, in the Pieza de

25 Antonio de Pereda, 1611–78
Still Life with Walnuts
Signed and dated, bottom right: *AP/1634*
Oil on panel, 20.7 cm diameter
Spain, Private collection

Meeting the challenge of designing a stable composition within a circle, the young Pereda has used the circular form of this tiny still life almost like a magnifying glass, to focus our scrutiny on the subject matter. The few walnuts resting on a narrow shelf are somewhat larger than life-size and assume a certain monumentality. At the right is a whole, uncracked walnut; the strong light falling from the upper left turns imperceptibly into velvety shadow on its wrinkled shell. To the left of it are two other walnuts whose shells have been cracked and partly peeled away. With breathtaking skill, the artist begins to reveal the anatomy of his subject. He shows us a cross-section of the shell and the membranes and fibrous dividers of the internal architecture. And finally, in the fragments towards the front, he shows us the treasure, the kernel, held like a gemstone in a setting; he has managed to convey the moist and oily quality of the kernel, in contrast to the brittle quality of the shells. In fact, almost every aspect of the nature of a nut has been addressed. Certainly in 1634, no artist in Madrid was painting still lifes so brilliantly.

Españoles, a special gallery of the Almirante's palace designated for paintings by eminent Spaniards:

> Another painting on canvas, one and one-half *varas* less one finger high by two and one-third *varas* less one finger wide, which they call the Disillusionment, in which is seen a figure of an angel with outstretched wings and a jewel as a clasp of its clothes, and in the left hand a miniature with a half-length portrait of an emperor, and the right [hand] pointing to a globe, and on a table a clock with little towers and three portraits of women, a necklace of pearls, a gold chain, some gold and silver coins and three playing cards of spades, and on the other side there is an hour-glass, some armour, books and skulls and a candlestick with a candle, [valued] at two thousand *reales*.[15]

The symbolic language of this painting has been explored by several authors.[16] The picture's power as a work of art derives, however, from Pereda's ability to give such a compelling physical presence to the meaningful objects in his still life, and from the restraint he exerted in order to achieve a coherent and focused message. Late in life he treated the subject again, in a canvas which, Palomino said in 1724, was still in the possession of the artist's heirs. The *Vanitas* today in the Uffizi (fig. 59), which is composed along similar lines, with an angel presiding over two adjacent tables laden with symbolic objects, and holding in his left hand a portrait miniature of a ruler, is probably that work.[17] The picture is painted in Pereda's late style, as can be seen by

26 **Antonio de Pereda, 1611–78**
Vanitas
*c.*1634. Oil on canvas, 139.5 x 174 cm
Vienna, Kunsthistorisches Museum

One of the greatest masterpieces of the Spanish Baroque, executed when Pereda was in his early twenties, this allegory of death was evidently famous from the beginning. Pereda's friend Lázaro Díaz del Valle wrote during the artist's lifetime, in 1657, that it had been painted just prior to the *Relief of Genoa* (fig. 58) – that is to say, about 1634 – and described it as 'the canvas of the Disillusionment of the World (*el desengaño del mundo*), with some skulls and other spoils of death, which is everything that the art of painting can achieve...'. Palomino referred to the picture again in 1724, saying that, because it was such a famous work, the Almirante de Castilla had placed it in a special hall of his palace designated for paintings by eminent Spaniards.

Pereda's gift for portraying the objective reality of things has underscored the symbolic power of a great variety of significant objects: the magnificent gilt clock, measurer of the process of dying that begins at birth; the terrestrial globe shown to us by the angel, domain of earthly rulers like the Emperor Charles V and his ancient counterparts; coins and jewels and portraits of ladies, signifying the hollow comforts of wealth and the affections of this mortal life; a gun, the armour and baton of command, signifying the futility of worldly authority; the extinguished candle, familiar reminder of the instantaneous advent of death; and the most astonishing presence of all, the mound of human skulls, shown to us with an objective focus and sense of drama never before achieved so compellingly in Spanish art. Perhaps the most poignant hieroglyph in the entire painting, however, is the cameo portrait of the Emperor Charles V, who abdicated his thrones in 1556 and retired to the monastery of Yuste in western Spain in order to prepare for his own death, thus becoming for Catholics the very paradigm of virtue in the face of the inevitable.

Fig. 59 Antonio de Pereda, *Vanitas*, *c*.1670. Oil on canvas, 163 x 295 cm. Florence, Uffizi.

Fig. 60 Antonio de Pereda, *Saint William of Aquitaine*, 1671. Oil on canvas, 110 x 165 cm. Madrid, Real Academia de Bellas Artes de San Fernando.

27 Antonio de Pereda?, 1611–78
The Dream of the Knight
*c.*1650. Inscribed on the banner: *AETERNE PUNG[I]T CITO VOLAT ET*
OCCIDIT (It pierces perpetually, flies quickly and kills)
Oil on canvas, 152 x 217 cm
Madrid, Museo de la Real Academia de Bellas Artes de San Fernando

One of the most famous and beloved of Spanish Baroque paintings, this masterpiece has recently become the subject of a debate over its authorship (see text). This should not detract, however, from our perception of it as one of the most compelling images of its time. Apart from the matter of its style, it differs from the Vienna *Vanitas* (cat. 26) by Pereda, in the way in which the moral message is delivered. In addition to the angel, the artist of this work has included the figure of a fashionably dressed young gentleman asleep in a chair beside a table heaped with emblems of power, riches and transience. The angel's message concerning the swift and unexpected advent of death is presented to us only indirectly: he is really addressing the dreaming *caballero*. The philosophical question of whether the dreaming or the waking state is a closer approximation of reality was the theme of one of the most famous and quintessential works of Spanish Golden Age theatre, Calderón de la Barca's *La vida es sueño* (Life is a Dream), first performed in Madrid in 1637. There is, in fact, no connection between what is depicted in this painting and anything that happens in Calderón's play. But the artist has, nevertheless, tapped into one of the richest veins of Baroque thought in his implication that attachment to the pleasures and glories of this life is tantamount to embracing the illusion of a dream. A picture more or less this size by Francisco de Palacios, known only from a document which identifies it as 'a hieroglyph that signifies the Disillusionment of the World' has been tentatively identified with this work.

comparing it to his *Saint William of Aquitaine* (fig. 60), dated 1671. One of the numerous ways in which the Uffizi canvas differs from the Vienna picture is that in the late work Pereda has added a further dimension of the theme of Vanity: the notion that the fame even of works of art will fade. This is symbolised by the wrinkled and torn engraving at the lower right corner. Little did he suspect, however, how true this was; for within twenty-five years of his death, his famous *Disillusionment of the World* painted for the Almirante would be taken out of Spain and would languish in oblivion, the name of its painter unknown, for two centuries.[18]

With no trace of Pereda's masterpiece remaining on Spanish soil, it is not surprising that by 1800 Díaz del Valle's and Palomino's references were generally associated with a related painting by another hand: the magnificent and no less eloquent *Dream of the Knight*, now in the Academia de San Fernando in Madrid (cat. 27). The attribution to Pereda, which is still upheld by the Academia, dates from 1800, when the diarist Pedro González de Sepúlveda saw the painting in the palace of Manuel Godoy.[19] This attribution to Pereda was universally accepted without the slightest question until 1959, when Martin S. Soria astutely observed in passing that its style seemed so strongly influenced by Carreño that it might be by him rather than Pereda.[20] This suggestion found no immediate adherents, but in 1985 it was proposed that the painting be removed from the canon of Pereda's oeuvre and assigned to an anonymous follower of Velázquez.[21] In 1992 Pérez Sánchez tentatively linked the painting with the name of the little-known artist Francisco de Palacios (*c.*1622/5–1651), whom we shall consider presently and in whose recently discovered will a painting of similar dimensions is cited: a 'hieroglyph that signifies the Disillusionment of the World'.[22] So little is known of Palacios's style at present (see cats 33 and 34) that it is not possible to be certain that the painting in the Academia is his; it is clear from the artist's will that the picture he had painted was very important, since the price agreed with his patron, to be paid in cash and in kind, was very high. The *Dream of the Knight* is testimony to the fame of the Vienna *Vanitas*; it is, however, an original masterpiece in its own right, and, if it is by Palacios, it establishes him as a major talent, and bears out Palomino's assertion that he was one of the best followers of Velázquez. Certainly the flickering brush strokes that define the gold embroidery of the knight's garments, the plumes in his hat and the bouquet of flowers at the right of the table have nothing to do either with Pereda's early style, seen in the Vienna *Vanitas*, or with his more diffuse but still sensuous late style, seen in the Uffizi painting. They have everything to do, however, with the revolution of the brush inspired by the style of Velázquez.

Soria suggested that Pereda's *Vanitas* in Vienna might have been inspired by a Dutch engraving such as *Finis Coronat Opus* (1626) by Hendrick Hondius (fig. 61).[23] There does not seem to be a strong relationship, however, between the painting and the print, which depicts an artist's studio strewn with books and the instruments of his craft. But, as has recently been discovered, Pereda did paint a work, now lost, on the theme of the vanity of artistic creation. In the 1683 death inventory of Don Andrés de Villarán, a noble member of the royal Council of the Treasury, was cited a 'hieroglyph of the Disillusionment, original by Pereda, with a skull, a palette, brushes, a clock and other papers'.[24] It seems that it was indeed Pereda who popularised the *Vanitas* theme among Spanish still-life painters. Numerous anonymous paintings of this type have been attributed to him, most without reason; the most beautiful of them, *Still Life with Books and an Hour-glass* (cat. 28), has taxed the imagination of art historians for generations, but as yet no convincing attribution has been found.

Fig. 61 Hendrick Hondius I, *Finis Coronat Opus*, 1626. Engraving. Amsterdam, Rijksmuseum.

28 Unknown artist
Still Life with Books and an Hour-glass
*c.*1640. Oil on canvas, 35 x 55 cm
Berlin, Staatliche Museen, Gemäldegalerie

13.5" x 21" ?

Reflecting the influence of Pereda's introduction of the *Vanitas* theme into Spanish still-life painting, this exceptionally beautiful still life has been regarded by nearly every scholar who has written about it as one of the finest works of its kind. Simple but highly sophisticated in its design and structure, it reveals the hand and mind of a remarkable artist. The well-used, vellum-bound volumes are laid in a natural way on a scholar's table covered with a rose-coloured cloth. On the largest tome sits an hour-glass, just inverted and about to begin to mark its measure of time. But the effects of time are already to be noted in the worn pages and crinkled bindings of the books, caught by the strong light which endows their silhouette against the blackness of the background with grandeur, and casts strong shadows toward the right from the smallest volume and the ink-well with its pen. The theme of the vanity of learning is clear, even without the ubiquitous skull found in Northern, and some Spanish still lifes of the type.

Over the years unconvincing attempts have been made to attribute the painting to Velázquez, Pereda, Murillo, Ribera, Collantes and Alonso Vázquez. One of the few great painters whose name has not been suggested is Alonso Cano (1601–67). But, although the elegant and restrained colour and stylish profile are not inconsistent with his Madrid period (1638–52), there is no indication that he ever painted this type of picture. At present the painting must remain one of those masterpieces that affect us deeply without the prejudice of an artist's name.

29 Antonio de Pereda, 1611–78
Still Life with Vegetables
Signed and dated on ledge at left: *PEREDA.
F./1651*
Oil on canvas, 74.5 x 143 cm
Lisbon, Museu Nacional de Arte Antiga

This still life and its pendant, *Still Life with
Fruits* (fig. 62), are seminal works from the
most productive moment of Pereda's career as a
still-life painter. Around them can be grouped
several related works, which share some of the
same motifs and explore in various ways the
artist's ability to describe the sensual reality of
the life around him. A contemporaneous second
version of this composition, somewhat larger
and with many changes, is in a private collection in Finland (fig. 63). Vaguely organised
around a series of parallel diagonals receding
into the depth from right to left, the composition is knitted together by the overlapping and
piling up of forms. The many lines of force suggested by jutting vegetables and tilted utensils
infuse a sense of movement or unrest into the
painting, an energy that replaces the noble stasis
of works of Sánchez Cotán and Juan van der
Hamen. Pereda's idea of naturalism is also more
theatrical. He floods our senses with tactile allu-
sions and contrasts, but works the surface so
vigorously as to call attention to his virtuoso
technique. The result is a kind of Baroque
maniera, or purposeful artificiality, that was to
characterise much painting from the second half
of the seventeenth century in Spain.

Fig. 62 Antonio de Pereda, *Still Life with
Fruits*, 1651. Oil on canvas, 75 x 143 cm.
Lisbon, Museu Nacional de Arte Antiga.

Fig. 63 Antonio de Pereda, *Kitchen Still Life*,
1651. Oil on canvas, 108 x 166 cm. Finland,
Private collection.

Although the mainstay of Pereda's livelihood, following Crescenzi's death, was his work for religious institutions, still lifes seem to have accounted for a significant part of his output. He appears to have been prosperous and extremely conscious of rank; he is reputed to have lived like a gentleman, affecting the use of the distinguishing *Don* with his name.[25] He rescued his son, Joaquín, from marriage to one of his servants, a situation that curiously calls to mind the subject matter of his only known genre painting (cat. 31).[26] He also managed to gain for his son a position in the royal household.[27] Pereda himself, however, remained rooted in the artisan class, if Palomino is to be believed that he could not read and write.[28]

Pereda may have produced still lifes at a steady rate throughout his life, but the only dated examples after Crescenzi's death were executed in the early 1650s.[29] In two rather large paintings dated in 1651 (cat. 29 and fig. 62), he adopted the format of the kitchen still life, recently popularised by Neapolitan painters, and created works of enormous strength and energy, whose most distinguishing feature is the brimming virtuosity with which they are executed. Attesting to the success of one of them (cat. 29), the artist painted a larger version in the same year, adding several items that were not depicted in the earlier work and increasing the height, so as to evoke a greater sense of ambient space (fig. 63).

Pereda was at the peak of his artistic powers when he painted his two signed still lifes of 1652 (cat. 30 and fig. 64), pictures in which his innate sense of elegance, his visual acuity and technical accomplishment were functioning in perfect balance. Both works seem once again to reflect a familiarity with imported still lifes – from both Italy and Northern Europe – which he may easily have known in collections he was invited to appraise,[30] but the results are anything but imitative. They simply reflect the mind of a great artist who was not working in a provincial vacuum. The luxury objects depicted recall the subject matter of Northern *pronk* (ostentation) still lifes but were probably things Pereda himself owned, since some of them reappear in his other still lifes.[31]

The large and impressive *Kitchen Scene* from Penrhyn Castle (cat. 31), published here for the first time in the modern literature of art, has not until now been associated with Pereda. Although no other such genre painting by Pereda is known, it seems clear that no other artist could have painted it. The picture generally conforms to a Neapolitan format – as seen, for example, in a large monogrammed *Kitchen Scene* (fig. 65), attributed by Salerno to Giovanni Battista Ruoppolo (1629–97) – but it nevertheless exhibits no significantly Italian pictorial qualities. It is not executed on the *pavimento* canvas usually found in Neapolitan pictures of this kind. Furthermore, it depicts a great variety of articles from all over Europe, including Spain, and from Spain's American dominions; some of these objects appear in other still lifes by Pereda.

As in the two Lisbon kitchen still lifes (cat. 29 and fig. 62), the artist has defined the objects he depicted with a varied brushwork, achieving thin, fluid passages in the modelling of textiles and ceramics, alongside thick and crusty ones in the highlighting of fruits and metal objects. A limpid light illuminates the scene which is set against a cool grey background, much as in the Hermitage *Still Life with Sweets, Vessels and an Ebony Chest* (cat. 30). More than anything else, however, Pereda's hand is identifiable in the characteristic combination of high illusionism on the one hand and the sensuous materiality of paint on the other. Parallels to the figures, and particularly to the broad execution apparent in the face and arms of the female figure, are not readily found in Pereda's religious oeuvre. This is not surprising, however, because there is no other mature work in which the human figures are almost

30 Antonio de Pereda, 1611–78
Still Life with Sweets, Vessels and an Ebony Chest
c.1652. Signed on round wooden box: *pereda f.*
Oil on canvas, 80 x 94 cm
St Petersburg, State Hermitage Museum

This well-preserved masterpiece reveals Pereda at the peak of his creative powers. In its composition which, like the Lisbon still lifes (cat. 29 and fig. 62), affects a studied disarray, we can see the impact of recently imported foreign still lifes that Pereda must have known in the great collections of Madrid. Against a relatively light grey background, an arrangement of sweets and vessels, some of them associated with the drinking of chocolate, is laid out upon a table-top spread with a sumptuous red cloth. The inlaid ebony chest in the centre supports a variety of vessels, one of them a lac-quered gourd bowl of the type imported from Mexico. Two of the cups on the silver plate at the left foreground appear possibly to be Chinese export ware. The decorated faïence vase with handles at the right is a typical product of the Spanish ceramics centre of Talavera. In general, the composition conveys an impression of intimate luxury, reinforced by the heightened sense of corporeality, which Pereda has achieved through his lush technique and chromatic richness.

Fig. 64 Antonio de Pereda, *Still Life with Shells and a Clock*, 1652. Oil on canvas, 78 x 91 cm. Moscow, The Pushkin Museum of Fine Arts.

subordinated to the still-life element. The buckskin jerkin, the sword and, especially, the shoes of the male figure can be related to the execution of similar details in his early *Relief of Genoa* (fig. 58).

To understand this picture fully, we must try to determine the subject. Amid the disarray following an elaborate meal, a young man dressed as a soldier leans nonchalantly on the end of the table, about to pour a drink from a copper pitcher. Kneeling, pausing in her work to make an imploring gesture towards the young man, is a stocky maidservant (*fregona*), plainly dressed as a member of the lower class. She is surrounded by heaps of dirty vessels associated with the preparation of the meal; the broken plate, overturned vessel and extinguished candle on the floor suggest the theme of lost virtue, common enough in the literature of the time. The table that the young man leans on is covered with rich, half-eaten food and imported luxury articles. The two figures, as well as the two parts of the still life, define this as a familiar situation in which a glib youth has taken advantage of a young woman, who now realises that what the encounter has brought her is not romance, but broken promises. Pereda has surely not illustrated here any specific scene from the theatre of his time, but the painting would have had a familiar moral resonance for his audience. This theme must certainly have had a personal significance for the artist himself, in view of his son's liaison with a household servant.

Pereda's role in the development of the still life at mid-century was rather comparable to Van der Hamen's role twenty or thirty years earlier. Although the still life did not predominate in his oeuvre, those he produced were extraordinary; like Van der Hamen, he creatively absorbed the best achievements of European still-life painting, thus opening many doors for the Spanish artists who followed him at the court. Like Van der Hamen, he probably exerted this kind of leadership from the very beginning of his career.

Fig. 65 Giovanni Battista Ruoppolo, *Kitchen Still Life*, mid-seventeenth century. Oil on canvas, 147 x 195 cm. Naples, Astarita collection (in 1964).

31 Antonio de Pereda, 1611–78
Kitchen Scene (Allegory of Lost Virtue)
c.1650–5. Oil on canvas, 179.2 x 226 cm
Penrhyn Castle, The Douglas-Pennant collection
(The National Trust)

This extraordinary painting, unpublished in modern times and never before reproduced, formed part of the Galerie Espagnole at the Louvre between 1842 and 1848, where it was exhibited as the work of Velázquez. However, its sensuous naturalism, dense coloration and pastose brushwork relate it closely to the mature style of Antonio de Pereda. Indeed, several of the objects depicted are exactly the same as those in Pereda's signed still lifes from the 1650s. The terracotta pitcher at the right rear of the table and the white ceramic jar on the footed dish nearer the centre, for example, are the same as those in the Pushkin *Still Life with Shells and a Clock* of 1652 (fig. 64), and the stoppered glass decanter and upturned wine glass at the table's left appear in the Lisbon *Still Life with Fruits* (fig. 62). The large copper jug on the floor at the left, with the very same dints and discolorations, is seen in the Lisbon *Still Life with Vegetables* (cat. 29).

The compositional disarray that characterises the pure still lifes of Pereda is taken a step further here and given an iconographic meaning. At the right foreground a maidservant is seen washing up after a lavish meal. She gestures imploringly to her male companion, whose attire suggests that he is a soldier. The table is covered with the aftermath of the opulent repast. Some of the vessels used to serve it are of foreign origin, such as the salt-glazed stoneware tankard from Germany, the Venetian glass goblet and the two small terracotta bowls, such as were made in both Portugal and Mexico. The floor under the table is strewn with the empty vessels used to prepare and serve the meal. Amid them are two candlesticks, one overturned, with its candle extinguished. This note, and the broken pottery and overturned copper vessel on the ground beneath the maidservant suggest the theme of lost virtue, so common in contemporary Spanish literature.

Two artists who shared Pereda's initiative in pursuing a more painterly style and a less formal mode of composition would not have given all the credit to him, for both appear to have been to a certain extent followers of Velázquez: Francisco de Burgos Mantilla (1609/12–1672) and Francisco de Palacios (1622/5–1652). Their few known still lifes were painted when each was quite young, and Velázquez may have encouraged them in the painting of such pictures from nature as a means of honing their skills.

In the late 1650s Lázaro Díaz del Valle wrote a brief sketch of the life of Burgos Mantilla, in which he stated that the artist had come to Madrid from Burgos as a boy, to study drawing with Pedro de las Cuevas (Pereda would have been a fellow-pupil). But Díaz del Valle goes on to say that he soon became a disciple of Velázquez, 'whom he always tried to imitate in his admirable manner'.[32] Burgos Mantilla himself provides conflicting evidence as to his date of birth. In 1658, when he appeared as a witness in support of Velázquez's patent of nobility, he said he had known the artist for almost thirty-four years, or from 1624, and gave his own age as forty-nine, implying a birth date of 1609.[33] In an unpublished document of 1650, however, the artist gave his age as thirty-eight, implying a birth date of 1612.[34] In either case, the master-pupil relationship of Velázquez and Burgos Mantilla would seem to be borne out by both the painter and his early biographer.[35]

Díaz del Valle does not mention Burgos Mantilla's still lifes, but says that he had become 'famous for making portraits from the life, as shown by the many which he has made of various gentlemen in this city of Madrid, with which he earned a great reputation'.[36] The identification of one of these would be of enormous benefit in clarifying the authorship of the numerous portraits tenuously attributed to Velázquez; alas, only one signed painting by Burgos Mantilla is known, and that is a small still

life dated in 1631 (cat. 32).

Burgos Mantilla may have been attracted to the still life as a challenge to his brush, but does not appear to have made much of a speciality of the genre. An inventory made of his studio in 1648 lists only five such pictures: two flower-pieces, a small painting with figures and flowers, a painting of grapes and a copy of a still life by Van der Hamen representing flowers and pomegranates.[37] Although the fact that he had copied a Van der Hamen might suggest a significant stylistic link with the older artist's work, this is not confirmed by his only known painting (cat. 32). Burgos Mantilla seems, in fact, to have made his living from his portraits and from his copies of other artists' works, a large number of which were described in his studio.

Francisco de Palacios had probably only reached his late twenties when he died on 27 January 1652.[38] Although he may have been as precocious as the young Pereda, his output must have been small. The quality of his work was sufficient, however, to merit a brief biography by Antonio Palomino in 1724, in which the author described him as a close disciple of Velázquez. Palomino acknowledged that he did not know of a single work of his in a public place but that there existed, and he had seen, excellent pictures by him in private houses, 'especially portraits, which he made excellently, and in which one recognises the good school in which he was formed, and how far he advanced in it'.[39] Of the three signed pictures by him that are known today, two are a pair of still lifes dated 1648 (cats 33 and 34). These works of exceptional beauty and refinement testify to the great loss that Palacios's early death inflicted on the school of Madrid.

The graceful nonchalance of Palacios's two still-life compositions recall that same quality in Pereda's Russian still lifes (cat. 30 and fig. 64), yet the way of painting is quite different. The young artist's subtle and diffuse brushwork does indeed seem to spring from Velázquez and confirms Palomino's account of his origins. A statement

32 Francisco de Burgos Mantilla,
1609/12–1672
Still Life with Dried Fruit
Signed and dated, lower right: *fr°. Burgensis*
Mantilla f¹ 1631
Oil on canvas, 29.1 x 58.9 cm
New Haven, Yale University Art Gallery,
Stephen Carlton Clark, B.A. 1903, Fund

Painted in the year of Van der Hamen's death, this remarkable little picture reveals how deeply its young painter had already been influenced by the art of Velázquez. Its close point of view and the random arrangement of dried fruits and nuts promote an intimacy of visual involvement quite distinct from that afforded by the cerebral formalism that had characterised earlier Spanish still lifes. The lively brushwork and controlled palette of silvery greys, blacks and earth tones remind one of the works of Velázquez, with whom Burgos Mantilla, according to his own later testimony, maintained a life-long relationship, beginning in 1624.

Fig. 66 Mateo Cerezo, *Immaculate Conception*, c.1665. Oil on silvered metal, 32 x 24.5 cm. Spain, Private collection.

in Palacios's will apparently gives an indication of the closeness of their realtionship: 'I have lent to Don Diego de Silva a sword and dagger set, which is the one he wears today. I order that they be recovered from him'.[40] There can be little doubt that Palacios, like Burgos Mantilla, painted his still lifes directly from nature, as Velázquez may have recommended. Three fruit still lifes by him, described as 'laid in from the life by the hand of Palacios' (manchados por el natural de mano de Palacios), were kept by his father-in-law, Francisco Bergés, for twenty years after the young painter's death.[41]

As indicated above, perhaps the most pressing question about Palacios today is whether or not the magnificent *Dream of the Knight* (cat. 27) could be the 'hieroglyph signifying the Disillusionment of the World', referred to in his will, which was painted for Luis de Carrión, harpist of the convent of the Descalzas Reales. Until more of his oeuvre is discovered, it may be difficult to decide; other artists of his generation were also capable of such an exalted work. But a confrontation with his two signed still lifes from the Harrach collection might prove instructive.

Younger than Palacios and enormously talented was Mateo Cerezo (1637–66), whose death before the age of thirty cut short one of the most promising careers of his generation. Like Burgos Mantilla, he left the provincial climate of his native Burgos, where his father was also a painter, and came to Madrid. There, in the mid-1650s, his artistic style was nourished by the richer and more sophisticated currents of art in the capital. Palomino wrote that around the age of fifteen he entered the workshop of Juan Carreño de Miranda (1614–85), but this has not been confirmed.[42] A recent assessment of his development presupposes an early influence from Pereda, followed around 1660 by a fuller assimilation of styles at the court, especially that of Carreño.[43] His mature work embraced the full range of sacred subject matter, and he worked both on a large scale for religious institutions and a small scale, in intimate, jewel-like paintings for private devotion. A recently discovered, signed *Immaculate Conception* (fig. 66), reveals, for example, the extent to which he had absorbed, probably through Carreño, a shimmering, light palette and more than a hint of the elegance of Van Dyck, so appreciated by his contemporaries in Madrid.[44]

Palomino spent most of his Life of Cerezo extolling his religious compositions on view in churches and convents in and around Madrid. He did, however, make a passing reference to still lifes: 'He also painted still lifes with such superior excellence that none surpassed him, if indeed a few equalled him: even if they be by Andrés Deleito, who made excellent ones in this court'.[45] Only two signed still lifes by Cerezo are known, the pair now in the Museo de San Carlos, Mexico (fig. 69). Those may have been the paintings Palomino had in mind; they were sufficiently well known to have been copied several times in the seventeenth century.[46] Other kitchen still lifes have been attributed to Cerezo (cat. 35), but the handling varies among them, and few are close enough to the Mexican pair to be regarded as conclusively his.[47] It could be that, although he painted still lifes with 'superior excellence', he did not paint a great many of them. Nevertheless, at least one other was documented in the eighteenth century, in the collection of the architect and painter Teodoro Ardemans (1664–1726).[48]

Although the condition of the signed still lifes by Cerezo in Mexico is not perfect, the paintings completely support Palomino's enthusiasm for the artist's abilities in this genre.[49] The *Kitchen Still Life with Meat*, which is the better preserved, depicts the interior of a kitchen with all the ingredients of a Castilian stew (*olla*) beside a fire. The casual arrangement of the heaped foodstuffs and utensils suggests that Cerezo admired the still lifes of Pereda (cat. 29). But his handling of paint is entirely different

33 Francisco de Palacios, 1622/5–1652
Still Life with Fruit and a Wine Cooler
Signed and dated, lower right: F*co*. DE PALACIOS. F*T*./1648
Oil on canvas, 59 x 78 cm
Schloss Rohrau, Austria, Graf Harrach'sche Familiensammlung

These two still lifes are the only signed examples by Palacios. Their remarkable state of preservation is no doubt due to the fact that they have always belonged to the same family since they were acquired in Madrid by Count Ferdinand Bonaventura Harrach, who was Austrian Ambassador to the Spanish court in the reigns of Philip IV and Charles II. Both paintings seem to bear out the statement made by Antonio Palomino in 1724 that Palacios was a close follower of Velázquez. They wholly lack any vestige of the hieratic or symmetrical mode of composition that characterised much earlier still-life painting at the court. Absent, too, is any implication of pictorial space based on linear perspective. As in the art of Velázquez, Palacios's optical focus is softer, his contours less hard-edged. Coherence is achieved by a soft, unifying light that falls from the upper left, casting shadows, but not the sharp, emphatic ones of Van der Hamen. The sensitive, interlaced brushwork approximates to Velázquez's in the decade of the 1640s, especially in the definition of such details as the plate with a pie and loaf topped by a folded napkin in cat. 33, or the loaves of braided bread and the silver pitcher in cat. 34. The pitcher, very similar to one in Pereda's great *Kitchen Scene* (cat. 31), is a *tour de force*, whose surface seems to have depth like a mirror and to reflect flashes of light at the same time. Near the centre of the same picture, Palacios has painted a tall-necked terracotta vase (*búcaro*) almost exactly like one painted by Francisco de Zurbarán more than a decade later (cat. 38). Such objects, imported from Estremoz (Portugal) or Tonalá (Mexico), were in common use in Spain.

34 **Francisco de Palacios**, 1622/5–1652
Still Life with Braided Bread
Signed and dated, lower left: *F. DE PALACIOS.*
F^T./1648
Oil on canvas, 60 x 80 cm
Schloss Rohrau, Austria, Graf Harrach'sche
Familiensammlung

and bears out, as do his mature religious works, Palomino's comparison of Cerezo's style to that of Carreño. The rich coloration and thickly massed impasto in the modelling of meat and fat, as well as the spontaneous highlights on the earthenware cookpot, seem deeply indebted to Cerezo's reputed master. Yet Carreño was not a still-life painter, and it is to Cerezo that we owe the application of this fiery technique to painting the humblest things in the kitchen.[50]

Francisco de Herrera the Younger (1627–85)[51] was among Cerezo's extremely gifted contemporaries in Madrid who occasionally painted still lifes. Having studied with his father (for whom see below) in his native Seville, Herrera left home around the age of twenty in order to perfect his skills in Rome. Returning to Spain around 1653, he settled first in Seville, where in 1660 he was elected co-president, with Murillo, of the newly founded academy in that city. However, shortly afterwards he moved permanently to the court in Madrid, where about 1673 he became painter to King Charles II. Trained as a architect as well as a painter, Herrera exerted a wide-

35 Attributed to Mateo Cerezo, 1637–66
Kitchen Still Life
c.1660–75. Oil on canvas, 100 x 127 cm
Madrid, Museo del Prado

This powerful still life, which brilliantly depicts freshly butchered meat, fowl, bread, cloth, and utensils of glass, metal and wood, is among the finest works of its kind executed in Spain. Of unknown Spanish provenance, it was acquired by the Prado in 1970 and first catalogued as an anonymous work close in style to Pereda. In 1976 Xavier de Salas again catalogued it as an anonymous work; while he maintained the possibility of Pereda's authorship, he alternatively suggested that it might have been executed by Mateo Cerezo, under Pereda's influence, noting the similarity of its composition and subject matter to the two signed still lifes by Cerezo in the Museo de San Carlos in Mexico City (fig. 69). Since that time, Pérez Sánchez has argued for the attribution to Cerezo, and this idea has won general acceptance. Nevertheless, a new look at the supposed similarity to Cerezo's style may be worthwhile.

In its composition, this painting recalls the kitchen still lifes by Neapolitan painters such as Giuseppe Recco, which must have been known from the collections of Madrid. But as noted by others, its sensuous and compelling naturalism also owes a certain debt to the technique of Flemish masters such as Jan Fyt. Be that as it may, the virtuoso brushwork evident in the plumage of the hanging cock and in the dense white highlights throughout the painting is really quite different from the technique of Cerezo. As Cerezo was a follower of Carreño, his Venetian-oriented technique is much more reminiscent of Velázquez's. For example, in Cerezo's *Kitchen Still Life with Fish* (Mexico) the folds of a white napkin are defined by long, meandering strokes of white that could not be more different from the napkin in the Prado still life, in which light and dark are much more closely graded, albeit with thick globs of white and grey paint. All things considered, it seems to us that the Prado's initial caution about attributing this work was well advised. Beyond the superficial similarities of composition between this painting and Cerezo's signed works, profound differences of technique can be observed, and it may be a disservice to this great painting to consider the matter closed.

Fig. 67 Unknown artist, *Still Life with a Barrel, a Hake and a Tortoise*, c.1660s. Oil on canvas, 65 x 98 cm. Formerly Bergamo, Pietro Lorenzelli.

Fig. 68 Unknown artist, *Still Life with Rabbit and a Mortar*, c.1660s. Oil on canvas, 65 x 98 cm. Formerly Bergamo, Pietro Lorenzelli.

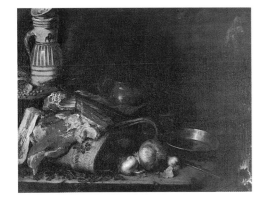

Fig. 69 Mateo Cerezo, *Kitchen Still Life with Meat*, 1664? Oil on canvas, 79 x 97 cm. Mexico, Museo de San Carlos.

ranging influence on the appearance of Late Baroque Madrid, being named, along with his other posts, *Maestro Mayor* of the royal works in 1679. He was also active as a designer for the theatre. Palomino records that, while studying and working as a young man in Rome, Herrera:

> applied himself to painting small still lifes, for which he had great talent; especially some with fish, painted from nature, in order to make himself stand out more and to help to meet his needs in that city, where he was without protection. He attained such superior excellence with these trifles that he earned in Rome the nickname *il Spagnolo degli pesci*, whereby he attained not only fame but also profit.[52]

On the basis of Palomino's account, many fish still lifes, most of them Neapolitan works related to Giuseppe Recco, have been gratuitously attributed to Herrera the Younger, but these attributions have not won general acceptance.[53] Nevertheless, there is no reason to doubt that he painted such pictures, or that he painted other still lifes during his long residency in Madrid. Copies of three of his still lifes belonged to Palomino's friend Teodoro Ardemans (mentioned above).[54]

It is tempting to speculate, although it is the merest conjecture at this point, that two paintings last recorded in the possession of Pietro Lorenzelli in Bergamo in the 1970s may be by Herrera the Younger (figs 67 and 68).[55] They are almost certainly identical with two of a group of four pictures that were attributed to Herrera the Elder in 1840, when they were in the Madrid collection of Serafín García de la Huerta.[56] They are of exceptional quality and are characterised by the painterly dash and rich colour one would expect from a successor to Pereda in Madrid. The hand is quite distinct from Pereda's, however, as can be seen in the spontaneous manipulation of the impasto in the rabbit's fur and the highlights on the copper pot (fig. 68). In both these respects, these paintings resemble more closely the Prado's great *Kitchen Still Life* attributed to Cerezo (cat. 35), in which the impasto on the copper vessels, in particular, lacks the representational specificity observed in Pereda's signed still lifes. Confirmation or denial of the younger Herrera's authorship of these still lifes is impossible at this point, because no signed example by him is known and because, as we know from the case of Mateo Cerezo, an artist's style as a still-life painter may be quite different from his style as a figure painter. Whether they are by him or not, however, they indicate by their quality that there is still much to learn about still-life painting in Madrid in the late seventeenth century.

36 José Antolínez, 1635–75
Still Life with Papillon
Signed and dated lower right: *Joseph Antolinez F./70*
Oil on canvas, 55.9 x 41.3 cm
Spain, Private collection

This painting is remarkable in the history of Spanish still life, as well as in the oeuvre of the artist, who was primarily a religious painter. Perhaps his independence of established convention contributed to the originality of his only known foray into this area. Whether the picture is considered a still life with a portrait of a dog or a portrait of a dog with a still life, it affords an intimate and evocative glimpse of upper-class domesticity in the reign of Charles II.

Antolínez's ability to portray the little dog's nervous energy and imminent movement is no less remarkable than his shimmering suggestion of the still life with a blue-and-white beaker in the background. Like Palacios and Cerezo before him, Antolínez was an exponent of the neo-Venetianism that overtook the School of Madrid in the wake of Velázquez. This small masterpiece realises the pictorial aims of that tradition, perhaps as fully as any of the artist's paintings.

Brought to England in the early nineteenth century by General John Meade, Consul General at Madrid, the painting was acquired in 1851 by Sir William Stirling-Maxwell of Kier, to whose descendants it belonged until 1990.

37 Andrés Deleito, active 1680
Vanitas
*c.*1680. Signed on cartellino: *ANDRES DE/LEITO F.*
Oil on canvas, 73 x 93 cm
Madrid, María Begoña García-Diego y Ortiz

Deleito's bizarre and mannered technique seems particularly unrelated to that of his Spanish contemporaries and has been seen by Pérez Sánchez (Madrid 1983) as possibly inspired by Tuscan artists. In this *Vanitas*, the heavy, golden atmosphere seems almost perfumed, as though by the jewel-encrusted atomizer at the right of the red-draped table-top. Heaped on the table with it are familiar symbols of the vanity of life and futility of earthly ambition: the open and well-used book; the mirror reflecting nothing as it points into the darkness of the corner; the clock; an empty coffer, the jewels and coins it once contained spilled out on the table as though having been fingered by appreciative hands; a miniature portrait of a beautiful young woman; a gauze-like veil of the type worn out of conventional modesty by women, when going in public; and in the shadows of the background, behind the mirror, a large bronze urn, difficult to decipher, except as a swirl of profane putti. In the background, above all this, is a luminous painting of the Virgin Mary and Saint John the Baptist kneeling before Christ at the Last Judgment. Deleito's technique, in which light glints fleetingly across the surfaces of objects, shatters the objective certainty of everything, leaving us with an ambiguous mist of reality, more than faintly decadent, full of moral import.

Another gifted contemporary of Cerezo, José Antolínez (1635–75), shared his ability to paint shimmering images of the Virgin and saints, but also embraced the occasional genre subject, such as the remarkably original *Picture Vendor* in Munich (fig. 70).[57] With the wit and anecdotal quality of the Bamboccianti, but with the large scale and sensuous technique of the neo-Venetian style that characterised the School of Madrid in the third quarter of the seventeenth century, Antolínez has depicted an artist (who may be himself) standing in a doorway in the background, directing the actions of a buffoonish huckster who is trying to sell a painting of the Madonna and Child. It is the contrast of the two faces – the alert, acutely intelligent one of the artist and the addled, cloddish one of the pedlar – that gives the painting particular resonance and reminds us of Palomino's verbal portrait of Antolínez's arrogant, self-confident personality.[58] The artist's only other known foray into genre is the beautiful *Still Life with Papillon* (cat. 36), painted in 1670.

Although several good painters produced the occasional still life in the final years of the seventeenth century,[59] the last artist by whom a significant body of work is known today is Andrés Deleito, to whom Palomino devoted no biography and whom he only mentioned in order to give relief to his praise of Cerezo's still lifes. The eighteenth-century writers on art Antonio Ponz and Ceán Bermúdez refer to his work in the cloister of the Franciscan monastery in Segovia, which Ceán described as being painted with 'better taste in colour than correction in drawing'.[60] Ceán also dates his work in Madrid to around 1680 and quotes Palomino on his still lifes. Beyond this, nothing at all is known of him, except what can be seen in his signed paintings.[61]

Deleito seems to have made a speciality of the *Vanitas* theme, which in the wake of Pereda enjoyed a certain vogue in Madrid. The several signed still lifes of this type (cat. 37) are the artist's best-known works. However, he also did kitchen still lifes with figures; and the large pair in the Instituto Amatller, in Barcelona (figs 71 and 72), are particularly impressive. Pérez Sánchez has noted the possible religious significance of the pairing of still lifes of meat and fish, but the appeal of the works is largely visual. In the play of light dancing across the surfaces of things, but failing to endow the forms with any sense of substantiality, and in the flickering, nervous movement of the artist's brush, we see what might be described as the dying embers of the impulse to describe reality that had been so solidly encouraged decades earlier by the example of Pereda, and subsequently by that of Cerezo.

Fig. 70 José Antolínez, *The Picture Vendor*, *c*.1670. Oil on canvas, 202 x 125 cm. Munich, Alte Pinakothek.

Fig. 71 Andrés Deleito, *Kitchen Still Life with Meat*, *c*.1680. Oil on canvas, 104 x 164 cm. Barcelona, Instituto Amatller.

Fig. 72 Andrés Deleito, *Kitchen Still Life with Fish*, *c*.1680. Oil on canvas, 104 x 164 cm. Barcelona, Instituto Amatller.

Still-Life Painting in Seville

In his discussion of the practice of fresco painting in *Arte de la pintura* (1649), Francisco Pacheco named the Andalusian artists who had pioneered the art of grotesque decorations. Some of them, we now know, also painted still lifes;[1] but in his discussion of the still life *per se*, Pacheco specifically mentioned only painters from Toledo and Madrid: Blas de Prado, Juan Sánchez Cotán and Juan van der Hamen.[2] All the evidence indicates that the practice of still-life painting became widespread in Seville later than in Castile.

The fourteen still lifes of fruit baskets by Antonio Mohedano (*c*.1561–1626) inventoried in the Sevillian residence of the Duque de Alcalá, were perhaps done before the artist left Seville for Antequera in 1610, and may have been unusual works for their time.[3] The modestly talented painter Blas de Ledesma of Granada (doc. 1602–14) painted still lifes of fruit baskets (fig. 7) that perhaps reflect Mohedano's, but little else is known of early Andalusian still life.[4] Pacheco considered that for great artists, still-life painting was no more than a pastime. During the first third of the century it probably remained a sideline for Sevillian painters, whose training and practice were closely geared to painting religious subjects and to polychroming wood sculptures for ecclesiastical patrons.

Francisco de Herrera the Elder (*c*.1590–*c*.1656) painted still lifes, but none is known today.[5] His still lifes do not begin to appear in inventories until the middle of

Fig. 73 Francisco López Caro, *Boy in a Kitchen*, 1620s. Oil on canvas, 58.5 x 98 cm. Private collection.

Fig. 74 Francisco de Zurbarán, *Still Life with Basket of Oranges*, 1633. Oil on canvas, 62.2 x 109.5 cm. Pasadena, California, The Norton Simon Foundations.

the seventeenth century, so we cannot be sure whether he was among the originators of the genre in Seville, or merely came to it late in his career.[6] Francisco López Caro (1598–1661), a pupil of Pacheco who imitated Velázquez's *bodegones* (fig. 73), painted still lifes in the 1620s. These are unknown today, but seventeen fruit still lifes were listed in López Caro's studio inventory, dated 19 January 1629, a document witnessed by the painter Pedro de Camprobín.[7] Camprobín's presence in Seville can now be documented from at least November 1628, and, although we know nothing of his early work, it is possible that he brought with him from Toledo an interest in still-life painting that influenced painters in Seville.[8] Two statistical surveys of seventeenth-century Sevillian picture collections document the greatly increased popularity of still-life painting by the middle of the century.[9] In chronological terms, this phenomenon of collecting corresponds to the period of known activity of the principal painters of still life in Seville, Juan de Zurbarán and Pedro de Camprobín, and to that of less prolific figures, such as Pedro de Medina and Francisco Barranco. It also covers the period when the greatest of all non-specialist still-life painters in Spain, Francisco de Zurbarán (1598–1664), painted his masterpiece, *Still Life with Basket of Oranges* (fig. 74).

The painting is signed and dated 1633, by which date Zurbarán had become Seville's leading religious painter. He was not then, nor subsequently in his lifetime, particularly known as a still-life painter. Because of this and of the compositional similarity of his famous still life to the symmetrical works of Van der Hamen, it has been suggested that his foray into this field may have had something to do with his forthcoming journey to the court in Madrid, where the still life was enjoying a great

102

Fig. 75 Francisco de Zurbarán, *Family of the Virgin*, c.1627–30. Oil on canvas, 128.2 x 106.6 cm. Spain, Juan Abello collection.

Fig. 76 Francisco de Zurbarán, *Agnus Dei*, c.1635–40. Oil on canvas, 38 x 62 cm. Madrid, Museo del Prado.

vogue, and where he was to work in 1634 on the decoration of the Hall of Realms in the Buen Retiro Palace.[10] Whatever the source of its composition, it is a painting of such inspired simplicity and eloquence that it has no peer. More than any other still life, it seems to embody an ennobling vision of Nature's simplest things. Indeed, the sense of mystery or import that one perceives in the works of Sánchez Cotán, and the sense of elegant restraint that characterises the still lifes of Van der Hamen, are, if anything, magnified in this work. Roberto Longhi was the first, in 1930, to try to explain the picture's allure as an expression of religious devotion, observing that the objects are arranged 'like flowers on an altar, strung together like litanies to the Madonna'.[11] Soria (1955) and many others, particularly Gállego, have developed this interpretation of the painting to a fine degree.[12] Indeed, the symbolic significance of the fruits depicted may have been readily apparent to the artist's contemporaries, and may have enriched their enjoyment of the painting. Yet, as in the case of other artists' still lifes, there can be little doubt that the picture was also conceived as a *tour de force* of painterly skill.

Zurbarán had always shown a gift for still-life details in his figurative works, and it may be that his interest in pure still life developed out of this. Those details that were sometimes repeated from one religious composition to another may have derived from small painted studies kept by the artist. Thus, in the early *Family of the Virgin* (fig. 75), painted in the late 1620s, Zurbarán painted the same silver plate with a ceramic cup of water and a pink rose that appear at the right of his still life of 1633; however, in the earlier work the proportions of the cup are more squat than in the still life, and the rose is observed from a different angle.[13] In both these respects this detail of the *Family of the Virgin* is closer to a small canvas representing just this motif which was acquired by Sir Kenneth Clark in the 1930s (fig. 79).[14] Although it has not been cleaned in years, the Clark painting is of extremely high quality. The left and right edges are intact, folded around the stretcher, so the picture is not a fragment of a much larger canvas: the front and back edges of the table on which the plate and cup rest are also parallel to the upper and lower limits of the canvas, unlike the larger religious compositions in which it is only a motif. It seems certain that this small picture is an autograph study. Thus, when he came to paint his monumental still life several years later, Zurbarán was able to take advantage of it, rethinking the placement of the rose and the proportions of the cup.

X-radiographs of *Still Life with Basket of Oranges* (fig. 77) reveal no hesitation in arriving at the forms we see; but they show that before Zurbarán painted the basket or the plate of lemons, he painted nearer the front edge of the table something we no longer see at all: a silver plate of *batata confitada* (candied sweet potato), a popular confection of the period in Spain. He suppressed this, however, in favour of the symmetrical arrangement of fruit. Recently a small painting has been discovered which is obviously a study for the plate of *batata confitada* (fig. 78); it is exquisite in its spontaneous execution and abbreviated notation of light and shadow. Clearly, a painting as carefully constructed as *Still Life with Basket of Oranges* would not have been made by setting out the objects on a table and painting them from the life; it was rather preceded by the same kind of methodical preparation that was carried out by Sánchez Cotán and Van der Hamen.

No other still life from this period of Zurbarán's career has been convincingly identified.[15] Several times, however, he did paint a kind of still life, *a lo divino* – a symbolic representation of a bound lamb. The most pointedly symbolic of these is the version in the San Diego Museum of Art, inscribed *Tanquam Agnus*, in which the lamb is haloed; the reference is to the biblical text 'he is brought as a lamb to the

Fig. 77 X-Radiograph of *Still Life with Basket of Oranges* (fig. 74).

Fig. 78 Francisco de Zurbarán, *Sweetmeats on a Silver Plate*, *c.*1633. Oil on canvas, 28.5 x 39 cm. Spain, Private collection.

slaughter' (Isaiah 53: 7). The most beautiful, though, is the version in the Prado (fig. 76), in which the sacrificial victim is a young ram.[16] The artist's genius for naturalistic portrayal has given palpable expression to the animal's fleece and pathetic form lying helpless on the same kind of stone ledge that still-life painters used to display their secular subject matter. In his later years, probably after moving permanently to Madrid in 1658, Zurbarán again took up the still life with aplomb in *Still Life with Four Vessels* (cat. 38).

Much more drawn to the still life was Zurbarán's son, who became something of a specialist in the genre. Juan de Zurbarán (1620–49) was trained in his father's studio, and as a young painter surely benefited from the elder Zurbarán's great reputation in Seville. In 1644 Juan was commissioned to paint two religious subjects for the Confraternity of the Rosary at Carmona, near Seville, but none of his figurative paintings is known today.[17] Juan's earliest known still life, *Plate of Grapes* (cat. 39), which somewhat recalls his father's *Sweetmeats on a Silver Plate* (fig. 78), was painted when he was nineteen years old. A few other still lifes can be attributed to this early stage of his development (e.g. cat. 40), but his style seems to have matured quickly thereafter. During his very brief career, he emerged as one of the most creative and gifted painters of still life anywhere in Spain, attracting imitators and copyists. His promising career was cut short, however, by his death at twenty-nine in the great plague that devastated Seville, killing half the population within a few months.[18]

Juan de Zurbarán was not content to live as a member of the artisan class. He always used the aristocratic *Don* before his name (even in some of his signatures) and was cultivated and stylish, with literary inclinations and a penchant for the courtly art of dancing.[19] The genteel subject matter of his *Still Life with Chocolate Service* (cat. 41), with its Chinese export porcelain, is perhaps revealing of his personality and lifestyle. In 1641, he made a spectacular marriage to Mariana de Quadros, the daughter of a procurator in the Real Audiencia of Seville, and a year later baptised their son with the grand name Francisco Máximo.[20] Juan's bride brought him a substantial dowry valued at 50,000 *reales*.[21] The fact that he had squandered a large part of this by the time of his death, some eight years later, is perhaps not surprising in a man who sought social distinction and tended to live beyond his means.[22]

Fig. 79 Francisco de Zurbarán, *Cup of Water and a Rose on a Silver Plate*, *c.*1627–30. Oil on canvas, 21.4 x 31.2 cm (without additions). Saltwood, Lord Clark family collection.

38 Francisco de Zurbarán, 1598–1664
Still Life with Four Vessels
c.1658–64. Oil on canvas, 46 x 84 cm
Madrid, Museo del Prado

Given to the Prado in 1940 by the Catalan collector Francisco Cambó, this painting has become one of the best known and most frequently exhibited Spanish still lifes. Cambó also owned a second autograph version of this same composition, with only slight differences, which he bequeathed in 1949 to the Museu Nacional d'Art de Catalunya in Barcelona. The somewhat less incisive draughtsmanship and softer modelling of these two works in comparison with the Norton Simon still life (fig. 74) of 1633 have led to some doubt that they were actually painted by Zurbarán. But the attribution seems perfectly sustainable within his stylistic development if one dates the paintings to the period 1658–64, when Zurbarán moved permanently to Madrid in search of new work opportunities. The vogue for still-life painting at the court may have led him to return to the genre he had tried decades earlier. Once again adopting a compositional mode introduced by Van der Hamen in the 1620s (cat. 12), he created a solemn masterpiece. Typical of Zurbarán's practice throughout his career is his use of at least one element of this composition in a painting of quite different character. The same white faïence vessel (*alcarraza*), which, because of its porosity kept water cool through evaporation, appears at the right in the large *Annunciation*, dated to the late 1650s, in the March collection, Mallorca. Furthermore, the red clay jar with two handles is exactly the same type (probably of Mexican origin) that appears in the still life, dated 1648, by Francisco Palacios in the Harrach Collection (cat. 34).

39 Juan de Zurbarán, 1620–49
Plate of Grapes
Signed and dated, l.l.: *Juan deZurbaran
façie.../·1639*
Oil on copper, 28 x 36 cm
Bordeaux, Private collection

Belonging to the same French collection since
the mid-nineteenth century, this important
picture was unknown to scholars until it was
shown in the exhibition *L'Age d'or espagnol* at
Bordeaux in 1955. It is of such a high quality
that at least one scholar found it difficult to
believe that it was not actually painted by the
father, though it is clearly signed with the son's
name. Painted when the artist was nineteen
years old, it is the earliest of the three signed
works known today. Although superficially
similar to his father's still lifes of plates, and to
similar details in his figural compositions, it
reveals a quite different vision. It has been compared to the works of certain Dutch painters,
but it is perhaps even closer in its preciosity to
such Lombard artists as Panfilo Nuvolone (doc.
1581–1631). In the young Zurbarán's painting,
the attentive observation of detail in the fruit
and its reflection in the flange of the silver plate
is paralleled by the great pains the artist took to
render the cracks and chips in the edge of the
stone ledge on which the plate rests. This focus
on accidental details was alien to his father's
sensibility. It is also somewhat more insistent
than in Juan's more mature style, as revealed in
a similar work executed about four or five years
later (cat. 42).

40 Juan de Zurbarán, 1620–49
Plate of Fruit with a Linnet
c.1639–40. Oil on canvas, 40 x 57 cm
Barcelona, Museu Nacional d'Art de Catalunya

This sensitive and remarkable little still life has
been attributed to Camprobín on the basis of its
compositional similarity to a signed *Plate of
Fruit* exhibited in 1947 at Sala Parés in
Barcelona (fig. 85). A recent examination of
both works, however, has revealed a marked
dissimilarity in the way the two are painted.
Camprobín's modelling is broad and cursory in
comparison to the nuanced gradations which
describe this plate of fruit. The grapes, in particular, have the subtlety seen in Juan de
Zurbarán's *Plate of Grapes* from Bordeaux (cat.
39). The definition of the silver plate, with its
high degree of reflectivity, is also similar to the
one in the Bordeaux still life, and to that in the
Kiev *Still Life with Chocolate Service* of 1640
(cat. 41), which suggests it should be dated to
about the same time. As in many of the younger
Zurbarán's known still lifes, the background
has darkened considerably.

Camprobín depicted a butterfly in his early
Plate of Fruit, and Juan de Zurbarán shows one
as well, hovering near the pomegranate blossom
at the top of the composition. The artist has
also portrayed with precision and sensitivity a
wasp that has alighted on the grapes and a drop
of dew on the iridescent skin of the plum. In a
clear reference to the classical literature of still-
life painting, he has depicted a linnet which has
plucked a grape from the bunch on the plate.

41 Juan de Zurbarán, 1620–49
Still Life with Chocolate Service
Signed and dated, l.l.: *Juan deZurbaran
fati.../1640*
Oil on canvas, 48 x 75 cm
Kiev, Museum of Western and Oriental Art

When it was first published in 1916, while still
in a private collection in St Petersburg, this still
life was believed to be by Francisco de
Zurbarán. Only in 1938, following the painting's cleaning, was a transcription of the artist's
signature published (upon a recent examination
it was not possible to see this signature). No
one had previously been aware that Zurbarán's
son had been a still-life painter. The twenty-
year-old artist reveals here a style distinct in
many ways from his father's. The setting is
extremely dark. The bright light that gives relief
to the forms neither fully penetrates the shadows nor defines a lucid space, as in Francisco's
Still Life with Basket of Oranges (fig. 74). The
objects in the Kiev still life – a silver plate,
Chinese export cups, a silver pitcher and another of white faïence, a wooden box of preserves,
a colourful napkin, a Mexican gourd bowl, a
chocolate mill and a spoon – emerge from the
darkness in a grouping that seems intuitively
balanced. The forms overlap one another,
achieving a cohesive overall design that gives
the artist an opportunity to study the reflections
and sensuous surface characteristics of a variety
of patterns and materials. Several unsigned still
lifes of this type have been attributed to Juan de
Zurbarán, but none achieves the level of quality
evident here.

A breakthrough in understanding the younger Zurbarán's style is represented by his *Still Life with Basket of Fruit and Cardoon* (fig. 80), which is signed and dated 'D.*Juan de Zurbaran, faciebat/1643*'.[23] The dramatic tenebrism and sensuous surface of this painting were inspired by contemporary Neapolitan still lifes, such as those of Luca Forte (active 1625–55) (fig. 81), which by this time were beginning to reach Spain.[24] The effect of the dynamic composition and earthy textures could hardly be less like the measured, cerebral calm of the elder Zurbarán's *Still Life with Basket of Oranges* and was certainly not what picture collectors in Seville were used to. The ledge on which the objects are arranged, as well as the background of the painting, have darkened considerably as a result of chemical changes inherent in the artist's technique. Such changes have also occurred in the glazes with which the fruit were modelled, lending them a slight brownish cast. These factors typify other still lifes that can be attributed to Juan de Zurbarán, such as the superb *Plate of Quinces, Grapes, Figs and Plums* (cat. 42) and the monumental *Still Life with Basket of Apples and Quinces* in the Museu Nacional d'Art de Catalunya (fig. 82).[25]

Until recently, the few known still lifes by Juan de Zurbarán, when compared with his father's *Still Life with Basket of Oranges* (fig. 74), were regarded as falling short of the lofty values that work was seen to embody.[26] In fact, Juan's style is so different from his father's that there are few valid points of comparison; but within the limitations imposed by his tenebrist style, his works are not inferior in quality.[27] Deciding to specialise to a certain extent in a genre that was just becoming fashionable among collectors in Seville, Juan further asserted his independence by embracing a style of painting that must have seemed novel to his audience.[28]

Little is known at present about the work of Juan de Zurbarán's Sevillian contemporaries in the 1640s. Ceán Bermúdez mentioned an Andalusian still-life painter named Francisco Barranco, by whom he had apparently seen works dated in 1646, which were 'well coloured and painted naturalistically'.[29] Recently, a beautiful painting by Barranco, *Still Life with Chocolate Service and Dead Birds*, signed and dated 1647, has come to light (fig. 83).[30] This obscure artist probably lived in Seville, where three of his still lifes were recorded in 1650.[31] The accoutrements of the chocolate service recall the subject matter of Juan de Zurbarán's still life of 1640 (cat. 41), and it should be recalled that he, too, is documented as having painted still lifes with dead birds.[32] Such subject matter was also painted by Pedro de Camprobín, whose beauti-

Fig. 80 Juan de Zurbarán, *Still Life with Basket of Fruit and Cardoon*, 1643. Oil on canvas, 74.5 x 106 cm. Mänttä, Finland, The Gösta Serlachius Fine Arts Foundation.

Fig. 81 Luca Forte, *Still Life with Fruit and Birds*, *c*.1640s. Oil on canvas, 79 x 104.5 cm. Sarasota, Florida, The John and Mable Ringling Museum of Art.

42 Juan de Zurbarán, 1620–49
Plate of Quinces, Grapes, Figs and Plums
c.1645. Oil on canvas, 33.5 x 47 cm
Private collection

We are able to recognise this small still life as the work of Juan de Zurbarán because of the closeness of its style to the signed *Still Life with Basket of Fruit and Cardoon*, dated 1643 (fig. 80), in the Gösta Serlachius Foundation in Mänttä, Finland. By that date, the polish and preciosity of the early *Plate of Grapes* (cat. 39) had been abandoned in favour of a robust naturalism, no doubt inspired by the Italian followers of Caravaggio, whose still lifes are documented as entering Spanish collections at about this time. The young Zurbarán has endowed the fruit with an extraordinary plasticity by the liberal use of a brownish glaze that brings the individual character of each quince into high relief. This same technique is seen in the Serlachius still life and in the *Basket of Apples and Quinces* in the Museu Nacional d'Art de Catalunya (fig. 82), which, although unsigned, is doubtless by the same hand. It is instructive to compare the artist's style, as seen in this picture, with the subtler manner of his *Plate of Fruit with a Linnet* (cat. 40), which must be among his earlier works.

Fig. 82 Juan de Zurbarán, *Still Life with Basket of Apples and Quinces*, *c*.1645. Oil on canvas, 72 x 105 cm. Barcelona, Museu Nacional d'Art de Catalunya.

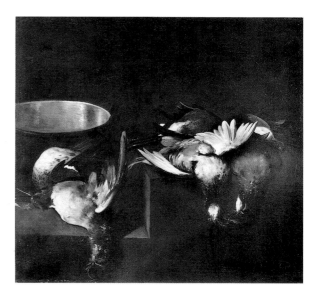

ful and fluently painted *Still Life with Game Fowl* is dated 1653 (fig. 84). But Barranco's free and vibrant style of painting, suggesting parallels with painters in Madrid, is unlike that of either of these artists. It establishes him as a worthy newcomer to the ranks of known practitioners of the still life in Seville.

By dint of his specialisation and his long career, the most prominent still-life painter active in Seville was Pedro de Camprobín Passano (1605–74), who more than any of his contemporaries gave lasting expression to the charm and elegance of life in one of Europe's most beautiful cities. Camprobín was trained in Toledo between 1619 and 1624 under Luis Tristán (*c*.1590–1624), who is not generally known as a still-life painter but by whom at least one fruit still life is documented.[33] Some time after the death of his master Camprobín decided to leave Toledo, which was rapidly losing its vitality as an artistic centre. His presence in Seville is first documented in November 1628, when he married María de Encalada, the daughter of a painter, Antonio de Arnos.[34] On 3 June 1630, Camprobín passed his examination to become a member of the Seville painters' guild.[35] The son of a *familiar de la Inquisición* (member of the Inquisition administration), in Seville Camprobín joined a cathedral confraternity, and in 1660 became, along with Murillo, Valdés Leal and other leading artists of the city, a founder member of its Academy. He died in 1674, apparently in comfortable circumstances.[36]

Camprobín's only known religious painting is a *Magdalen*, signed and dated 1634.[37] The absence of documented religious commissions, along with his large extant oeuvre of still lifes and flower paintings and the frequent reference to these in inventories, suggests the extent to which he specialised. The earliest dated still lifes by Camprobín that have been known until now are from the early 1650s, but it has been assumed that he must have painted such works much earlier. His career as a still-life painter may have benefited from the early death of his potential rival, Juan de Zurbarán, in 1649, but that a relationship of some kind existed between them is suggested by Camprobín's signed *Plate of Fruit* (fig. 85). The painting was published in 1947, but it was only realised in the course of editing this catalogue that it also bears a restored date which appears to read '1632' or '1652'.[38] If the painting indeed dates from 1632, then it suggests that Camprobín, who would have known such works from his youth in Castile, was developing this format in Seville at the same time that Francisco de Zurbarán was painting his studies of still-life motifs (figs 76

Fig. 83 Francisco Barranco, *Still Life with Chocolate Service and Dead Birds*, 1647. Oil on panel, 30.5 x 50.8 cm. Madrid art market.

Fig. 84 Pedro de Camprobín, *Still Life with Game Fowl*, 1653. Oil on canvas, 70.3 x 78.7 cm. Dallas, Southern Methodist University, Meadows Museum, Algur H. Meadows Collection.

Fig. 85 Pedro de Camprobín, *Plate of Fruit*. Oil on canvas, 51 x 65 cm. Barcelona, Private collection.

and 78). If it dates from later, it would simply suggest that he knew the works of Juan de Zurbarán (cat. 39), which is more likely to have been the case. Camprobín's modelling is less developed and his drawing less incisive than Juan de Zurbarán's, but the closeness in format of the two painters' works of this type has led to confusion in the past. The superb *Plate of Fruit with a Linnet* (cat. 40) in the Museu Nacional d'Art de Catalunya, Barcelona, has been attributed to Camprobín on the basis of its similarity to this small painting by the artist.[39] But a closer knowledge of both pictures requires us to revise that view and attribute the picture to the younger Zurbarán.

Camprobín's skill and personal style seem to have developed considerably by the 1650s. His *Still Life with Game Fowl* (fig. 84) of 1653 is an understated picture, compared to the copious kitchen still lifes being painted in Madrid at this time, and its great beauty derives largely from the verve and fluency of his brush in depicting the feathers and the sheen on the copper cauldron. The extremely well-preserved, small *Still Life with Hamper of Peaches and Glass of Wine* (fig. 86), signed and dated 1654, is painted with the same fluent touch. Its relaxed, intimate composition, unlike anything painted at the court, speaks of the easy elegance of affluent life in Seville.

The apogee of Camprobín's career was the decade of the 1660s, by which time he had evolved a truly original repertory of still-life types. They encompass fruit still lifes, flowerpieces and dessert still lifes, as well as banquet pieces that combine all of these elements – some of them with landscape or architectural backgrounds and such accoutrements of leisure as musical instruments. In their quiet refinement, these works are unlike any others painted in Spain, and they establish Camprobín as one of the most distinctive masters of still-life painting in Spain. Yet it was in this decade too that the artist began to alter his technique, relying to a much greater extent on

Fig. 86 Pedro de Camprobín, *Still Life with Hamper of Peaches and Glass of Wine*, 1654. Oil on canvas, 36 x 46.5 cm. Madrid, Naseiro collection.

43 Pedro de Camprobín, 1605–74
Still Life with Sweets
Signed and dated on table at right: *Pº de Camprouin passano fᵗ. 1663*
Oil on canvas, 42.5 x 62.5 cm
Private collection

44 Pedro de Camprobín, 1605–74
Still Life with Chestnuts, Olives and Wine
1663. Oil on canvas, 42 x 62 cm
Private collection

Camprobín's exquisite sensibility and delicate touch can be seen in this pair of small still lifes as in few other works. They have never been subjected to the neglect and harsh restoration that have seriously compromised much of his fragile oeuvre, and the balance between the velvety modelling of the forms and the subtly graded ambience is unaltered. Both paintings convey an atmosphere of intimacy and charm typical of the Sevillian school and of Camprobín in particular. In one of the still lifes, a silver-gilt tazza supports a heap of sweetmeats, something which Francisco de Zurbarán had depicted in 1633 (figs 77 and 78); but here the results are redolent of the relaxed elegance of Sevillian society, something one is not so conscious of in the older artist's work. The other still life of the pair depicts a simple silver plate of roasted chestnuts, a cup of olives, an ordinary bottle of red wine and a silver wine cup. Both silver objects are of the types manufactured at the silver mines of Peru and imported ready-made, to save on cost, to Seville.

the use of glazing to achieve delicacy in modelling, a technique that doomed many of his works to be robbed of the very qualities that once distinguished them. Over time the high oil content of these glazes has led to a darkening of the images; this in turn has often led unwitting restorers, using solvents that were too harsh, to strip away the darkened glazes, leaving only the underpainting. It is difficult today to find examples that reveal just how refined and exquisite his sensibility was. Among his best-preserved paintings must be placed *Still Life with Sweets* and *Still Life with Chestnuts, Olives and Wine* (cats 43 and 44), which were carefully cleaned in England in the early 1980s.

One of Camprobín's most beautiful paintings from the 1660s is *Still Life with Sweets and Flowers* (fig. 87), from the collection of the late Julio Cavestany, Marqués de Moret, who did more than anyone to launch the serious study of Spanish still-life painting. The unpretentious bouquet of roses, irises and jonquils in a simple faïence vase rests elegantly on a wooden table beside a small, ivory-inlaid walnut chest of drawers, on top of which is a glass salver of candied fruit. A butterfly hovers between the flowers and the sweets, and the atmospheric background lightens perceptibly towards the right.

Camprobín was the first distinctive flower painter in Seville and perhaps the only artist of real stature to paint flowers in the city. A sign of his pre-eminence was the set of twelve flower paintings on public display in the chapel of Our Lady of the Sorrows in the church of San Pablo.[40] Decorating churches with flower paintings became increasingly common in seventeenth-century Spain, and the pictures probably reflected the practice of bringing actual bouquets on feast days.[41] Camprobín's flower still lifes are highly varied: some depict single vases (simple or ornate ones) on tables, in niches, or on balustrades with landscape backgrounds and curtains. Others depict baskets of flowers.[42]

One of the most original formats explored by Camprobín was that of the grand banquet piece, a type of picture which might ultimately descend from mannerist works like Alonso Vázquez's famous *Lazarus and the Rich Man* (fig. 9), but which the artist made entirely his own (fig. 88). These highly decorative paintings depict

Fig. 87 Pedro de Camprobín, *Still Life with Sweets and Flowers*, c.1660s. Oil on canvas, 48 x 76.5 cm. Madrid, Private collection.

Fig. 88 Pedro de Camprobín, *Still Life with Sweets and Musical Instruments*, c.1665. Oil on canvas, 109 x 136 cm. Private collection.

Fig. 89 Pedro de Medina, *Still Life with Apples, Walnuts and Sugar Cane*, 1645. Oil on canvas, 43 x 60 cm. Madrid, Naseiro collection.

serving tables with ostentatious displays of silver-gilt plate, fruit, flowers and sweet-meats, and with musical instruments – guitars, violas, clavichords and sometimes harps – in colonnaded interiors, overlooking vistas of palatial structures. As in the case of Van der Hamen's dessert still lifes with dogs (cats 9 and 10), the theme would appear to be that of cultivated hospitality, for which the noble houses of Andalusia were famous.

The velvety modelling and warm colour that can be observed in the best-preserved of Camprobín's still lifes also characterised the works of his younger contemporary Pedro de Medina Valbuena (c.1620–91), who was about the same age as Juan de Zurbarán and, like him, was already painting still lifes in the 1640s. Medina's well-preserved *Still Life with Apples, Walnuts and Sugar Cane* (fig. 89), signed and dated 1645, has, however, little in common with the younger Zurbarán's work.[43] His brush-work is less vigorous; his contours, much softer. An even light falls on the forms, which are gently modelled and not consumed by shadow. Like Camprobín, Medina was a founding member of the Seville Academy in 1660, and seems to have painted still lifes throughout his career.[44] In 1682 he signed a grand, symmetrically composed fruit still life (present whereabouts unknown), which, like his earlier work, is arranged on a shaped stone plinth that helps to give depth to the composition.[45] Medina died in poverty in 1691.[46]

It is known from documents that some of the great figurative painters working in Seville in the second half of the seventeenth century occasionally turned to the still life; the greatest of them was Bartolomé Esteban Murillo (1617–82). Among the most sublime genre painters of all time, Murillo was no doubt able to endow his paintings of fruit and flowers with the same panache and sensuous presence as the images of bread, fruit and pastry in his famous paintings of beggar children. Following the artist's death in 1682, two small fruit still lifes and two flowerpieces, probably two pairs, were listed in the inventory of the contents of his studio; in 1709 the same paintings, identified as originals by Murillo, still belonged to his son Gaspar Esteban.[47] In 1685 two flowerpieces by Murillo – one representing lilies and the other roses – belonged to the great collector and patron of the artist Justino de Neve.[48] Regrettably, no such pictures have been identified among surviving works.

Any consideration of still-life painting in Seville would be incomplete without mention of Juan de Valdés Leal (1622–90); although not a still-life painter, he showed an imaginative genius for the portrayal of significant objects that makes it impossible to leave him out of any account of Spanish still-life painting. His famous allegories in the Hospital of Charity in Seville – *In Ictu Oculi* (In the Twinkling of an Eye) and *Finis Gloriae Mundi* (The End of Worldly Glory) – rank among the supreme master-pieces of Spanish art (figs 14 and 15).[49] These chilling, large-scale works were known in their day (1672) as 'Hieroglyphs of the Four Last Things' (*Jeroglíficos de nuestras postrimerías*). As in the case of Pereda's earlier 'Disillusionment of the World' (*Desengaño del mundo*) (cat. 26), the paintings' moral message was couched in the representation of objects charged with symbolic meaning, signifying the futility, in the face of death, of all worldly attainments and ambitions. Valdés's suitability for the commission to paint the 'Hieroglyphs of the Four Last Things' was possibly deter-mined by another pair of canvases he executed much earlier. In 1660 he treated this theme quite differently in a pair of paintings, now separated: *Allegory of Vanity* and *Allegory of Salvation* (cats 45 and 46).

45 Juan de Valdés Leal, 1622–90

Allegory of Vanity

Signed and dated on the engraving in the open book to the right of the skull: *1660 Juᵒ de baldes Leal FA.*

Oil on canvas, 130.4 x 99.3 cm

Hartford, Connecticut, Wadsworth Atheneum. The Ella Gallup Sumner and Mary Catlin Sumner Collection Fund

Separated in 1938, Valdés Leal's *Allegory of Vanity* and its pendant, the *Allegory of Salvation* (cat. 46), have not since been exhibited as a pair. Hung together, however, they can be seen as they were intended, as one great work, replete with symbolism: one of the most beautiful expressions in Spanish art of the Christian's path to salvation. In *Allegory of Vanity*, the putto at left blows a soap bubble, as fragile and fleeting as human life, and as empty as earthly ambition. All around him are tokens of temptation, pride, transience and death. On top of the disorderly mound of profane books, most of which have been identified, we can make out pages from Carducho's *Diálogos de la pintura* and Vignola's *Le due regole della prospettiva*, reminders that attainments of the arts, like those of all human science and learning, weigh nothing in the final balance. At the lower left, a laurel-crowned skull rests on a copy of Father Juan Eusebio Nieremberg's *De la diferencia entre lo temporal y eterno y crisol de desengaños* (On the Difference Between the Temporal and Eternal and Crucible of Disillusionments), an essential key to the painting's meaning. Behind the armillary sphere, an angel lifts a curtain and points to a luminous painting of the Last Judgement, a deliberate counterpoint to Carducho's engraving in which an artist's brush is poised before a blank canvas. Indeed, not only are symbols abundant in this painting, but their meanings are subtly elaborated into a kind of visual poetry at which Valdés Leal was unrivalled among Spanish Baroque painters.

46 Juan de Valdés Leal, 1622–90
Allegory of Salvation
1660. Oil on canvas, 130 x 99 cm
York City Art Gallery (presented by F.D. Lycett Green through the National Art-Collections Fund)

In contrast to the promiscuous disorder of Valdés Leal's *Allegory of Vanity*, the *Allegory of Salvation* is buttressed by an orderly structure in which relatively few symbols lead us to a quick and clear grasp of the picture's meaning. In front of a painting of the Crucifixion, whose frame is decorated with gilded emblems of the Passion, an angel holding a triple hour-glass, in which the measure of time has run out, points over its head to a luminous crown emblazoned with the words 'QUAM REPROMISIT DEUS', a reference to the General Epistle of James: 'Blessed is the man that endureth temptation: for when he is tried, he shall receive the crown of Life, which the Lord hath promised to them that love him' (James 1:12). In the foreground a young man holding a rosary is reading from an open volume, perhaps that very Epistle. About him are other well-known devotional texts, such as Fray Antonio de Alvarado's *Arte de bien vivir y guía de los caminos del cielo* (The Art of Living Well and Guide to the Paths of Heaven), and Antonio del Castillo's account of the Holy Land, *El devoto Peregrino, viage de tierra santa* (The Devout Pilgrim, Journey to the Holy Land) (Madrid 1656), which is opened to the plate depicting Mount Calvary. Emerging from the pages of this book is a penitential flail, and behind it is a glass vase with a stem of lilies, signifying chastity. When viewed together with the *Allegory of Vanity*, the two paintings tell us that the way to salvation is to turn one's back on the vanities of life and to follow a disciplined path of prayer, penitence and chastity. The potentially tedious sermonising is, however, transfigured by Valdés Leal's sense of visual poetry, his discreet taste and lustrous technique.

117

Hiepes and Still-Life Painting in Eastern Spain

Valencia in the seventeenth century was, like Seville, an important provincial capital, with active trade and cultural ties with the rest of the Iberian peninsula and Italy. As in Seville, still-life painting, with a few exceptions, did not begin to flourish there until the 1640s. Once it did, the products of the school were characterised by a distinctive, if somewhat archaistic charm, reflecting a different way of life from that of the court. Unquestionably the dominant figure in this development was the painter Tomás Hiepes (or Yepes), who was born around 1610.[1] From his earliest known works, dated 1642, until his death on 16 June 1674, he created still lifes of a strongly individual character that deeply affected the work of other artists in and around Valencia. Very little factual information about Hiepes's life has so far emerged from the archives of his native province, but his great local reputation has left traces in the early literature of art. Midway through his career, in 1656, the local chronicler Marco Antonio Ortí wrote of his *fruteros*:

> There were many pictures in which many kinds of fruits were painted, all children of the brush and hand of Yepes, the painter who in this line of the imitation of fruits has succeeded in acquiring a very singular fame and reputation.[2]

The primary source of information on Hiepes as an artist is the account written in the eighteenth century by Marcos Antonio Orellana.[3] After wasting much ink in scolding Palomino for not mentioning Hiepes in his *Lives of the Eminent Spanish Painters and Sculptors*, Orellana writes of Hiepes's work:

> His flowers are subtle, translucent and light, his fruits very natural and everything done with admirable perfection. His paintings are equally copious as they are esteemed and celebrated, and one does not see baskets with fruit, flowers, etc., biscuits, pies, cheeses, or pasties and other similar things which are well executed in conformity with the real things, without thinking and esteeming them to be works by Yepes. The houses of this city and Kingdom [Valencia] are filled with these kind of paintings by his hand...and I myself have by his hand a basketful of grapes, which I esteem. The limpid and translucent grapes with the vine leaves could deceive the birds, like those other celebrated grapes by Zeuxis.[4]

Orellana's account of Hiepes's oeuvre suggests that he was prolific, that the range of his subject matter was broad and that his skill was considerable. All this is confirmed by his surviving still lifes. The earliest works known today are a pair of still lifes signed and dated 1642 on the reverse of the original canvas,[5] one of which depicts a table-top covered in a lace-trimmed white cloth, on which are placed two decorated Manises bowls of fruit (fig. 90). This distinctive format, with the use of identical lace-trimmed tablecloths, but not always employing symmetrical compositions, was used

Fig. 90 Tomás Hiepes, *Still Life with Two Bowls of Fruit*, 1642. Oil on canvas, 67 x 96 cm. Private collection.

several times by Hiepes in the 1640s. Three somewhat larger paintings of this type, representing tables laden with sweets or with fruit and flowers, are in private collections in Spain (fig. 91).[6]

By the mid-1650s Hiepes had further developed this format, producing several large still lifes, strictly symmetrical in their compositions, in which the table-top is covered with a red damask cloth. In the centre of the table is a small ebony-and-ivory

Fig. 91 Tomás Hiepes, *Still Life with Baskets of Nuts and Wafers*, 1640s. Oil on canvas, 76.5 x 112 cm. Madrid, Plácido Arango.

Fig. 92 Tomás Hiepes, *Still Life with Flowers and an Ebony Chest*, 1654. Oil on canvas, 114 x 145 cm. Private collection.

Fig. 93 Tomás Hiepes, *Flowerpiece*, 1664. Oil on canvas, 150 x 98 cm. Oviedo, Masaveu collection.

chest of drawers (known in Castile as *escritorio* or *papelera*, and in Catalonia and Aragón as *arquimesa*), on top of which is an ebony-framed painting (probably a copper panel), in the Flemish style, representing a biblical subject such as the *Judgement of Solomon* (fig. 92). In two of the known examples, a pair of decorative jasper orbs is placed on top of the chest in front of the painting.[7] The chest is flanked on the table by a pair of *floreros*. Reliance on such rigid symmetry had passed from favour at the court long before the 1650s, but, in the *retardataire* spirit of his style, Hiepes still employed it occasionally to create impressive and highly decorative still lifes. (The innovation of depicting a chest of drawers on a table-top was a motif also developed by the prolific artist we shall call Pseudo-Hiepes [see below].)

As noted by Orellana, and as seen in the still life just discussed, Hiepes was a skilful painter of flowers. Dated paintings from at least the last decade of his career depict elaborate vases of cut flowers or Manises pots of flowering plants. The grandest of these is the pair of large flowerpieces in the Masaveu collection, dated 1664 (fig. 93).[8] In contrast to the fluently painted, and nearly contemporary vases and baskets of flowers by Arellano (cats 50 and 51), what is most impressive about these pictures is the artist's obsession with minutiae.

One aspect of Hiepes's repertory not mentioned by Orellana was the painting of game. A signed and dated still life of 1643 in a Madrid private collection depicts a butcher's stand with assorted game fowl and a hare hanging from a rail along the top of the composition (fig. 94). Underneath, a table-top covered with a patterned textile serves to display plates of meat and entrails, two eggs, a knife and a plucked bird.[9] This work, perhaps more similar in type to Italian than to Castilian models, reveals something else distinctive about Hiepes's way of painting. The brushwork is smooth, with little variation in texture and little spontaneity of touch; yet the painting is rich and glowing. This is due to the importance of glazing in the artist's working process,

Fig. 94 Tomás Hiepes, *Still Life with Game Fowl and Hare*, 1643. Oil on canvas, 102 x 160 cm. Madrid, Naseiro collection.

and in this regard his technique closely resembles that of his contemporary, the Valencian religious painter Jerónimo Jacinto de Espinosa (1600–67).[10] As in the case of Camprobín, this technique gives a certain radiance to Hiepes's well-preserved still lifes, but it renders them extremely vulnerable to rash restorers. As the glazes naturally darken with age, unwitting restorers have often mistaken them for discoloured varnish and have dissolved them with harsh cleaning agents. This has often left exposed the rather cursory, but less vulnerable underpainting, which was never intended to stand on its own.

One of Hiepes's finest and best-preserved works is *Still Life with Grapevine, Marigolds and Fruit*, in the Arango collection, Madrid (cat. 47). Much of its powerful impact stems from its extraordinarily good state of preservation: the glazes that were such an integral part of the artist's technique are largely intact. Only in the mound of pears and apples at the right have they been partially removed by some overzealous attempt at cleaning in the past. During the course of a careful recent cleaning, the difference in the quality of form between the pears and the fruit at the left was striking.[11] Hiepes's technique, so much praised by Orellana for its 'perfection' and 'great naturalism', is indeed impressive in such well-preserved examples. But in other works, even signed examples, it can seem crude, cursory and naïve by comparison.

Among the known paintings by or attributed to Hiepes, the quality varies greatly, suggesting that he may have had an active workshop. This may, indeed, account for his habit of occasionally including in his signatures an indication that the painting being signed is an 'original', as in the case of the Arango still life illustrated here (cat. 47). But apart from this, appreciable variations in quality can have a great deal to do with the condition in which a painting has come down to us.

A final aspect of Hiepes's repertory that deserves special mention is the painting of still-life compositions in landscape settings. A number of signed pictures are known that depict the corners of gardens, with paved terraces and flower beds planted with climbing roses, jasmine and morning glories, orange trees, lilies, marigolds, etc.

47 Tomás Hiepes, *c.*1610–74
Still Life with Grapevine, Marigolds and Fruit
Signed and dated on pot in foreground: *ORIGINAL DE THOMAS HIEPES, EN V^c. 1654...*
Oil on canvas, 110.5 x 134.6 cm
Madrid, Plácido Arango collection

Departing from the familiar formulas of still-life composition, Hiepes has depicted a darkened interior, perhaps a potting shed, with a window opening to the left. On a simple wooden table sits a large Manises pot, a type of decorated earthenware typical of the region around Valencia, containing a well-pruned grapevine heavily laden with fruit. Surrounding the pot on the table are mounds of pomegranates, quinces, pears and apples, arranged as though they had just been picked by a gardener and left there for later use. In the window-sill sits a Manises flowerpot containing a robust African marigold plant, as though it had been placed there momentarily in the course of working in a garden.

The picture's treatment of an everyday scene is the source of much of its charm. But the painting's impact stems also from the artist's technique, seen here with the glazes that were an integral part of it still intact (see text). Because of its extraordinarily good state of preservation, the painting bears out the opinion of Hiepes's Valencian contemporaries that he excelled all others at the painting of fruit.

Valencia was famous for its gardens and the fruits and flowers they produced. Some of Hiepes's paintings of this type depict live fowl strutting on a terrace in the manner of the Dutch animal painter Melchior d'Hondecoeter (1636–95). All have distant vistas of hilly landscapes, which recall the backgrounds of some religious paintings by Jerónimo Jacinto de Espinosa.[12] One of the most spectacular of these pictures represents a young woman seated on the ground making nosegays (fig. 95). Surrounding her are baskets of cut flowers and pots of carnations, hyacinths, peonies and irises. In a version of this composition, known only from an old photograph, the young woman is replaced by a monkey (fig. 96).

Related to this type of painting by Hiepes are the monumental outdoor game pieces by his short-lived Valencian contemporary Miguel March (c.1633–c.1670) (fig. 97), who, according to Orellana, had travelled to Italy in the 1650s. In addition to painting still lifes, March, it seems, had a much more active career than Hiepes as a traditional figurative painter.[13]

Fig. 95 Tomás Hiepes, *Girl Making Nosegays in a Garden*, c.1660s. Oil on canvas, 102 x 160 cm. Private collection.

Fig. 96 Tomás Hiepes, *Monkey in a Garden with Potted Flowers*, c.1660s. Oil on canvas. Location unknown.

Fig. 97 Miguel March, *Landscape with Game*, 1663. Oil on canvas, 114 x 158 cm. Valencia, Montortal collection.

The appearance in recent years of a body of related still-life paintings has high-lighted the existence of a problematical artist whose identity has yet to be estab-lished.[14] Because all his known pictures are unsigned, over the past century and a quarter he has been confused with other Spanish artists; he has even been considered by some to be Italian. The paintings in question vary occasionally in size and format, but most are oblong canvases, over one metre in width. They seem to have been col-lected in series.[15] The compositions are usually arranged on foreshortened, free-stand-ing stone plinths with decorated cornices, or on red table-tops trimmed with fringe and gimp, attached with brass nails. Although a single artistic personality seems to be behind them all, the quality varies from work to work: from quite good to quite bad. Because of the large number of works involved – about forty are known today – and the wide variation in quality, it is obvious that they derive from a workshop, headed by a master who could himself paint on an impressive, if not brilliant level, and supported by one or more subordinates, who helped him to address an appar-ently large commercial market. Beside the distinctive supports (table-tops and plinths), what unites these still lifes is a common repertory of objects and motifs that are used interchangeably. In most of them also, a strong light falls diagonally across the background, creating a dramatic effect reminiscent of the followers of Caravaggio, although nothing else about these pictures is Caravaggesque.

In 1983 John Spike attributed a still life by this master (fig. 98) to an anonymous Lombard artist.[16] The following year, Luigi Salerno, who dated the same painting *circa* 1600, picked up the idea and named the artist the Master of the Lombard Fruit Bowl.[17] For want of a better name, this appellation has generally been retained. But the artist was not Italian; nor, probably, was he even born until after 1600. What has passed for 'Italian' was no doubt the result of Italian influence, and what has passed for 'early' would probably be better called 'provincial'. Because of certain decorative objects depicted in the still lifes, we can be certain that they were painted nearer the middle of the seventeenth century.[18] Because of similarities to the works of Tomás

Fig. 98 Pseudo-Hiepes, *Still Life with Bowl of Cherries, Pears, Apricots and Peas, c.*1650–75. Oil on canvas, 49 x 74 cm. Formerly Bergamo, Pietro Lorenzelli.

Fig. 99 Pseudo-Hiepes, *Still Life with Fruit Bowl and Artichokes, c.*1650–75. Oil on canvas, 67.3 x 111.7 cm. Private collection.

Hiepes, himself an archaising artist, we may conjecture a familiarity with his still lifes.

As an example of both the range of quality and the reuse of motifs evident in this large group of paintings, we can compare the still life attributed to a Lombard artist by Spike (fig. 98) to another, depicting the same rather generic-looking fruit bowl with a similar arrangement of cherries, apricots, pears and peas (fig. 100). The latter painting, darkened by old varnish and of less good quality, spreads the composition out on a plinth with a decorated cornice. To the left of the fruit bowl are two artichokes, identical in design to those in *Still Life with Fruit Bowl and Artichokes* (fig. 99), attributed by Salerno[19] to the Master of the Lombard Fruit Bowl. To the right of the bowl is a glass vase of lilies and roses, derived from the superb *Still Life with Honeycomb, Fruit and a Vase of Flowers* (cat. 48), which is one of a group of six unpublished still lifes by this artist in a private collection in Madrid, paintings whose quality is as high as he ever attained.

These six paintings have belonged to the same family since at least the mid-nineteenth century. Confusion surrounding the identity of the artist was already evident

Fig. 100 Pseudo-Hiepes, *Still Life with Fruit Bowl, Artichokes and a Vase of Flowers, c.*1650–75. Oil on canvas. Location unknown.

48 Pseudo-Hiepes
Still Life with Honeycomb, Fruit and a Vase of Flowers
c.1650–75. Oil on canvas, 77 x 115 cm
Madrid, Private collection

The author of this elegant still life has thus far eluded identification, but he obviously enjoyed great popularity in the last half of the seventeenth century. Nearly forty still lifes by the artist and his prolific workshop are known today, a far larger number than exist by most of his contemporaries. The frequent repetition of motifs and whole compositions, varying greatly in quality, suggests that a large workshop may have been involved. The uniformly large scale of most of the still lifes, the fact that many of them seem to have belonged to series, and the depiction of objects that can be dated to the second half of the 1600s, suggest a studio that did a brisk business in supplying works for the ambitious decorative schemes of late seventeenth-century houses. The somewhat archaic style of the artist, however, has often led to an earlier dating and to confusion with older artists, one of whom is Tomás Hiepes. A suggestion of a provincial origin, such as Valencia, may be helpful in resolving some of the problems that the paintings present.

in 1870, when Vicente Poleró Toledo catalogued the collection of Don Manuel Salvador López, then the owner of the paintings.[20] In his manuscript inventory, Poleró described in detail the six still lifes, measuring 77 x 115 cm, which he catalogued as by Tomás Hiepes, probably reflecting what was already then a traditional assumption. In deference to this tradition, until the painter in question has been identified, he should perhaps be called Pseudo-Hiepes.

Indeed, several things about *Still Life with Honeycomb, Fruit and Vase of Flowers* (cat. 48) suggest a possible Valencian origin. One is the foreshortened support or pedestal on which the objects are arranged; this recalls the table-top still lifes of Hiepes (figs 90 and 91) and is not a format often found elsewhere in Spain.[21] Another is the glassware, the simple shapes of which are adorned, if at all, with *latticinio*, or stripes of opaque white glass; such glassware appears in Hiepes's still lifes (fig. 91) and was a common product of the glass furnaces of Catalonia and Valencia from the sixteenth to the end of the eighteenth century.[22] Valencian glass in the seventeenth century was more ordinary than Barcelona glass and, unlike it, was not made in the Venetian manner.[23] Glassware in such simple shapes decorated with *latticinio* does not appear in Castilian still lifes, but is a common feature in those of Hiepes and Pseudo-Hiepes. The white lace underneath the bread and pastry at the right is quite different from Hiepes's snowflake lace of the 1640s (figs 90 and 91) and probably dates from later in the seventeenth century. Perhaps the most striking motif in this beautiful picture is the plate containing a moulded white cheese, on top of which is a honeycomb with a rose stuck into it. It is typical of the *modus operandi* of Pseudo-Hiepes and his workshop that this motif should be used in works of widely varying quality.[24]

Among the objects most commonly depicted in this corpus of still lifes are the small chests of drawers mentioned earlier (*papeleras*). These luxury objects were ubiquitous in seventeenth-century Spain.[25] We have already seen one in Pereda's *Still Life with Sweets, Vessels and Ebony Chest* of 1652 (cat. 30), and another in Hiepes's *Still Life with Flowers and an Ebony Chest* of 1654 (fig. 92). At least seven examples

Fig. 101 Pseudo-Hiepes, *Still Life with Ebony Chest, Fruit and a Vase of Flowers*, c.1650–75. Oil on canvas, 77 x 115 cm. Madrid, Private collection.

are known by Pseudo-Hiepes and his workshop.[26] The series of still lifes in Madrid includes one in which an ebony-and-ivory *papelera* is placed on a red fringed table-top (fig. 101). On top of it are two decorative jasper orbs and a sliced melon on a plate.[27] In the foreground are an elegant white openwork faïence fruit bowl, a ripe melon, a dead bird and a ceramic vase of flowers. Although openwork fruit bowls had been depicted since Labrador (cat. 23), this one resembles nothing in Castilian still lifes of the mid-seventeenth century. The modelling of the fruit in the bowl, especially of the quinces, with shadows defined by glazing, is similar to Hiepes (cat. 47). The artist used both the melon on the table-top and the flower arrangement in many other still lifes, and the rather hard, almost metallic modelling of the flowers is characteristic.

Although the subject matter of Pseudo-Hiepes's works would seem to date them to the last half of the seventeenth century, an accurate assessment of his style is difficult, unless it is understood as the product of a provincial culture. It has none of the painterly richness that characterised the School of Madrid from Pereda and Palacios onwards, and has nothing to do with such *retardataire* artists at the court as Antonio Ponce, whose repertory of forms and manner of painting are nowhere visible in these works. Archaising as the style of these still lifes is, it also lacks the delicacy in draughtsmanship and glazing that can be seen in the best of Hiepes's still lifes. Because of this peculiar combination of factors, the identity of this mysterious workshop should probably be sought somewhere in the region extending from Valencia, in the south, northwards to the region of Zaragoza. We shall probably not know who the master was until a signed example is discovered.

There were certainly still-life painters in this region, mentioned in the early literature of art and about whom little or nothing is known. Two of them were Valencian artists, father and son, to whom Orellana devoted a lengthy discussion: Joaquín Eximeno the Elder and the Younger.[28] Eximeno the Elder is said to have studied with Jerónimo Jacinto de Espinosa and to have married his daughter, although the latter fact seems improbable.[29] Eximeno the younger is said to have been born around 1676 and to have lived until around 1754. Several very archaising flowerpieces by the son are known.[30] Orellana says that the two Eximenos painted all manner of still lifes and that the houses of Valencia were full of them.[31] He compares their works to Hiepes's, but says they lack the subtlety of his lighting and modelling and the bite of his naturalism. He says that the works of father and son were virtually indistinguishable but that, if pressed, one would have to say that the father was the better painter of the two.

It would be rash to propose that Pseudo-Hiepes can be identified with two painters about whom we know practically nothing, and we cannot make this assumption. There were many other painters, little-known or unknown today, who were active in the regions of Valencia and Zaragoza, and who also could have been responsible for this body of work. At present, we can do no more than ask: who is this painter and where did he work? The answer may yet be surprising.

Flower Painting in Madrid, 1650-1700

From around 1600 there were, in Northern Europe, artists who specialised in flower painting; in Spain, however, artists did not specialise in that genre until around the middle of the seventeenth century. Juan van der Hamen had incorporated flowers into his still lifes of fruits and sweets and was recorded as having painted independent flowerpieces, or *ramilleteros*, though none of these is known today. He was the first artist in Spain to adopt the Flemish format of the devotional image or landscape in a garland, but he was far from being a specialist in flowers. As we have seen, in the mid-1630s Sir Arthur Hopton persuaded Juan Fernández, El Labrador, to try his hand at flowers, and the results were spectacular (cat. 24, fig. 57). Nevertheless, Labrador was better known for his still lifes of fruit.

Towards the middle of the century, two principal currents could be discerned among painters of flower still lifes in Madrid. One, descended from the courtly, cerebral art of Van der Hamen, was represented by his pupil Antonio Ponce (cat. 19); the other, influenced by the taste for flower paintings imported from Antwerp and Rome, was represented by Juan de Arellano (1614–76), eight years younger than Ponce, and beginning to specialise in flowers after an unsuccessful attempt at becoming a figure painter.[1] The first of these currents was soon to die out; the second, developing many offshoots, eventually became one of the most visible and varied features of painting in Late Baroque Madrid.

Ponce's emblematic *Cupids with Cartouche and Festoons of Flowers* (fig. 102), probably executed in the late 1640s or early 1650s, shows that he was affected by both of these currents. The compositional type, in which a cartouche and floral decorations embellish a central sacred or allegorical subject, emulates the format popularised by the Flemish Jesuit painter Daniel Seghers (1590–1661), known in Spain as El Teatino, who around 1650 was the most famous living flower painter in Europe. By that time, Seghers's pictures of this kind (fig. 103) were well known to connoisseurs in Madrid,[2] and Ponce was consciously adopting a format that was *à la mode*. In doing so, he did not reject his formation in the school of Van der Hamen: his flowers, like those in his master's garlands and bouquets, are drawn with perfection, but they have a rather abstracted and artificial quality, lacking the suppleness of Seghers's touch. Ponce's beautiful (and perhaps somewhat later) *Still Life with Artichokes and a Talavera Vase of Flowers* (cat. 19), has the same exquisite precision of contour, but in its rich chiaroscuro and close viewpoint, it reveals a more intimate aspect of his style.

Arellano's earliest dated work of 1646 is similar to Ponce's cartouche (fig. 104). Following the example of Flemish flower specialists, such as Brueghel and Seghers, he had the central *Allegory of Vanity* painted by his fellow artist Francisco Camilo (*c*.1614–73), who was the better figure painter.[3] At first glance, Arellano's garland

seems to lack the architectural clarity of Ponce's, but on close inspection, one can see that in depicting (doubtless inspired by Seghers) the delicacy and ephemerality of a rich variety of blossoms, birds, insects and molluscs, he brings something wholly new to flower painting in Spain. The sensuous, almost palpably fragrant, atmosphere conjured up by the garland provides the perfect foil to the moral lesson depicted in the centre: that the pleasures of this life will pass.

The following year (1647), Arellano painted a pair of large flowerpieces with birds and fruit, which afford further insight into this early stage of his development (fig. 105). Their tall, narrow format, with the depiction of bouquets raised on stepped pedestals, is one to which he returned occasionally throughout his career (e.g. cat. 50).[4] But the sparse and awkward grouping of flowers in the bouquet, to say nothing of the leaden butterflies, suggests the effort of a beginner.[5] The modelling of the flowers, with its acute observation of detail, is similar to that in the garland of the previous year, and reaffirms the artist's early focus on Seghers's style. On the other hand, the historiated bronze vases and ornamented pedestals are indicative of the Italianate taste that dominated the decorative arts at the court of Philip IV.

By 1652, when Arellano signed the spectacular pair of festoons with landscape views in the Prado (cat. 49), he had completely absorbed the manner of his Flemish

Fig. 102 Antonio Ponce, *Cupids with Cartouche and Festoons of Flowers*, *c.*1650. Oil on canvas, 148 x 104 cm. Madrid, Private collection.

Fig. 103 Daniel Seghers, *Garland of Flowers with Virgin and Child*. Oil on copper, 84 x 55 cm. Madrid, Museo del Prado.

Fig. 104 Juan de Arellano and Francisco Camilo, *Garland of Flowers with Allegory of Vanity*, 1646. Oil on canvas, 146 x 124 cm. Spain, Private collection.

Fig. 105 Juan de Arellano, *Flowerpiece with Birds and Fruit*, 1647. Oil on canvas. Madrid, Private collection.

49 **Juan de Arellano**, 1614–76
Festoon of Flowers with Cartouche Surrounding a Landscape
Signed and dated: *Juan de Arellano, 1652*
Oil on canvas, 58 x 73 cm
Madrid, Museo del Prado

By 1652, when this painting and its pendant were executed, Arellano was thirty-eight years old and had reached the peak of his early maturity. Although his style continued to evolve for the rest of his career, the level of quality established here was rarely, if ever, surpassed. Like the collection inventories of these years, the painting attests to the prestige then enjoyed in Madrid by the most famous of living flower painters, the Flemish Jesuit Daniel Seghers (1590–1666), known in Spain as 'El Teatino'. But unlike Seghers's many close imitators in Flanders, Arellano has shown originality and self-confidence in adapting the cartouche and garland format to his own purposes. Rather than seeming to encircle or enclose something, his cartouche, with its shell-like forms, opens on an expansive natural vista. Whether or not Arellano himself painted the landscape is perhaps arguable, since he is known to have collaborated with other painters, but the ensemble has a striking unity of conception and design. The delicately delineated festoon of roses, tulips, hyacinths, morning glories and daffodils, with its court of admiring insects, hangs like an honorific decoration before the rustic landscape.

Fig. 106 Mario Nuzzi, *Flowerpiece*. Oil on canvas, 68 x 49.8 cm. Formerly London art market.

Fig. 107 Juan de Arellano, *Flowerpiece*, *c*.1650s. Oil on canvas, 71 x 58 cm (with additions). Oviedo, Masaveu collection.

models and was working with a degree of competence and self-confidence that established him as one of the finest flower painters active at the court. By his maturity, as Palomino wrote in his brief biography, 'none of the Spaniards surpassed him in eminence in this skill'.[6] Early in his career he had opened a shop for the sale of his paintings, near that of Francisco Barrera, facing the church of San Felipe.[7] Throughout the 1650s he may have been competing with Ponce for dominance in an ever-growing market for flower paintings. By the 1660s, when many of his dated pictures were made, he had developed a repertory of flowerpiece formats which he and his workshop continued to elaborate with considerable diversity until his death in 1676. When asked as an old man why he had devoted himself so much to flowers and had abandoned figures, he answered wryly, 'Because this way I work less and earn more.'[8]

Palomino, who was sometimes readier with the illuminating anecdote than with fact, tells us that when Arellano realised that he could not make his mark as a figure painter in Madrid, he tried copying some flower paintings by the Roman specialist Mario Nuzzi (1603–73), called Mario de' Fiori (fig. 106), thus discovering his natural gift for the genre. Although this story is unlikely to be historically accurate, Arellano probably did know Nuzzi's works from early on. Nuzzi, who was thirteen years younger than Seghers, had built a great reputation by 1650, and his works were already represented in Madrid collections by this date.[9] Arellano drew cautiously from both artists as he proceeded to forge his own style – one which became, in fact, as individual as either of theirs. It is clear, however, that as time went on, Arellano felt a greater affinity with the more robust, Baroque manner of Nuzzi; he even adopted certain formats readily identified with that artist, such as the painting of flowers on mirrors, the most famous examples of which were Nuzzi's works in the Galleria Colonna in Rome.[10]

The pair of small overdoors in the Masaveu collection (fig. 107) are datable on the basis of their style to Arellano's early maturity.[11] With their very low point of view, it is obvious that they were conceived for a specific location, and this serves as an example of the growing role of flower painting in the decoration of Madrid's palatial homes and richly decorated ecclesiastical interiors. However, the artist more usually produced bouquets observed at eye level, arranged in bulbous glass vases (cat. 50), decorated urns or open-work baskets (cat. 51). But we find surprising and original variations, such as the large canvas in the Museo de Bellas Artes, La Coruña, in which a basket and an urn of flowers are depicted on different levels, with the basket reflected in a mirror (fig. 108). A characteristic feature of Arellano's bouquets is the careful balance he maintains between blossoms rendered in shades of the primary colours – red, blue and yellow – and others, of a lusciously glazed white, with which these are mixed.

It is noteworthy that Arellano's famous specialisation in flowers was not quite absolute. While he may have devoted himself primarily to painting high-quality flowerpieces, his unpublished will and the inventory of his estate reveal that his prosperous workshop was organised like a factory, turning out a wide variety of no doubt ordinary pictures to supply his shop; these included flowerpieces, garlands, fruit still lifes, portraits, landscapes, hunting scenes, religious images and allegories of the Senses, Seasons and Elements.[12] The Museo del Prado recently acquired a signed *Plate of Peaches and Plums*, the first pure fruit still life by Arellano to be discovered.[13] A number of unattributed paintings of the Five Senses that have appeared on the art market in recent years are very likely to have come from Arellano's studio.[14]

Fig. 108 Juan de Arellano, *Flowerpiece with Mirror*, c.1660s. Oil on canvas, 126 x 106 cm. La Coruña, Museo Municipal.

Fig. 109 Attributed to Juan de Arellano, *Sense of Smell*. Oil on canvas, 108 x 162 cm. Oviedo, Masaveu collection.

50 Juan de Arellano, 1614–76
Still Life with Flowers and Fruit
c.1665–70. Signed on plinth at left: *Juan. deArellano*
Oil on canvas, 98.5 x 63 cm
Spain, Masaveu collection

For the grace and balance of its composition, the lightness of its background and the fluency of its technique, this still life stands out as one of Arellano's greatest late works. It belonged successively to Goya's friend Bernardo de Iriarte, one of the most remarkable Spanish collectors of the late eighteenth century; to José de Madrazo, director of the Real Museo del Pintura y Escultura, now the Prado; and to the Marqués de Salamanca, perhaps the most colourful and ambitious Spanish collector of the later nineteenth century.

In raising a *florero* on a small stone plinth, which in turn rests on a larger one laden with fruit and attracting moths, Arellano was returning to a format first employed in his youth. But comparison with those early still lifes (e.g. fig. 105) reveals the extent of the transformation which twenty years or more had wrought in his style. The polish, ornamentation and crowding of the earlier works have given way to vivacity, airy unity and chromatic harmony. The lidded glass vessel on the lower level is apparently only sketched. Since the paint layer seems to be contemporary with the rest, one can only wonder if the painting was actually finished when signed, or if this was an afterthought, never quite resolved.

51 **Juan de Arellano,** 1614–76
Basket of Flowers
*c.*1670–5. Signed on plinth at right: *Juan de Arellano*
Oil on canvas, 84 x 105 cm
Madrid, Museo del Prado

Monumental open-work flower baskets like this, profusely stuffed with stems and blossoms as though these had just been picked and were awaiting arrangement, constituted a major achievement of Arellano's late career. Most of the known examples are nearly identical in size and may have served as overdoor or overwindow decorations in a single grand room in one of Madrid's noble mansions. Two of them are dated 1671 and 1672 respectively; they were thus painted in the last five years of the artist's life. The selection of flowers varies from basket to basket, but the lilies, tulips, hortensias, anemones and carnations seen in this example are characteristically animated by a dynamic energy that bends and twists every stalk, petal and leaf. This sense of movement, originating not from any external force but from the ebbing life of the flowers themselves, combines with the fluid chiaroscuro and incidental animal accents, such as insects and lizards, to convey a generous and suggestive image of nature. It was this that assured Arellano's place as the pre-eminent flower painter of seventeenth-century Spain.

Fig. 110 José de Arellano, *Basket of Flowers*, 1683. Oil on canvas, 64.8 x 64.8 cm. Formerly New York art market.

One such intact series is in the Masaveu collection, Oviedo, where it still bears the faked signature of Van der Hamen, no doubt placed there in recent years to make it more desirable. The *Sense of Smell* (fig. 109) may be attributed to Arellano and his workshop on the basis of the style of the flowers, which is unmistakable. The landscape setting with a scene from Genesis is reminiscent of the works of Juan de Solís, Arellano's master.[15] Although not great works of art, these series of *Senses* add significantly to our understanding of one of the most important still-life painters of his time.

Among the artists working in Arellano's workshop were several members of his family. Juan, his son by his first marriage, died at the age of eighteen, before he could have completed his training. José, his son by his second marriage to María de Corcuera, was trained as a painter by his father but was only twenty-one years old when the latter died.[16] Trying, no doubt to carry on the family business as best he could, he followed in his father's speciality until about 1705, imitating his style in a very rudimentary way. But his dry and pedestrian works (fig. 110) cannot be confused with those of his father.

Arellano's most gifted pupil was Bartolomé Pérez de la Dehesa (1634–98), who must be ranked among the greatest flower painters that Spain produced.[17] We know nothing for sure about his training, but he married Arellano's daughter Juana in 1663 and probably joined his father-in-law's workshop. At his death in 1676, Arellano owed Pérez money for paintings that the latter had supplied.[18] By that time, Pérez had long been practising as an independent painter, and his distinctive style, already evident in his earliest dated pictures in the 1660s, shows originality and extraordinary sensitivity. Pérez was more gifted than Arellano as a figure painter, and Palomino says that he assisted the latter by painting the figures in some of his garlands. Indeed, when Ceán Bermúdez saw his now unknown *Virgin and Child Appearing to Saint Rose of Lima* in the collection of Bernardo de Iriarte around 1800, he wrote that Pérez ought to be regarded as one of the best painters of the *fin de siècle*.[19] Such hyperbole probably derived from Ceán's surprise that a flower painter could also be a 'good painter'. What is probably an example of Pérez's figural style can be seen in his *Garland of Flowers with Saint Anthony and the Christ Child* (cat. 53).

Flower painting at the end of the seventeenth century has been so little studied, that Bartolomé Pérez's personality as an artist is very ill-defined today. Such, at least, is the situation on the art market, where most of the works attributed to him are by Italian painters. As Pérez Sánchez has observed, even in the Museo del Prado, where in the nineteenth century flower paintings not by Arellano were routinely ascribed to Pérez, many attributions are in need of revision.[20] In seeking to come to grips with his style, therefore, it is important to focus on signed or documented works; from this, a consistent personality emerges, one whose subdued range of colour, fluid touch and delicate chiaroscuro are as distinct from Arellano's style as they are from the pastose brushwork and agitated rhythms of the Roman and Neapolitan flower painters, with whose works those of Pérez are most often confused.

Among the earliest signed paintings by Pérez that are known is one dated 1665 (fig. 111). It represents a glass vase of flowers on a stone plinth, beside which is a slightly lower plinth supporting loose blossoms, probably those left unused from the making of this bouquet.[21] It is painted neither like the early, Flemish-oriented works of Arellano nor like that artist's robust works of the 1660s. There is, instead, a preciosity of line and a delicacy of modelling – a certain exquisiteness – that is distinctly Pérez's own.

In the following year, 1666, Pérez painted the magnificent floral overdoor now in

Fig. 111 Bartolomé Pérez, *Flowerpiece*, 1665. Oil on canvas, 53.3 x 71.1 cm. Formerly London art market.

the Fitzwilliam Museum (cat. 52), a painting whose original octagonal shape is still discernible. This distinctive and decorative format, which had been tried before in Spain by other painters (see cat. 20), is one which the artist used on several occasions.[22] Today, with the corners filled in, the pedestal on which the urn rests seems awkward in shape, but were the corners removed as intended, it would brilliantly echo the canvas's edge.

Among Pérez's greatest gifts were his varied talents as a designer. Palomino tells us that he was much in demand as a scenographer for the spectacles presented in the theatre of the Buen Retiro Palace, and Ceán Bermúdez states that it was for this reason that he was appointed Painter to the King on 22 January 1689. From near the beginning of his royal service, Pérez worked, under the direction of the architect José de Churriguera (1665–1725), in applying his skill as a flower painter to one of the most ambitious and spectacular decorative projects of Charles II's reign, the now almost forgotten gilded bedchamber of the king ('Camón Dorado de Su Magd') in the Royal Palace of Madrid.[23]

It has been known since the 1930s from published documents that Pérez painted bouquets and garlands of flowers on gold-ground panels (cat. 54), some of them painted on both sides, and it has been assumed that these were intended as folding screens (*biombos*).[24] The 1734 inventory of the old Royal Palace lists twenty-two such panels, of various sizes, by Pérez. Eight of them were gilded and painted on both sides but were rather small. In the inventory of 1747 there are five additional ones said to be by Pérez: 'Twenty-seven panels of different sizes, which altogether comprise a *camón*, and on them are painted *floreros*, originals by D. Bartolomé Pérez, and some of them are painted on both sides.'[25] By 1772 the panels had been moved to the Buen Retiro Palace, and thirty-five of them – some with vases and some with garlands – were described in a single lot as by Pérez.[26] The word '*camón*' used to describe the original context of the panels in the 1747 inventory is not commonly used today, but

52 Bartolomé Pérez, 1634–98
Flowers in a Sculptured Vase
Signed and dated on plinth: *B^{me} Perez Faciebl/..66*
Oil on canvas, 82.6 x 62.2 cm
Cambridge, Fitzwilliam Museum

Works of the quality of the Fitzwilliam flowerpiece, fully signed and dated, must be the guideposts in the overdue process of redefining the personality of Bartolomé Pérez after generations of confusing misattributions. As this paradigmatic example reveals, his dramatic lighting and fluid, velvety chiaroscuro set him quite apart from his father-in-law, Arellano. His sensual bouquet in its historiated bronze urn emerges from the shadowy surrounding space with the utmost subtlety. There are few overt mannerisms in his handling of paint, and his observation of flowers, especially roses near the end of their life, is more acute than Arellano's. Yet we know that, like the older artist, he used drawings or studies in composing his bouquets: another flowerpiece (formerly Newhouse Galleries, New York), dated twelve years later, repeats many of the blossoms and part of the vase design from the Fitzwilliam example, and his style appears to have altered little meanwhile. The Fitzwilliam flowerpiece was originally octagonal in shape, however, while the later version was rectangular. The very low viewpoint evident in this work indicates that it was intended as an overdoor. Obviously influenced in this and other respects by the robust Baroque flowerpieces of the Roman painter Mario Nuzzi, Pérez nevertheless remained a strong, independent personality. He was, in fact, an artist of subtler sensibility than Nuzzi, and, if one looks closely, there is no real reason to confuse their styles.

53 **Bartolomé Pérez, 1634–98**
Garland of Flowers with Saint Anthony and the Christ Child
After 1689. Signed: *B^me. Pérez RP (Regis Pictor)* interlaced and crowned
Oil on canvas, 65 x 84 cm
Madrid, Museo del Prado

Like the Fitzwilliam flowerpiece, this signed *Garland* by Bartolomé Pérez helps us to distinguish his style from those of his Spanish and Italian contemporaries. As has often been noted, Pérez eliminated the stone cartouche employed by Arellano and derived from Daniel Seghers (see cat. 49). His flowers are arranged neither in a highly organised wreath nor in a classic festoon. Their loosely controlled and natural-looking groupings serve simply to set off the mystical scene revealed in the centre of the picture. It has always been assumed, probably correctly, that Pérez painted this figural scene himself, since Palomino wrote in 1724 that he was a skilled figure painter and sometimes painted such scenes within garlands by Arellano. The intensely dark background, which has perhaps darkened over time due to chemical changes in the pigment, sets off dramatically the delicacy with

which the flowers are realised. Their presence and natural grace is achieved with fluid brush strokes and sparing use of impasto. Occasional highlights of white are applied to give volume to tulips and peonies, while silken shadows of umber are applied over the whites of apple blossom and narcissi. The autonomy of the religious scene in the centre is frequently infringed by unruly blossoms that overlap the space inhabited by the figure of Saint Anthony, uniting the two parts of the composition without recourse to artificial devices.

After the recent cleaning, the last element in the signature, which has always been interpreted as a capital 'F', for *Fecit*, proved to be the artist's designation of himself as Painter to the King, which effectively dates the picture after 22 January 1689.

54 Bartolomé Pérez, 1634–98
Garland of Flowers on a Gold Ground
*c.*1689–91. Oil and gold on panel, 63.5 x 54 cm
Madrid, Private collection

The discoveries of this panel and its related documentation give new insight into the sumptuous decorations of the royal apartments of the old Royal Palace in the reign of Charles II, and into Bartolomé Pérez's late style. The delicate technique with which the flowers are painted is nearly identical to that seen in Pérez's *Garland of Flowers with Saint Anthony and the Christ Child* (cat. 53). The gold-ground panel, however, makes the flowers stand out in brilliant relief. The *trompe l'oeil* wood border is slightly truncated at the top and bottom (the strong shadow at the top of the panel was cast by a feigned carving no longer there). Palace inventories, beginning in 1734,

record dozens of gilded panels, in a variety of sizes, painted with garlands and vases of flowers, 'all originals by Bartolomé Pérez'. Newly published documentation reveals that these panels were originally part of the gilded bedchamber of the king ('Camón Dorado de Su Magd'), an amazingly sumptuous structure designed by the architect José de Churriguera and built at great cost between 1689 and the end of 1691. Attached to the gilded and carved structure were fifty-four gilded floral panels by Pérez. After the *Camón* was dismantled in the eighteenth century, these remained in the royal collection for many decades and were devoted to other decorative purposes. This *Garland* is the only one known today which can definitely be associated with Pérez's work on this project, and it reveals that his late style was not as loose nor as pastose as many Italian and Spanish flower paintings often erroneously attributed to him.

the authoritative eighteenth-century dictionary of the Spanish language defines it as a sort of alcove intended to shield and enclose the bed of an important person.[27]

The recently published research of J.M. Barbeito reveals that the *Camón Dorado* was a large and extremely complex structure made of carved and gilded wood, which was placed in the Hall of the Furies (Pieza de las Furias), comprising two alcoves which served as 'Dormitorio y Real Cámara de Su Magd'.[28] Designs for the *Cámon* were finished by José de Churriguera by 13 August 1689, shortly before the king's second marriage, to Mariana de Neoburgo, but due to the complexity and great cost of the project (78,550 *reales*), it was not completed until the end of 1691. The walls and ceilings of the structure were adorned with fifty-four painted and gilded panels (*tableros*) of flowers. Many of these, as well as the window panes intended to let in light and keep out draft, were movable and were controlled by a complicated system of weights and pullies devised by the clockmaker Francisco Filipin.[29]

Pérez, who began to execute the flower panels in November 1689, had finished eight of them, measuring about one *vara* (84 centimetres) square, by 4 February 1690 and was working on ten others twice as large. By 30 July 1691, eighteen more panels had been placed on the ceiling of the *Camón*, and eighteen remained to be painted. He asked for two months to finish them and had the assistance of three other painters, only one of whom, the Granadine José de Ziezar (d. 1692), was identified.[30] In the 1701 inventory of the Royal Palace, made after the king's death, the floral panels are not described among the paintings, but the *Camón Dorado* is referred to in the inventory of the hangings.[31] The rest of the room in which the *Camón* was assembled was hung with scarlet English wool. The windows had scarlet curtains lined with taffeta and trimmed with gold braid and fringe from Milan. In the midst of all this the king's canopied bed, valued at 107,310 *reales*, was hung with voluminous curtains and panels embroidered with images of flowers and fruits in gold, silver and coral. Accustomed as we are today to seeing seventeenth-century Spanish palaces stripped of their furnishings, it is surprising to realise how opulent palace life was.

Pérez also carried out decorative projects for members of the aristocracy; in fact, we know from Palomino that this is how he met his death. In 1698, while painting the staircase landing of the palace of the Duque de Monteleón, he fell from scaffolding while trying to demonstrate to a young assistant that he should not be afraid to walk on it. He was greatly mourned in Madrid, since his reputation as a skilled artist was equalled by that of his kindness and good nature.[32]

The last important native flower painter of the century in Madrid was Gabriel de la Corte (1648–94), about whose life very little is known. Palomino (1724) wrote that he was the son of one Francisco de la Corte, a painter of perspective views. It is more probable that Ceán Bermúdez (1800) was correct in stating that Gabriel was the son of Juan de la Corte, the well-known painter of battles and mythological subjects, who died when his son was only twelve.[33] According to Ceán, the young orphan, left without a master, turned to flower painting as a way of making a living, becoming in time extremely skilled. However, lacking the connections that would enable him to compete with such artists as Arellano and Pérez, he was reduced to painting garlands and cartouches to surround other artists' figural subjects and to making sets of flower paintings that were sold in the shops and public places of Madrid.[34] Barely able to eke out a living from the low prices he received for such work, he died in poverty.

On the basis of the few signed paintings that are known, it is possible to arrive at a certain understanding of Gabriel de la Corte's style. Few of his paintings are dated, however, so we have only a few guide-posts to account for what seems to be a con-

Fig. 112 Gabriel de la Corte, *Flowerpiece*, *c.*1670s. Oil on canvas, 41.2 x 25.7 cm. Spain, Private collection (formerly Meadows Museum, Dallas).

Fig. 113 Gabriel de la Corte and Matías de Torres, *Garland of Flowers with Saint Anne*, *c*.1670s. Oil on canvas, 124.5 x 95.2 cm. USA, Private collection.

siderable stylistic evolution over the span of his career. In its dash and fundamentally decorative impulse, Corte's style is quite different from either Arellano's or Pérez's. In what one must infer to be his early works, he already showed himself elegantly adept at manipulating with his brush the thick impasto that gives his paintings a distinctly textured surface. The petals of flowers, for example, are thus given relief as well as shading. This is best illustrated by comparing one of a pair of small flower-pieces by Corte formerly in the Meadows Museum, Dallas (fig. 112), with Antonio Ponce's small flowerpiece (fig. 50) in a Madrid private collection. The richly worked and glazed surface and the dark background of Corte's picture, which dates perhaps from the 1670s, are the very opposite of the calm and clarity of Ponce's works. Unsigned paintings in this style, often misattributed to Bartolomé Pérez, such as the splendid flowerpiece in the Prado (cat. 55), are much more closely related to Corte's style at this date and may be by him.

Among the figure painters for whom Palomino said that Corte painted garlands were Antonio Castrejón (*c*.1625–*c*.1690) and Matías de Torres (1635–1711). A pair of rather large garlands with images of Saint Joachim and Saint Anne has been convincingly attributed to the collaboration of Corte and Torres (fig. 113).[35] As in his straightforward flowerpieces, the artist here shows himself less concerned with botanical accuracy than with spontaneity of touch, evidently relishing the swirling patterns left by the brush as it passes through the viscous paint. He confidently applied this same technique to the painting of purely decorative cartouches, as can be seen in a signed *Floral Decoration* (fig. 114), in which the eddying rhythms of blossoms, tendrils and architectural elements are reinforced by the graceful energy of execution. We lose much, however, by not knowing the context in which such a work originally figured. It was perhaps part of the decoration of some sumptuous room in late seventeenth-century Madrid: but we can only speculate whether it was contained

Fig. 114 Gabriel de la Corte, *Floral Decoration*, *c*.1670s. Oil on canvas, 60 x 80 cm. Formerly Madrid art market.

in some architectural setting, or in an altarpiece, or was one of several overdoors.

Two works, similarly puzzling in origin, are the pair of canvases of unknown provenance, signed and dated 1687, belonging to the Department of Chemistry of the University of Madrid (fig. 115). Obviously fragments of some decoration, they make no sense as independent compositions.[36] The sweeping grey, fragmentary cartouches with swags and vases of flowers have no focal point and seem to be parts of some much larger whole. The execution is brilliant, however, and suggests a definite stylistic evolution away from the dark, sensuous works we have already considered. The lighter coloration is coupled with a more incisive draughtsmanship and a great facility in the brushwork, which together result in a highly decorative superficiality. Perhaps the single most surprising feature of the style is the almost complete absence of glazing in the modelling of the flowers and leaves. One might be tempted to conclude that these features stemmed from the nature of these works as decorations rather than straightforward flowerpieces, except that the same characteristics can be seen in flowerpieces of a similar date.[37]

In the pair of *floreros* by Corte which in 1935 belonged to the Duques de Valencia (fig. 116), the blossoms and leaves are defined with the almost schematic notation of details and highlights that is characteristic of a fresco or tempera painter. Modelling of form is defined by applying discrete strokes of colour several shades lighter or darker than the underlying one, which has been allowed to dry, with no effort made to blend or shade tonal transitions. The resulting crispness and schematisation of detail makes one wonder if Corte's style in oil painting might not have been decisively affected by working with Matías de Torres and other artists on ephemeral decorations carried out in tempera.[38] Perhaps the eventual discovery of additional dated paintings will help us to arrive at a better understanding of his development.

55 Attributed to Gabriel de la Corte, 1648–94
Flowerpiece
c.1670s. Oil on canvas, 62 x 84 cm
Madrid, Museo del Prado

This magnificent flowerpiece epitomises the forgotten opulence of Late Baroque Madrid, when the vogue for flower painting was at its peak. It was one of six anonymous canvases of approximately the same size that were brought to the Museo de la Trinidad following the suppression of the monasteries in 1836; it then entered the collection of the Prado, where it has traditionally been considered the work of Bartolomé Pérez. No signed work by Pérez, however, is painted even remotely in this manner. The coarse canvas and thick brush strokes, which mould the impasto into an actively textured surface, are alien to the finesse of Pérez's sensibility. But the resulting effect is of a richness that is altogether beautiful and admirable. The hand is much closer to that of Gabriel de la Corte, as revealed in the small pair of signed *floreros* formerly in the Meadows Museum (fig. 112). However, other signed works by that artist, particularly those which are obviously fragments of decorative ensembles (fig. 115), reveal a lighter and more superficial and decorative touch. In the present very incomplete state of our knowledge of Corte's development, we cannot know exactly how this painting fits into it, but suppose it to be an early work. In our view, it does not fit into any stage of Pérez's development.

Fig. 115 Gabriel de la Corte, *Floral Decoration*, 1687. Oil on canvas, 151 x 98 cm. University of Madrid, Department of Chemistry.

Fig. 116 Gabriel de la Corte, *Flowerpiece*, c.1680s. Oil on canvas, 74.7 x 51 cm. Spain, Private collection.

If fruits, especially grapes, were a primary concern of still-life painters and patrons earlier in the seventeenth century, there is no question that flowers were the favoured subject nearer the century's end. To satisfy the demand for variety and quality in flower paintings, large numbers of them were imported from Naples and Rome. Over the years, many of these became attributed to Spanish masters, and much work remains to be done in sorting out the resulting confusion.[39] We are only beginning to understand the true role of flower painting at the Spanish court in the late seventeenth century; and, despite the fact that the names of certain artists are household words in Spain, we have to admit that we do not, in fact, know them well.

The End of the Golden Age

Few periods in the history of Spanish art leave us with more unanswered questions than the shadowy years of transition from the seventeenth to the eighteenth centuries. One of the most perplexing aspects of this period is the almost total eclipse of the still life after a century of unprecedented creativity. While countries such as France, Italy and Holland continued throughout the eighteenth century to enjoy unbroken traditions of still-life painting, there is not a single signed and dated Madrilenian still life of great quality from the first half of the eighteenth century. Occasional sparks of life appeared in the regional schools; but for these, too, this was not a great period.[1] This loss of creative energy seems to have affected not only this particular genre, but painting in general. As the golden century and the Habsburg dynasty had slowly ebbed together, the generation of painters who had helped to make Baroque Madrid a resplendent capital – the generation of Pereda, Arellano, Carreño, Rizzi and Herrera the Younger – had died out, after long and fulfilling careers. But during this same period, an alarmingly large number of gifted younger artists, including Mateo Cerezo (1637–66), José Antolínez (1635–75) and Juan Antonio de Frias y Escalante (1633–70), who might have carried the torch well into the 1700s, as both artists and teachers, died prematurely. Several talented painters who succeeded them, such as Claudio Coello (1643–93) and Gabriel de la Corte (1648–94), did not live to see the new century. There were, of course, survivors: artists such as Antonio Palomino (1655–1726), appointed court painter in 1688, who continued the Late Baroque style well into the eighteenth century. But there were few high points. Some still-life painters must certainly have continued to work along the lines laid down by their predecessors, creating works that today may be misattributed to masters of the seventeenth century. But no native counterparts appeared to the defining talents of Largillierre, Huilliot, Deportes or Oudry in France; to Bimbi, Belvedere, Munari or Caro in Italy; or to Weenix, van Huysum or Ruysch in Holland. The decadence that had overtaken Spain's monarchy, economy and institutions appears to have also sapped its cultural lifeblood. The recovery under the new Bourbon monarchy would take time, and, with isolated exceptions, this cultural limbo was to last for nearly sixty years.

If not in recognition of this course of events, then at least in order to obtain better options, the Habsburg monarchy began, in the 1690s, to import artists and works of art from other parts of the Spanish empire, principally from Italy. The most significant action in this regard was the summoning to Madrid in 1692 of the leading Neapolitan painter, Luca Giordano (1634–1705), who remained for a decade decorating the royal palaces with frescoes and canvas paintings. These exerted a strong influence on local painters at the court, notably Antonio Palomino.

Among the foreign still-life painters long favoured at the court was the Neapolitan

Fig. 117 Giuseppe Recco, *Still Life with Flowers and Sweets*, *c*.1680s. Oil on slate, 40.5 x 53.7 cm. Madrid, Private collection.

Fig. 118 Giuseppe Recco and Luca Giordano, *Marine Still Life with Neptune and Two Nereids*, *c*.1680. Oil on canvas, 234.5 x 296 cm. New York art market.

Giuseppe Recco (1634–95), who had worked for a succession of viceroys in Naples, and whom a document of 1682 calls 'painter to the Marqués de los Vélez'.[2] He was knighted by Charles II, and made ample use of this distinction in signing many of his still lifes 'EQUES' (fig. 117).[3] It was probably during the vice-regency of Vélez, around 1680, that Recco, together with Luca Giordano, executed for the king a pair of enormous marine still lifes with Neptune and Galatea (fig. 118). These have long been thought lost, but were, in fact, among the works stolen by Joseph Bonaparte, which he brought to America; there they have remained, unpublished, since 1813.[4] The classical subjects of these pictures served merely as a pretext for the display of Recco's virtuosity in depicting the impressive array of marine life heaped in the foreground. Smaller still lifes of this type, by Recco and his followers, were also imported to Spain in large numbers, in order to accommodate the seemingly insatiable appetite of Spaniards for images of delicacies of the sea. In 1695, the king summoned Recco himself to join Giordano in Madrid, but the painter died *en route* in Alicante.[5]

It was surely, in part, the great fashion for paintings of flowers that prompted the king to summon from Naples the flower painter and decorator Andrea Belvedere (*c*.1652–1732). He arrived in 1694 and stayed until 1700, when, if we are to believe the eighteenth-century biographer Bernardo de Dominici, a heated dispute with Giordano caused him to return to Naples in a rage.[6] However, in November 1700, the grateful Charles II awarded the artist a pension, which enabled him to live comfortably in Naples.[7] Belvedere's style in many ways prefigures the eighteenth century, and he had a great and lasting impact on his students in Naples; but the new approach to painting flowers and fruit that he brought to Madrid made very little impression in Spain.[8] His still lifes show the influence of Abraham Brueghel; they are often set out of doors, in deftly brushed, pale landscapes with columns, balustrades,

Fig. 119 Andrea Belvedere, *Still Life with Fruit and Flowers in a Landscape*, c.1694–1700. Oil on canvas. Madrid, Duque del Infantado.

bas-reliefs, herms, fountains and other classical motifs. His delicate sensibility and fluid technique can be seen at their best in the four beautiful signed still lifes belonging to the Duque del Infantado (fig. 119).[9]

Another Italian whose works appear to have enjoyed a great vogue at the Spanish court was the Lombard painter Margherita Caffi (1650/1–1710).[10] There is no record that she ever came to Spain, but her flower paintings were imported in large numbers at the end of the seventeenth century, perhaps because of the prestige bestowed on her works by the patronage of the Medici court in Florence, with which the Spanish court maintained extremely close ties.[11] Like Belvedere, she prefigures the eighteenth century with her use of a pale palette, and the predominantly horizontal format of her compositions. But, unlike Belvedere, Caffi almost never opened the backgrounds of her compositions with luminous vistas of trees and sky. Her vases and flowers growing directly from the ground (fig. 120) are cloaked in a darkness that has obviously intensified over time, resulting in a characteristic discontinuity between the pale, delicately brushed flowers and the dark, enshrouding ambience. However, despite their popularity among Spanish collectors, Caffi's works do not seem to have had much effect on the practice of flower painting in the Iberian peninsula.[12] In fact, the large numbers of late seventeenth-century Italian flower paintings in Spanish collections suggest that, after the deaths of Pérez and Corte, the taste for flowers was satisfied largely by imported works, which subsequently came to be mostly attributed to Pérez. An example of this is the beautiful *Still Life with Roses, Tulips and Petunias* (fig. 121), which in 1889 came to the Prado from the collection of the Duques de Pastrana, with an attribution to Pérez. Pérez Sánchez has attributed the painting, with reservations, to Caffi, but it seems more likely to be by her North Italian contemporary Elisabetta Marchioni.[13]

One aspect of early eighteenth-century still-life painting in Spain that has received

Fig. 120 Margherita Caffi, *Still Life with Flowers*. Oil on canvas, 75 x 103 cm. Madrid, Real Academia de Bellas Artes de San Fernando.

Fig. 121 Elisabetta Marchioni, *Still Life with Roses, Tulips and Petunias*. Oil on canvas, 152 x 196 cm. Madrid, Museo del Prado.

a good deal of attention is one unashamedly appropriated from Dutch and Flemish practice, the *trompe l'oeil*.[14] But there may be less to this phenomenon than has been supposed, and we may know less about it than we thought. Palomino (1724) reliably informs us that *trompe l'oeil* painting was practised in Valencia at the end of the seventeenth century by Vicente Victoria (1650–1713), whom he knew personally.[15] Born in Denia, in the province of Alicante, of an Italian father, Victoria was educated in Valencia in the liberal arts, as well as in painting. After the age of twenty-one, he went for ecclesiastical studies to Rome, where he also studied painting with Carlo Maratta (1625–1713). He returned to Valencia in 1688; there he was ordained a priest, became a canon of the collegiate church of Játiva and worked as a painter until the end of the century. Around 1700 he returned to Rome, where he became salaried antiquarian to the Pope and painter to the Grand Duke of Tuscany. His superior education and literary bent bore considerable scholarly fruit and were recognised in both countries. Apart from his portraits and religious works painted in both fresco and oil, Victoria attained a certain fame in his time for his *trompe l'oeil* images. In his extensive biography of the painter, Palomino described examples he had seen:

> I saw in his studio some *trompes l'oeil* that I mistook for reality until he himself gave me reason to doubt it, such as a simulated board done on canvas from which hung some papers, drawings, and other trifles, which I must sincerely confess did fool me. There was also a section of simulated bookshelves that filled up a gap in the very select library he had, which I, not finding any difference between the simulated ones and the real ones, for both had the same highlights and the same relief, believed were all of one piece. And there were many other things by his hand of this tenor, done from nature with wonderful observation and accuracy.[16]

Unfortunately, there exists not a single signed example of this type of painting by this obviously very interesting artist. Several unsigned works of this type have recently been attributed to Victoria, on the strength of a late eighteenth-century description of a *trompe l'oeil* of arms, then in the O'Cruley collection, Cádiz, which was being attributed to him at the time.[17] The most spectacular of these works is the pair of large canvases in the Osuna collection, which depict rolled-up banners and an assortment of arms attached to a white wall. The attribution of these paintings is almost certainly incorrect, however, since an extremely similar *trompe l'oeil* in the New York collection of Bill Blass is signed and dated: 'J. Biltius, fat. 1661' (fig. 122).[18] The two

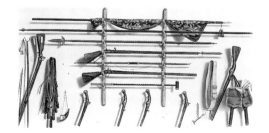

Fig. 122 Jacobus Biltius, *Trompe l'Oeil of Arms*, 1661. Oil on canvas, 169 x 343 cm. New York, Bill Blass.

Osuna paintings are slightly less long than the Blass picture, but appear to be cut down on all sides, especially the left and right. All three would seem to be by Jacobus Biltius (1633–81), who worked in The Hague, Amsterdam, Maastricht and Antwerp in the second half of the seventeenth century. He specialised in hunting still lifes and, especially in the 1660s, produced large numbers of *trompe l'oeil* paintings of arms and hunting implements against luminous, light backgrounds.[19]

In Seville several minor artists of the eighteenth century, about whom nothing at all is known except their signed works, produced large numbers of the sort of charming and decorative *trompe l'oeil* pictures popularised in Northern Europe by Cornelis Norbertus Gysbrechts (doc. between 1659 and 1678), Wallerand Vaillant (1653–77) or Evert Collier (1640–after 1706). That such foreign works should have been known in the cosmopolitan city of Seville, in which northerners abounded, is not surprising.[20] There are signed pictures of this kind by Pedro de Acosta, Carlos López and Francisco Gallardo.[21] Based on a brief biography included in the dictionary of artists by Ceán Bermúdez in 1800, this tradition has been thought to have begun in Seville with a seventeenth-century painter named Marcos Correa, a graduate of the Sevillian Academy, whose activity between 1667 and 1673 Ceán was able to document from archival finds.[22] Ceán described having seen paintings by Marcos Correa 'which depicted pine boards with various papers, trifles, ink-wells and other things copied from nature with much truth, mastery and good effect'.[23] In all likelihood, the paintings he described are the ones preserved today in the Hispanic Society of America, in New York (fig. 123), one of which is signed simply *Correa*.[24] Stylistically, however, these paintings hardly differ at all from the other *trompe l'oeil* works executed in Seville between the 1730s and the 1760s, and it is difficult to believe that they were painted in Spain in the third quarter of the seventeenth century. The Marcos Correa whose activity Ceán knew from the archives has been identified by modern research as Marcos Fernández Correa (b. 1646), who in 1661 was apprenticed to the sculptor Francisco Dionisio de Ribas.[25] The identification of this artist, who appears to have been a sculptor, with the painter of the Hispanic Society *trompe l'oeil* pictures has been called into question by Duncan Kinkead, who concludes that 'the belief that Seville was an important [seventeenth-century] centre for the development of the *trompe l'oeil* still life in Spain needs to be restudied'.[26] While it would not have been unusual for a sculptor also to practise as a painter, it is not likely that one who devoted himself primarily to orthodox *retablos* would have painted this type of decorative work so far ahead of its time in Seville. It appears more likely, therefore, that the Correa who painted these two pictures was an eighteenth-century painter about whom a great deal remains to be discovered.

Among the most competent examples of *trompe l'oeil* painting from eighteenth-century Seville are two examples in the Louvre signed by Bernardo Luis Lorente y Germán (1680–1759), an artist of considerable reputation, best known for his imitations of Murillo's works.[27] Executed around 1730, the Louvre pictures may be among the earliest such works done in Seville (fig. 124). Both represent elements of an artist's studio, displayed on wooden shelves and tacked to walls panelled with pine planks. A fictive painting in one of them represents Bacchus drinking; a painting in the other represents smokers. The subject matter suggests the Sense of Taste and the Sense of Smell and the pictures may have belonged to a series of the Five Senses.[28]

Ironically, although the art of painting languished in the early years of Bourbon rule, it was during this very period that Antonio Palomino, himself a devotee and occasional practitioner of the still life, wrote his influential treatise on the theory and practice of painting (1715). Neither did the collecting of pictures diminish under the

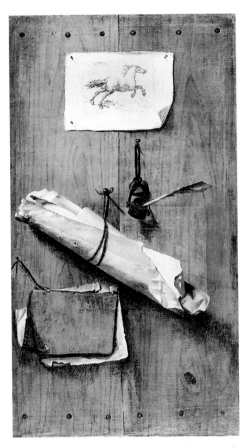

Fig. 123 Correa, *Trompe l'Oeil with Ink-well*, *c.*1730–60. Oil on canvas, 98 x 55 cm. New York, The Hispanic Society of America.

Fig. 124 Bernardo Lorente y Germán, *Trompe l'Oeil*, *c.*1730. Oil on canvas, 70 x 50 cm. Paris, Musée du Louvre.

Fig. 125 Giacomo Nani, *Still Life with a Salad*. Oil on canvas, 35 x 47 cm. Segovia, Palacio de Riofrío, Patrimonio Nacional.

new monarchs: Philip V's second queen, Isabella Farnese, was a passionate collector. Her catholic taste encompassed Flemish, Dutch, French and Italian masters of the seventeenth century, as well as contemporary artists, and she enriched the royal collections by the addition of hundreds of paintings. Her interest in the so-called minor masters, and her fondness for genre paintings and still lifes, served to complement the collections inherited from her Habsburg predecessors. Her taste had a profound effect on the royal collection; and, perhaps more importantly, she instilled this love of pictures in her sons, Ferdinand VI, Charles III and the Infante Don Luis, all of whom were to make a genuine contribution to the renewal of the cultural life of the realm.

Among the acquisitions made by Queen Isabella Farnese that are most often cited in relation to the development of still-life painting in Spain are the twenty-four small still lifes by Giacomo Nani (1698–1770); by 1746 these were to be found at the country palace of La Granja (Segovia), which was finished in 1723. Very probably the commission for this series originated in Naples, where Isabella's son the Infante Don Carlos, Duke of Parma and Grand Duke of Tuscany, had reigned since 1734 as King Charles VII of Naples. Nani's series of still lifes (fig. 125), preserved intact in the palace of Riofrío (Segovia), has been cited as a precedent for the works that Meléndez was later to paint for Charles IV.[29] Although executed without the skill and sophistication that Meléndez would bring to bear on still-life painting, they are works of considerable interest, characterised by compact, intimate and straightforward compositions.[30]

The Eighteenth Century:
Still-Life Painting at Court

The renewal of painting in eighteenth-century Spain came about largely through the initiatives of the Bourbon monarchy in founding the Academies, which became the primary vehicles for the training of artists, and also through the importation of foreign artists, who brought fresh outlooks and provided powerful examples. For nearly 150 years, artists at the court had been struggling in vain for approval for the foundation of an academy, and for the recognition of painting as a noble and liberal art.[1] When this finally came about, it was as part of an integrated, enlightened plan to revive all the institutions of Spain, a plan that proved largely successful. In Madrid the Real Academia de Bellas Artes de San Fernando was officially established in 1752, during the reign of King Ferdinand VI, after a provisional Academy (*Junta preparatoria*) had been set up in 1744.[2] The Valencian Academia de Bellas Artes de San Carlos was established in 1768. These institutions and others like them were dedicated to the cultivation of the Three Noble Arts – Painting, Sculpture and Architecture – and to the training of young artists in life drawing and history painting in the Grand Manner. These priorities might seem unpromising for the revival of still-life painting, but there was, within the academic view of things, room for the encouragement of secondary genres.

The Academia de San Fernando inherited its doctrine of the hierarchy of the genres from its French predecessor, the Académie Royale de Peinture et de Sculpture, founded in 1648, which had elevated the theory and practice of narrative history painting to the most elevated status.[3] The painting of edifying moral subjects from classical antiquity, the Bible and Spanish history required the depiction of expressive, idealised figures in action, and posed a significant artistic challenge. Compared to this, the genre of still life was considered decorative rather than didactic, and merely depended on the artist's ability to imitate exactly the objects in front of him. Artists of the seventeenth century had needed no academy to reach the same evaluation of the still life, but the new institution was able to bring discipline and encouragement to the cultivation of the lesser genres, which, in any case, had probably ceased to be the subject of heated debate since the early days of the Velázquez-Carducho rivalry.

The Academy officially acknowledged artists who were specialists in the minor genres. But it is indicative of the low state to which the still life had fallen during the first half of the eighteenth century in Spain, and of the domination of the field by foreign artists, that the first academician in this genre in Madrid was a Neapolitan, Mariano Nani (*c.*1725–1804), the son of Giacomo Nani.[4] Mariano had been trained by his father in Naples and like him, had worked as a designer and painter in the porcelain factory of Capodimonte, established in 1743 by the enlightened King Charles VII of Naples and Sicily. When, in 1759, Charles succeeded his brother Ferdinand as Charles III of Spain, he brought Nani with him and put him to work in

Fig. 126 Mariano Nani, *Kitchen Still Life*, 1764. Oil on canvas, 140 x 110 cm. Madrid, Real Academia de Bellas Artes de San Fernando.

Fig. 127 Mariano Nani, *Still Life with Game*. Oil on canvas, 72 x 48 cm. Madrid, Museo del Prado.

the royal porcelain factory of the Buen Retiro, which he founded in order to create an important new industry in his realm. Reluctantly, Nani worked for this enterprise for many years, but was eventually able to pursue his preferred career as a painter in oils; he also became drawing master to the Infante Don Luis (1727–85), Charles III's younger brother. In 1775 Mengs recognised his talents and recommended him as a designer for the Royal Tapestry Factory, where he worked alongside Goya and others. In 1764 he applied for and was awarded entry into the Academy. His large entrance piece (fig. 126) shows considerable skill in his chosen speciality, combining fruit, flowers, game and kitchen utensils, as well as a *trompe l'oeil* nail on the back wall. The depiction of live animals in this painting, considered more demanding than that of dead ones, perhaps elevated this work above the average still life in the judgement of the academicians. Like other artists of his time, Nani drew inspiration from seventeenth-century Flemish painters, such as Frans Snyders, who enlivened his pictures with animal incident, and Jan Fyt, who skilfully evoked the textures of fur and feathers. Fyt's influence is especially noticeable in the beautiful *Still Life with Game* (fig. 127), one of a pair of works in the Prado in which the powerful rendition of textures is combined with an airy suggestion of landscape.

In the first twenty-five years of its existence, the Academia de San Fernando admitted a handful of still-life painters to the rank of Académico de Mérito: Mariano Nani (1764), the flower painter Cándido García Romeral (1765), José Garcés (1772) (fig. 140), and Ramón de Castellanos (1774).[5] Although Luis Meléndez (1716–80),[6] who became the greatest still-life specialist of eighteenth-century Spain, was excluded after 1748 from membership of the Academy, his roots were in this same tradition. The body of work he left, which comprises well over one hundred still lifes dated between 1759 and 1778, constitutes one of the great achievements of eighteenth-century Spain, and places him alongside the greatest still-life painters of Europe.[7] However, the still life would probably not have been Meléndez's principal activity, if his career had not been blighted by his expulsion from the provisional Academy. The cause of this terrible blow was Meléndez's father, who was, ironically, one of the founders of the institution.[8] Francisco Antonio Meléndez (1682–after 1758), a royal miniaturist who had lived in Italy for eighteen years, was the artist who in 1726 officially petitioned the king for the establishment of an Academy of Fine Arts. But his petition was so strongly coloured by expressions of personal resentment at not having been more adequately rewarded for his own service to the crown, that nothing came of it for several years. Finally, in 1744, Philip V santioned a provisional Academy under the directorship of the royal sculptor Giovanni Domenico Olivieri; Francisco Meléndez was appointed as its honorary professor of painting. In March 1745, his son Luis was unhesitatingly ranked first among the students examined for admission to the academy.[9]

Fig. 128 Luis Meléndez, *Self Portrait*, 1746. Oil on canvas, 98 x 81 cm. Paris, Musée du Louvre.

In 1746, Luis Meléndez celebrated his prospects as a figure painter and portraitist in a superb *Self Portrait* (fig. 128). In it he holds up a prize-winning academic figure study in red chalk, to demonstrate his mastery of figure drawing, which was regarded as fundamental to figurative history painting. This unusually elegant and self-congratulatory portrait, painted while he was still a student, reflects the temperament of pride and vanity that Meléndez inherited from his father and which was to mar his relations with the court. On 8 March 1748 Francisco Meléndez, irate, it seems, that someone else had sat in the seat assigned to him at an Academy convocation and that the Director General, Olivieri, had allowed it, printed and had circulated a denunciation of the directors of the Academy, which he characterised as 'a very small organisation for my talents'.[10] Embittered that his own initiatives towards the foundation of an academy had received so little credit, Francisco had his son Luis deliver the written diatribe personally. This affront caused Francisco to be relieved of his teaching post and expelled from the Academy; Luis was likewise formally expelled on 14 June 1748.

Luis Meléndez's career never recovered from this blow.[11] He could not take up an academic scholarship to Italy, and his visit to Rome and Naples in the years 1748–52 had to be financed by his father. Luis was denied the official credentials afforded by graduation from the Academy, as well as the privileged status conferred by membership. The episode closed the doors on easy artistic advancement at court, on the possibility of royal commissions and, certainly for a long while, on the patronage of influential individuals.[12]

While living in Italy, Meléndez did, in fact, attract the attention of the future Charles III, then King of Naples and Sicily, who received him at court and purchased three paintings celebrating his own 'virtuous deeds'.[13] Back in Madrid, Meléndez earned a living by painting miniatures. Between 1753 and 1758 he and his brother José Agustín worked as part of the team of artists assembled by Francisco Meléndez to help with the commission he had received from Ferdinand VI to paint the choir books for the chapel of the new Royal Palace.[14] In 1760 Meléndez referred to this service as a miniaturist in the royal employ in an unsuccessful petition to the newly crowned Charles III for the post of court painter.[15] A second petition in 1772 may have brought him the commission for a miniature of the Holy Family, which he painted in 1773 for a portable oratory of the Príncipe de Asturias, the future Charles IV.[16]

Meléndez's earliest dated still life is from 1759, but his petition of 1760 made no mention of this aspect of his activity, which he had probably undertaken to augment his income. However, the petition of 1772 dwelt on his work as a still-life painter, as he no doubt thought that this would appeal to the enlightened Príncipe de Asturias. In keeping with the spirit of his times, he referred to his still lifes as part of an ambitious project:

whose representation consists of the four Seasons of the year, or, more properly, the four Elements, with the aim of composing an amusing cabinet with every species of food produced by the Spanish climate in the said four Elements, of which only those belonging to the Fruits of the Earth are finished, because [the painter] has not the means to continue, nor even those necessary to feed himself.[17]

In his petition, Meléndez asked for support to continue the series of still lifes, and his plea for financial assistance to meet the barest needs of subsistence may not have been much of an exaggeration. He appears never to have made much money from painting, and at his death was officially declared a pauper.

The project that Meléndez proposed to the Príncipe de Asturias had arisen from an audience he was granted by the heir to the throne and his consort, María Luisa of Parma, on 6 January 1771. It is not clear who initiated the meeting, but, knowing of the prince's great interest in natural history, Meléndez gave the royal couple a Christmas present of a number of still lifes, and secured a verbal agreement that he should paint more of these for the king's recently acquired Nuevo Gabinete de Historia Natural, the natural history collection soon to be installed on the second floor of the building on the Calle de Alcalá, which also housed the Academia de San Fernando.[18] Between 6 January 1771 and 5 January 1772, Meléndez delivered to the royal couple thirty-seven (or possibly forty-one) still lifes, some of them older pictures and some newly painted ones on larger canvases.[19] A few others were supplied, until the total number had reached forty-four. By 1776, however, a dispute had arisen over how much money the artist was owed. His haughty and irascible nature once again worked against him, and the commission was terminated in 1776, despite the 'high opinion which Meléndez has of his own merit and his work', according to a report written in 1778 in an effort to resolve the dispute.[20]

The still lifes that Meléndez sold to the prince, which, according to his own statement of 1773, he had begun painting fourteen years earlier, were certainly not planned as part of a coherent programme for a specific patron. He probably gave the series a post-facto thematic rationale in the hope of securing a salaried appointment at the court and future sales. A significant precedent for Meléndez's group of paintings is the set of twenty-four small still lifes by Giacomo Nani, mentioned in the previous chapter (fig. 125).[21] As in Nani's series, much of the appeal of Meléndez's still lifes depended on their depiction of basic Spanish foodstuffs, ordinary pottery and kitchen utensils.[22] However, an even more germane precedent for the thematic content, and one certainly known by reputation to the Príncipe de Asturias and his consort, was the series of naturalist paintings documenting the botanical culture of Tuscany, which was executed between 1694 and 1719 by Bartolomeo Bimbi for the Grand Duke Cosimo III de' Medici.[23] Bimbi's 'portraits' of fruits and plants, which by this date belonged to the prince's brother-in-law, the Grand Duke Leopoldo II of Tuscany, have a marked scientific character, unlike Meléndez's still lifes, and are, in fact, much more like what the Spanish artist proposed to do than what he actually did. It is conceivable that the opening of a possibility of patronage at court for Meléndez resulted at least as much from the prince's desire to have such a series of paintings, as from the artist's own initiative.

In looking at the body of still lifes which Meléndez sold to the Príncipe de Asturias, it is clear that he was not required to alter the style of his kitchen still lifes of the late 1750s and 1760s to suit the pseudo-scientific rationale that apparently lay behind the commission. There is much repetition in the species of fruits and vegetables represented; there are very few species of fish or fowl; and there is an almost equal emphasis on man-made kitchen implements. While the realism of Meléndez's style could have lent itself to a 'scientific' description of Nature, there is no evidence of any systematic exploration of flora and fauna, and the artist did not employ any of the conventions of naturalist illustration.[24] Nevertheless, the prince appears to have liked his paintings, which were never hung in the Gabinete de Historia Natural, as originally proposed.[25] Instead, just as Bimbi's naturalist series had been hung in the Medici *casino* 'La Topaia' at the Villa di Castello, Meléndez's forty-four still lifes were placed in the prince's country villa, the Casita del Príncipe, at El Escorial. A report of 1778 implies that the original plan for the series had not been fulfilled: 'a large collection of paintings of different sizes that were to contain the natural history of Spain, that is, the depiction of all the fruits, meats, fowl, fishes, flowers, foods and other natural produce of these kingdoms'.[26]

The Casita del Príncipe, an Italian-style villa with gardens, built in 1772 by Juan de Villanueva in the rural setting of the foothills of Escorial de Abajo, was a recreational retreat, comfortably removed from the strict protocol of the court at Madrid. As with earlier royal *casas de campo*, its interior decoration included nature paintings, among which still lifes and flowerpieces figured prominently; to these, works by Paret and Espinós were subsequently added. By 1800, Meléndez's series of still lifes had been transferred to the dining-room of the royal palace at Aranjuez, the Spanish royal family's traditional spring and summer retreat, whose gardens were regarded as the most beautiful in Spain.[27]

From his earliest still lifes, such as the Prado's *Oranges, Watermelons, a Jar and Boxes of Sweetmeats* (fig. 129), Meléndez capitalised on the basic geometric shapes of the objects depicted, playing one off against another with the skill of a consummate academician. Novel in his approach are the low vantage point and very close-

Fig. 129 Luis Meléndez, *Still Life with Oranges, Watermelons, a Jar and Boxes of Sweetmeats*, c.1760. Oil on canvas, 47 x 34 cm. Madrid, Museo del Prado.

Fig. 130 Luis Meléndez, *Still Life with Jug, Bread and a Basket*, c.1760s. Oil on canvas, 48 x 34 cm. Madrid, Museo del Prado.

156

Fig. 131 Luis Meléndez, *Still Life with Figs, Wine, Cheese and Bread*, c.1760s. Oil on canvas, 49.5 x 36 cm. Formerly Antwerp, Museum Ridder Smidt van Gelder (destroyed).

up view of the table-top. As a result, the narrow, upright canvas seems almost unable to contain the powerfully modelled forms, which take on an unprecedented monumentality. In the Prado's famous *Still Life with Jug, Bread and a Basket* (fig. 130), Meléndez's extraordinary descriptive skill is abundantly evident. Placing the lower objects in the front of the composition, as he habitually does, he has defined the substance of the simple crockery vessel at the left with a palpability reminiscent of Velázquez's *Waterseller* (cat. 8). The basket, largely hidden behind the jug and the bread, contains a dark wine bottle and a glass, three pottery plates placed on the diagonal and a coarsely woven napkin embroidered with the artist's initials. The folds of the napkin have a plasticity worthy of Zurbarán. Indeed, there can be little doubt that Meléndez, like Mariano Nani and other European still-life painters of his time, looked to the masters of the seventeenth century for inspiration.

It may be assumed that Meléndez's travels in Italy, and his familiarity with the collections of Madrid, had acquainted him with the various national traditions of still-life painting and the works of his European contemporaries. In spite of this, and notwithstanding the suggestions that he was influenced by contemporary Neapolitan still lifes, his style is so original and so highly personal, that the question of possible influences is a moot one. With the exception of his French contemporary Chardin, with whose works there is no evident relationship, there was hardly another still-life painter of the time who surpassed him in the force of his works, the size of his oeuvre or its consistently high quality.

Meléndez, like most still-life painters, made use of things he owned, often repeating these objects in different contexts. Each composition is unique, however, and none appears formulaic. The objects and foodstuffs which comprise a given composition were often chosen, it seems, to provide the artist with a rich variety of patterns, textures and surfaces to imitate and contrast. As may be seen in the fine *Still Life with Figs, Wine, Cheese and Bread* formerly in the Museum Ridder Smidt van Gelder, Antwerp (fig. 131), he had a preference for juxtaposing contrasting textures, such as the black glass bottle and the porous cork wine cooler. His descriptive insistence on the roughness of the cork makes the bottle seem all the smoother. He carefully defined the chip in the glaze on the edge of the faïence plate in the middle distance and lingered over modelling the velvety skin of the figs and the wood grain, knots and nicks in the table-top. His is a virtuoso technique, but supported by an unfailing sense for the underlying structure of a composition. In the case of this still life, we perceive a faint diagonal recession into space, which is enlivened by opposing planes of light against dark: the cheese silhouetted against the cork of the wine cooler and the bright bread roll which contrasts with the darkness of the bottle. The few X-radiographs we have seen of Meléndez's still lifes suggest that he occasionally made alterations in such arrangements, adjusting the compositions and the objects represented until he was satisfied he had achieved the right balance.

All of Meléndez's still lifes were painted in the studio from arrangements on table-tops. Some of them, such as *Still Life with Fruit, Cheese and Containers* (cat. 56) and *Still Life with Sea Bream and Oranges* (cat. 57), exist in two or more versions. While sharing the principal motifs, these versions are never identical, which suggests that either before the primary version left the studio, or on the basis of drawings, the artist painted variations of the compositions made for the Príncipe de Asturias, so that he could sell them to private patrons. The fact of having received royal patronage, however restricted, probably helped Meléndez's career in its final phase. Certainly some of his most ambitious works (cat. 58), executed on a larger scale, date from this period and do not have a royal provenance.

56 Luis Meléndez, 1716–80
Still Life with Fruit, Cheese and Containers
Signed and dated on box at right: *Lˢ. Mᶻ./1771*
Oil on canvas, 40 x 62 cm
Madrid, Museo del Prado

One of the still lifes presented to the Príncipe de Asturias in 1771 or early 1772, this work is a reprise of a signed but undated composition of nearly the same size (Tufts, no. 76). The artist has made certain substitutions and additions which clarify the organisation of the space. The result is a virtuoso performance with some very impressive passages, such as the wrinkled crust of the fresh cheese, whose shadowed side leads the eye through the paper-lidded jar behind it into the centre of the composition. Meléndez has described the fall of light on a great variety of surfaces: the rough-planed, oblong boxes of *turrón*; the flat, round boxes of jelly in the rear, almost consumed by shadow; the thick glaze on the red-and-white Manises honey jar (an object he depicted several times, in a variety of colours); the grainy wood of the olive barrel and table-top; the skin of the fruit; and the smooth surface of the stoppered wine bottle. The acutely observed play of light and shadow works together with the purposeful placement of the objects to bind this seemingly random array into a balanced, harmonious whole.

57 Luis Meléndez, 1716–80
Still Life with Sea Bream and Oranges
Signed and dated: *L^s E^o M^{es} D^{ra} D^{zo} IS^{to} p^e/Ano 1772*
Oil on canvas, 41 x 62.8 cm
Spain, Masaveu collection

This spectacular composition gave Meléndez's virtuosity free rein to display itself, and is among his most successful late inventions. Long known from the famous version in the Prado, which was delivered to the Príncipe de Asturias in early 1772, the same composition was used in two other signed still lifes that have only come to light in recent years. One of these, sold by Newhouse Galleries in New York in 1988, is undated. This version, like the Prado example, is dated 1772 and was unknown in the literature before being offered at auction in London in 1992. Each of the three has in common the central element of the two sea breams. All three also share the motif of the dish towel and two oranges at the right, although the exact arrangement of the folds in the towel is different in each. The ceramic jug and the bowl with a wooden spoon at the left rear of this composition also appear in the New York version, but not in the Madrid one. There is a conical oil can in all three, but its placement varies. Beyond this, each version contains elements unique to itself. This one, for example, has the tilted copper pot in the right background, which gives the overall composition a decidedly diagonal orientation, something the other two do not have. Qualitatively, this painting is equal to the Prado's. The three together illustrate how Meléndez, like his earliest seventeenth-century predecessors, used remarkable inventiveness in rearranging his basic repertory of forms.

58 **Luis Meléndez**, 1716–80
Still Life with Oranges and Walnuts
Signed and dated on wooden box at right: *L^s. E^o. M^z. D.N (?)/ANO 1772.*
Oil on canvas, 61 x 81.3 cm
London, The National Gallery

The year in which this monumental work was painted must have been one of deep professional satisfaction for Meléndez, because during the previous twelve months he had supplied a large number of still lifes to the Príncipe de Asturias, thus realising, if only briefly, his lifelong ambition to attain royal patronage. As in some of his still lifes from 1771, the scale and complexity of the composition are considerably more ambitious than those of the 1760s, perhaps reflecting the optimism of his outlook. The intensity of his earlier works has not, however, diminished. If anything, his apparently wilful manipulation of geometric form, in a manner reminiscent of Van der Hamen, has intensified, and the use of perspective as an organising principle has become markedly more prominent. Objects of larger volume are ranged along the rear of the composition, their scale gradually diminishing towards the foreground. Moreover, emphatic vanishing lines, implied by the table-top, the oblong wooden boxes, the paper stopper on the jug at right, the rings around the olive barrel and the tops of the round jelly boxes, and by the recession of the oranges at the left, create a space as rationally organised as any composition by Poussin: a connection which this proud, rejected academician may have intended us not to miss.

Fig. 132 Luis Meléndez, *Still Life with Watermelons and Apples in a Landscape*, *c*.1771. Oil on canvas, 62 x 84 cm. Madrid, Museo del Prado.

Fig. 133 Luis Meléndez, *Picnic (La Merienda)*, *c*.1771–80. Oil on canvas, 106 x 154 cm. New York, The Metropolitan Museum of Art, Jack and Belle Linsky Collection.

The four largest still lifes sold to the prince, which date from between 1771 and about 1774, have landscape settings (fig. 132). These works, which are clearly examples of a response to Neapolitan tradition, were particularly appropriate for the rural setting of the Casita where they were placed, and inscriptions on the back – 'P.ᵉ N.ʳᵒ S.ᵒʳ' (*Príncipe Nuestro Señor*) – denote their provenance from the prince's collection there.[28] During the 1770s, Meléndez pursued this innovation – the most dramatic departure from his accustomed style – for other patrons also (cat. 59). Some of his still lifes in landscapes were much smaller than those for the Príncipe de Asturias, and some were much larger.[29] In the largest of them, the expansive composition in the Metropolitan Museum of Art, New York (fig. 133), objects familiar from Meléndez's kitchen still lifes are situated beneath a grove of trees, as though set out for a picnic. Since Meléndez had for many years consistently pursued his personal style on a small scale, it is remarkable that he was able, in the final years of his life, so successfully to adapt and expand his compositions. It lends a poignant dimension to his life, so tragically blighted by flaws of character and official censure, and encourages speculation about what the artist's career might have been, had he received the nurture and encouragement that his talents obviously deserved.

The life of Luis Paret y Alcázar (1746–99) could hardly have differed more from that of Meléndez, even though the trajectory of the younger man's career was also diverted into some unexpected directions.[30] Born of a French father and a Spanish mother, the precocious youth began his studies at the Academia de San Fernando at the age of eleven. In 1760 he won second place in the drawing competition for his class. In 1763, when he was seventeen, he competed with the advanced class, and, although Mengs accorded him his vote for first place, the professors as a whole once more awarded him the second prize. The boy's innate talent and promise were, however, recognised by the Infante Don Luis, who immediately took him under his wing and personally funded a visit to Rome lasting two and a half years, so that he could perfect his skills. This relationship between patron and painter proved to be an

59 **Luis Meléndez**, 1716–80
Still Life with Artichokes and Tomatoes in a Landscape
*c.*1771. Signed on small stone at right: *L. Mz*
Oil on canvas, 61.6 x 81.9 cm
Collection of Lila and Herman Shickman

Four still lifes with landscape settings, all approximately the same size as this large canvas, were among the paintings Meléndez delivered to the Príncipe de Asturias in 1771 and 1772. All four are today in the Prado. Although in some respects works of this type represent a dramatic departure from the artist's usual practice, in others, they are perfectly consistent. There are none of the man-made, rectilinear forms with which he usually articulated space; only rotund, natural forms. The compositions are structured along emphatic diagonals, facilitating grouping in pairs. Instead of the usual table-tops, the compositions are arranged on natural ledges in the foreground that drop away at the pictures' lower edge. The landscape backgrounds are not topographical, but are simply suggestive of the Spanish landscape, whose bounty in this case included the New World tomato, artichokes, pears and peas. Rather than diminishing the scale of the fruits and vegetables depicted, the setting enhances their monumentality. Although many non-Spanish artists before him, especially Neapolitans, had painted still lifes in landscapes, few, if any, ever achieved a more compelling sense of Nature's grandeur.

Fig. 134 Luis Paret, Frontispiece to *Colección de las Aves que contiene el Cavinete de Historia Natural del Serenísimo Señor Infante Don Luis*, c.1774. Watercolour on paper. Private collection.

Fig. 135 Luis Paret, *Golden Oriole (Oropendola)*, c.1774. Watercolour on paper, 34 x 27 cm. Madrid, Museo del Prado.

enduring one. The Infante, who had been made a cardinal at the age of eight, and had been appointed Archbishop of both Toledo and Seville, had renounced his ecclesiastical posts in 1754 and was leading the life of a bon vivant and patron of the arts. By the summer of 1766, Paret was back in Madrid. In that year or the following, he signed the *Masked Ball*, now in the Prado, which is characteristic of the elegant genre scenes of court life that became a speciality, and which have lent him the sobriquet 'the Spanish Watteau'. It is unconfirmed whether he journeyed to France in the late 1760s, as proposed by Baticle,[31] but he became the most 'French' of all his contemporaries and was proud to have studied in Madrid with Charles de la Traverse (d. 1787), a disciple of Boucher. As well as Spanish, Paret knew Latin, Greek, French and Italian, and appears to have been extraordinarily cultivated. After his return from Italy, the Infante treated him as his unofficial court painter and acquired a number of his paintings.[32] Paret's most interesting commission, at least for the purposes of this study, was one relating to the Infante's abiding interest in natural history. Don Luis had assembled in the Royal Palace a cabinet of natural history, completely distinct from the king's; it contained an extraordinary collection of stuffed birds and quadrupeds, and dried insects. Around the time that this collection was moved from Madrid to the Infante's palace at Arenas de San Pedro (1774), Paret was commissioned to execute in watercolour a volume illustrating his patron's collection of birds (fig. 134).[33] Unlike Meléndez's series painted for the Infante's nephew, Paret's watercolours are not really still lifes; they conform to the prevailing standards of scientific illustration (fig. 135). But as in the case of Meléndez's still lifes, their quality as works of art is so high that they must be ranked at the very pinnacle of this category of European art.

In 1774 Paret was officially named as salaried court painter on the list of the Infante's household staff, which numbered more than 550;[34] his name remained on the list until Don Luis's death eleven years later. By a quirk of fate, however, he did not actually work for the Infante during most of this time and after 1775 never saw him again. In that year a tremendous scandal concerning the Infante's libertine habits erupted at the court, and Paret was implicated as one who procured women for his patron's pleasure. Although the details of this scandal have never become known, it was evidently so embarrassing to the king that Don Luis was banished to his country palaces for life and Paret was exiled to Puerto Rico for two years. He was then allowed to return to Spain, residing in the northern port of Bilbao, but was not permitted to return definitively to Madrid until 1789, four years after the Infante's death. However, during this time his art continued to flourish, and he continued to enjoy royal patronage. In 1780 he was admitted *in absentia* as Académico de Mérito to the Academia de San Fernando. While living in the north, Paret began in 1783 to execute some of his most beautiful works, a series of landscapes depicting the ports of Cantabria, no doubt inspired by Joseph Vernet's *Ports de France*. In 1786 Charles III, already looking forward to Paret's rehabilitation at the court, responded to these works with a royal commission to supply, at a salary of 15,000 *reales*, at least two such paintings each year, an arrangement that lasted until 1792.

Paret must have painted the extraordinarily beautiful pair of flower paintings in the Prado (cats 60 and 61), around 1780, before his return to Madrid. They were acquired by the Príncipe de Asturias and hung in the Casita del Príncipe along with Meléndez's still lifes. Paret was far from being a specialist in flowers, but his two signed flowerpieces are among the most beautiful of the eighteenth century. Perhaps inspired by the designs of Jean Pillement or Charles-Germain de Saint-Aubin, they reveal that Paret remained in touch with contemporary developments in France.[35]

60 and 61 **Luis Paret** 1746–99
Pair of Floral Bouquets
c.1780. Each signed, lower right: *L. Paret fec*[t]
Oil on canvas, 39 x 37 cm
Madrid, Museo del Prado

Often called, with justification, the most beautiful flower paintings of the Spanish eighteenth century, this pair of floral bouquets has been dated to the artist's maturity, around 1780. Evidently acquired by the Príncipe de Asturias, the future Charles IV, they were hung at his Casita at the Escorial, in the company of the many still lifes acquired from Meléndez. Both bouquets are tied with blue-and-white ribbons, which recall the heraldic colours of the royal Order of Charles III, established by the prince's father in 1771. Although comparisons have been made between some flowerpieces attributed to Paret and those of his French contemporary Vallayer-Coster, or those of the much older artist M.-N. Micheux, it might be more apposite to relate these pictures to the bouquets designed by Jean Pillement and popularised by the engravings he published in Paris in 1767. In their incisive draughtsmanship, jewel-like colour and soft lighting, they reveal a taste for the Dutch and Flemish flowerpieces so avidly collected by the French aristocracy. In this respect they recall Paret's words of praise for his own master, Charles de la Traverse, written down for inclusion in Céan Bermúdez's dictionary of Spanish artists: 'In coloration he adopted the principles and cast of the best Flemish Painters, whose works he had copied and which he continually celebrated with enthusiasm'.

The School of Valencia

In the last third of the eighteenth century, the city of Valencia became a flourishing centre for the education of flower painters in Spain, its influence extending even to Madrid.[1] This was not the result of a thriving tradition, because the same decline in the quality of still-life painting had occurred in Valencia as elsewhere; it resulted from the establishment in the city in 1768 of the Academia de San Carlos, and from Charles III's programme of reviving the silk industry, which had formerly flourished there, in order to stem the outflow of capital spent on the importation of luxury textiles from France. Valencian silk manufacturers made textiles in imitation of French designs, and several masters were brought from Lyon, the principal centre of the French textile industry.[2] At Lyon itself a school of drawing to support the silk industry had been established in 1757 and, as was to occur also in Valencia, the by-product of this was a great number of distinguished flower painters. Among the most celebrated artists to work in Lyon was Jean-Baptiste Pillement (1727–1808), who was in Madrid as a young man and who published an influential set of engraved floral designs for textiles in 1767 (fig. 136).[3] The parallel between what existed in Lyon and what was established in Valencia is essential to understanding the rapid development that was about to take place.

In 1775 the Valencian silk guild, the Colegio del Arte Mayor de la Seda, moved to establish an academy to train artists to produce floral motifs and designs for the region's silk manufacture. In 1778 a royal decree established the Sala de Flores within the Academia de San Carlos, with places for twelve students.[4] The royal decree stipulated that only the less promising students, those least likely to progress in history painting, sculpture or architecture, were to study there.[5] This seems to have been the case with José Ferrer (1746–1815), one of the first students to enter the Sala de Flores. Ferrer, a native of Alcora (near Valencia), had, several years earlier, been among the first painters to enrol in the newly established Academia de San Carlos. Not notably successful in his early efforts as a figure painter, in 1780 he submitted to the Sala de Flores a pair of floral studies in grisaille (fig. 137), obtaining a prize, but not without controversy as to the applicability of his designs to textiles.[6] These are elegant paintings with a pronounced Neo-classical flavour, retaining something of the character of exercises. Ferrer eventually became a prolific painter of small colourful flowerpieces, although he remained somewhat distanced from the Academy, because of his full-time association with the porcelain factory at Alcora, where he worked with his father, becoming its director in 1799. In 1795, however, he was created Académico de Mérito of the Valencian Academy.[7]

In 1784 the Sala de Flores became the Escuela de Flores y Ornatos Aplicados a los Tejidos (School of Flowers and Ornaments Applied to Textiles) under the direction of the flower painter Benito Espinós (1748–1818), Maestro de Flores.[8] The Valencian

Fig. 136 Jean Pillement, *Bouquet of Roses.* Engraving from *Oeuvres de Jean Pillement,* Paris 1767.

Fig. 137 José Ferrer, *Vase of Flowers*, 1780.
Oil on canvas, 38 x 41 cm. Barcelona, Reial
Acadèmia Catalana de Belles Arts de Sant Jordi.

Academy's attitude to the Escuela de Flores was marked by its concern that the
Academy's status would be debased by links with industry.[9] Even Espinós was reluc-
tant to instruct pupils in textile designs, a mechanical activity that he considered
unworthy of his artistic talents.[10] Prizes in the annual competitions in the Escuela de
Flores were awarded for the flower study, in oil, pastel or watercolour, made from
life during a two-hour session, which was deemed most adaptable to a textile design;
and also for an actual textile design.[11]

During the spring semester, students made timed drawings from fresh flowers,
usually in black and white on toned paper. Espinós set the standard, and works like
his *Flower Study* (fig. 138), clearly inspired by the type of drawings produced by the
School of Flowers at Lyon, were typical of these exercises. Espinós's beautiful *Sprig
of Orange Blossom* (cat. 62), is typical of the oil studies undertaken by the students.
In winter, master drawings by Espinós were copied, as were prints of ornamental
motifs from antiquity and Raphael's Vatican *Loggie*.[12] The drill of drawing and copying inculcated a normative style among students, which carried over into finished
paintings, and made necessary the inclusion of prominent signatures on both drawings and paintings. Benito Espinós dominated the whole school of Valencian flower
painters during his long career as director of the Escuela de Flores (1784–1814), and
his drawings were sent as models to other regional academies. The worn condition of
many of them testifies to their frequent use by students.

As early as 1789 it was clear that the Escuela de Flores was not proving the strong
stimulus to the textile industry it was planned to be, and that even prize-winning
studies could not easily be translated into fabric designs. One critic attributed the
school's failure to achieve the king's purpose to Espinós's 'vanity' in being unwilling
to adapt himself to its practical exigencies.[13] It was clear that under Espinós's direc-

Fig. 138 Benito Espinós, *Flower Study*. Pencil
and chalk on blue-grey prepared paper, 471 x
362 mm. Valencia, Museo de Bellas Artes San
Pío V.

62 Benito Espinós, 1748–1818
Sprig of Orange Blossom
c.1783. Signed, lower right: *Benito Espinós, f.^t*
Oil on canvas, 43 x 29.5 cm
Barcelona, Reial Acadèmia Catalana de Belles
Arts de Sant Jordi

This fresh and spontaneous nature study is a
beautiful example of the sort of exercise that
was a fundamental element of the curriculum of
the Valencian Escuela de Flores, of which
Espinós was named director in 1784. Painted
life-size from a cutting in the studio, it exemplifies the systematic, disciplined approach to
learning adopted by the Valencian Academy
from the School of Flowers at Lyon, which had
been founded in 1757. Botanical accuracy was a
primary goal of these exercises, but so was
speed. Students were usually allowed two hours
to accomplish a study of this kind. The fluency
and lightness of touch that resulted from a well-
executed study were considered essential ana-
logues to the 'freshness' and 'naturalness' of the
blooms represented.

tion, the Escuela de Flores had become a school in which every student wanted to be a flower painter, rather than a textile designer. Notwithstanding its partial commercial failure, it continued to turn out the best-trained painters of flower still lifes in Spain until well into the nineteenth century.[14]

The flower painting that won Benito Espinós the first prize in 1783 and launched his career at the Academia de San Carlos (fig. 139) is signed by the artist as inventor and painter.[15] Such a flowerpiece was known as a *florero de invención* and was far from being a literal transcription of an arrangement set up in front of the artist. This dimension of flower painting was being referred to by Ferrer, when he said that Espinos's paintings 'were both intelligent and natural'.[16] The judges must have been impressed by the studied composition of the varied blooms, the distribution of masses in light and shade, the drawing of contour and form and the graceful turning of the stems. The same values and procedures that prevailed in academic figure painting were applied to flower painting: an idealised version of nature was sought, in which the artist's creative imagination 'improved on' what was observed in studies from the life. The Late Baroque painter and theorist Antonio Palomino had likewise advised in 1715 that a flower painting should be composed according to the precepts of history painting.[17] The flowerpiece that José Garcés presented to the Madrid Academy in 1772 (fig. 140) is a similar type of work, with a faintly Neo-classical quality; it is a refined and carefully composed picture, whose restraint and polish are surely the result of painstaking study and preparation.[18]

Even though he enjoyed the financial security of a regular salary and a pension from the Academy (a contrast to the precarious existence led by Meléndez in Madrid), Benito Espinós still hankered after royal favour and the patronage of influential collectors at the court. As was customary among eighteenth-century artists seeking advancement, he tried to secure royal favour with gifts of paintings. In 1788 he travelled to Madrid and was received by the Príncipe de Asturias, to whom he presented three flower paintings for the Casita at the Escorial (fig. 141).[19] Painted with

Fig. 139 Benito Espinós, *Flowerpiece*, 1783. Oil on canvas, 78 x 55 cm. Valencia, Museo de Bellas Artes San Pío V.

Fig. 140 José Garcés, *Flowerpiece*, 1772. Oil on canvas, 73 x 58 cm. Madrid, Real Academia de Bellas Artes de San Fernando.

Fig. 141 Benito Espinós, *Flowerpiece*, 1788. Oil on canvas, 60 x 42 cm. Madrid, Museo del Prado.

22 x 15 ?

63 Juan Bautista Romero, 1756–after 1802

Vase of Flowers

1796. Signed, lower centre: *Juan bauta romero*
Oil on panel, 55 x 37 cm
Madrid, Museo de La Real Academia de Bellas
Artes de San Fernando

This small flowerpiece and its dated pendant are
among the best-known works of Romero, who
was one of the most distinguished graduates of
the Valencian Escuela de Flores before establishing himself at the court. They passed into the
collection of the Academia de San Fernando in
Madrid in 1808, when Manuel Godoy, the
prime minister and the Academy's protector,
was deposed from office and his property confiscated by the state. It is likely that the artist
presented them to him in the expectation that
such a gift would advance his career. Perhaps it
did, for between 1800 and 1802 Romero was
working as a flower painter in the royal porcelain factory of the Buen Retiro. Compared to
the verve of Espinós's style of painting flowers,
Romero's technique is more controlled, with
areas of impasto contrasting with thin glazes.
The delicate modelling is enhanced by a soft,
atmospheric lighting that highlights the tiny
dewdrops on petals and pedestal, achieving a
convincing evocation of freshness.

great verve, these accomplished works reveal the artist at his best. Years later, in 1802, Espinós gave the same prince, by then King Charles IV, six more flower paintings. In 1803 he was still in Madrid, where he signed two drawings of bouquets of flowers.[20] In 1814 he gave the restored King Ferdinand VII, on his visit to the Valencian Academy, two flower pictures, one on panel and another on glass.[21] Espinós was thus represented by at least eleven flower paintings in the royal collection; but he never received a royal appointment, nor did he obtain the pension he asked for when he went blind in 1816.[22]

Juan Bautista Romero (1756–after 1802) was one of the most distinguished graduates of the Valencian Escuela de Flores, obtaining first prize in 1785. He lived for a time in Madrid and claimed to have studied at the Academia de San Fernando. Between 1800 and 1802 he worked as a painter for the Buen Retiro porcelain factory in the capital.[23] Romero's *Vase of Flowers* (cat. 63) is one of a pair painted in 1796 and given to Manuel Godoy, the prime minister and royal favourite, probably in the hope of winning advancement at court.[24] These paintings follow a standard Valencian format, as exemplified by Espinós's works (fig. 141), and are executed with great subtlety. Compared to the spirited handling of Espinós's flowerpieces, Romero's reveal a more refined sensibility, which dwells even on the tiny drops of dew that cling to the flower petals.[25]

Even before enrolling in the Valencian Academy, Romero practised as a still-life painter. Two unpublished still lifes representing foodstuffs on crude wooden tabletops, inscribed 'Spring' (PRIMAVERA) and 'Winter' (INBIERNO), are signed and dated 1781.[26] These pictures, no doubt originally part of a set of the Four Seasons, are poorly composed and badly drawn, revealing how far Romero was able to progress as a result of receiving a sound academic training.

Romero was far more versatile than most graduates of the Escuela de Flores, and

Fig. 142 Juan Bautista Romero, *Still Life with Strawberries and Chocolate*. Oil on panel transferred to plywood, 43.2 x 58.4 cm. Raleigh, North Carolina Museum of Art, Gift of the North Carolina Art Society (Robert F. Phifer Funds).

Fig. 143 Juan Bautista Romero, *Still Life with Tea, Chocolate and Biscuits*. Oil on canvas, 46 x 63 cm. Location unknown.

some of his best mature works are still lifes in the strict sense. A pair of paintings in the North Carolina Museum of Art, Raleigh, depicts two courses of a summer picnic laid out of doors for one person, the viewer: in one, a country paté, meat pies, a salad and wine are represented; in the other a dessert of strawberries, sugar, chocolate, biscuits and bread is laid out on a crisply laundered white cloth trimmed with lace (fig. 142).[27] While recalling the outdoor still lifes of Giacomo Nani (fig. 125), they offer a glimpse of the elegance of upper-class society in late eighteenth-century Spain.

Another pair of remarkable still lifes by Romero, whose location has been unknown for many years, also depict two courses of a meal, or two types of meals. One represents an intimate table spread with plates of salad, dried fish, bread, olives and nuts, with a beautifully wrought silver knife and fork on top of a folded napkin; the other represents a dessert, or perhaps a tea service (*merienda*) (fig. 143). Featured on the polished wooden table-top in the latter picture are a silver teapot with a bowl of sugar, a Chinese export teacup and saucer with a silver spoon, a plate of sweets, a cup of chocolate similar to the one in the Raleigh still life, and a footed metal tray with four tumblers of water. This elegant work, while reminiscent of the still lifes of Jean-Etienne Liotard (1702–89), with which the artist was probably not familiar, also recalls the courtly dessert still lifes of Van der Hamen (cat. 10), painted for the aristocracy of Madrid more than a century and a half earlier.

Although Valencian by birth, José López Enguídanos (1760–1812) enrolled in the Madrid Academia de San Fernando at the age of fourteen. He won prizes in 1781 and 1784 and became a well-known printmaker, publishing engravings of the cast collection of the Academy (1794) and a collection of images for the instruction of young artists (1797).[28] His dry Neo-classical style found favour with the Academy's protector, Manuel Godoy, and it was Godoy's support that was instrumental in the artist's appointment in 1806 as Pintor de Cámara to Charles IV. As a sign of gratitude, the artist gave Godoy a set of four still lifes, now in the collection of the Academia de San Fernando (cat. 64, fig. 144).[29]

64 José López Enguídanos, 1760–1812

Still Life with Melon, Birds and a Glass of Water

1807. Signed on table edge, at right: *Josef Lopez Enguídanos f.*

Oil on canvas, 51 × 68 cm

Madrid, Museo de la Real Academia de Bellas Artes de San Fernando

This is the best-known of four still lifes presented by the artist to Manuel Godoy, perhaps as a token of gratitude for Godoy's support for his appointment in 1806 as Pintor de Cámara to King Charles IV. Frédéric Quilliet's inventory of the Godoy collection, made in 1808, indicates that these pictures were painted in 1807. López Enguídanos's still lifes usually depict – as this work does – game, fruit, vegetables and utensils on wooden table-tops, thus inviting comparison to those of Meléndez. Indeed, he knew Meléndez's still lifes well, but the style of the two artists could hardly be more different. López Enguídanos painted in a limpid, earnest, if somewhat dry, style consistent with his academic background. In contrast to the dramatic, monumental works of Meléndez, with their roots in seventeenth-century naturalism, his still lifes are characterised by an intimacy and charm that can be noted in the bourgeois still lifes of Neo-classically trained artists from other countries at the turn of the nineteenth century.

Fig. 144 José López Enguídanos, *Still Life with Ducks, a Partridge, Oranges and a Copper Pot*, 1807. Oil on canvas, 47 × 61 cm. Madrid, Real Academia de Bellas Artes de San Fernando.

**65 Francisco Lacoma y Fontanet,
1784–1849**
Vase of Flowers with Lute and Lyre
Oil on canvas, 116 x 90 cm
Barcelona, Museu Nacional d'Art de Catalunya

Francisco Lacoma's flowerpiece betrays the international flavour of the artist's biography. He was a Catalan who lived most of his adult life in Paris; it is not easy to detect in his work a 'Spanish' character that would differentiate his style from that prevalent in Paris in his day. It is, in fact, only the saturnine, greyish light, so unlike the sunny atmosphere of similar works by French artists, that reminds us at all of Barcelona. In this diligent, meticulous painting, in which contours are precisely delineated, the controlled application of paint produces a smooth, enamel-like surface, very unlike the fresh spontaneity sought by Espinós and his Valencian followers. But this is not surprising coming from an artist who frequented the studio of Gérard van Spaendonck, the most influential flower and fruit painter in Paris, and who certainly knew and admired the works of his successors Redouté and Van Dael. For all these painters, the ideal of painterly perfection was still to be found in the works of such late Baroque artists as Jan van Huysum and Rachel Ruysch, whose still lifes were abundant in Paris collections but would have been rare in Spain. Lacoma's development is too little known to enable us to date this work.

López Enguídanos's paintings are kitchen still lifes, with foodstuffs, birds, game and utensils arranged on plain wooden table-tops. At their best, they are executed with a great subtlety of colour and delicacy of touch. Although his still lifes are sometimes compared to those of Meléndez, the handling of paint is very dissimilar and they reveal a very different attitude towards composition; they are products of a different age. His *Still Life with Ducks, a Partridge, Oranges and a Copper Pot* (fig. 144) is one of his most sensitive works. Although its composition may recall the kind of *bodegón* painted 150 years earlier by an artist such as Francisco Barranco (fig. 83), its refined execution is a product of the academic tradition. Unlike Meléndez, the artist establishes recession into depth by skewing the table at an angle; the objects, never approaching the monumentality of Meléndez's forms, reside comfortably within the intimate, domestic space he defines.

Francisco Lacoma y Fontanet (1784–1849) was trained in the School of Drawing of La Lonja in Barcelona and excelled in flower painting and ornamental design.[30] In 1804 he was sent to Paris with a five-year grant from the Barcelona Chamber of Commerce, to perfect his art and to learn lacquer work and gilding. In 1805 and 1808 he won prizes from the Academia de San Fernando in Madrid for examples he had sent of his flower and fruit paintings and for his portraits. The superb *Branch of Cherry Blossoms* (fig. 145), painted in 1805, is an example of the kind of academic exercise Lacoma must have been required to execute in Paris, not unlike the sort required by the Valencian Escuela de Flores (cat. 62). His finished works, like the fruit still life he sent in 1808 to the Barcelona Chamber of Commerce,[31] display the meticulous, highly polished technique for which he is admired; this reflects the Parisians' admiration for the style of eighteenth-century Dutch still-life painters such as Rachel Ruysch and Jan Van Huysum. Lacoma made his career in Paris and exhibited at the annual Salons. He stayed in France during the Peninsular War and was instrumental in securing the return of Spanish paintings looted for the Musée Napoléon, a service which earned him the title of Académico de Mérito of the Madrid Academy in 1819.

The refinement seen in Lacoma's *Still Life with Fruit* is taken even further in his mature flower paintings (cat. 65), in which we see one current of eighteenth-century style taken to its logical conclusion, under the impulse of the Neo-classical imperative to 'improve on' nature in works of precious near-perfection. Lasting until the mid-nineteenth century, and even beyond, in the hands of a few *retardataire* French and Northern artists, this approach to flower painting and the still life was, however, a dead end. The seeds of what might replace it were already planted when the young Lacoma was perfecting the polish of his enamel-like technique. It would have needed an artist completely indifferent to the painterly niceties so beloved by contemporary bourgeois society to offer a vigorous alternative to still-life painting as it had evolved; and such an artist, approaching his sixty-fifth birthday, was then living in Spain.

Fig. 145 Francisco Lacoma, *Branch of Cherry Blossoms*, 1805. Oil on paper laid on canvas, 58 x 45 cm. London art market.

Goya and the Still Life

Francisco José de Goya y Lucientes (1746–1828) did not paint many still lifes; so far as we know, he did not paint any until he was over sixty years old. Seen against the backdrop of eighteenth- and early nineteenth-century still-life painting, Goya's still lifes represent a rupture with tradition as abrupt and shocking as that produced by any aspect of his work. They are at once beautiful and poignant objects; all but one depict dead animals. Not the courtly game of a hunter's trophy, nor the meat on a butcher's stall, nor the dead beasts traditionally symbolising life's brevity or Nature's bounty – but animals that have been slaughtered, from whom life has been violently torn, in whose images there is a depth of pathos as life-affirming as anything to be found in the greatest works of Velázquez or Zurbarán. In the unorthodox technical explorations of these works, Goya expanded the reach of his medium beyond the limits previously known: using his brushes, his knife, his fingers, combining patches of heavy impasto with the thinnest of glazes, producing shimmering transparencies and iridescences and the most desolate voids of darkness. Considering the impact of these works, one might well wonder why Goya waited so long to paint a still life, as well as why he painted any at all. We have to understand how they fit into his overall oeuvre, because, when he finally did approach the genre, he changed it for future generations, just as he reinvented nearly every form of painting and graphic art that he embraced.

Unlike his exact contemporary Luis Paret (see page 161), Goya was not a prodigy. He was born in Fuentetodos, a small town forty kilometres southwest of Zaragoza. At the age of sixteen he was apprenticed to José Luzán, a painter of modest talents in Zaragoza.[1] In 1763, aged seventeen, he made his first trip to Madrid, where he competed unsuccessfully in the triennial competition sponsored by the Real Academia de San Fernando.[2] Paret, who had been attending classes at the Academy since the age of eleven, won second place in the very same competition, attracting the notice of the Infante Don Luis, the king's brother, who immediately sent him to Rome on a pension.[3] That same year, Goya entered the Madrid workshop of Francisco Bayeu (1734–95), where he gained a solid grounding in the fundamentals of his craft. At that time the leading artists at the court were Anton Raphael Mengs (1728–79) and Giovanni Battista Tiepolo (1696–1770). Finally in 1770–1, at the age of twenty-four, Goya was able make his own trip to Italy.[4] On his return, he secured several commissions for fresco decorations in Zaragoza. In 1774, on the recommendation of Mengs, who headed the Royal Tapestry Factory, he was summoned to Madrid and asked to submit cartoons for nine tapestries, thus enabling him to establish a foothold at the court. Less than two years later, Mengs put him on salary to continue supplying designs for tapestries for the decoration of the royal households; he continued to do this until 1792, with diminishing enthusiasm for what he considered to be 'undignified' work.[5] In 1780 he caught up with Paret (who in the meantime was serving a fourteen-year exile from the court, for having abetted the Infante's pursuit of a libertine lifestyle);[6] both artists (Paret *in absentia*) were admitted to the Academia de San Fernando at the same time, at the age of thirty-four.

From then on, Goya's rise was steady. In 1781 he defeated Francisco Bayeu, his former mentor – and by now his brother-in-law – in an important competition for a royal commission to paint an altarpiece for the church of San Francisco el Grande.[7] He gained the patronage of the Infante Don Luis; and in 1785, the year of the Infante's death, he was appointed court painter to King Charles III. In that same year Goya began his lifelong association with the Duques de Osuna, the wealthiest and most enlightened private patrons in Spain, for whom he was to paint some of his most memorable works. In 1789 he was promoted to Pintor de Cámara to the newly crowned Charles IV; from him, and from his queen, María Luisa de Parma, he received numerous commissions for portraits, consequently becoming the foremost portrait painter to the Madrid aristocracy and intellectual society.

Following his disastrous illness of 1792–3, which left him totally deaf for the rest of his life, Goya slowly recovered his strength and embarked upon his remaining thirty-four years like an artist reborn. In January of 1794, he sent to Bernardo de Iriarte, vice-protector of the Academy, the now-famous series of eleven small cabinet pictures in which he gave free rein to 'fantasy and invention', and which mark the turning-point of his career.[8] The following year, he was appointed director of painting at the Academy. Before the century had ended, he had completed the suite of eighty etchings known as *Los Caprichos*, frescoed the interior of the small church of San Antonio de la Florida, and executed many of his greatest portraits.

The early years of the new century were difficult and dangerous ones for Spain; normal life was disrupted again and again by political upheavals and violent war against the French. Maintaining a façade of neutrality, Goya painted masterly portraits of men on all sides in the conflict: the most despotic or the most liberal of

Fig. 146 Francisco de Goya, *Hares*, *c.*1808–12. Oil on canvas, 45.1 x 62.9 cm. New York, Wildenstein & Co., Inc.

Spaniards, the occupying French and the liberating English. During the worst years of the war, 1808–14, he worked increasingly in solitude and for himself. Among the greatest works of art he produced during this period were the drawings for his private use and his second series of eighty etchings, derived from them, which have come to be known as *The Disasters of War* (figs 151 and 152). Many of his greatest and most original paintings also date from this time, as do all of his surviving still lifes. Indeed, as has been astutely observed by José López-Rey, there is a creative link between the still lifes and *The Disasters of War* that is crucial to understanding the artist's mind at this time in his life.[9]

In June 1812, Josefa Bayeu, Goya's wife of thirty-nine years, died in their house on the Calle de Valverde, Madrid. The documents concerning the settlement of her estate are extremely informative about the artist's way of life, and it is from the inventory made at that time that we learn of Goya's activity as a still-life painter.[10] According to the will which Josefa and her husband had signed in 1811, the estate of whichever one of them died first was to be divided equally between the surviving marriage partner and their only son, Javier. The documents confirm that, although not wealthy, Goya lived quite comfortably, having managed to accumulate property, cash, valuable jewellery, silver, a library of several hundred volumes and, of course, a large number of his own paintings, drawings and prints. In the division of property, Goya, quite surprisingly, gave all the paintings and prints to Javier. Xavier de Salas has convincingly suggested that this was done intentionally, to protect Javier's principal eventual inheritance – his famous father's works of art – against the consequences of a possible second marriage or liaison.[11] Such a precaution would not have been unwarranted, as Goya's relationship with Leocadia Zorilla de Weiss, who was to be his companion until his death, had probably begun before his wife's death. Javier, who chiefly desired material comfort and social standing, no doubt felt reassured that his inheritance was guaranteed.

In the inventory of paintings given to Javier in 1812, item 11 mentions 'Twelve still lifes', without describing them individually. They are valued collectively at 1,200 *reales*, far less than their actual worth at the time.[12] The paintings are assumed to have decorated the dining room of Goya's house and probably remained there until 1819, when Goya moved to the Quinta del Sordo on the outskirts of Madrid and began work on a set of decorations for his new dining room – the works we know as the *Black Paintings*.[13] Ten still lifes certainly by Goya are known today; all can probably be identified with item 11 in the inventory of 1812.[14] Thanks to the records of the process of distributing Josefa's estate, and to subsequent documents, it is possible to trace the movements of the paintings in some detail.

Salas has demonstrated that all the paintings described in the inventory of 1812 that were given to Javier, were marked with a white 'X' followed by an inventory number.[15] The 'X' stood for 'Xavier', the alternative spelling of Javier's name. In some instances, these numbers, or remnants of them, are still visible on the paintings. Two of the still lifes known today (cats 66 and 69) bear remnants of this inscription, 'X11' (Xavier, item 11 of the inventory).[16]

Javier Goya left the still lifes he had received from his father to his own son, Mariano, who also inherited his father's social aspirations. In 1846 Mariano Goya, going by the unauthorised title 'Marqués Conde del Espinar', defaulted on a loan he had received from the Conde de Yumuri; he had used this money to finance his claim to nobility. The still lifes had been security for the loan;[17] consquently, for the next two decades Yumuri was able to display the paintings in the dining-room of his villa at Carabanchel Alto, close to Madrid. Thanks to the documents relating to Yumuri's

66 Francisco de Goya, 1746–1828
Still Life with Golden Bream
*c.*1808–12. Signed, right foreground (almost vertically): *Goya*
Oil on canvas, 44.1 x 61.6 cm
Houston, Museum of Fine Arts. Museum purchase with funds provided by the Alice Pratt Brown
Museum Fund and the Brown Foundation Accession Endowment Fund.

This painting, which was acquired in Paris by the influential art critic Zacharie Astruc, Manet's friend,
resembles *Still Life with Woodcocks* (cat. 67) in conception. The scene is illuminated by moonlight,
which glints across the wet, scaly bodies of the fish and is reflected in their large, staring eyes, which,
arranged in an ellipse, seem to encapsulate the startling instant of transition between life and death.
The eye of the beholder is allowed to construe the foam of the wave breaking diagonally on the beach
from the quick, half-blended strokes of white, umber and black. The fish's bodies, deftly drawn and
foreshortened, are modelled by a combination of unorthodox techniques. Working from a ground of
warm, light grey, which is allowed to show in parts, Goya has rubbed light brownish and bluish grey
pigment on top. He has defined the gleaming bellies by jabbing at the canvas with a brush heavily
loaded with white paint, overlaid in places with a yellowish glaze. Details of the scales and gills are
defined in black and grey applied with the brush and the knife. The fins are painted in a salmon-
coloured paint, with unblended streaks of white applied with a stiff brush. The yellow pigment of the
eyes is boldly placed with single, circular strokes. Touches of red along the gills and mouths, which
appear to be applied with the knife and the butt-end of a brush, provide the final accent to this vibrant,
coherent work.

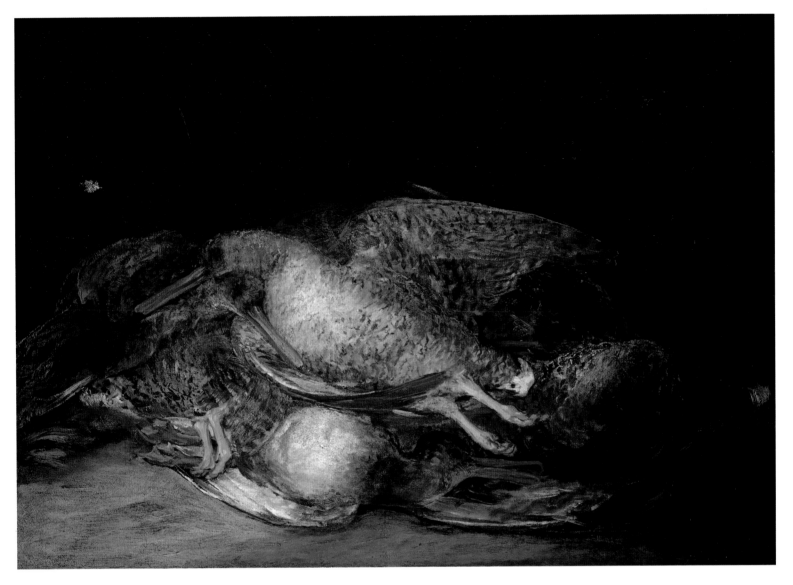

67 **Francisco de Goya**, 1746–1828
Still Life with Woodcocks
*c.*1808–12. Oil on canvas, 45.2 x 62.6 cm
Dallas, Texas, Southern Methodist University, Meadows Museum, Algur H. Meadows Collection

This painting corresponds to one in the possession of the Conde de Yumuri, recorded as representing 'three dead woodcocks'. Although usually known as *Still Life with Woodcocks*, the painting also represents other game birds, thrown into a heap in the marsh grass as though by a hunter. A waterfowl with a broader bill and reddish webbed feet is situated at the bottom of the pile in the foreground, and a larger bird with a white-ringed neck, probably a duck, is seen at the right. Goya removes the birds from the realm of anecdote, however, by casting the scene at night, when no hunter could possibly shoot. As López-Rey has observed (Newark 1964–5), the gracefully curved, outstretched wings of the topmost bird seem to retain the 'élan of life', even though they are frozen in death. Especially touching is the apparent embrace, as though part of some mating ritual, of the two birds' heads at the middle left – a poignant and ironic allusion in the dark solitude of this setting. Painting on a warm, light ground, Goya has worked wet paint into wet, both with his brushes and with a palette knife, creating an incredibly rich variety of textures and nuances of colour. In the foreground, however, he has brushed the light green of the marsh floor over a black ground, giving the impression of cold, saturated damp.

collection and his dealings with Mariano, we have a more detailed description of the still lifes, which can be related to paintings now dispersed throughout the world:[18]

'A still life with dead game' (Un bodegón de caza muerta). Wildenstein & Co., New York (fig. 146).

'Two representing a dead chicken and a duck' (Dos representando un pollo muerto y un pato). Prado, Madrid, and Bührle Collection, Zurich (figs 147 and 148).

'One with fruits and fish' (Uno con frutas y pescado). Oskar Reinhart Collection, Winterthur (fig. 149), and Museum of Fine Arts, Houston (cat. 66). This almost certainly refers to two pictures, 'one with fruits' and 'fish', since the only still life by Goya with fish (cat. 66) is one of those which retains traces of the inventory number 'X11'.

'An unplucked turkey and a plucked one' (Un pavo sin pelar y otro pelado). Prado, Madrid (cat. 68), and Alte Pinakothek, Munich (fig. 150).

'A still life with pieces of rib, loin and a head of mutton' (Una naturaleza muerta con trozos de costilla, lomo y cabeza de carnero). Louvre, Paris (cat. 69).

'Three slices of salmon' (Tres ruedas de salmón). Oskar Reinhart Collection, Winterthur (fig. 153).

'Three dead woodcocks' (Tres chochas muertas). Meadows Museum, Dallas (cat. 67).

Following the death of the Conde de Yumuri in 1865, the group of still lifes was sold and dispersed. Shortly thereafter, some of them were taken to Paris, where, during the formative years of Impressionism, they were acquired by collectors of avant-garde taste. Their impact on French painting has not been adequately studied.

The one signed still life by Goya that does not represent dead animals is *Still Life with Fruit, Bottles and a Cask* in the Oskar Reinhart Collection (fig. 149). The most conventional of all, it is the only one with a composition reminiscent of Meléndez. Could it be that, having decided to paint a series of still lifes for his dining-room, Goya painted this one first, then abandoned the usual formulas as he became preoccupied with his work on *The Disasters of War*? He was certainly familiar with the works of Meléndez, which may have represented to him the best precedents. The other nine of his still lifes, however, are completely different and seem to be variations on a single theme, conforming to his tendency to conceive works in series.

Fig. 147 Francisco de Goya, *Dead Birds*, *c*.1808–12. Oil on canvas, 46 x 64 cm. Madrid, Museo del Prado.

Fig. 148 Francisco de Goya, *Duck*, *c*.1808–12. Oil on canvas, 44.5 x 62 cm. Zurich, Bührle Collection.

Fig. 149 Francisco de Goya, *Still Life with Fruit, Bottles and a Cask*, *c*.1808–12. Oil on canvas, 45 x 62 cm. Winterthur, Oskar Reinhart Collection.

Fig. 150 Francisco de Goya, *Plucked Turkey and Frying Pan*, *c*.1808–12. Oil on canvas, 44.8 x 62.4 cm. Munich, Alte Pinakothek.

68 Francisco de Goya, 1746–1828
Still Life with Dead Turkey
*c.*1808–12. Signed, bottom centre (almost vertically): *Goya*
Oil on canvas, 45 x 63 cm
Madrid, Museo del Prado

Goya's *Dead Turkey* in the Prado is one of his most powerful still lifes. Its bold expressiveness derives in part from its sombre chromatic scale of intense blacks and earth tones, relieved by a single passage of red in the head and wattle of the bird, whose beak and brow are grandly silhouetted against the black background. Its outstretched wing and rigid legs seem charged with the energy of its dying gesture. As in all the still lifes, Goya has contrasted areas in which only a thin film of paint covers the canvas with others in which impasto is thickly built up. In the bird's wing and tail, single, bold strokes of black, grey and ochre denote whole feathers with sure-handed verve. The basket is suggested by quick, decisive strokes that create an anchoring pattern in marked contrast to the black void above. The foreground is laid down with thick, overlapping strokes of white mixed with burnt umber. In the middle of the wet paint, Goya has boldly inscribed his name, just as he did in the Houston *Still Life with Golden Bream*. As the brightly lit foreground meets the shadowed corner at the left, the thick brush strokes feather out to thinness and disappear, leaving the bird's clawed feet splayed against the dark ground.

69 Francisco de Goya, 1746–1828
Still Life with Pieces of Rib, Loin and a Head of Mutton
c.1808–12. Signed in red in the shadow underneath the head: *Goya*
Oil on canvas, 45 x 62 cm
Paris, Musée du Louvre

In his catalogue of the 1952 exhibition of still lifes at the Orangerie in Paris, Charles Sterling tried to place this great still life in historical perspective by comparing it to Rembrandt's *Flayed Carcass of Beef*, to Géricault's pictures of human body parts, to Daumier's *Butcher* and to Soutine's *Plucked Chickens*. Goya knew none of these, of course, although he surely did know such seventeenth-century still lifes of butchered meat as that attributed to Cerezo (cat. 35). But Sterling noted a unique and distinctive element of Goya's picture that seemed to anticipate the concerns of a later generation: its sense of pathos. While we cannot compare these sections of a sheep's carcass to the works of Géricault, we can indeed compare them to Goya's own equally unforgettable invention, *Great Deed! With Dead Men! (Grande hazaña! Con muertos!)*, plate 39 of *The Disasters of War* (fig. 152). With consummate artistry and chilling, feigned indifference, Goya has propped one rack of mutton against the other, so that it towers monumentally against the black background. He has poised the brainless face of the sheep at the left as an integral element in the composition. The dismembered animal seems a blind witness to the brutal artifice committed on its former self. With a note of irony, Goya has signed his name, as though in blood, with tiny red letters in the shadow underneath the sheep's head.

In his essay linking Goya's still lifes to *The Disasters of War*, López-Rey eloquently drew a parallel between Goya's treatment of human corpses and those of animals; both are made to express 'the life force as it is turned into the grimace of death under the impact of violence'.[19] As López-Rey pointed out, the tense, rigid bodies of the chickens in the Prado's *Dead Birds* (fig. 147), which retain, as if frozen by death, vestiges of their dying agony, recall such plates in the *Disasters* as plate 22, *So Much and More* (*Tanto y más*) (fig. 151). In others, such as *Plucked Turkey and Frying Pan* (fig. 150), the denuded and broken body of the bird rests unnaturally upon its neck, while its bulk is thrust upward and silhouetted against the barren sky, endowing the cruel image with the same incongruous monumentality as is observed in *Disasters* plate 39, *Great Deed! With Dead Men!* (*Grande hazaña! Con muertos!*) (fig. 152), where the monstrous act is so at odds with the nobility of the human bodies upon which it is inflicted. None of the still lifes better reveals Goya's departure from tradition than the brilliant *Three Slices of Salmon*, in the Oskar Reinhart Collection (fig. 153). Unlike Meléndez's still lifes in which a slice of salmon is depicted within the context of a kitchen (fig. 154), Goya has isolated the three cross-sections of the fish's body from all context. Looming, brightly lit against a dark void, and observed with extraordinary sensitivity to their pliant flesh, clotted blood and iridescent skin, these forms, recalling body parts in a morgue, seem to prefigure Géricault, or even Henry Moore. They have nothing to do with the sensibility of Chardin or Meléndez.

It is not surprising that Goya did not normally paint still lifes. He was a great artist, trained in the Neo-classical tradition, which disparaged such pictures as the province of *petits maîtres* and decorative painters. Although unorthodox, he was enormously successful and respected in his maturity. Growing sick of painting what others wanted him to paint in his youth, such as the tapestry cartoons, he had no need, unlike Meléndez, to paint still lifes for a living; but in the bitter years of the Peninsular War, preoccupied with death and violence, he seized on this genre as something relevant to his larger concerns. In doing so, he was not wholly unlike the first generation of still-life painters, who acted out of a commitment to deeply held ideas about the nature of art. If there is an important legacy from Goya's still lifes, it is that he made the still life respectable again, by elevating it to a level of seriousness not to be found in the pretty, bourgeois works of his contemporaries. The legitimate heirs of this legacy were not his immediate Spanish followers; they were, perhaps, Cézanne, Picasso and all who finally saw the potential he rediscovered.

Fig. 151 Francisco de Goya, *So Much and More* (*Tanto y más*), c.1810–11, plate 22 of *The Disasters of War*, Madrid 1863. Etching, 16.1 x 25.4 cm, London, British Museum.

Fig. 152 Francisco de Goya, *Great Deed! With Dead Men!* (*Grande hazaña! Con muertos!*), c.1810–11, plate 39 of *The Disasters of War*, Madrid 1863. Etching, 15.7 x 20.8 cm, London, British Museum.

Fig. 153 Francisco de Goya, *Three Slices of Salmon*, *c*.1808–12. Oil on canvas, 44 x 62 cm. Winterthur, Oskar Reinhart Collection.

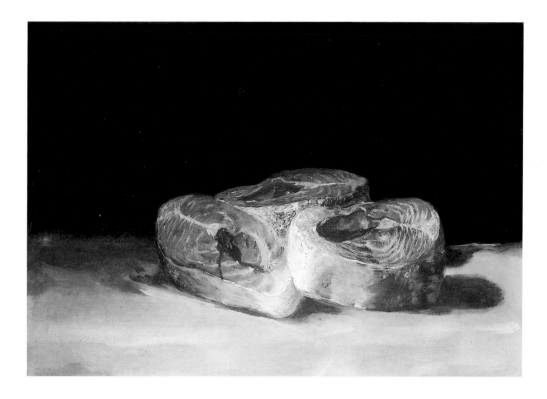

Fig. 154 Luis Meléndez, *Still Life with Salmon, a Lemon and Three Vessels*, 1772. Oil on canvas, 42 x 62 cm, Madrid, Museo del Prado.

Notes

Abbreviations
AGP: Archivo General de Palacio
AHPM: Archivo Histórico de Protocolos, Madrid
AHPT: Archivo Histórico de Protocolos, Toledo
APS: Archivo de Protocolos, Seville

The Still Life in Spain: Origins and Themes

1. The phenomenon is not wholly explained by reference to artists' 'conquest of reality' over the course of the fifteenth and sixteenth centuries (the phrase is the title of the chapter devoted to the art of the early fifteenth century in E.H. Gombrich's *The Story of Art*, London 1950).

2. 'muy bien pintados', Pacheco 1649 (edn 1990), p. 511.

3. For the document concerning Prado's trip to Morocco, see Serrera 1986. It states that Prado 'fue a Berveria ... a servir al Xarife', and that he was in the pay of the Duque de Medina Sidonia. Prado is most likely to have worked as a portraitist in Morocco, and a parallel may be drawn with Gentile Bellini's visit to the Sultan of Turkey.

4. See Madrid 1983, p. 30, nos 1–2; Fort Worth 1985, pp. 10–11.

5. Malvasia (1678, edn 1841, I, p. 289) refers to the still lifes and flower paintings of Carlo Antonio Procaccini (*c*.1551–1605) and says that the Spanish governors of Milan returned to Spain with some of his pictures, and gave them to Philip IV. Baldinucci (1681–1728, edn 1845–7, III, pp. 384–5) comments that Procaccini's landscapes, fruit and flower paintings were sought after in Spain. A still life by the Cremonese artist Panfilo Nuvolone (1581–*c*.1651) was in the collection of the Marqués de Leganés, possibly acquired during his governorship of Milan (1635–41): 'una pintura de melocotones y ubas con una salba de panfilo nuvolone en tabla', López Navío 1962, no. 1115. A painting of a very similar description (the same work?) is listed in the inventory of 1628 of the Marqués de la Hinojosa, Governor of Milan, who had been recalled to Spain in disgrace in 1615: 'Un quadro de unas hubas y persigos [sic] sobre una salva y el marco dorado y color de nogal', AHPM, Prot. 2350, fols 666–9. The description suggests a version of Nuvolone's still life dated 1620 in a private collection in Milan, see Zeri and Porzio 1989, I, pl. 257.

6. Sterling 1952, 1959 and 1981; Gombrich 1959. Gombrich cites a fruit picture sent to Isabella d'Este in 1506. It would not be surprising if some still lifes were painted earlier than the 1590s.

Illusionistic images, such as Jacopo da Barbari's *Dead Bird* of 1504 (Munich, Alte Pinakothek), which has been adduced as a precedent for the modern revival of still-life painting, have been related to classical prototypes. For three paintings of dwarf fruit trees in pots, perhaps copies of works by Giovanni da Udine of the 1530s, see Sterling 1959, p. 37; Dacos and Furlan 1987, p. 195; Zeri and Porzio 1989, I, pp. 55–6.

7. Examples of this attitude are apparent in Cristóbal de Villalón's *Ingeniosa comparación entre lo antiguo y lo presente*, Valladolid 1539, and Pablo de Céspedes's *Discurso de la comparación de la antigua y moderna pintura*, 1604, see Ceán Bermúdez 1800, V, pp. 273–352.

8. Jerónimo de la Huerta's translation of Pliny was published in 1599. Juan van der Hamen painted a portrait of de la Huerta, see Jordan 1967, p. 361, no. 124, where the sitter is incorrectly identified as Sebastián Gómez de la Huerta.

9. See Bialostocki 1966; Glendinning 1978; Toledo 1982, p. 83; Edinburgh 1989, pp. 11–23, 50–9; Marías 1993.

10. Bann 1989, pp. 27–40; Bryson (1990, pp. 18–20) quotes the Elder Philostratus' detailed descriptions of two still lifes, or *xenia*.

11. Pliny 1984, XXXV, p. 375.

12. Pliny 1984, XXXV, pp. 309–11.

13. Pliny 1984, XXXV, pp. 309–11; Villalón 1539 (edn 1898), p. 151.

14. Jan Bialostocki, 'The Renaissance Concept of Nature and Antiquity', in Bialostocki 1988, pp. 64–8. A *topos* of artistic thought was also that of the superiority of art over nature, still lifes could be seen as immortalising and surpassing the beauties of nature, as is made clear by a madrigal by Gregorio Comanini on the reverse of Figino's *Still Life with Peaches on a Plate* (fig. 2): 'Questi sì vaghi pomi/ non è d'arte fattura;/ che a far opre sì belle arte non vale./ Nè può tant'anni conservar natura/ frutto caduco e frale,/ che brevissimi giorni appena dura./ Ma questa è sol, Figin, forza o possanza/ del tuo stile immortale/ che l'arte vince e la natura avanza', see Ciardi 1968, pp. 104–5, and Zeri and Porzio 1989, I, pp. 220–1. Another poem by Comanini of 1594 celebrates the naturalism of

Figino's picture, see Zeri and Porzio 1989, I, p. 220.

15. It is not clear whether either Caravaggio's or Sánchez Cotán's still lifes were framed or displayed to exploit their illusionistic qualities. *Trompe l'oeil* was regarded as a demonstration of the artist's *ingenio*, or creative skill, and was often associated in the sixteenth century with paintings of fictive landscape views, see Marías 1989, pp. 579–80.

16. Dacos 1969. Pacheco 1649 (edn 1990, p. 113) notes the existence of ancient frescoes in Spain.

17. Dacos 1977; Dacos and Furlan 1987, pp. 61–93. For festoons as a precedent for still life, see Zeri and Porzio 1989, I, pp. 55–68. In manuscript illumination, *trompe l'oeil* flowers, fruit and dead animals are depicted in the margins of the pages of Books of Hours. They also appear on tapestry borders, which often include natural motifs, such as landscapes, flowers and baskets of fruit; in Spain these borders were called *verduras*. For manuscript margins, see Bergström 1956, pp. 30–2 and DaCosta Kaufmann 1993, pp. 11–48.

18. Ceán Bermúdez 1800, V, pp. 280, 288–92, 311–12. For Céspedes, see Angulo Iñiguez 1954a, pp. 310–14 and Brown 1991, p. 117.

19. For the garland image, see Freedberg 1981 and Jones 1993, pp. 84–7. The classical precedent for this type of painting, cited by Pacheco (1649, edn 1990, pp. 509–10), was the story of the painter Pausias Sconius' love of the garland maker Glisera, whom he painted weaving a garland. The story is the subject of a picture by Rubens and Osias Beert the Elder (Sarasota, The John and Mable Ringling Museum of Art).

20. Pacheco 1649 (edn 1990), p. 461. Writing in 1539, Cristóbal de Villalón (edn 1898, p. 170), says that Aquiles and Mayner 'hicieron obras al gentil y antigüedad', which were the most perfect of their time.

21. López Torrijos 1986.

22. 'su cuarto de las frutas [in the Alhambra]/ fresco, vistoso y notable,/ injuria de los pinceles/de Apeles y de Timantes/ donde tan bien las fingidas/ imitan las naturales,/ que no hay hombre a quien no burlen/ ni pájaro a quien no engañen', quoted in López Torrijos 1986, pp. 48–9.

23. For Mohedano, see Valdivieso and Serrera 1985, pp. 174–88. Pacheco 1649 (edn 1990), p. 511, particularly praises his festoons, now lost, in the cloister of the convent of San Francisco, Seville.

24. Pacheco 1649 (edn 1990), p. 461.

25. Brown and Kagan 1987, pp. 238, 251, VII, no. 1. Mohedano left Seville for Antequera in 1610.

26. See Madrid 1983, pp. 70, 79–82 for the tentative attribution to Mohedano. For the whole ceiling, Valdivieso and Serrera 1979, pp. 75–9.

27. Jordan (Fort Worth 1985, pp. 13–14) emphasised the classical dimension of this decoration and its relation to the comments of Pliny the Elder.

28. 'donde, en un aparador de vasos de plata vidrio y barro puso mucha diversidad de colaciones y otras frutas, y un frasco de cobre puesto en agua a enfriar, todo pintado con mucha destreza y propiedad. Pero hizo lo que no hacen otros pintores de frutas, que dio a las figuras igual valentía que a las demás cosas', Pacheco 1649 (edn 1990), pp. 511–12.

29. Pliny 1984, XXXV, pp. 309–11; Pacheco 1649 (edn 1990), p. 520.

30. This is the point of the story for Carducho, 1633 (edn 1979), pp. 197–8.

31. Pacheco 1649 (edn 1990), p. 521, cites the example of the *trompe l'oeil* vase in Pablo de Céspedes's *Last Supper* of 1595 (Córdoba, Cathedral), which attracted far more interest than the heads and hands of the sacred figures. The implication is that this kind of diversion can disturb the clarity of the doctrinal message of paintings.

32. Pacheco 1649 (edn 1990), p. 512.

33. Pacheco 1649 (edn 1990), p. 511. Elsewhere Pacheco speaks of 'puntual imitación', p. 512.

34. Quoted in Hibbard 1983, p. 83.

35. On flower paintings Pacheco says 'Y alguna vez se pueden divertir en ellas buenos pintores, aunque no con mucha gloria', (1649, edn 1990, p. 511) and speaking of paintings of dead game and still life objects: '... y todas estas cosas, hechas con valentía y buena manera, entretienen y muestran ingenio en la disposición y en la viveza' (p. 517).

36. Morán and Checa 1985.

37. Bergström 1956, pp. 40–1. On natural history and still life see G. Luther in Münster/Baden–Baden 1979, pp. 46–67 and G. Olmi in Zeri and Porzio 1989, I, pp. 69–91.

38. Morán and Checa 1985, p. 222; Cherry 1991, p. 30.

39. Checa 1992, pp. 245–9.

40. For exotica in Spanish collections, see Morán and Checa 1985, pp. 41–53, 129–38; for flora from the Indies planted in Spanish gardens, Morán

and Checa 1985, pp. 148–50. The 1623 inventory of Nicolas Morel in Seville listed 'tres liencos [sic] de frutas de indias', which had possibly been sent by his brother Francisco, who was a merchant living in Peru, Cherry 1991, p. 388, n. 21.

41. Jones 1988; Jones 1993, pp. 76–84. Caravaggio's *Supper at Emmaus* (London, National Gallery) contains a significant detail of surprising wit in the basket of fruit that casts a shadow in the shape of a fish, the emblem of Christ. This observation was made in conversation by Jennifer Fletcher of the Courtauld Institute of Art, London University.

42. 'cosas de cocina', Benito Domenech 1980, p. 174, no. 29. See p. 198, no. 306, for the archbishop's genre painting of 'una labradora en el mercado de jenova [Genoa]'.

43. Longhi and Mayer (1930, no. 65) were the first to explore the painting's 'spiritual' qualities, and the idea has most recently been restated by J. Baticle in Madrid 1988b, p. 91.

44. Gállego 1968, p. 195.

45. Denny 1972.

46. For the Carthusian rule regarding food, see Madariaga 1596, pp. 130–68. Also relevant in this context is a painting by Sánchez Cotán of the *Virgin and Child* at Guadix (Granada), destroyed in 1936, which represented a homely 'Carthusian' supper of cardoon, fruit and bread on a ledge in front of the Virgin, see Angulo Iñiguez and Pérez Sánchez 1972, no. 75, p. 77.

47. 'Dos bodegones grandes: Navidad y Cuaresma' are listed in the 1646 inventory of Don Alvaro de Posada y Mendoza, Agulló 1978, pp. 196–7. In the Seville collection of Cristóbal Coello in 1644 there were 'ocho fruteros de quaresma y carnal', Cherry 1991, p. 364, n. 53.

48. Bryson (1990, p. 66) sees an 'anorexic', monastic quality to Sánchez Cotán's depiction of foodstuffs, in which references to appetite and sustenance are suppressed by the artist. This idea is further developed by Taggard 1990.

49. See Diego de Granada's *Libro de arte de cozina*, Madrid 1599, and Francisco Martínez Montiño's *Arte de la cocina*, Madrid 1611, and for sweets, Juan Gracián's *Cuatro libros del arte de la confitería*, Alcalá 1592.

50. Jan Bialostocki, 'Books of Wisdom and Books of Vanity' in Bialostocki 1988, p. 47.

51. For the *Vanitas* in Spain, Gállego 1968, pp. 197–204. For the theme in general, C. Klemm, 'Weltdeutung–Allegorien und Symbole in Stilleben' in Munster/Baden-Baden 1979, pp. 191–218, and Caen 1990.

52. Marcos Villanueva 1973, pp. 232–3 and p. 234, n. 84.

53. Gállego 1968, pp. 198–9.

54. The cartellino in Alejandro de Loarte's *Poultry*

Vendor (fig. 44) bears a laurel-crowned skull, suggesting that the painter's fame will live on after his death, see Madrid 1983, pp. 38–9.

55. They are called 'Jeroglíficos de nuestras postrimerías' in 1672, Brown 1978, p. 136, n. 35c; Palomino (1715/24, edn 1947, p. 1053) called them 'Jeroglíficos del Tiempo y de la Muerte'. For these paintings in the context of the decorative programme of the church, see Brown 1978, pp. 128–46; Valdivieso and Serrera 1980. A *Vanitas* by Francisco Palacios (1622/5–52), tentatively identified in this catalogue with cat. 27, was called 'un geroglifico que significa el Desengaño del mundo', see catalogue entry.

56. In Calderón de la Barca's *El gran mercado del mundo* (edn E. Frutos Cortés, Madrid 1979, p. 131), Gluttony offers the World 'Pinturas que pintadas/ todas mis glorias son imaginadas'.

57. AHPM, leg. 1811, ff. 1494–1666, cited by Scroth in Fort Worth 1985, p. 29. Schroth believed that the earliest reference to still lifes was the group of nine pictures of *verduras* recorded in the collection of Don Alonso Téllez de Girón in 1590. These are more likely to have been landscape paintings.

58. 'otro quadro en q[ue] [h]ay fruta pintada de melon menbrillo [sic] granada çanaoria y Cardo', Schroth in Fort Worth 1985, p. 29. The picture hung beside a genre painting depicting fruit and vegetables and laughing figures (Otro quadro de pinturas de frutas melon datiles escarola y la rrisa y otras) in Loaysa's study with portraits of famous men, some religious subjects and sixty pieces of Valencian pottery painted with animal motifs. Loaysa's other still life is described in general terms, 'otra pintura en quadro de cossas de cocina y frutas'.

59. For Sandoval, who patronised leading Spanish artists and imported important Caravaggesque paintings by Carlo Saraceni, see Pérez Sánchez 1969.

60. No inventory of Sandoval's collection is known, but some of his pictures were later listed in the possession of Don Francisco de Oviedo, former gentleman of his chamber, and in other court collections. For Oviedo's inventory of 1663, see Barrio Moya 1979 and Burke 1984, pp. 16–22. Cherry (1991, pp. 306–7, nn. 21 and 22) cites an earlier Oviedo inventory, dated 3 March 1631. El Greco's pupil Luis Tristán appears to have been a favourite artist of Oviedo's and among the paintings by Tristán which he owned were a still life of fruit and an ironic self-portrait as a *picarón*.

61. The Duque de Lerma's still lifes were hung at his country estate of La Ribera at Valladolid. For still lifes which were kept in the country house near Baeza of Sandoval's *mayordomo*, Don Pedro Ocón in 1618, see Cherry 1991, p. 79.

62. Carducho (1633, edn 1979, p. 330) recommended landscapes, hunting scenes, animal paintings, pictures of birds, fish and fruit, views of cities and foreign parts and different regional costumes as appropriate decoration for a 'Casa de campo de recreación'.

63. Saltillo 1953, p. 168; Jordan 1967, I, p. 14; Schroth in Fort Worth 1985, p. 35.

64. For the inventory, see Fernández Bayton 1975–85, II, pp. 143–5. Cherry (1991) and Jordan (Madrid 1992) realised independently that the paintings were still *in situ* in 1701. Jordan (Madrid 1992, pp. 47–52) proposed the tentative identification of them with those in Sánchez Cotán's inventory.

65. Schroth in Fort Worth 1985, pp. 28–39.

66. Lerma owned seasonal still lifes and by 1603 he owned a large picture with 'mucha diversidad de frutas ... de Buena mano', and a small picture of 'Un Platillo de Fructas', which is reminiscent of contemporary Spanish and Lombard still lifes, see Schroth 1990.

67. Cherry 1991, p. 277, n. 61.

68. For a survey of still lifes in inventories of collections in Madrid before 1615, see Cherry 1991, pp. 30–2.

69. In 1628 the painter Pedro de San Martín agreed to paint fruit still lifes for 6 *reales*, flower pieces for 9 *reales*, and paintings of saints for 16 *reales* each; see Cherry 1991, pp. 502–3.

Sánchez Cotán and Still-Life Painting in Toledo around 1600

1. Sterling (1959, pp. 70–1), who wrote eloquently about the picture, found it difficult to understand the naturalism of Sánchez Cotán without the influence of Caravaggio.

2. For the best account of Sánchez Cotán's life and work, see Angulo Iñiguez and Pérez Sánchez 1972, pp. 39–102.

3. Sterling 1952 (English edn 1959), pp. 70–1; Orozco 1965, pp. 224–31; and, most recently, Bryson 1990, p. 66, are among those who take this point of view. A view of the paintings as largely profane works was proposed in Fort Worth 1985, pp. 43–63, and by Cherry 1991, pp. 33–67.

4. Orozco Díaz 1966.

5. Pacheco 1649 (edn 1990), p. 511.

6. On 13 December 1599, Dr Martín Ramírez de Zayas, a professor of theology at the University of Toledo, who had commissioned from El Greco a magnificent family chapel dedicated to Saint Joseph, signed a document settling on a payment of 2,850 ducats for the work. Of this amount, 636 ducats were to be paid to El Greco's creditors, among them Sánchez Cotán, who was owed 500 ducats. See Toledo 1982, p. 105.

7. For a discussion of El Greco's artistic ideas in relation to Italy see Marías and Bustamante 1981; Toledo 1982.

8. Excerpts from this document are published by Cavestany 1936–40, pp. 134–8.

9. Cherry 1991, p. 35.

10. Sánchez Cotán's inventory listed a few books related to his art, including the second part of Alonso de Villegas's *Flos sanctorum* (Toledo 1584), the standard lives of the Virgin and saints, and Jacopo Barozzi da Vignola's *Le due regole della prospettiva prattica* (Rome 1583), as well as a book of music. Vignola was a standard reference work for artists and appears in Valdés Leal's *Allegory of Vanity* (cat. 45).

11. Because Cavestany (1936–40, p. 70), in the context of a discussion of the documents, refers figuratively to the artist's still lifes as 'offerings to the Virgin' (ofrendas a la Virgen), many writers have propagated the notion that the artist gave everything to the church.

12. Cherry 1991, p. 283, n. 13.

13. The twelve entries in the inventory relating to Sánchez Cotán's still lifes are analysed and related to existing paintings in Fort Worth 1985, pp. 47–8, and Madrid 1992, pp. 41–2;

14. In 1614 one of the artist's clients, Don Antonio Manrique de Vargas, a knight of Calatrava, owned four small oil paintings of the Four Seasons, 'painted in the manner of fruits' (pintados a manera de frutas), but the author of these works is not specified. For details of this collection, see Cherry 1991, pp. 75, 304, nn. 7 and 8.

15. On Salazar de Mendoza as a collector, see Kagan 1984.

16. The inventory cites 'A primed canvas for a window' (Un lienzo emprimado para una ventana). The underlying plane of the window shelf, showing through some of the superimposed forms, can be seen with the naked eye.

17. Technical examination revealed that the artist achieved this rich blackness by first painting the background a dark grey mixed with an orange red. Over this he applied a glaze of black mixed with red lake, a practice still used by painters today to achieve intense black. Extremely vulnerable to cleaning solvents, this black glaze has been stripped from many Spanish still lifes. We are grateful to Yvonne Szafran, of the Paintings Conservation Department of the J. Paul Getty Museum, who cleaned the picture, for this insight.

18. Young (1976, pp. 204–5), made this point. Held (in Münster/Baden-Baden 1979, pp. 382–90) called it a *despensa*, a niche in a cellar which was used for the same purpose.

19. Soria (1945, pp. 225–30) first made this observation, which was taken up by Pérez Sánchez (Madrid 1983), who aptly related it to the Neo-Pythagorean preoccupations of the scholars and artists gathered around El Escorial at the time.

20. Bryson (1990, p. 65) writes eloquently about this aspect of Sánchez Cotán's style.

21. Gudiol (1977, pp. 311–18), was the first to identify this picture with the one mentioned in the artist's inventory.

22. Another entry in the inventory describes 'Two cartoons, one with a sandgrouse and another with two ducks' (Dos cartones uno con una ganga y otro con dos ánades). In addition to using cartoons, it is obvious that the artist copied motifs from one finished picture to another. None of the still lifes of which X-radiographs have been made reveals any pentimenti, indicating that they must have been painted after very careful preparation.

23. The inventory refers to the still life in the Piasecka Johnson collection (fig. 18) as: 'Another with a cardoon and a francolin' (Otro con un cardo y un francolin). In subsequently itemising the still life now in the Prado (cat. 3), however, it refers to 'Another picture of *the* cardoon' (Otro lienzo *del* cardo), implying that it was a recognisable design.

24. For a detailed discussion of this picture and its fragmentary state, see Jordan 1990, pp. 96–9; Madrid 1992, pp. 66–9.

25. This painting is a good example of how, in an old cleaning, the topmost glaze of black has been removed from the background, except around the francolin itself, where the black is much more intense than around the cardoon.

26. For a consideration of this series, see Angulo Iñiguez and Pérez Sánchez 1972, pp. 70–1, nos 31–46.

27. It is worth keeping in mind that Sánchez Cotán had a number of relatives who were artists active in Toledo. One of them was Juan Gómez Cotán (documented as a painter in Toledo from 1603 until at least 1631), to whom Sánchez Cotán, in his testament, gave four cases of colours, models and materials, as well as five of his paintings, including his *Bearded Woman of Peñaranda (Brígida del Río)* (fig. 17). For full bibliography on Gómez Cotán's activity and his relations with Luis Tristán, see Cherry 1991, p. 294, n. 5.

28. A related still life of somewhat weaker execution, recently on the Madrid art market, depicts the very same basket of apples at the right. The other elements in the composition, including a vase of flowers in place of the fish, are different, however, although they are organised in a similar fashion within a window frame.

29. A contemporary copy, similar in its execution to the one mentioned in the previous note, is to be found in another private collection in Madrid.

30. The 1603 inventory describes the composition thus: 'A canvas with a hamper of cherries and a little basket of apricots' (Un lienzo de un zenacho de Zerezas y cestilla de Albarcoques [sic]). The painting was probably the one described in the royal collection in 1701: 'A small fruit still life with a basket of apricots' (Un fruttero pequeño con Un Cesto de albaricoques...). See Fort Worth 1985, p. 48, and Madrid 1992, pp. 42–3, 51–2, for a detailed discussion of this work and the various copies of it.

31. Space does not permit the reproduction of the other two works, but parallels with the still lifes of Sánchez Cotán exist in both of them as well.

32. For detailed cataloguing of this picture, see Madrid 1992, pp. 82–4.

33. For a discussion of everything known about Ramírez, see Angulo Iñiguez and Pérez Sánchez 1972, pp. 107–8.

Velázquez and the *Bodegón*

1. Pacheco 1649 (edn 1990), p. 202: '...después de cinco años de educación y enseñanza casé con mi hija, movido de su virtud, limpieza y buenas partes, y de las esperanzas de su natural y grande ingenio', quoted in translation from Harris 1982, p. 191.

2. The earliest dated use of this term is found in the descriptions of two Flemish paintings of edibles and human figures given by Philip II to El Escorial in 1593, Zarco Cuevas 1930, p. 93, nos 1494 and 1496.

3. Pacheco 1649 (edn 1990), pp. 407, 519. Sterling 1959, p. 39, notes that the humanist Hadrianus Junius likened Pieter Aertsen to Peiraikos in his *Batavia* (Antwerp 1588).

4. Pacheco 1649 (edn 1990), p. 519: '¿Los bodegones no se deben estimar? Claro está que sí, si son pintados como mi yerno los pinta alzándose con esta parte sin dexar lugar a otro, y merecen estimación grandísima; pues con estos principios y los retratos...halló la verdadera imitación del natural alentando los ánimos de muchos con su poderoso exemplo...', quoted in translation from Harris 1982, p. 194. Apart from copies and pastiches after Velázquez, only one signed response of the sort Pacheco alluded to is known: *Boy in a Kitchen* (fig. 73) by Francisco López Caro (1598–1661), published by Harris 1935, pp. 258–9. This painting may derive from a lost *bodegón* described by Palomino 1715/24 (edn 1947), p. 893.

5. Carducho 1633 (edn 1979), pp. 338–9: 'cuadros de bodegones con baxos y vilisimos pensamientos ... sin mas ingenio, ni mas asunto, de aversele antojado al Pintor retratar quatro picaros descompuestos, y dos mugercillas desaliñadas , en mengua del mismo Arte, y poca reputacion del Artifice'. This passage is usually considered an attack on the naturalistic painting of Velázquez, Carducho's main rival at court. Pacheco (1649, edn 1990, p. 407) himself admitted that painters could excel in genre ('fish paintings, *bodegones*, animals, fruit and landscapes'), but should also 'aspire to greater things'.

6. Pacheco 1649 (edn 1990), p. 519: '...pinté un lencecillo con dos figuras del natural, flores y frutas y otros juguetes ... y conseguí lo que bastó para que las demás cosas de mi mano pareciesen delante dél pintadas.'

7. Schroth (in Fort Worth 1985, pp. 31–4) explores and documents this.

8. See Kusche 1964, p. 231, for three *bodegones de Italia* which the royal painter Juan Pantoja de la Cruz painted for Agustín de Toledo, a member of the Council of Indies, in 1592. For Campi's paintings in Spain, see Fort Worth 1985, p. 33.

9. Pacheco's treatise quotes liberally from the first edition of Van Mander's *Het Schilder Boeck* (Haarlem 1604), the second part of which is devoted to biographies of Flemish and German painters. See Bassegoda i Hugas in Pacheco 1649 (edn 1990), pp. 33, 343 n. 7. Van Mander's account emphasises Aertsen and Beuckelaer's early mastery of their art in working from nature, and, in the case of the latter, stresses the danger of undervaluing genre painting.

10. Brown and Kagan 1987, p. 250, III, no. 33, for an unframed 'lienco grande de diversos pescados de mano de Pedro Longo'. Cherry 1991, p. 382, n. 43, notes that Aertsen's Italian nickname, Pietro Lungo, was used here.

11. Bergström 1970, p. 56, brought this painting into the discussion of Velázquez's *bodegones*. For Flemish collections in Seville, see Cherry 1991, p. 195.

12. '... más quería ser primero en aquella grosería que segundo en la delicadeza.' Palomino 1715/24 (edn 1947), pp. 893–4, probably extrapolated Velázquez's supposed antipathy to Raphael from G.B. Bellori's life of Caravaggio in his *Vite de' pittori scultori ed architetti moderni*, Rome 1672.

13. Van Mander emphasised Caravaggio's radical artistic independence and characterised him as a painter who 'will not make a single brushstroke without the close study of life, which he copies and paints', Hibbard 1983, pp. 343–5.

14. Cherry 1991, pp. 357–8, documents examples of these.

15. The depiction of smiling and laughing faces was long considered a difficult artistic challenge. Pacheco (1649, edn 1990, pp. 527–8) relates how Velázquez drew from a young model, laughing and crying, which was excellent training in the depiction of emotions.

16. López-Rey 1963, pp. 159–60, nos 110–12.

17. López-Rey 1963, pp. 160–1, nos 114–18.

18. A painting described as '*Un picaro*' was inventoried in the collection of a Madrid surgeon, Juan de San Vicente, in 1616. Two years later the same picture was described as representing a kitchen hand (un rretrato de un picaro de cocina). This collector's library included Cervantes's *Don Quixote*, two copies of Mateo Alemán's picaresque novel *Guzmán de Alfarache* (1599/1604) and Francisco López de Ubeda's *La pícara Justina* (1605), Cherry 1991, pp. 360–1, n.38.

19. Kahr 1976, pp. 18–19, related the Russian picture to an episode from *Lazarillo*. Many critics have thought the old man blind, recalling Lazarillo's notorious first master; however, the figure's eye is open.

20. For Paleotti, see Wind 1974; for G.B. Lomazzo (1584) on these subjects, see Meijer 1971. Campi's *Cheese Eaters* (Madrid, Prado) was listed in the Madrid Alcázar in 1666 (Pérez Sánchez 1967, p. 311). A painting of the same subject was inventoried in a Madrid collection as early

as 1616 (Cherry 1991, p. 357, n. 24). For at least four versions of the work, see Bocchi and Spike 1992, pp. 24–7, no. 1.

21. See Miedema 1977, for the peasant satirised in painting. For a contrasting interpretation, see Alpers 1972–3; Alpers 1975–6.

22. Wind 1987, pp. 81–94, exaggerates this dimension of Velázquez's pictures.

23. Braham 1965, pp. 362–5. Gállego 1968, p. 252, called these 'bodegones a lo divino'.

24. See Mann Phillips 1967, p. 42: '*Ollas ostentare*' (to make a show of kitchen pots). See also Moxey 1971, pp. 335–6.

25. From 1618, the year in which Velázquez painted *Kitchen Scene with Christ in the House of Martha and Mary*, Pacheco served as artistic censor (veedor de pinturas sagradas) for the Seville Tribunal of the Inquisition. We do not know what he thought about his son-in-law's moralised *bodegones*, because he is silent on the subject. We do, however, know how Carducho felt about them: 'Tambien es justo se repare en otras Pinturas de devocion, pintadas con tanta profanidad, y desacato, que apenas se conoce: y vi los dias pasados pintada aquella santa visita de Christo a las hermanas de Lazaro, la devota Madalena [Mary Magdalene], y la solicita Marta, cercados todos con tanta prevencion de comida, de carnero, capones, pavos, fruta, platos, y otros instrumentos de cocina, que mas parecia hosteria de la gula, que hospicio de santidad, y de cuidadosa fineza, y me espanto de la poca cordura del Pintor, que tal obra saca de su idea y manos', Carducho 1633 (edn 1979), pp. 350–1.

26. For the importance of volume (relievo) in painting, see Pacheco 1649 (edn 1990), pp. 123, 404–7. In the context of the *paragone* debate between the relative merits of painting and sculpture, Pacheco (pp. 94–142) discusses at length ways in which paintings on a flat surface can achieve effects of volume and lifelikeness.

27. Pliny (edn 1984), p. 299; and see Pacheco 1649 (edn 1990), pp. 104–6, 499–500. Pliny (p. 329) emphasises the illusionistic effects in a painting of Alexander painted in this way by Apelles.

28. Pacheco 1649 (edn 1990), p. 519.

29. Pacheco 1649 (edn 1956), I, p. xxxii.

Van der Hamen and Still-Life Painting in Castile

1. For literary references to Van der Hamen, see Jordan 1967, pp. 307–21. An extensive monograph on the artist by William B. Jordan is in preparation and is scheduled for publication by the Yale University Press in late 1996.

2. Jordan 1967, pp. 21–30, 80–91, 107; see also Fort Worth 1985, pp. 103–5, 116–17, for Van der Hamen's literary circle and his portraits of per-

sonas ilustres. Van der Hamen was the only artist mentioned in Montalbán's *Indice*, which was otherwise clearly limited to men of letters.

3. For these paintings, see Fort Worth 1985, pp. 121, 144–6.

4. Lope de Vega's sonnets are reproduced in Fort Worth 1985, pp. 104, 122.

5. For some details of Van der Hamen's family, see Jordan 1967, pp. 163–75. The forthcoming monograph (see note 1 above) will document the family history in detail.

6. Cherry 1991, p. 130–1.

7. Martín González 1958, p. 59.

8. It is worth noting, however, that González himself may occasionally have painted still lifes, since four 'lienços pequeños de frutas' were listed in his death inventory by Antonio de Lanchares (Cherry 1993, p. 6). Moreover, the unpublished death inventory (1630) of Lanchares himself, who won the competition for the post of the king's salaried painter, lists appreciable numbers of still lifes and flower paintings, some of which were unfinished at the time of his death.

9. Pacheco 1649 (edn 1990), p. 512: 'Juan de Vanderramen las [flores] hizo extremadamente, y mejor los dulces, aventájandose en esta parte a las figuras y retratos que hacía y, así, esto le dio, a su despecho, mayor nombre'.

10. Brown 1991, p. 140.

11. Cardinal Barberini first sat to Van der Hamen on 28 July 1626, and the portrait was finished in a second sitting on 1 August, during which the artist's brother Lorenzo, a distinguished literary figure in Madrid, presented some of his books to the legate and read extracts from his forthcoming biography of Don Juan de Austria. Van der Hamen's picture caused Cassiano to compare it favourably to the 'melancholy and severe air' (aria malinconica e severa) of Velázquez's portrait of the legate, see Harris 1970, p. 364; Fort Worth 1985, pp. 117–19.

12. For these, see Tormo 1917, pp. 131–4; Jordan 1967, pp. 119–43; Ruiz Alcón 1977, pp. 29–36; Fort Worth 1985, pp. 114–15. It may be significant that the royal architect, Juan Gómez de Mora, who was responsible for the Encarnación and its pictorial decoration (Madrid 1986b, pp. 103–4, 246, n. 83), was a friend of the artist, who painted his portrait (Jordan 1967, p. 365, no.131).

13. Van der Hamen married Eugenia de Herrera in the parish church of San Ginés (*Libro de matrimonios*, 7 March 1615, fol. 330); the marriage was confirmed (*velado*) in the parish of San Sebastián (*Libro de matrimonios* 3, 22 November 1615, fol. 392v), when the groom was called a painter (Cherry 1991, p. 458). The reason for the long delay between the marriage and the confirmation (instead of the usual three weeks) was that the young artist, as he stated in his petition to marry (Jordan 1967, p. 176–83), had to leave Madrid for professional reasons. He may well have gone abroad.

14. Van der Hamen received 100 *reales* on 10 September 1619, for 'un lienço de frutas y caça'. Saltillo 1953, p. 168. See Madrid 1992, pp. 47–52, for the court architect Juan Gómez de Mora's role in this decoration.

15. Jordan (1964–5, p. 53–4) questioned Palomino's assertion that Van der Hamen studied with his father, mistakenly believed by Palomino to have been a painter from Flanders; he likewise questioned the supposed Flemish roots of Van der Hamen's style. See Fort Worth 1985, pp. 107–9, 125–8, for Van der Hamen's still lifes in a Flemish mode.

16. Robels 1989, p. 263, no. 128, pointed out that Snyders's still life was Van der Hamen's prototype.

17. Van der Hamen received 3,000 *reales* for these pictures, paid in two instalments on 18 August and 14 November 1629. Jordan 1967, II, pp. 260, 268.

18. Volk 1981, pp. 526–9.

19. Volk 1981, p. 526, 'Otros dos quadros de pintura al olio ... el uno bara y media de alto y en el esta pintado un frutero grande de frutas y flores y un muchacho desnudo que las tiene – el otro de tres baras de largo y de ancho tres quartas poco mas o menos en que esta un feston de todas flores y frutas y tres muchachos desnudos que las dos de ellos le tienen y el otro encima y en medio con un paxaro en la mano hizquierda – estos hizo Balderamen para esta pieça' (1636, Madrid Alcázar inventory).

20. Orso 1993, pp. 152–7, no. 17.

21. For Van der Hamen still lifes in collections at court, see Cherry 1991, pp. 142–53.

22. For the importation of exotica from Mexico, see Aguiló Alonso, 'El coleccionismo de objetos procedentes de ultramar a través de los inventarios de los siglos XVI y XVII', in Arias Anglés et al., 1990, pp. 129–30; Seseña, 'El búcaro de "Las Meninas"', in *Velázquez y el arte de su tiempo*, 1991, pp. 39–48.

23. Whole sets of still lifes by Van der Hamen are documented in his studio inventory and in contemporary collections, see Jordan 1967. Popular demand for his paintings necessitated studio intervention and led to a market for imitations, see Fort Worth 1985, p. 113.

24. Jordan 1967, pp. 373–4. Although described in documents, no paintings by Van der Hamen in these formats are known.

25. Both Longhi (1950, p. 39) and Sterling (1952, p. 66) note the similarity between this arrangement and the frescoed still lifes from classical antiquity. Although the examples we know today were not discovered until the eighteenth century, some antiquarians may have known of others. It is perhaps significant in this regard that the visit to Madrid of Cassiano dal Pozzo, the most learned antiquarian of his time, coincided exactly with the year in which Van der Hamen first adopted this format. Contemporary Neapolitan still lifes in a similar

format exist, suggesting a possible common source, see Fort Worth 1985, pp. 132–3.

26. For Lope's sonnet in praise of the artist's flowers, see Fort Worth 1985, p. 122; Pacheco 1649 (edn 1990), p. 511.

27. Jordan 1967, pp. 373–4.

28. Valued highly (2,400 *reales*) in the 1638 Solre inventory, the paintings were described as: 'Dos quadros de dos diosas una de flores, y otro de fructas que tienen de cayda tres varas poco mas o menos y de ancho dos Varas menos sesma poco mas o menos'; they were sold on 29 December 1638 to Bartolomé Barrilaro, in whose death inventory of 1651 (Agulló 1981, pp. 210–11) they no longer appeared, Cherry 1991, p. 135. The *Offering to Flora* has been reduced slightly in size.

29. Pérez de Montalván 1633, fol. 1!r: '...que si viviera, fuera el mayor Español he huviera avido de su Arte'.

30. For the dowry Loarte received see Méndez Casal 1934, p. 202. Loarte married María del Corral, the young widow of a court notary, in the Madrid parish of San Sebastián on 27 June 1619 (Madrid, Parroquia de San Sebastián, *Libro de matrimonios* 4, fol. 171).

31. Loarte's *Miracle of the Loaves and Fishes* was recently rediscovered. The signature and date that Ceán Bermúdez (1800, III, pp. 42–3) saw on the painting have been removed.

32. Loarte is last documented in Madrid on 2 August 1620, when he valued the pictures in the estate partition of one Antonio de Heredia (AHPM, Prot. 5158, fols 116v–18v). He is first documented in Toledo on 13 February 1624, when he took as an apprentice Francisco de Molina (AHPT, Prot. 3092, fols 177–8v; Marías 1978, p. 422). Loarte's move may have been due to family connections, since a number of individuals with his surname were living in Toledo at the time (Cherry 1991, p. 296, n. 2).

33. Loarte drew up his last will and testament on 9 December 1626 (Méndez Casal 1934, pp. 188–91) and died on 13 December (Toledo, Parroquia de Santos Justo y Pastor, *Libro de difuntos* 3, fol. 121v). His estate was valued on 17 December (Méndez Casal 1934, pp. 191–4).

34. For Loarte's religious paintings, see Angulo Iñiguez and Pérez Sánchez 1972, pp. 212–21; Toledo 1982, p. 171, no. 141; Noval Mas 1984. In 1625 Loarte signed a contract for 550 *reales* for a painting of the Martyrdom of Saint Catherine for the parish church of Bórox (AHPT, Prot. 2490, fol. 564; Cherry 1991, p. 440), which was found still *in situ* by Mazón de la Torre (1977, pp. 85–6).

35. Méndez Casal 1934, p. 194; 'un lienco de una despensa', which was, however, worth only eight *reales*.

36. Méndez Casal 1934, pp. 188–9, figs 1 and 2. Jordan examined these paintings several times in the 1960s and 1970s in the Casa Torres collection, Madrid. Their exact location is unknown today.

37. The latter painting is also close in the details of its execution to the Várez Fisa *Kitchen Still Life*, but, being unlined and on its original stretcher, it is much better preserved. It is the pendant of a symmetrical fruit still life of identical dimensions, which disposes the composition on a simple stone ledge with no background scene. The close-up focus on the hanging birds makes one wonder if the painting has been trimmed around the edges, but the original tacking edge of the canvas, still intact on this work and its pendant, confirms that this is not the case.

38. For this picture, published by Méndez Casal (1934, p. 196), and a complete bibliography see Fort Worth 1985, pp. 99–102.

39. Pérez Sánchez in Madrid 1983, p. 38. Loarte's inventory listed five portraits of unidentified 'famous painters' and six paintings of the Liberal Arts, images suggestive of his concern for the humanistic dimension of the art of painting.

40. Méndez Casal 1934, pp. 188–9: 'Una gallinera firmada de mi nombre'. The clause of Loarte's will detailing business with Martínez Heredia shows that the latter commissioned portraits of himself, his wife and his children, owned a large painting of *Judith* by Loarte, a small, signed fruit still life (liencecito con su quadro dorado de frutas firmado de my nombre) and a pair with cardoons (dos liencos de dos fruteros de cardos); he had also ordered a set of eight fruit still lifes (liencos de frutas) at an agreed price of 60 *reales* each. These were worth more than the still lifes in the inventory, valued for as little as four *reales* each. In his transcription of Loarte's will, Méndez Casal omitted to mention the two still lifes with cardoons. Martínez Heredia's profession is not specified in the documents.

41. For the erotic significance of female poultry vendors in paintings by Bartolomeo Passerotti, see Wind 1974, p. 31; London, Matthiesen Gallery, *Around 1610: The Onset of the Baroque*, 1985, no. 2.

42. In 1603 in Valladolid, Juan de Espinosa was among a number of painters who received money from Vicente Carducho (Martí y Monsó 1898–1901, p. 606). In 1606, Juan de Espinosa signed a receipt for the dowry of his wife Ana Aguado (AHPM, Prot. 1331, unpaginated; Matilla Tascón and Martín Ortega 1983, p. 221).

43. Espinosa attended a meeting of the chapter of the Cofradía del Sacramento of the Madrid parish of San Sebastián on 16 October 1611 (Madrid, Parroquia de San Sebastián, *Libro de entradas de cofrades del Santísimo* 12, fols 31–2v) and is cited as a brother in the following year (Agulló Cobo 1981, p. 77). On 28 August 1613 he rented a property in Madrid and was called 'pintor y pintor del sr. duq del ynfantado' in the document (AHPM, Prot. 1459, fols 530–530v). For a signed portrait of Don Iñigo López de Mendoza, 2nd Conde de Tendilla and an ancestor of the Duque del Infantado, see Gutiérrez Pastor 1988, p. 212. This picture is probably identifiable with one previously recorded at the Infantado palace, Guadalajara, by Barcia 1898, p. 36.

44. Harris 1967a; Gutiérrez García-Brazales 1982, pp. 215, 335, 338, for documentation of Espinosa's work for the Consejo de la Gobernación del Arzobispado. He is recorded as dying in the course of work for the church of Lugar Nuevo.

45. Cherry 1991, p. 452.

46. In a document of 26 September 1620, Espinosa gave his age as thirty-five. See Marías 1978, p. 426.

47. See Cavestany 1936–40, p. 154, cats 27 and 28, pl. XXII. Both paintings appear to be severely cropped around the edges. See Madrid 1983, p. 58, no. 31, for discussion of the unsigned painting.

Madrid: Barrera, Ponce, Labrador

1. See Brown and Elliott 1980, pp.105–40, especially p. 118, for the decoration of the Buen Retiro Palace and its effect on collectors.

2. For Merchant de la Cerda's collection, see Agulló 1981, pp. 213–16. The inventory of Soria Arteaga's collection will be published shortly by Burke and Cherry (Getty Provenance Index). He owned still lifes by Van der Hamen, Labrador, Espinosa, Ponce, Francisco de Rómulo and Pietro Paolo Bonzi.

3. Illustrative of the activities of these minor and often anonymous painters is a document concerning Juan de Argüelles, a picture dealer (tratante en pinturas). An inventory of his stock in 1634 was listed no fewer than twenty-eight dozen fruit and flower paintings, as well as paintings of heads: 'Veinte y ocho docenas de lienços ordinarios pintados de diferentes [sic] Los unos de frutas y otros de rramilletes y otras cavecas pintadas que por ser todas de un precio se ponen todas juntas Y son de tres quartas de largo y media bara de ancho...excepto la una docena que son los doce meses del año que son de bara de largo', AHPM, Prot. 6439, fol. 1444; Cherry 1991, p. 404, n. 13. Another case in point is that of the painter Pedro de San Martín, who on 1 July 1628 agreed to a piece-rate contract to paint fruit still lifes for six *reales*, flowerpieces for nine *reales* and paintings of saints for sixteen *reales* each, AHPM, Prot. 3987, ff. 696–9. Cherry 1991, pp. 502–3.

4. Palomino (1715/24, edn 1947, pp. 161–2) acknowledged Barrera's successful lawsuit of 1639–40. Barrera owed 800 *reales* in 1 per cent sales tax on his work for 1636–7, the highest amount among the artists listed in a document of 1638 (Gállego 1976, p. 256). For further documentation on Barrera's career, see Fort Worth 1985, pp. 183–4; Cherry 1991, pp. 489–501.

5. Barrera signed in 1633 a rental agreement for the two shops on the corner of the street now called Travesía del Arenal (Gállego 1976, p. 224). However, he had probably opened his shop much earlier, since he was living at the same address in 1625; he was still there in 1644.

6. Carducho 1683 (edn 1979), p. 440.

7. Don Miguel Ibañez, *Capellan* of the Council of the Inquisition, declared he had seen the paintings 'a la puerta de un pintor q vive enfrente de san Felipe'. Ibañez did not know Barrera's name, but said he was fat and of medium height (es un hombre gordo de mediana estatura). Later in the document (in which concern was expressed at the names of the angels written on the pictures), the offender is identified as Barrera. AHN, Inquisición leg. 4456, no. 14; Paz y Mélia 1947, p. 135, no. 373.

8. *Varia Velazqueña* 1960, II, doc. 53, pp. 236–7.

9. Although uncreative, this decorative work appears to have been lucrative; Brown and Elliott 1980, pp. 205, 210, 212–13; Agulló 1978, pp. 28; Agulló 1981, p. 164. For Ponce's decorative painting in 1649, see Saltillo 1947b, pp. 378–9; Agulló 1978, pp. 130–1.

10. Madrid 1983, pp. 64–6; Fort Worth 1985, pp. 185–7.

11. This subject matter is documented from the beginning of Barrera's career. In 1623 he painted for the Conde de Montalbán twelve landscapes and twelve fruit still lifes, which may have had a seasonal theme (Cherry 1991, p. 490). The artist received relatively little money (757 *reales*) for the twenty-four paintings.

12. For other still lifes by Barrera, see Fort Worth 1985, pp. 183–90.

13. Ponce, the son of Francisco Ponce, a servant of the Duque de Peñaranda, and Antonia de Villalobos, was born at Valladolid in 1608. His baptism was confirmed in Madrid on 15 August 1609 (Madrid, Parroquia de San Juan, *Libro de bautismos* 3, *Confirmaciones* fol. 47v), and his death certificate was signed on 13 December 1677 (Madrid, Parroquia de San Ginés, *Libro de difuntos* 11, fol. 145v). On 26 October 1624, Antonia, by this date widowed, apprenticed her seventeen-year-old son to Van der Hamen for three years (AHPM, Prot. 1465, fols 245v–6). Ponce married Van der Hamen's niece Francisca de Alfaro on 10 December 1628 (Madrid, Parroquia de San Ginés, *Libro de matrimonios* 5, fol. 33v), and thus the older artist became his uncle. For Ponce's family connections and a review of his life and work, see Fort Worth 1985, pp. 171–3; Cherry 1991, pp. 504–12.

14. For *May* and *September* in this series, see Fort Worth 1985, pp. 173–4, figs. IX.1–2. *November* was offered at Sotheby's Peel, Madrid, 18 May 1993, lot 11; *December* is in a private collection, Madrid.

15. See Fort Worth 1985, pp. 177–8, no. 29, where three of these are reproduced. Doubt as to whether the date on the Strasbourg picture should be read as 1630 or 1650 was resolved during the exhibition in Fort Worth in 1985. Two similar paintings were offered by Sotheby's Peel, Madrid, 27 October 1992, lot 5.

16. Ponce may have found it increasingly difficult to sell his work. His widow, Francisca de Alfaro, drew up a declaration of poverty some two weeks after his death (AHPM, Prot. 12.472, f. 124, 30 December 1678) and was buried as a pauper in 1685 (Madrid, Parroquia de San Ginés, *Libro de difuntos* 12, fol. 19v, 22 March 1685), Cherry 1991, pp. 511–12.

17. The date of Espinosa's marriage is deduced from information in the will of his wife Ana de Roa in 1640 (AHPM, Prot. 5530, fols 709–11). One of her executors was the picture dealer Juan de Argüelles (see note 3 above).

18. Espinosa witnessed the dowry agreement of Burgos Mantilla on 22 June 1645 (Agulló 1978, pp. 183–4) and his marriage three days later (Madrid, Parroquia de San Juan, *Libro de Matrimonios* 1, fol. 251v). He is last documented in Madrid when he signed the will of the painter Pedro Núñez del Valle in 1659 (Agulló 1978, pp. 117–18). The hypothetical identification of this Juan de Espinosa with an artist of the same name who was involved in the lawsuit of the Cofradía Real de Nuestra Señora de los Siete Dolores in 1677 (cf. Fort Worth 1985, p. 165; Gutiérrez Pastor 1988, pp. 214–15) is untenable. The latter artist gave his age as thirty when he signed a collection inventory on 11 January 1678 (AHPM, Prot. 8181, unpaginated; estate of Juana de Heras). The same artist, whose signature is different from that of the still-life painter, also signed picture valuations in 1672 and 1675, Cherry 1991, p. 408, n. 36.

19. Jordan (Fort Worth 1985, p. 166) noted that Espinosa's *Still Life with Dead Finch* (Madrid, Prado) was in the collection of the Marqués de Eliche in 1651.

20. For both these works, see Fort Worth 1985, pp. 167–70.

21. It is worth noting that the fifteen paintings by Espinosa in the collection of Don Francisco Merchant de la Cerda in 1662 included a still life of flowers (lienzo de flores), a painting with fish (vnos pezes y otras cossas) and six *bodegones*. Agulló 1981, pp. 213–16.

22. The most common meaning of the word *labrador* today is someone who farms the land, which the artist could, of course, also have done. However, he appears to have painted for a living, and it is more likely that his nickname corresponds to the third definition of 'labrador' in the *Diccionario de autoridades*, published by the Real Academia Española, Madrid 1732, III : 'Signifying every man or woman who lives in a small village or hamlet, even though he does not cultivate the land'. It was pointed out by Jordan (1967, pp. 34–5) that the artist is referred to as 'el labrador de las nabas [sic]' in the inventory of the Marqués de Leganés (1655). Pérez Sánchez (Madrid 1983, p. 43) thought this might refer to the place called Las Navas del Marqués (Avila). Twice in the year 1660 he is called 'el Labrador de las navas', once in the death inventory of Ramiro de Quiñones (AHPM, Prot. 6689, ff.1080v–3, 18 February 1660) and again when the picture dealer Francisco Berjés, father-in-law of Francisco de Palacios, bought from the same estate the following: 'Un quadrito de barroz y bidrios Y mas otros dos de el Labrador de las navas todo ello en quin.tos Y cinquenta R.s que fue su tassa' (ibid., f.1122v, 3 March 1660).

Rather than referring to a specific place, it is more likely that 'Las navas', which literally means 'the plains', was intended in a more generally descriptive way, as, in English, it is said that someone from the country is from 'the sticks'.

23. The effort to link Labrador with a real farmer named Juan Fernández living outside Madrid is not convincing (see Nottingham 1981, p. 26, which cites the document published by Agulló 1978, p. 182).

24. Trapier (1967) published the correspondence of Labrador's English patrons that documented his activity in the 1630s, and Valdivieso (1972) published the *Vase of Flowers*, which gave Labrador's full name and the date 1636. Harris (1974) documented Arthur Hopton's encouragement of Labrador's flower paintings in 1635. For a study of what is known about the artist and his paintings to date, see Fort Worth 1985, pp. 147–63.

25. For four landscapes, see note 30 below. In 1670, Antonio Pereda valued eight religious subjects by him in the collection of a silversmith Alonso González: 'Eight paintings of the holy scripture by the Labrador, one *vara* more or less wide, with black frames' (ocho Pinturas de la sagrada escritura del Labrador de Una Vara Poco mas o menos de largo Con marcos negros), worth 100 *reales* each. AHPM, Prot. 8142, unpaged, 7 January 1670; Cherry 1991, 417, n. 28.

26. Lord Cottington referred to Labrador as 'the poore fellow', perhaps suggesting the artist's lowly class or fairly abject circumstances. Hopton, in letters from Madrid to Cottington in London in 1632 and 1633, speaks of Labrador's irregular and overdue visits to Madrid with his pictures, and in an undated letter, probably of 1633, writes '...the Labrador never comes hither but about Easter...' (Trapier 1967, pp. 239–42). Pérez Sánchez (Madrid 1983, p. 43), related Labrador's preference for the country to Antonio de Guevara's *Menosprecio de corte y alabanza de aldea* (Scorn of the court and praise of the village) of 1539, a theme which informs Golden Age writing. Indeed, in his life of the artist Palomino said he grew the things he painted, and may have called him 'Juan Labrador' after the noble rustic character in Lope de Vega's *El villano en su rincón*.

27. This artist was nicknamed *dei Crescenzi* because of his close association with the Crescenzi family; see Pérez Sánchez 1964a and Seville 1973, nos 18–20.

28. For Crescenzi's still life given to the king, see Baglione 1642 (edn 1935), p. 365; Díaz del Valle 1657–9 (edn 1933), pp. 347–8; Palomino 1715 (edn 1947), p. 890; Ceán Bermúdez 1800, I, p. 373. Pacheco (1649, edn 1990, p. 206) names Crescenzi as one of the judges of the competition held between royal painters for a painting of the *Expulsion of the Moriscos*, and says he was 'of great knowledge about painting' (de gran conocimiento en la pintura). See also Carducho 1633 (edn 1979), p. 421; Brown and Elliott 1980, pp. 44–5. No still lifes have been convincingly attributed to Crescenzi; for a review of attempts to do so, see Zeri and Porzio, II, 1989, pp. 675–6, 710.

29. For Crescenzi's academy, see Grelle 1961. For

Bonzi, see Zeri and Porzio, II, 1989, pp. 678–81, 698–701. Pérez Sánchez (Madrid 1983, p. 49, no. 14) suggested that *Kitchen Scene* (Ávila, Palacio de los Aguila), possibly an early work by Bonzi painted *c*.1606, came to Spain with Crescenzi.

30. See Sainsbury 1859, pp. 354–5, for a list of pictures offered to Charles I by Crescenzi, including 'Four landscape pieces of Labrador'. Shakeshaft (1981, pp. 550–1) showed that the note dates from 1630; Crescenzi's original Spanish reads, 'Quatro piecas de Vicas del mano del Labrador'. They appear to have remained in Crescenzi's collection and were inventoried with his pictures in 1635 as 'quatro Payses de a dos tercias de ancho y media bara de alto con sus molduras negras'.

31. Some forty pictures from Crescenzi's estate, including copies after Titian, a picture of *Christ* by Rubens and a *David* by Ribera, were transferred for safekeeping to the painter Francisco Gómez on 12 October 1635, in a document witnessed by Antonio de Pereda. AHPM, Prot. 6385, fols 451–2v (Cherry 1991, pp. 516–18). Further goods, books and pictures were inventoried on 12 May 1637 (AHPM, Prot. 6387, fols 180–5v; Cherry 1991, p. 516). Among the pictures listed in the 1635 inventory were three fruit still lifes, a picture of fish and a still life with glasses and vessels (bidrios y bucaros). One of the fruit still lifes had been borrowed from the royal collection for Crescenzi to frame (un lienço de frutas Granadas y benbrillos [sic] y ubas con su moldura negra que ... la avia traido El marq.s de palazio a Echar moldura). The only attributed still life was 'un liençecito pequeño de un plato de ubas de El labrador'.

32. First suggested by Pérez Sánchez in Madrid 1983, p. 44.

33. See note 2 above. Soria Arteaga's collection was valued by Francisco de Burgos Mantilla. Two of the paintings were described as follows: 'otro lienço de Ubas del Labrador mas pequeño Con una moldura ondeada de evano (350 reales), otro lienço algo mayor q los de ariba con un gajo grande de Ubas moradas q no tiene marco y no es del Labrador (50 reales)'. From an earlier undated inventory of Soria Arteaga's capital, we learn that after his marriage he exchanged a *Repentant Magdalen* for the single small painting of grapes by Labrador and the one by Bonzi, called by a garbled form of his nickname, 'the hunchback of Naples' (*el Corcobado de napoles*).

34. See, for example, the inventory of Merchant de la Cerda (Agulló 1981, p. 215).

35. Cavestany 1936–40, p. 66.

36. The attribution to Espinosa was made by Pedro de Madrazo in the 1872 catalogue of the Prado; it remained unchallenged until 1985 (Fort Worth 1985, pp. 160–2), when, for stylistic reasons, an alternative attribution to Labrador was proposed. Pérez Sánchez (1987, p. 63) was unconvinced by this attribution, but we persist in proposing it.

37. Cavestany 1936–40, p. 142: 'Un racimo de uvas en su vástago colgante tres cuartas de alto, dos tercios de ancho, de Juan Labrador'. The sale of paintings by Crescenzi to Philip IV is documented in Harris 1980, p. 564.

38. Sainsbury 1859, p. 157, n. 214; p. 298, n. 29. Crescenzi was also invited to visit England. Shakeshaft 1981, p. 550.

39. Van der Doort 1639 (edn 1757), p. 4.

40. See Harris (1974) for Hopton's letter of 25 February 1635 to Lord Cottington, in which he says, 'I have had him [Labrador] to try his hand at flowers, which I have not yet seen; if they turn out as good as his fruits, I shall send some of them to your Lordship'.

41. Valdivieso (1972) first published this picture and the inscription on the reverse: *el. labrador./ Ju. fernãdez./ 1636*.

42. For a survey of references to Labrador's paintings in collection inventories, see Fort Worth 1985, pp. 150–3.

43. Fort Worth 1985, pp. 160–2.

44. Many of the darker hues in Labrador's paintings have sunk into the ground and become almost indistinguishable from the black background. He seems to have modelled certain forms, such as red and black grapes and foliage, by applying thin glazes of colour directly on to an absorbent, dark ground, rather than underpainting them with white lead. This may have created a luscious effect originally, but eventually all the colour was leached out by the ground, leaving the forms indistinct. This has happened in the Hampton Court painting (cat. 23) and in the black grapes in the Prado's *Still Life with Grapes and Apples* (fig. 54), but not in the small still lifes of hanging white grapes (cat. 21 and fig. 53), because in these he has glazed over an underpainting in white lead.

Madrid: Pereda to Deleito

1. Díaz del Valle 1657–9 (edn 1933), pp. 374–6: 'deseoso de ayudarle para q^e aprendiese'.

2. Ibid.: '...debajo de sus documentos cuando llegó a edad de 18 era pintor excelente, tanto qe sus primeras obras qe salieron a luz parecieron de artifices muy experimentados'.

3. Ibid.: 'hizo mucho ruido en esta corte y despertó muchas envidias'. Angulo Iñiguez and Pérez Sánchez (1983, p. 181, no. 41) plausibly suggest that this is the painting now in Lyon, although their dating, c.1634, does not correspond to the one given by Díaz del Valle, who may have erred in this respect.

4. Cherry 1987.

5. Brown and Elliott 1980, pp. 141–92. The picture was signed in Latin and gave the artist's age, twenty-three, as evidence of his precocious gifts.

6. Díaz del Valle 1657–9 (edn 1933), p. 375: 'Todo muy bien conducido y con exc^{te} colorido,

así en los paños como en las cabezas. Con esta pintura dio de todo punto muestras de su gallardo ingenio, junto con su valiente natural...y me atrevo a decir qe compite en lo grande con la mejor de todas'.

7. Tormo 1916 (1949), p. 264: '...la [alma] del Marqués, mi Señor'.

8. According to Díaz del Valle 1657–9 (edn 1933), p. 372, Pereda painted this work just prior to the *Relief of Genoa*; that is, in 1634 or before: 'Tambien pinto (entiendo qe antes deste) un lienzo del desengaño del mundo, con unas calaveras y otros despojos de la muerte, que son todo a lo que puede llegar el arte de la pintura, por qe este artifice pinta muy al natural, tierno y fresco; su dibujo disposicion y pincel es de la escuela veneciana....' It was long dated in the later art-historical literature as *c.*1650, the period of Pereda's best-known signed still lifes; Pérez Sánchez (Madrid 1978, no. 7) recognised the stylistic similarity between this work and Pereda's *Immaculate Conception* at Lyon and proposed a date corresponding to Díaz del Valle's account.

9. Fort Worth 1985, pp. 214–18.

10. Carducho 1633 (edn 1979), p. 417.

11. Letter to Lord Cottington, 5 August 1638. Quoted from Brown and Elliott 1980, p. 115.

12. The inventory is partially transcribed in Fernández Duro 1903, pp. 184–215.

13. '880...un fruterico Pequeño del Mro Perea', valued at 200 *reales*. The copy of the 1647 inventory from which we quote is a different one from that partially transcribed by Fernández Duro (1903). It will be published shortly by Burke and Cherry (Getty Provenance Index). The inventory transcribed by Fernández Duro gave the number of Pereda's fruit still life as 515.

14. The painting was described with a garbled Latin title as '610. A canvas of a *respice finem* ['behold the end'] with four death's heads by the hand of the Spaniard' (un Lienço de un respice finem con quatro cavezas de muertes de mano del español). Fernández Duro (1903) had mistakenly transcribed the name as '*esparido*'. Art historians could argue indefinitely whether the Italianised '*español*' might refer to Pereda, the only Spaniard mentioned in the inventory, which gave no dimensions; but it is clear that it did not refer to Ribera, who was consistently called throughout by his full name.

15. Unpublished 1691 inventory, ff. 41–41v. Among the eighteen pictures in the 'Pieza de Españoles': 'Otra Pintura en lienzo que tiene de altto vara y media menos un dedo y de ancho dos varas y tercia menos un dedo que llaman el desengaño, en que se ve una figura de un Angel con las alas tendidas y per broche del ropa de Una Joya, y en la mano Yzquierda una tarxetta con un Rettratto de medio cuerpo de un Emperador y la derecha arrimada a un glovo y sobre una messa un Relox de torezilla y tres retrattos de muxer una sarta de perlas una cadena de oro unas monedas de oro y platta y tres naypes de espadas, y al otro

lado ay un Relox de Arena unas Armas libros y calaveras y un Candelero con una bela en Dos mill Reales 2000'. The valuation, lower by half than in 1647, reflects the intervening revaluation of the Spanish currency. The paintings in this inventory, which was overseen by Claudio Coello, were not attributed. Interestingly, Ribera was not included in the Pieza de Españoles, since there was an entire gallery devoted exclusively to his works.

16. See Gállego 1984, p. 246; Madrid 1978, no. 7; Fort Worth 1985, p. 215.

17. Pérez Sánchez (Madrid 1978, cat. 7) identified this work with the second version cited by Palomino (1724, edn 1947, p. 958). See also Angulo Iñiguez and Pérez Sánchez 1983, p. 224, no. 149. Kinkead (1974, pp. 153–5 and 1978, p. 352, no. 39) had erroneously attributed the Uffizi painting to Valdés Leal.

18. The Vienna *Vanitas* was inherited in 1691 by the 11th Almirante de Castilla, who in 1703 was declared a traitor by the new Bourbon regime, because his sympathies lay with the Austrian Habsburgs in the War of the Spanish Succession. He fled the country with some of his belongings, but most of his property was confiscated. During this time the Archduke Charles of Austria, later Emperor Charles VI, was leading an allied army on Spanish soil in defence of his claim to the throne (which the Almirante supported). The painting now in Vienna was first inventoried in the Austrian Imperial collection in 1733, the name of its artist forgotten. Not until 1911 (Mayer 1911, p. 199) was Pereda's name again associated with his early masterpiece.

19. Pardo Canalís 1979, pp. 300ff.

20. Soria 1959, p. 282.

21. Fort Worth 1985, p. 218. Pérez Sánchez (Madrid 1978, no. 39) and Angulo Iñiguez and Pérez Sánchez (1983, p. 228) recognised the problem of fitting the painting into Pereda's chronological development but believed that the traditional attribution should be maintained.

22. Pérez Sánchez 1992, p. 246. Palacios's will was published by Barrio Moya 1987, pp. 425–35: 'Declaro que de horden de luis de Carrion, Arpista de la real capilla de las Descalzas franciscas desta dha. villa e echo un quadro grande de un geroglifico que significa el Desengaño del mundo, de tres baras escasas de largo y dos de ancho que esta en mi casa acavado en toda forma con su masco negro y conçerte con el me havria de dar por su echura quinientos reales en dinero y un buffete de caoba grande y una lossa de moler colores de Pintura = y tres laminas de cobre para pintar = y mas una yluminazion de mano de Geronimo ypigalle que es nra. ssa. = y una caja de concha de tortuga que tiene dentro sus divisiones para reliquias y una caja de madera con algunos colores y esta en señal de dho. quadro y de todo lo referido solo tengo en mi poder la dha. caja de colores. Mando que si el suso dho. quisiere el dho. quadro se le entregue pagando los dhos. quinientos reales y entregando las demas cosas referidas en esta clausula por que asi fue el conçierto.' (I declare that by order of Luis de Carrión, Harpist of the

Royal Chapel of the Discalced Franciscans of this city, I have made a large painting of a hieroglyph that signifies the Disillusionment of the World, nearly three *varas* long and two high, which is in my house completely finished with its black frame; and that I agreed with him that he would give me for making it 500 *reales* in cash and a large mahogany buffet and a stone for grinding pigments = and three copper plates for painting = and a miniature by the hand of Gerónimo Ypigalle, which represents Our Lady = and a tortoiseshell box which has divisions inside for relics, and a wooden box with some colours, and this as a token for the said picture, and of all this I have only in my possession the said box of colours. I order that if the above mentioned [Carrión] wants the said picture, it be delivered to him upon payment of the 500 *reales* and delivery of the rest of the things referred to in this clause because thus it was agreed.)

23. Soria 1959, p. 281.

24. 'Gerolifico del desengaño orijinal de Pereda Con una Calabera Paleta y Pinsseles un relox y otros Papeles...'. Measuring about 80 x 64 cm, the painting was given the relatively high value of 1,000 *reales*. To be published shortly by Burke and Cherry (Getty Provenance Index).

25. Díaz del Valle (1657–9, edn 1933, p. 376) gave an account of the noble lineage of Pereda's name. See Palomino (1724, edn 1947, p. 960) for the story of Pereda making a painted lady-in-waiting for his second wife, Mariana Pérez de Bustamante, whom he calls a 'muy gran señora'. Pereda's second wife was the widow of Juan Roldán de Tejada, of the Papal Nuncio's Tribunal, and the artist received with her a substantial dowry of 10,000 ducats in property and an allowance from the Queen's household, as well as a quantity of silver.

26. Tormo 1914, p. 263; see also Angulo Iñiguez and Pérez Sánchez 1983, p. 144, for the novelistic episode with Pereda's servant (*criada*). Joaquín had taken money and jewellery from his father's house and gone to marry in Castrejón. Pereda was forced to spend over 2,000 ducats in lawsuits to prevent the union, and in paying off the bride. Pereda himself brought up the child, Antonia, born of the relationship.

27. In 1661 Joaquín was nominated for the place of Ujier de la Saleta, an office which had been awarded to Pereda by the Marqués de la Lapilla, Secretary of the Despacho Universal, for his painting of *Saint Dominic in Soriano*, executed in 1655 for the Madrid church of Santo Tomás, Palomino 1715/24 (edn 1947), pp. 193, 959; Tormo 1916 (1949), pp. 262–3, 303–6.

28. Palomino (1715/24, edn 1947, p. 959) found this fact remarkable, and especially unworthy of an artist like Pereda who owned a large library. But he goes on to describe how skilfully the artist was able to dissemble this deficiency and how he overcame it by having his books read to him. The frequent orthographic mistakes in Pereda's signatures, on paintings and documents, lend credibility to Palomino's account. Martí y Monsó (1898–1901, pp. 571–3) published, however, a facsimile of a let-

ter dated 22 August 1645, from Pereda to Diego Valentín Díaz, written and signed in a single hand. Jordan (Fort Worth 1985, p. 210) has suggested that the artist was possibly dyslexic, a condition that would certainly not have been understood at the time.

29. A set of six still lifes attributed to Pereda and bearing awkwardly written inscriptions with his surname were recorded in 1785 in the estate of the Infante Don Luis de Borbón (Saltillo 1951, p. 47). Four of these are today in the Palacio de Riofrío (see Lozoya 1966, pp. 13–20), and two others have appeared in private collections. Angulo Iñiguez and Pérez Sánchez (1983, pp. 222, 233–4), following the Pereda retrospective exhibition in 1978, were inclined to reject them from the artist's oeuvre. The matter should perhaps remain open, however, since we know so little about the artist's activity as a still-life painter after 1651.

30. The most important collection valued by Pereda was that of the Conde de Monterrey, in 1653, see Pérez Sánchez 1977.

31. As an indication of the type of luxury objects Pereda owned, he is documented in 1664 as buying a pair of elegant chests of drawers at public auction for the extremely high price of 7,000 *reales* (dos escritorios de concha y évano con bufetes, cajas de caoba y évano y las garras de bronce y oro molido), Agulló 1981, p. 14.

32. Díaz del Valle 1657–9 (edn 1933), p. 372: '...al cual siempre ha procurado imitar en la admirable manera'. For Burgos Mantilla's life see: Saltillo 1947a, pp. 642–6; Agulló 1978, pp. 35, 183–5; Agulló and Pérez Sánchez 1981, pp. 359–82; Fort Worth 1985, pp. 196–8.

33. Varia Velazqueña 1960, II, p. 330, testigo 87.

34. AHPM, Prot. 7681, unpaginated, 10 October 1650, for Burgos Mantilla's appraisal of the collection of Miguel Enríquez.

35. Two original paintings by Velázquez and four copies after his works were listed in Burgos Mantilla's studio in 1648, suggesting a close link with the artist, see Agulló and Pérez Sánchez 1981.

36. Díaz del Valle 1657–9 (edn 1933), p. 372: '...famoso en hacer retratos por el natural como lo manifiestan muchos qe ha hecho en esta villa de Madrid de diferentes señores con que ha ganado grande opinión'.

37. Agulló and Pérez Sánchez 1981, pp. 373–5: 'Vn ramilletero y vn Espíritu Santo'; 'Otro ramilletero de açuçenas y rosas, pequeño'; 'Vn lienço de bara de figuras y flores, orixinal'; 'Vn raçimo de vbas negras con sus ojas, orijinal'; 'Vn lienço de tres quartas de flores y granadas, copia de Balderamen'.

38. See Barrio Moya 1987, pp. 425–35 for reference to Palacios's marriage contract, signed on 10 January 1646, when he and his wife gave both their ages as older than twenty and younger than twenty-five (p. 426: 'ambos cónyuges son menores de veinticinco años pero mayores de veinte'); also for the receipt of payment for his wife's dowry,

dated 30 January 1646; and for the artist's last will and testament, signed on 22 December 1651.

39. Palomino 1715/24 (edn 1947), p. 984: '...especialmente retratos, que los hizo con excelencia; y en que se conoce la buena escuela en que se crió, y lo mucho que adelantó en ella'.

40. Barrio Moya 1987, p. 431: '...que tengo prestado a Don Diego de Silva un adereço de espada y daga, que es la que trae puesta al presente. Mando se cobren del'. It cannot be considered certain that the Diego de Silva mentioned here is Velázquez, although he was, in fact, known by his maternal surname at this date.

41. Barrio Moya 1987, p. 434. These three unfinished paintings were valued at 99 *reales*. Palacios's father-in-law was also a painter, who dealt in pictures. At his death in 1672 he owned another, more valuable, still life by Palacios: 'un lienço pintado en el una mesa con unos melocotones y unas aceitunas y un barro tasada por original de Palacios en veinte ducados'. It could well be that Count Ferdinand Bonaventura Harrach, owner of Palacios's two known still lifes, acquired them from Bergés when he arrived in Madrid in the 1660s as ambassador from the Austrian Archduke.

42. Palomino 1715/24 (edn 1947), p. 977.

43. For the life and work of Cerezo, see Buendía and Gutiérrez Pastor 1986; especially pp. 27–30 for his early development.

44. Sold at Christie's, London, 20 July 1990, lot 104 (attributed to Valdés Leal) to Thos. Agnew & Sons. This exquisite small picture, signed at the lower right, is a reprise of the composition, praised by Palomino as '*cosa peregrina*', commissioned by the convent of San Francisco in Valladolid and today belonging to the City Hall of San Sebastián. It is probably the painting inventoried in the collection of the late Doña Petronila de Torres Bricianos on 27 April 1748: 'Una laminita de Nuestra Señora de la Concepción, con su marco dorado, copete y caídas talladas, de más de media vara de alto y poco menos de ancho, de Matheo Zerezo, en 1.000 reales' (Barrio Moya 1984, p. 156), recorded as a lost work in Buendía and Gutiérrez Pastor 1986, p. 172, no. A-14.

45. Palomino 1715/24 (edn 1947), p. 978: 'Pintó también bodegoncillos, con tan superior excelencia, que ningunos le aventajaron, si es que le igualaron algunos: aunque sean los de Andrés de Leito, que en esta Corte los hizo excelentes'.

46. For the copies, see Buendía and Gutiérrez Pastor 1986, pp. 153–4.

47. For a review of still lifes attributed to Cerezo, see Buendía and Gutiérrez Pastor 1986, pp. 95–100, 131–4, 154, nos 63–4; p. 160, no. 69; p. 197, nos A215–A219. The most promising examples, known only from old photographs, would appear to be a set of four oblong overdoors representing fruits and vegetables, meat, fish, game and fowl, formerly in the Arasjauregui collection, Bilbao, which are catalogued by Buendía and Gutiérrez Pastor as nos 32–5. To judge from the photographs they reproduce, these paintings seem

closely related in style to the Mexican pair, as well as to certain details in Cerezo's figurative works.

48. The painting was cited in 1733 among the property left by Ardemans: 'Un jaualí muerto y diferentes animales y frutas, orixinal de Mateo Cerezo, con marco negro y oxas de laurel tallado y dorado', Agulló 1978, p. 207; cited in Buendía and Gutiérrez Pastor 1986, p. 197, no. A215.

49. As a result of damage, the date on the painting of fish is not fully legible. The pictures were first reproduced by Angulo Iñiguez (1935, p. 69ff.), who read the date as 1666. Soria (1959, p. 287) read it as 1664. See also Madrid 1983, p. 114, nos 74 and 75, which discusses the possible religious significance of the pairing of still lifes of meat and fish (bodegones de Navidad y Cuaresma).

50. The excessively dark pool of shadow in which half of the painting is now shrouded was not the artist's intention: an old copy of the picture shows this area of the kitchen more clearly, Buendía and Gutiérrez Pastor 1986, p. 154.

51. For a general account of Herrera's life and work, see Madrid 1986a.

52. Palomino 1715/24 (edn 1947), p. 1020: '...y habiéndose aplicado a pintar bodegoncillos, en que tenía gran genio; y especialmente con algunos pescados, hechos por el natural, para hacerse por este camino más señalado, y socorrer su necesidad en el desamparo de aquella Corte. Llegó a tan superior excelencia en estas travesuras, que mereció en Roma ser conocido con el nombre de il Spagnole de gli-pexe; por cuyo medio logró, no sólo la fama, sino la utilidad'.

53. See Cavestany 1936–40, nos 73–5. See Pérez Sánchez 1987, p. 148, for comment on these attributions.

54. Agulló 1978, p. 207: 'Tres pinturas de bodegón, copias de Don Francisco Herrera, con marquitos dorados, de tres quartas de alto y quarto de ancho, en 450' (Three still lifes, copies of Don Francisco Herrera, with little gold frames, three-quarters [*vara*] high by one-quarter wide, 450 [*reales*]).

55. Bergström in Bergamo 1971, unpaginated, as Pereda.

56. '1. Bodegón con jamones y un pastel, de Herrera "el Viejo", de tres cuartas escasas de alto por cuatro largas de ancho, en seiscientos reales. 2. Otro bodegón con un conejo y un almirez, de Herrera "el Viejo", de tres cuartas escasas de alto por cuatro largas de ancho, en seiscientos reales. 3. Otro bodegón con castañas y un frasco [sic], de Herrera "el Viejo", de tres cuartas escasas de alto por cuatro escasas de ancho, en seiscientos reales. 4. Otro bodegón con un barril, una merluza y una tortuga, por Herrera el Viejo, de tres cuartas escasas de alto por cuatro escasas de ancho, en seiscientos reales.' (The numeration is ours), Saltillo 1951, p. 188, nos 410–13, quoted from Martínez Ripoll 1978, pp. 191–2, nos Pp. 9–Pp. 12. The Lorenzelli paintings under discussion are almost certainly nos 2 and 4. They were the same pictures as those exhibited in Madrid in 1935 as anony-

mous works close to Pereda, see Cavestany 1936–40, pp. 161–2, nos 87 and 89.

57. For the life and work of Antolínez, see Angulo Iñiguez 1957.

58. Palomino 1715/24 (edn 1947), pp. 981–3.

59. For a review of these painters and their works, see Madrid 1983, pp. 97–8.

60. Ponz 1772–94, X, para. 36 (edn 1947, p. 924); 'mejor gusto de color que corrección de dibujo', Ceán Bermúdez 1800, III, p. 34.

61. For Deleito, see Madrid 1983, pp. 112–13, 205.

Still-Life Painting in Seville

1. Pacheco 1649 (edn 1990), pp. 453–66.

2. Pacheco 1649 (edn 1990), pp. 511–12. The name of the artist who painted three still lifes that Pacheco valued in a Sevillian collection in 1601 is not given (López Martínez 1932, p. 194). These 'tres lienços de cazas, frutas y pescados', worth 800 *reales* each, were owned by Hernando Díaz de Medina, Seville postmaster, and the high valuations assigned to them perhaps reflected their rarity at the time. Pacheco himself painted symbolic vases of lilies and roses as emblems of the Immaculate Conception in an altarpiece of 1610–15, Valdivieso and Serrera 1985, p. 115, nos 291–2.

3. Alcalá's collection was inventoried between 1632 and 1636. See Brown and Kagan 1987, pp. 238, 251, VII, no. 1.

4. Pacheco (1649, edn 1990, p. 461) mentions Ledesma in connection with the painting of frescoed grotesques; for this, see Galera and Mañas 1986, pp. 401–7. For other still lifes attributed to Ledesma and the problems associated with them, see Fort Worth 1985, pp. 65–8; Pérez Sánchez 1987, pp. 86–90.

5. Palomino 1715/24 (edn 1947), p. 881: 'He also had singular taste in painting still lifes with different trifles from the kitchen, painted from nature with such skill that they deceive' (Tuvo también singular gusto en pintar bodegoncillos con diferentes baratijas de cocina hechas por el natural, con tal propiedad, que engañan).

6. Ceán Bermúdez (1800, II, p. 277) said that by his time Herrera's *bodegoncillos* had been taken off by foreigners. The dowry of Ana de Carriaga, widow of Bartolomé Ria, master surgeon, on her marriage to the silversmith Alonso Rodríguez Canillo in 1650, included 'tres bodegones de mano de fran[cis]co de herr[er]a', valued at 66 *reales* each, and 'otros tres de mano de fran[cis]co de barranco', worth 50 *reales* each (APS, Oficio 5, 1650, libro 1, fols 248–52). Eighteen still lifes by Herrera were listed in the collection of Joseph Belero in 1654 (see note 28 below). An inventory of the collection of Maria Teresa Escobar y Rey in 1722 listed thirteen 'bodegones...de mano de herrera' (APS, Oficio 7, 1722, fols 304–6). For these references,

see Cherry 1991, p. 372, nn. 11 and 14; p. 391, n. 32; p. 428, n. 19. For nineteenth-century inventory references to still lifes by Herrera the Elder, see Martínez Ripoll 1978, p. 210, nos Pp.113–14: two fruit still lifes were in the collection of Francisco de Bruna y Ahumada – 'dos fruteros, por Herrera el Viejo, a trescientos reales cada uno' – and probably entered the collection of Deán López Cepero, where they were inventoried in 1860. For four other still lifes which, although described as by Herrera the Elder, may have been by his son, see discussion in preceding chapter.

7. APS, Oficio 16, 1629, libro 1, fols 256–9 for López Caro's inventory of capital, on his marriage to Ana Bermudo. The document lists two valuable still lifes with flowers ('dos Liencos de flores y frutas con sus molduras de caoba') worth 700 *reales*; thirteen fruit still lifes; and two paintings listed as 'un lienco de frutas de bodegon', whose average value was only 24 *reales* each. For further documentation of López Caro's life and career, see Cherry 1991, pp. 182–5, 473–80.

8. Camprobín, described as a resident in Seville, drew up a dowry contract on 5 November 1628 (APS, Oficio 18, 1628, libro 4, fols 467–71). He rented a property on 21 November (APS, Oficio 19, 1628, libro 6, fol. 836); by 28 January 1629 he had married María de Encalada, daughter of the painter Antonio de Arnos (Seville, Parroquia del Sagrario, *Libro de matrimonios*, 1627–31, fol. 168v). For further documentation of Camprobín's life and career, see Cherry 1991, pp. 525–30.

9. Duncan Kinkead ('Artistic Inventories in Seville 1650–1699', in *Boletín de Bellas Artes de la Real Academia de Santa Isabel de Hungría*, 2ᵉ, XVII, 1989) surveyed 158 collections between 1655 and 1665, and found that still lifes constituted the second most popular secular subject pictures, after landscapes: in that one decade alone, he documented 457 still lifes in 57 collections. *Bodegones* in the strict sense and genre paintings were among the least popular subjects at this date. The study by Martín Morales (1986) of 224 inventories from the period 1600–70 confirms these findings. By the second half of the century, fruit still lifes made up an important part of shipments to South America and were twice as common in this trade as in Sevillian collections, perhaps reflecting the colonists' nostalgia for their native land, see Kinkead 1983; Kinkead 1984.

10. Pérez Sánchez (Madrid 1983, p. 76) observes that Zurbarán could easily have known Van der Hamen's still lifes in Seville collections; both he and Young (1976) suggest that the artist might have made a trip to Madrid prior to 1634, in anticipation of his commission there.

11. Rome 1930, no. 65.

12. Gállego (1968, pp. 121–2) argues that the fruits usually identified as lemons are, in fact, citrons, a paschal symbol. Gállego (1972, 1984 edn, p. 202) further interprets the basket of oranges and the orange blossoms as symbols of virginity and fecundity; the cup of water as a symbol of purity, and, placed as it is on a silver plate with a rose, as a symbol of divine love.

13. Around the same time, Zurbarán also painted this motif in the *Miraculous Cure of the Blessed Reginald of Orléans* (Seville, Santa María Magdalena).

14. See London 1938, no. 13; see also Seckel 1946, p. 286, fig. 4. This painting and the small *Sweetmeats on a Silver Plate* (fig. 78) are extremely close in the manner of execution. Another small version of this motif is on loan to the Museo de Bellas Artes, Pontevedra, from a Spanish private collection. The latter work, however, is a fragment of a mutilated still life by Camprobín, formerly belonging to the Conde de Ibarra, Seville (see Fort Worth 1985, p. 23, fig. 26, for the painting before mutilation). Photographs of that work after it was cut to pieces are preserved in the Instituto Amatller, Barcelona (neg. nos E–85471 and E–6562). The craquelure is identical to that of the fragment now in Pontevedra.

15. For a critical review of those still lifes that have been attributed to Zurbarán, see Guinard 1960, pp. 280–2. What may be still-life fragments from authentic religious compositions by the artist are known, such as the *Quinces* in the Museu Nacional d'Art de Catalunya, Barcelona. See Pérez Sánchez 1987, p. 98, fig. 82. Also, recently offered on the Madrid art market was a beautiful, small *Talavera Plate of Figs*, obviously a fragment of a late religious painting.

16. Pérez Sánchez (in Madrid 1988b, pp. 435–6, no. 115) argues persuasively that even a horned sheep could be taken to symbolise Christ, as in Calderón de la Barca's *El cordero de Isaías*.

17. See Caturla 1957, p. 281, for Juan de Zurbarán's contract with the Cofradía del Rosario in Carmona dated 3 April 1644. The contract called for two paintings (196 x 280 cm) with large figures, of 'Miracles of the Virgin of the Rosary', for a price of 737 *reales*.

18. See Caturla 1957, p. 283, for Juan's burial on 8 June 1649.

19. In 1642, Juan de Esquivel Navarro's *Discursos sobre el arte del danzado* included a sonnet to the author from Juan de Zurbarán, who was also listed among the distinguished pupils of the dancing master José Rodríguez Tirado as 'Don Juan de çurbaran, hijo de Francisco de çurbaran el gran pintor'.

20. Caturla 1957, pp. 252–3. Caturla (1957, p. 282) suggested that Jorge de Quadros, Juan's father-in-law, was a wealthy moneylender. In March 1646, Juan signed a general power of attorney to Quadros and two other procurators of the Real Audiencia de Sevilla to represent him and a minor in his charge in any lawsuits (APS, Oficio 22, 1646, libro 1, fol. 263v). In documents from 1649, Quadros is called 'agente de negozios de la Real Audiencia' and 'solizitador' (Cherry 1991, p. 522).

21. Caturla 1957, pp. 273–80. Apart from Mariana's clothes and household effects, Juan received silver, jewellery and cash worth 22,120 *reales*. Francisco de Zurbarán's dowry of 27,000 silver *reales* in money and jewellery on his third

marriage in 1644, was even more valuable than his son's (Guinard 1960, pp. 53–4). To place this in perspective, Pedro de Camprobín's dowry in 1628 was worth 4,257 *reales*, and Francisco López Caro's in 1629, 10,744 *reales*. These were closer to the average for artists.

22. In his last will and testament, dated 5 June 1649, Jorge de Quadros refers to the dowry of his widowed daughter Mariana and states that 'el d[ic]ho don ju.o de zurbaran le a disipado la mejor p[ar]te de su dote', leaving only 15,400 *reales*. In May 1650 Mariana married Don Joseph de Viana, the son of a physician; she had been able to recover only 17,500 *reales* of her dowry from her late husband's estate (APS Oficio 5, 1650, libro 1, fols 617–20), Cherry 1991, pp. 254, 523.

23. See Fort Worth 1985, pp. 230–2, no. 43. The painting had previously been included in the exhibition *La natura morta italiana*, Naples 1964, no. 132, organised by Raffaello Causa, with an attribution to Michelangelo da Campidoglio (1610–70). Causa had earlier (in correspondence with the Finnish owner) attributed the painting to Luca Forte (active *c*.1625–55). Pérez Sánchez (1987, p. 232, n. 86) pointed out that Causa (1972, p. 1051) eventually recognised the existence and authenticity of the signature, but this reference was somehow overlooked in the literature of Spanish still life until 1987. Under laboratory examination during the 1985 exhibition in Fort Worth, it was verified that the date on the painting reads 1643, and not 1645 as tentatively stated in the catalogue.

24. See Fort Worth 1985, pp. 230–2, for documentation of those belonging to the 9th Almirante de Castilla, who had served as Viceroy of Naples from 1644 to 1646.

25. For attribution of the latter to Juan de Zurbarán, see Fort Worth 1985, pp. 231–4.

26. Pemán (1958, pp. 193–211), however, put forward the bizarre theory that the Bordeaux *Plate of Grapes* (cat. 39), which he deemed, despite its signature, too good to have been painted by Juan, was actually painted by his father, who wrote his son's name on it in order to help launch his career.

27. For an effort to define the distinctive qualities of Juan de Zurbarán's still lifes, see Fort Worth 1985, pp. 222–34.

28. As an indication of the rising popularity of the new genre in Seville, in 1654 four fruit still lifes (probably by Juan) and one with two partridges were listed in the post-mortem inventory of Joseph Belero, a juror-bookseller: 'Cuatro fruteros de mano de Zurbaran a dos tercias de largo y media vara de alto, Otro del mismo con dos perdises'. Belero's collection also included seventeen still lifes by Camprobín and eighteen by Juan de Herrera (APS, Oficio 21, 1654, libro 1, fol. 297). We are grateful to Dr Duncan Kinkead for this reference.

29. Ceán Bermúdez 1800, I, p. 93: '...pintados con verdad y buen colorido'.

30. Sotheby's, New York, 19 May 1994, lot 107, where it was miscatalogued as by Francisco

Barrera. The painting had previously been published by Pérez Sánchez (1991, pp. 318–19, fig.5), who, on the basis of a photograph in which the signature was not entirely clear, tentatively identified the artist as one Francisco Sarabia. Assuming that the unrecorded artist was from Andalusia, Pérez Sánchez nevertheless pointed to certain Madrilenian qualities of the style. On close inspection of the original, it is clear that the signature reads: F^{co} *Barranco fac/1647*.

31. For Barranco's still lifes documented in 1650, see note 6 above.

32. For Zurbarán's still life 'with two partridges', recorded in 1654, see note 28 above.

33. On 15 April 1619, Pedro de Camprobín, a citizen of Almagro, apprenticed his fourteen-year-old son, Pedro, for five years to Luis Tristán (San Román 1924, pp. 129–30, doc. 7). For 'Un quadro pequeño de frutas orig.L del mismo [Tristán]', catalogued in the collection of Francisco de Oviedo in 1631, see Cherry 1991, pp. 306–7, nn. 21 and 22.

34. See note 8 above.

35. *Documentos para la historia del arte en Andalucía*, II, Universidad de Sevilla, Seville 1928, p. 270.

36. Camprobín's last will and testament, containing no information pertaining to his profession, was drawn up on 30 September 1670 (APS, Oficio 19, 1670, libro 3, fols 292–3v), and his death was recorded on 22 July 1674 in the registry of the Hermandad Sacramental del Sagrario of which he was a member (Valdivieso 1983, p. 73).

37. Torres Martín 1978, p. 37. See Madrid 1983, p. 90, no. 63 for attribution to the artist of the painting *Death and the Young Man*.

38. Barcelona, Sala Parés, *Floreros y bodegones (siglos XVI, XVII, XVIII, XIX) de colecciones barcelonesas*, May 1947, p. 31, pl. VII. The lower right corner of the painting, where the signature and date are placed, appears to have suffered some damage and restoration, and it is impossible to be sure, without technical examination, that the date has not been tampered with, or added altogether.

39. The attribution was made by Jordan in Girona 1987, no. 27.

40. Ceán Bermúdez (1800, I, p. 206), who first mentioned these paintings, did not consider them appropriate for this context. However, he said the same about flower paintings by Arellano in three Madrid churches (1800, I, pp. 53–4). Camprobín's flowerpieces for this church are unknown today.

41. See García Chico 1946, II, plate VI, for a fictive altar in the sacristy of San Miguel, Valladolid, representing eight large vases of flowers in niches.

42. For reproductions of some of Camprobín's flower paintings, see Pérez Sánchez 1987, figs 88, 92–6.

43. For the pendant to this picture, a quite damaged but signed *Still Life with Oranges, Bread and*

Shellfish, see Torres Martín 1971, p. 63, fig. 14, pl. 40. Two small still lifes of fruit in the Museo Lázaro Galdiano, Madrid, show a marked stylistic similarity to Medina's *Still Life with Apples, Walnuts and Sugar Cane*.

44. Nicolás Omazur owned two pairs of Medina still lifes with fruit, fish and seafoods, as well as six bird paintings (Kinkead 1986, p. 137, nos 74–5, 164–5 and 132–7).

45. Cavestany 1936–40, p. 36, fig. 14.

46. Medina's decline may have been due to illness. On 5 September 1691, he drew up a declaration of poverty, saying he was unable to make a will, owned nothing, and was living on the charity of his brother-in-law (APS, Oficio 3, 1691, fols 1223–1223v). His death certificate was dated 3 (sic) September 1691 (Seville, Parroquia de San Nicolás, *Libro de defunciones*, 1668–1705, fol. 93).

47. Angulo Iñiguez 1981, II, p. 337, nos 429–32.

48. Angulo Iñiguez 1981, II, p. 337, nos 433–4.

49. For these works, see Brown 1978, pp. 128–46; Valdivieso and Serrera 1980.

Hiepes and Still-Life Painting in Eastern Spain

1. For the modern literature on Hiepes, see Cavestany 1936–40, p. 83; Pérez Sánchez 1987, pp. 150–4.

2. 'Había muchos quadros, donde estaban pintados muchos géneros de frutos, todos hijos del pincel de la mano de Yepes, que es el pintor que en razón de este linaje de imitación de frutas ha sabido adquirir muy singular opinión y crédito', Ortí 1656, p. 168.

3. Orellana (edn 1967), pp. 220–3.

4. '...hizo las flores desperfiladas, diáfanas y ligeras: las frutas con mucha naturalidad, y todo con admirable perfección. Son igualmente copiosas, que estimadas y famosas sus pinturas. Y no se ven canastos con fruta, flores, etc., viscochos, empanadas, quesos, tortas, cubiletes, muebles, o ahinas de repostería y otras cosas semejantes, bien executadas, conforme al natural, que luego no se crea y estime por cosa de Yepes, de cuya clase de pinturas de dicha mano están llenas las casas de esta Ciudad y Reyno.... Y yo mismo conservo de su mano con estimación un canasto lleno de ubas, cuyos granos diáfanos, y transparentes, con sus pámpanos, pudieran engañar a las aves, como aquellas otras ubas tan celebradas de Zeuxis', Orellana (edn 1967), pp. 221–2.

5. Orellana (edn 1967), p. 222, cites a still life signed on the back exactly as these are: *Thomas Yepes me fecit en Val^a. 1642*.

6. These three paintings were photographed together when they were in one collection during the Spanish Civil War (Servicio de Recuperación de Obras de Arte). One of them, representing a lace-covered table with sugar cane, a plate of *turrón* and other sweets, was for many years after the war in a private collection outside Spain. It was offered for sale by the Matthiesen Gallery, London, in 1993 (see *Fifty Paintings (1535–1825)*, no. 17) and is now in a Madrid private collection.

7. See Pérez Sánchez 1987, p. 151, fig. 155, where one of this pair is illustrated; the other is unpublished. Jasper orbs, ebony pyramids, tortoiseshell boxes, pieces of ivory, small paintings and other such objects frequently placed on top of *escritorios* were known as 'galanterías para sobre escritorios' (Aguiló Alonso in Arias Anglés et al. 1990, p. 121; see note 22 on page 190).

8. It is evident, even in photographs, that these paintings have been enlarged by the addition of canvas along the top edge. In their original state, there was no more background visible above the bouquet than at the sides. Another signed painting of this type, measuring 113 x 91 cm, was sold at Jean-Louis Picard, Paris, on 24 June 1993. A further pair is in a private collection, Madrid.

9. In addition to still lifes of dead game, Hiepes also painted pictures of hunters with game in landscapes. Two such paintings, in overdoor format, were offered for sale by Sotheby's, New York, 19 May 1994, lot 108; a photograph of another, dated 1664, is in the photo archive of the Instituto Amatller, Barcelona (neg. no. RE 55).

10. See A.E. Pérez Sánchez, *Jerónimo Jacinto de Espinosa*, Madrid 1972, p. 25, for an excellent description of Espinosa's technique.

11. The restorer has tried to compensate for this loss, rendering the damage less noticeable than it was.

12. Two of these paintings by Hiepes belong to the RUA Foundation, Marseille; one is reproduced in Pérez Sánchez 1987, p. 154, fig. 158. Another, in a Madrid private collection, is reproduced in Angulo Iñiguez 1971, p. 252, fig. 251.

13. For Miguel March, see Pérez Sánchez 1987, pp. 154–8.

14. Curiosity about this painter's identity was spurred by the appearance in 1991 of five unsigned still lifes at the Madrid auction house of Edmund Peel y Asociados in 1991 (21 May 1991, lots 10, 11 and 12; and 29 October 1991, lots 12 and 13). The auction house catalogued the paintings as by the Valencian master Tomás Hiepes, supported by the opinion of William Jordan, who knew in a Madrid private collection a series of six other still lifes by the same hand, which in the nineteenth century had been attributed to Hiepes; two of these are published here for the first time. By the time that yet another painting by this same hand appeared at Christie's, London, on 29 May 1992 (lot 324), Jordan realised that the traditional attribution was in error and retracted his endorsement of it. He insisted on the Spanish origin of the paintings, however, which in some quarters were still considered to be early seventeenth-century Italian works.

15. All five still lifes auctioned by Sotheby's Peel (see note 14) came from one collection. A series of six, in a Madrid collection, is dealt with here. Another series of six is known.

16. New York 1983, p. 27. The painting in question had been attributed to the Spanish still-life painter Pedro de Camprobín by Ingvar Bergström (following the suggestion of Pietro Lorenzelli) in Bergamo 1971, no. 43. The use in this painting of the unadorned, cubic plinth instead of a decorated one is an anomaly that occurs more than once among the forty-odd pictures that can be attributed to the master and his workshop.

17. Munich 1984–5, p. 35; Salerno 1984, p. 18.

18. For example, in a still life of fruit and flowers auctioned by Sotheby's Peel in Madrid on 29 October 1991 (lot 13), the ceramic flower vase has a portrait medallion impressed on to its side, in which the long hair and distinctive collar and cravat of the sitter are unquestionably mid-seventeenth century in style.

19. Salerno 1984, pp. 18–19, fig. 5.2. This painting, formerly in the collection of Victor Spark, New York, was attributed by the owner to Sánchez Cotán. The same artichokes also appear in several other still lifes, including that auctioned at Christie's, London, on 29 May 1992 (lot 324).

20. Poleró was a well-respected painter, restorer and art expert at the Real Museo de Pinturas, who sometimes published scholarly articles. For Poleró's part in the creation of the present-day Museo del Prado after the Revolution of 1868, see Museo del Prado 1991, pp. 13–14.

21. A notable exception is Van der Hamen's *Serving Table* (fig. 34), a painting of the early 1620s that has no other stylistic connection whatsoever with works by Pseudo-Hiepes.

22. Frothingham 1963, pp. 30–51.

23. Almela y Vives, *La antigua industria del vidrio en Valencia*, Valencia 1954, p. 5.

24. A mediocre still life on the Madrid art market, measuring 48 x 72.5 cm, reproduces this motif on a fringed red table-top. Also represented is an ivory-inlaid ebony *papelera*, an ink-well and quill, and a letter inscribed: *Al l^do. Nicolas yniguez/Racionero dela Villa/de murillo de gallego que dios guarde*. Murillo de Gállego is a small, mountainous town near the border between the provinces of Zaragoza and Huesca, suggesting that, if the painting originated in Valencia, the studio had a far outreach. The individual mentioned in the inscription was probably Nicolás Iñiguez y Girón de Rebolledo, Señor de Fanlo y Espun, whose titles originated from exactly that area of Aragón (cf. Alberto and Arturo García Carraffa, *Diccionario heráldico y genealógico de apellidos españoles y americanos*, Salamanca 1932, vol. 43, p. 174). We cannot, of course, rule out the possibility that Pseudo-Hiepes was from Zaragoza. For a list of still-life painters active in that city whose works are unknown, see Pérez Sánchez 1987, p. 162. Bruñén Ibáñez et al. 1987, pp. 256–7, also cite documents concerning one Juan Espinosa (dis-

tinct from the painter of that name in Madrid), who apparently painted in Zaragoza around 1670 numerous *fruteros*, some of which were taken to Madrid to be sold.

25. Madrid 1990, pp. 115–21; Bruñén Ibáñez et al. 1987, p. 352.

26. Among them are two catalogued as by Camprobín in Sala Parés, *Pinturas españolas, siglos XVI– XVII*, Barcelona 1966, pls XXXVI and XXXVII. Another was sold as Hiepes in Paris, Hotel Drouot (Etude Couturier Nicolay), on 10 December 1993 (lot 26), and yet another, catalogued as 'Master of the Lombard Fruit Bowl', at Christie's, London, 8 December 1994, lot 68.

27. A similarly cut melon on a plate appears in a signed still life by Hiepes recently on the Madrid art market.

28. Orellana (edn 1967), pp. 312–13: 'Ambos a dos Eximenos, padre e hijo, dedicados al arte de la Pintura tubieron particular numen para pintar flores, frutas, aves, pezes y demás, copiando del natural, en cuya claze de pintar descollaron en su tiempo. Usaron un pintar franco y unas tintas muy frescas en las aves y frutas, aunque sin tanta fuerza de claro y obscuro como las de Thomas Yepes, ni con tanta naturalidad como las de este Professor, de quien ya hemos hablado. Tanto el Eximeno padre como el hijo trabajaron mucho y bien, aunque sin quedar ninguno inferior, parece que se aventajó el padre, bien que siendo una misma familia y una misma Escuela, se confunden sin descernirse quáles sean las obras del uno, y quáles las del otro....'

29. If Eximeno the Elder was Espinosa's apprentice, he must have been in the studio prior to 1667, when the latter died at the age of sixty-six. There is no record of a daughter from Espinosa's only known marriage, and his wife died in 1648. Pérez Sánchez (Madrid 1983, p. 104) has stated, without citing a source, that Eximeno married a granddaughter of Espinosa.

30. Ibid. These flowerpieces are unpublished, however, and are unknown to us.

31. Orellana (edn 1967), p. 313. According to Orellana, the Marqués del Moral in Valencia owned four or six (sic) horizontal still lifes of various fowl by Eximeno. In the house of the widow of Mariano Bello in Valencia there were sixteen or eighteen paintings by Eximeno, ' ...y otros muchos en casas particulares, que es donde más hay, por no ser los floreros (que es lo que más y mexor pintaron) asunto tan adequado para las Iglesias.'

Flower Painting in Madrid, 1650–1700

1. Palomino (1715/24, edn 1947, p. 964) writes that, after studying with the painter Juan de Solís and trying to make a career as a figure painter, Arellano reached the age of thirty-six without having achieved distinction of any kind. For an excellent, brief account of Arellano's career, see Pérez Sánchez 1987, pp. 129–38.

2. Among several works by El Teatino listed in the 1651 inventory of the collection of Don Gaspar Méndez de Haro y Guzmán, Marqués de Eliche, was one representing three festoons of flowers with a sacred image in the middle, see Burke 1984, II, p. 216.

3. For a full discussion of this painting and its iconography, see Valdivieso 1979, pp. 479–82; Madrid 1983, p. 118.

4. Arellano used this format also in a splendid mature work, formerly in the collection of the Infante Don Sebastián Gabriel de Borbón and now in a Madrid private collection (see Museo del Prado 1991, no. 307).

5. If these were among Arellano's earliest flower paintings, then he began painting flowers at least four years earlier than stated by Palomino.

6. Palomino 1715/24 (edn 1947), p. 964: '...ninguno de los españoles le excedió en la eminencia de esta habilidad....'

7. Ibid., p. 964.

8. Ibid.: '...por qué se había dado tanto a las flores y había dejado las figuras, y respondió: Porque en esto trabajo menos y gano más.'

9. In the 1647 inventory of the collection of the Almirante de Castilla, a garland of flowers by Nuzzi with an Immaculate Conception in the centre was valued at 2,000 *reales* (no. 172); another by Nuzzi's imitator Giovanni Stanchi was valued at 550 *reales* (no. 273); and two flowerpieces by Nuzzi were valued at 300 and 250 *reales* respectively (nos 266 and 267), see Fernández Duro 1903, pp. 195, 198–9. Two paintings of glass vases of flowers by Nuzzi were catalogued among the pictures of the Marqués de Eliche in 1651 (nos 94 and 98), see Burke 1984, II, p. 219.

10. No such works by Arellano are known today. Antonio Ponz (1772–94, edn 1947, p. 416) cites works of this type by Arellano, now destroyed, in the Madrilenian church of San Jerónimo el Real. Cavestany (1936–40, p. 82) considered the extant examples in Toledo Cathedral to be by Arellano, but these seem closer to the style of Nuzzi himself, or Stanchi. In specifying where in Madrid one could see works by Arellano, Palomino (1715/24, edn 1947, p. 964) mentions the palace of the Conde de Oñate; among the flower paintings listed in the 1685 inventory of the Oñate collection, to be published shortly by Burke and Cherry (Getty Provenance Index), are forty-five small, unattributed flowerpieces on mirror, with gilt frames. Perhaps these were by Arellano.

11. Pérez Sánchez (Oviedo 1988, nos 23–4) considers the possible symbolic significance of the pictures. These works formed part of a larger series; a picture from the same group, formerly in the Stirling-Maxwell collection, was auctioned at Christie's, London, on 14 December 1990, lot 42. Originally square, all three have been extended by the later addition of canvas at the top, which gives them a decidedly vertical format.

12. AHPM, Prot. 10431. A great many of these pictures were surely copies, such as the thirty

paintings listed as '*Caza de montería*', the seventy-seven portraits of members of the House of Austria, or the twelve portraits of kings and queens. In 1980 Irene Martín used this document in an unpublished master's thesis at Southern Methodist University, Dallas, under the supervision of William B. Jordan.

13. Edmund Peel & Asociados, Madrid, 29 October 1991, lot 10.

14. The paintings that have appeared on the market all measure approximately 165 cm in width. Those in the inventory and appraisal of Arellano's studio are described as: 'Zinco lienzos de a dos Varas [approximately 168 cm] delos Cinco sentidos a Ciento y diez Rs Cada uno.' See note 12 above for citation of the document.

15. For examples of the rare paintings of Solís, see Angulo Iñiguez and Pérez Sánchez 1983, plates 338–41.

16. Arellano had two other sons, Manuel and Julián, who were twelve and eight years old, respectively, when their father died. There is no indication that they were trained as painters.

17. For accounts of Pérez's life, see Palomino 1724, edn 1947, pp. 1058–9; Ceán Bermúdez 1800, IV p. 73; Cavestany 1936–40, pp. 85–6; Madrid 1983, pp. 99–100, 123–5, 215. In signing several documents relating to the settlement of Arellano's estate (see note 12 above), Pérez invariably signed with his full surname, *Pérez de la Dehesa*, which he did not customarily use when signing his paintings and which has not been known until now. He signed his testament (AHPM, Prot. 12610) on 2 January 1698, five years later than Palomino said. See A. Matilla Tascón, *Indice de testamentos y documentos afines*, II, Madrid 1987, doc. 1728.

18. These are alluded to in Arellano's testament, cited in note 12 above.

19. Ceán Bermúdez 1800, VI (Supplement), p. 83.

20. Madrid 1983, p. 100.

21. A related picture, formerly in the Cavestany collection, is reproduced in Pérez Sánchez 1987, fig. 137.

22. In 1728 four octagonal flowerpieces by Pérez in gilt frames with carved shells as topknots (*por remate*) were catalogued in the collection of the late Conde de Salvatierra in Madrid; see Agulló 1981, p. 72. Other painters also worked in this format. A large number of such pictures, from the Casa Moix collection in Mallorca, were sold through Sala Parés in Barcelona in the 1960s with untenable attributions to Pérez. Three of them are illustrated in Barcelona 1966, pls XXII–XXIV.

23. New documentation of this project has been published by Barbieto 1992, pp. 195– 6; see also the exhibition catalogue *El Real Alcázar de Madrid*, ed. Fernando Checa, Madrid, Palacio Real, Museo del Prado, Real Academia de Bellas Artes de San Fernando, Calcografía Nacional, Fundación Carlos de Amberes, 1994, p. 170, where it is briefly discussed.

24. Cavestany 1936–40, pp. 143–4; Madrid 1983, p. 215

25. Cavestany 1936–40, p. 143: 'Veintisiete tablas de diferentes tamaños que todas componen un camon y en ellas pintados unos floreros originales de D. Bartolomé Perez y algunas de ellas pintadas por ambos lados.'

26. Perhaps these were the paintings referred to by Ceán Bermúdez, 1800, VI (supplement, p. 83): 'There are many flower paintings by his hand...in the rooms of the palace of the Buen Retiro called the apartment of the Infantas' (Hay muchos floreros de su mano en...las piezas del palacio del Buenretiro, llamadas habitacion de las infantas).

27. *Diccionario de Autoridades*, Real Academia Española, Madrid 1726, II, p. 96: Camón: (1) 'A bed that is very large and adorned appropriately, like those used is the palaces and houses of great gentlemen' (La cama que es mui grande, y está adornada con toda decencia, como las suelen usar en los Palacios y casas de grandes Señores); (2) 'also an enclosure of glass panes made in palaces and other houses to put the bed in, to be warmer (cosier) and have more light, when it is desired' (Se llama tambien un cercado de vidros [sic] que se hace en los Palacios y otras casas, para poner dentro la cama, y estar con mas abrigo y mas luz, quando la quieren tener).

28. Barbeito 1992, p. 196.

29. Barbeito 1992, p. 196. 10 January 1692. José de Mendieta: 'Relazion de los gastos que se han hecho y coste que ha tenido la obra del Camon Dorado'. AGP, SA, leg. 712.

30. For José de Ziezar, or Ciezar, see Palomino, edn 1986, p. 328. The fact that some of the paintings from the *Camón* were executed by assistants working under Pérez's direction must explain why, in the Royal Palace inventory of 1734 (see Cavestany 1936–40, p. 143), nine gilded floral panels, apart from the twenty-two attributed to Pérez, were attributed to Arellano, an error that was not repeated in subsequent inventories. Recently on the Madrid art market there was a small *Vase of Flowers* painted on a gilded panel by a hand other than Pérez's. The background had been overpainted in black to make the picture seem like an ordinary *florero*, but traces of the gold could be seen underneath.

31. Fernández Bayton 1975, pp. 287–8.

32. Palomino 1715/24 (edn 1947), pp. 1058–9.

33. Cavestany (1936–40, p. 39, fig. 18) reproduced a *Basket of Flowers* said to be signed by Juan de la Corte. It is likely, however, that the signature was misread, since the style of the picture corresponds to others which can be attributed to Gabriel. A 'Francisco de la Corte', a painter of Flemish extraction, is referred to in a document of 1630, Agulló y Cobo 1978, p. 52.

34. Palomino 1715/24 (edn 1947), p. 1069; Céan Bermúdez 1800, I, p. 364.

35. Pérez Sánchez 1965, pp. 38–9, nos 8–9, plate

IV. The photographs reproduced by Pérez Sánchez show the paintings as they were before cleaning had removed several flowers that had been added in modern times to make the garlands appear fuller.

36. Three similar fragments depicting parts of cartouches and garlands, clearly by another hand (an Italian, close to Andrea Belvedere), are preserved in the storerooms of the Museo del Prado (inv. 3855, 6969, 7013). Coming from the Museo de la Trinidad, it is likely that they were salvaged from some larger whole, just as the fragments by Corte seem to have been.

37. For a flower still life by Corte signed and dated 1690, see Sotheby's, Monaco, 6 December 1991, lot 286. The signed flowerpiece, dated 1694 and belonging to the Marqueses de Moret (Cavestany 1936–40, no. 103), is known to us only from a poor reproduction.

38. Such an occasion might have been the marriage of Charles II and Marie Louise d'Orleans in 1679, when Torres was among those involved in painting the triumphal arches and other devices erected for the celebrations in the capital, Palomino 1715/24 (edn 1947), p. 1061 (cited by Pérez Sánchez 1965, p. 42).

39. Many flower paintings have apparently been attributed to Bartolomé Pérez simply because the flowers are arranged in historiated metal vases, a practice much more common among Italian painters. In fact, only two signed works of this type by Pérez are known, and both use the same vase. As an example of the error to which this approach can lead, see *Trafalgar Galleries at the Royal Academy III*, London 1983, no. 10.

The End of the Golden Age

1. For an excellent account of the exiguous activity among still-life painters from this period, see Madrid 1983.

2. Burke 1984, p. 301: the 1682 inventory of the paintings of the Marqués del Carpio, drawn up in Rome, describes a pair of fish still lifes by 'Gioseppe Reco, pittore del Marchese de los Velez'. Fernando Joaquín Fajardo de Requesens y Zúñiga, Marqués de los Vélez (d. 1693), was Viceroy of Naples from 1675 until 9 January 1683, when he was replaced in the post by Carpio.

3. For observations on Recco's knighthood see Pérez Sánchez 1988.

4. The paintings were described as being in the Buen Retiro Palace by Ponz (1772–94, VI, p. 28; edn 1947, p. 551) and Ceán Bermúdez (1800, II, pp. 343–4) (Fernández Bayton 1975–85, II, p. 295). Pérez Sánchez (1965, p. 429) listed these among the lost works and speculated that they might be among the many uncatalogued works by Giordano stored in the Royal Palace. Ferrari and Scavizzi (1992, I, pp. 119 and 403) likewise include them among the lost works. See also Barghahn 1986, pp. 213–25. As in the case of Sánchez Cotán's *Quince,*

Cabbage, Melon and Cucumber (cat. 1), however, both paintings were taken by Joseph Bonaparte, under the name of Comte de Survilliers, to his home in exile at Bordentown, New Jersey, where they were auctioned in 1847. *Marine Still Life with Neptune and Two Nereids* reappeared at auction in Baltimore in March 1993.

5. Recco's daughter Elena, who may have accompanied her father on the trip, did work in Spain; still lifes signed by her, and by her brother Nicola Maria, are represented in Spanish collections.

6. De Dominici 1742–5, III, pp. 570–6.

7. Prota Giurleo 1953, p. 25ff.

8. It is sometimes said that Belvedere influenced Bartolomé Pérez, but no signed work by Pérez bears this out. It is on account of this assumption that flower paintings by, or close to, Belvedere are often misattributed to Pérez.

9. See Madrid 1983, nos 101 and 102, for a pair of spectacular flowerpieces signed by Belvedere.

10. For Caffi, see Zeri and Porzio 1989, I, pp. 254–9.

11. For relations between Caffi and the Medici, see Celani Casolo in Florence 1988, pp. 107–11.

12. Pérez Sánchez (Madrid 1983, p. 100) held that Bartolomé Pérez 'owed much' to the style of Caffi, but no signed painting bears this out, and her works may not have begun to arrive in Spain until the end of his career.

13. In tentatively attributing this work to Caffi, Pérez Sánchez (Madrid 1983, cat. 107) noted the anomalous precision of detail, as in the carefully described thorns of the rose bush, and suggested that the painting might be a work only influenced by Caffi. Such would, indeed, seem to be the case, since the precise description of thorny rose bushes and the more attentive description of detail in general are features of Marchioni's style. For Marchioni, see Zeri and Porzio 1989, I, pp. 329–33.

14. See Madrid 1983, pp. 102–3, 140–53, for the most complete consideration of *trompe l'oeil* painting in Spain.

15. For Victoria, see Madrid 1983, pp. 140–1, 219. See also the annotations made by Nina Ayala Mallory to Palomino 1724 (edn 1987), pp. 380–2.

16. Palomino 1715/24 (edn 1947, p. 1135) (quoted in translation from edn 1987, p. 380): '...vi en su estudio algunas travesuras, teniéndolas por naturales, hasta que él mismo me dió motivo a el reparo. Como son, una tabla fingida en un lienzo, sobre la cual pendían algunos papeles, dibujos, y otras baratijas; que yo confieso con ingenuidad, que me engañé. Como también un trozo de librería fingido, para llenar un vacío de la que tenía muy selecta, que yo no hallando diferencia entre la fingida, y la verdadera; pues una, y otra estaban tocadas de una misma luz, y con un mismo relieve; la juzgué toda una. Y a este tenor tenía otras muchas cosas de su mano ejecutadas por el natur-

al, con gran observación, y puntualidad.'

17. For several *trompe l'oeil* paintings attributed to Victoria, see Madrid 1983, pp. 140–1; Pérez Sánchez 1987, p. 159.

18. Unpublished in art-historical literature until now, this painting is illustrated in several articles on the décor of Mr Blass's apartment: see, for example, *The New York Times Magazine*, 4 April 1993, p. 20. We are grateful to Mr Blass for corroborating the reading of the signature on his painting and to Christopher Gibbs for supplying the photograph.

19. For Biltius, see Sullivan 1984, pp. 49–50.

20. As Pérez Sánchez points out (Madrid 1983, pp. 102, 133, cat. 111), a pair of *trompe l'oeil* paintings by Franciscus Gysbrechts (doc. 1674), perhaps a relative of Cornelis Norbertus, was acquired in Seville by Queen Isabella Farnese before 1746.

21. See Madrid 1983, nos 126–35, for examples of their works.

22. Ceán Bermúdez 1800, I, 363; for this artist, see also Madrid 1983, p. 102; Kinkead 1986, p. 137; Valdivieso 1986, pp. 239–40.

23. Ceán Bermúdez 1800, I, 363; 'He visto algunas obras de su mano que figuraban tablas de pino con varios papeles, baratijas, tinteros, y otras cosas copiadas del natural con mucha verdad, valentía y buen efecto'.

24. Trapier (1938, p. 30) suggested that these could be the paintings seen by Ceán.

25. We are grateful to Dr Duncan Kinkead for this information and for his assistance with this problem.

26. Kinkead 1985, p. 137, n. 35. In private communication with us, Dr Kinkead informs that he has examined fifty-nine documents referring to Marcos Fernández Correa in the Sevillian Archivo de Protocolos and the archive of the Sevillian Academy dating from 1665 (at which time the artist was associated with the sculptor Pedro Roldán as an *oficial* rather than a *maestro*) to 1689. In these documents he is never referred to as a painter and, when his profession is stated, he is always identified as a sculptor. In documents of 1686 and 1687, Fernández Corea is reported to have emigrated to the New World.

27. A third signed example, representing a cupboard with a partially opened glass door revealing stored tableware, is in a private collection in Seville (see Valdivieso 1986, p. 306, fig. 255).

28. For more on these paintings, see Madrid 1983, nos 124–5.

29. For a reassessment of these neglected works, see Madrid 1983, pp. 157–60.

30. For more on these still lifes by Giacomo Nani, see Urrea 1977, pp. 342–51, pls CXVII–CXXI.

The Eighteenth Century: Still-Life Painting at Court

1. Gállego 1977.

2. For the history of the Academia de San Fernando, see Bédat 1989.

3. For history painting as the highest form of painting, see Bédat 1989, pp. 225–6. For academic values in the period, see León Tello and Sanz Sanz 1979.

4. For Nani, see Urrea 1977, pp. 163–70.

5. See Madrid 1983, no. 156, for *Basket of Fruit* by Castellanos, given to the Academy on the occasion of the artist's reception.

6. Meléndez's full name, to which his initialled signatures refer with varying degrees of completeness, was Luis Egidio Meléndez de Rivera Durazo y Santo Padre.

7. For Meléndez, see Tufts 1985; Madrid 1982–3; Dallas 1985. Tufts catalogues works dated from 1759 to 1774. A pair of signed still lifes dated 1778 was auctioned at Edmund Peel y Asociados, Madrid, on 29 October 1991 (lot 5).

8. For Francisco Antonio Meléndez's role in founding the Academy, and his subsequent involvement with it, see Bédat 1989, pp. 26–50.

9. Bédat 1989, p. 61.

10. For a thorough discussion of the elder Meléndez's difficulties with the Academy, see Bédat 1989, pp. 44–50, 61–2. See especially p. 45: '...es muy pequeña empresa para mis talentos'.

11. See Symmons 1988, pp. 31–41, for the importance of academic training.

12. See Symmons 1988, pp. 59–92, for the status of artists and relations with the monarchy.

13. They are untraced: Tufts 1985, p. 15.

14. Tufts 1985, pp. 16–19.

15. Tufts 1985, pp. 213–14, docs 7–8.

16. Ceán Bermúdez 1800, III, p. 117.

17. 'cuya representación consiste en las quatro Estaciones del año, y mas propiamente los quatro Elementos, a fin de componer un divertido Gavinete con toda la especie de comestibles que el clima Español produce en dichos quatro Elementos de la que solo tiene concluido lo perteneciente a los Frutos de la Tierra por no tener medios para seguirla, ni aun los precisos para alimentarse...' Tufts 1985, p. 214.

18. Tomlinson 1990, pp. 84–5. For the *Gabinete*, see Calatayud 1987. For Cristóbal Vilella (d. 1803), an artist trained at the Madrid Academy who was also a naturalist, see Dallas 1985, p. 35. Tufts 1985, p. 56, suggested that the more luxurious subject matter in some of the paintings by

Meléndez dated in 1770 (e.g. Tufts 1985, nos 25 and 26) may have something to do with his proposed gift to the royal couple.

19. Tomlinson 1990, p. 86. The uncertainty as to the number of canvases stems from the artist's admitted confusion in January 1772 as to the number he had delivered one year earlier.

20. Tomlinson 1990, pp. 87–8. In Meléndez's own account, probably written in 1773, of the delivery (*entrega*) of his still lifes to the prince, he wrote (in Tomlinson's paraphrase): 'that he hesitates to price his work, since perhaps no one will dare do so in the future; according to the artist, this claim is made not from arrogance but from the knowledge that he has been chosen by God to imitate the marvellous works of His knowledge'.

21. For Nani's paintings in the inventory of La Granja, see Cavestany 1936–40, p. 145. See also Madrid 1983, nos 141–3; Tomlinson 1990, p. 85.

22. For pottery in Meléndez's still lifes, see Gutiérrez Alonso 1983.

23. Tomlinson 1990, pp. 85–6.

24. The science of natural history was well established in Spain by 1771. The Real Gabinete de Historia Natural was founded by King Ferdinand VI in 1752. Charles III purchased the important natural history collection formed in Paris by the Spanish colonial Pedro Franco Dávila, and in 1773 the Nuevo Gabinete de Historia Natural was inaugurated. The Real Jardín Botánico had been founded in 1755 and in 1781 was moved to its present site on the Prado, at the end of the building, now the Museo del Prado, which was designed and constructed to house the Real Gabinete de Historia Natural, the Academia de Ciencias and the Laboratorio Química (see Puerto Sarmiento in Madrid 1988a, pp. 295–306). Botanical study also had a nationalistic dimension. The systematic cataloguing of the indigenous flora of the vast Spanish peninsula was begun in 1762 with the first volume of José Quer's *Flora española*, 1762–84, which was illustrated by the Madrid painter Lorenzo Marín; in 1784 this was revised according to the system of Linnaeus by the great botanist Casimiro Gómez Ortega. The most ambitious botanical enterprise begun during the reign of Charles III was the Real Jardín's inventory of Spanish, American and Philippine flora, which was then still largely unknown. Perhaps Meléndez counted on appealing directly to royal interests in aiming to represent comprehensively the foodstuffs produced by the Spanish climate, which could also be seen as fruits of Bourbon rule. In his review of Tufts 1985, Jonathan Brown in *Art in America*, LXXIII, 1985, p. 17, suggested that the still lifes may have been intended to glorify the fruits of Charles III's enlightened rule.

25. In stating that he had been chosen by God to imitate the marvellous works of His knowledge (see note 20 above), Meléndez may have been appealing to the view of botany as 'natural theology' that was common among Enlightened intellectuals. Thus, Miguel Barnades in his *Principios de Botánica* of 1767, wrote: '[Botany] es muy conduciente para la teología natural, llevando al hom-

bre por la mano al claro conocimiento y a la alabanza del Criador [...], pues en la hermosura de ellas [las plantas] resplandece su sabiduría en el orden de su conservación, proporción y renovación, se manifiesta su poder; y en la providencia de su utilidad para el uso del hombre se experimenta su inefable bondad' (quoted by Puerto Sarmiento in Madrid 1988a, p. 297, n. 4).

26. Tomlinson 1990, p. 89: '...una gran coleccion de Quadros de diferentes tamaños que debian contener la historia natural de España, esto es la pintura de todas las frutas, carnes, aves, pezes, flores, alimentos y demas producciones naturales de estos Reinos'.

27. The forty-four paintings at Aranjuez were mentioned by Ceán Bermúdez (1800, III, p. 118); forty-five were listed in the royal inventory (Tufts 1985, p. 218). For Aranjuez's famous gardens, see Iñiguez Almech 1952, pp. 140–54.

28. Madrid 1983, no. 150; Tufts 1985, nos 33–6.

29. See Luna 1989 for several examples on a smaller scale.

30. For Paret, see Delgado 1957; Bilbao 1991.

31. Baticle 1966.

32. For paintings by Paret in the Infante's collection, see Bilbao 1991, pp. 76–8.

33. For Paret's ornithological illustrations for the Infante, see the essay by Milicua (Bilbao 1991, pp. 137–54), which incorporates previous contributions to their study by Pérez Sánchez, Salas and Arnaiz.

34. See the essay by Rosario Peña in Bilbao 1991, p. 73.

35. For Pillement's floral designs, see Faré 1976, pp. 352–5. Other prints for floral designs were published by Charles-Germain de Saint-Aubin in 1771 (Faré 1976, pp. 355, 389–90). For the relationship of Paret's works to the work of Pillement in general, see Luna 1982, who does not, however, consider the relationship of the two artists' floral designs.

The School of Valencia

1. See Madrid 1983, pp. 177–89, for a fuller consideration of the School of Valencia, with discussion and illustration of many artists not mentioned here.

2. Partearroyo Lacaba in Bonet Correa (ed.) 1982, pp. 367–70.

3. See note 35 in the previous chapter.

4. Aldana Fernández 1970, pp. 57, 64; León Tello and Sanz Sanz 1979, pp. 30–2, 41–3.

5. Aldana Fernández 1970, pp. 65, 263.

6. Aldana Fernández 1970, pp. 67–9, 264–6.

7. For other works by Ferrer, see Madrid 1983, pp. 183–4; Pérez Sánchez 1987, pp. 202–4.

8. The royal decree of 1784 was published by Cavestany 1936–40, pp. 140–41, doc. VI. See also Aldana Fernández 1970, pp. 73–4, 267–71.

9. Aldana Fernández 1970, pp. 65–6; Bédat 1989, p. 227.

10. Members of the silk guild who were expert in transferring designs for textiles were not, however, admitted as teachers in the Academy, Aldana Fernández 1970, p. 280.

11. Aldana Fernández 1970, pp. 66, 71, 77, n. 72, 96, n. 129 for prizes. In 1783 Benito Espinós won first prize of 1,000 *reales* in the category of 'el mejor y más completo estudio de varias flores copiadas del natural...y un dibujo de una casulla, estola, manípulo, cubrecáliz y bolsa para las festividades de la Virgen, con expresión de algunos de sus atributos, con todo sus matices coloridos sobre papel, y las flores imitando las naturales, con buen gusto en su enlace y contraposición de colores', Aldana Fernández 1970, pp. 71–2.

12. In addition to works by the academicians and prizewinners, from 1806 the teaching collection at Valencia included three flower paintings by Daniel Seghers, see Aldana Fernández 1970, pp. 99, 140; seventeenth-century Valencian artists were also admired, including Tomás Hiepes, see León Tello and Sanz Sanz 1979, pp. 37, 125.

13. See the damning report of the engraver Manuel de Monfort in 1789 in Aldana Fernández 1970, pp. 84–7, 276–80, doc. 10.

14. Orations at prize-giving ceremonies at the Academia de San Carlos attributed the excellence of the native school of flower painters to the 'inspiration' of this fertile agricultural region, see León Tello and Sanz Sanz 1979, pp. 14, 72–82, 122–3. No credit was given there, and little has been given since in art-historical literature, to the effective educational model borrowed from the French, or to the example of French flower painters.

15. The painting is signed: 'Lo inventó y pintó Benito Espinós en Valencia el año 1783'.

16. Quoted in Dallas 1985, p. 50, n. 151.

17. Palomino 1715/24 (edn 1947), pp. 509–11.

18. Very little is known of this artist, except that he was dead by 1802. In 1772 a painter of this name, who was most likely the same man, was working in the royal porcelain factory of the Buen Retiro in Madrid.

19. Aldana Fernández 1970, p. 275, doc. 8. In the artist's petition for a royal pension of 1816 (ibid., p. 285), he claimed to have presented Charles with five '*floreros*'.

20. Aldana Fernández 1970, p. 285; León Tello and Sanz Sanz 1979, pp. 52–3. For Espinós's drawings, signed and dated in Madrid in 1803, see A.E. Pérez Sánchez, *Museo del Prado. Catálogo de dibujos*, III, Madrid 1977, pp. 32–3.

21. Aldana Fernández 1970, pp. 109, 285; León Tello and Sanz Sanz 1979, p. 20.

22. For Espinós's paintings in the royal collection, see Cavestany 1936–40, p. 146; Aldana Fernández 1970, pp. 176–7, n. 346.

23. For Romero, see Cavestany 1936–40, p. 100; Aldana Fernández 1970, pp. 76, 93–4, 200–1; Madrid 1983, pp. 158, 174, 217. Both of his sons, Juan Bautista and Vicente, were also flower painters.

24. Madrid 1983, p. 174, nos 160–1.

25. Two unsigned flower paintings in the North Carolina Museum of Art, Raleigh (Pérez Sánchez 1987, figs 206–7), have been attributed to Romero ever since they were acquired in 1952 from Newhouse Galleries in New York. Sullivan (1986, nos 26 and 27) noted that their style is closer to that of Espinós than it is to Romero's signed flowerpieces in the Academia de San Fernando and concluded from this that they might be early works, painted around the time that Romero was Espinós's student. It remains to be determined, however, whether these paintings are indeed by Romero, rather than by Espinós himself or some other of his Valencian followers.

26. These pictures, known to us only from photographs, were briefly on the London art market in 1977.

27. Sullivan 1986, nos 24–5. The piece of paper in the still life with pies bears an obscure fragmentary inscription (*de / su Altesa y Mandado por / Sor. Mio Gesucristo Dios*) which implies that the painting was intended for a noble.

28. For López Enguídanos, see Cavestany 1936–40, pp. 54, 101; Madrid 1983, p. 175, nos 162–3, p. 210. For his prints, see Carrete Parrondo et al. 1989, pp. 627–8.

29. Rose Wagner (doctoral thesis, Universidad Complutense, Madrid) 1983, II, pp. 253–6; see also Madrid 1983, p. 175, nos 162–3.

30. For Lacoma, see Cavestany 1936–40, p. 104; Madrid 1983, pp. 178, 187, 209; Dallas 1985, p. 41.

31. The picture is reproduced in Madrid 1983, no. 179.

Goya and the Still Life

1. For the fullest account of Goya's life and work, see Gassier and Wilson 1971.

2. Sambricio 1946, p. 8.

3. Delgado 1957, pp. 21–2.

4. See Calvo Serraller et al. 1994 for the implications of this journey for Goya's development.

5. Sambricio 1946, docs 128–35.

6. Delgado 1957, pp. 27–8. Paret was absent from Madrid, in Puerto Rico and in Vizcaya, from 1775 until 1789.

7. Sambricio 1955, pp. 20–3.

8. See Madrid 1993, pp. 189–209.

9. López-Rey 1948.

10. Sánchez Cantón 1946, pp. 73–109.

11. Salas 1964, pp. 317–20; Gassier and Wilson 1971, pp. 246–9.

12. Item 29 in the inventory records '*Unos pájaros*' at 25 *reales*. This may also have been a still life, so we cannot be certain whether there were twelve or thirteen such pictures in the house.

13. See Muller 1984.

14. An eleventh still life attributed to Goya, *Calf's Head* (Gassier and Wilson 1971, no. 913), in the Nationalmuseum, Copenhagen, is included in some discussions of the subject. Gassier and Wilson regard the attribution of the painting, which is of a different size and of unknown provenance, as somewhat problematical. We have not seen the work, and therefore omit it from the discussion here. Goya's first biographer, Laurent Matheron (*Goya*, Paris 1858, unpaginated), wrote that the artist also painted a large number of still lifes during his self-imposed exile in Bordeaux between 1824 and his death in 1828; but none of the artist's surviving still lifes reveals the stylistic features of his very late works. Nevertheless, several authors, especially those writing before Saltillo's 1952 publication (see note 17 below), in which the known still lifes were documented in the Yumuri collection, have dated some of them to the Bordeaux years; none of these authors any longer holds to that dating.

15. Salas 1964, pp. 317–20.

16. Remnants of the inscriptions were noticed by Juliet Wilson-Bareau at the Goya exhibition in the Mauritshaus in 1970 (see Gassier and Wilson 1971, p. 254). The 'X11' on cat. 66 was overpainted when the photograph used in this catalogue was made and only reappeared in its recent cleaning. During the same exhibition, Jeannine Baticle (reported by Gassier and Wilson) noticed that several of the known still lifes have plain wooden battens nailed to the stretchers. She deduced that these were simple frames devised by Goya. More probably, they were simply part of a framing apparatus placed on the pictures after the canvases had been relined, which they all were. In many nineteenth-century and earlier frames, the sight opening allowed for almost no overlap of the canvas, so that battens such as these were necessary in order to keep the pictures from falling forward out of the frames.

17. For documentation of the change of ownership of the still lifes in the Yumuri collection, see Saltillo 1952, pp. 47–8.

18. Saltillo 1952, p. 48; the identification of existing paintings with those mentioned in the document is proposed in Gassier and Wilson 1971, p. 254, nos 903–12.

19. López-Rey 1948, p. 253.

Bibliography

AGUILERA, E.M., *Pintores españoles del siglo XVIII*, Barcelona 1946.

AGULLÓ Y COBO, M., *Noticias sobre pintores madrileños de los siglos XVI y XVII*, Granada 1978.

AGULLÓ Y COBO, M., *Más noticias sobre pintores madrileños de los siglos XVI al XVIII*, Madrid 1981.

AGULLÓ Y COBO, M., AND PÉREZ SÁNCHEZ, A.E., 'Francisco de Burgos Mantilla', *Boletín del Seminario de Estudios de Arte y Arqueología*, (47) 1981, pp. 359–82.

ALDANA FERNÁNDEZ, S., *Pintores valencianos de flores (1766–1866)*, Valencia 1970.

ALPERS, S., 'Brueghel's Festive Peasants', *Simiolus*, (6) 1972–3, pp. 163–76.

ALPERS, S., 'Realism as a Comic Mode: Low-Life Painting Seen through Bredero's Eyes', *Simiolus*, (8) 1975–6, pp. 115–44.

ANGULO IÑIGUEZ, D., *La Academia de Bellas Artes de México y sus pinturas españolas*, Seville 1935.

ANGULO IÑIGUEZ, D., *Pintura del Renacimiento*, Ars Hispaniae, vol. 12, Madrid 1954. (Angulo Iñiguez 1954a)

ANGULO IÑIGUEZ, D., 'José Antolínez. Obras inéditas o poco conocidas', *Archivo Español de Arte*, (213) 1954, pp. 213–32. (Angulo Iñiguez 1954b)

ANGULO IÑIGUEZ, D., *José Antolínez*, Madrid 1957.

ANGULO IÑIGUEZ, D., *Pintura del siglo XVII*, Ars Hispaniae, vol. 15, Madrid 1971.

ANGULO IÑIGUEZ, D., *Murillo*, 3 vols, Madrid 1981.

ANGULO IÑIGUEZ, D., AND PÉREZ SÁNCHEZ, A.E., *Historia de la pintura española: Escuela toledana de la primera mitad del siglo XVII*, Madrid 1972.

ANGULO IÑIGUEZ, D., AND PÉREZ SÁNCHEZ, A.E., *Historia de la pintura española: Escuela madrileña del segundo tercio del siglo XVII*, Madrid 1983.

ARIAS ANGLÉS, E., et al., *Relaciones artísticas entre España y América*, Consejo Superior de Investigaciones Científicas, Madrid 1990.

BAGLIONE, G., *Le vite de' pittori, scultori et architetti. Dal Pontificato di Gregorio XIII del 1572 in fin a' tempi di Papa Urbano Ottavo nel 1642*, Rome 1642 (edn 1935).

BALDINUCCI, F., *Notizie dei professori del disegno da Cimabue in qua*, Florence 1681–1728 (edn 1845–7).

BANN, S., *The True Vine: On Visual Representation and the Western Tradition*, Cambridge 1989.

BARBEITO, J.M., *El Alcázar de Madrid*, Madrid 1992.

BARCELONA, SALA PARÉS, *Pinturas españolas, siglos XVI–XVII*, February 1966.

BARCÍA, A.M., 'Noticias de los retratos que se encuentran en la colección de dibujos originales de la Biblioteca Nacional', *Revista de Archivos, Bibliotecas y Museos*, (2) 1898.

BARGHAHN, B. VON, *Philip IV and the 'Golden House' of the Buen Retiro*, doctoral dissertation, New York University, 1986.

BARRIO MOYA, J.L., 'La colección de pinturas de don Francisco de Oviedo, secretario del Rey Felipe IV', *Archivo Español de Arte*, (82) 1979, pp. 163–71.

BARRIO MOYA, J.L., 'Una importante colección pictórica madrileña del siglo XVIII', *Boletín del Museo e Instituto 'Camón Aznar'*, (18) 1984, pp. 151–9.

BARRIO MOYA, J.L., 'El pintor Francisco de Palacios: algunas noticias sobre su vida y su obra', *Boletín del Seminario de Estudios de Arte y Arqueología*, (53) 1987, pp. 425–35.

BATICLE, J., 'Les attaches françaises de Luis Paret y Alcázar', *La Revue du Louvre et des Musées de France*, (16) 1966, pp. 157–64.

BÉDAT, C., *La Real Academia de Bellas Artes de San Fernando (1744–1808)*, Madrid 1989.

BELGRADE 1981, *Spanish Painting from El Greco to Goya*, exhibition catalogue, National Gallery, 1981.

BENITO DOMÉNECH, F., *Pinturas y pintores en el Real Colegio de Corpus Christi*, Valencia 1980.

BERGAMO 1971, *Natura in posa; Aspetti dell'antica natura morta italiana*, exhibition catalogue, Galleria Lorenzelli, 1971.

BERGSTRÖM, I., *Dutch Still Life Painting of the Seventeenth Century*, London 1956.

BERGSTRÖM, I., 'Juan van der Hamen y León', *L'Oeil*, (108) 1963, pp. 24–31.

BERGSTRÖM, I., *Maestros españoles de bodegones y floreros del siglo XVII*, Madrid 1970.

BERUETE, A. DE, *Velázquez*, London 1906.

BERUETE, A. DE, *Goya. Composiciones y figuras*, Madrid 1917.

BIALOSTOCKI, J., 'Puer Sufflans Ingues', *Arte in Europa: Scritti di storia dell'arte in onore di Edoardo Arslan*, Milan 1966, pp. 591–5.

BIALOSTOCKI, J., *The Message of Images*, Vienna 1988.

BILBAO 1991, *Luis Paret y Alcázar (1746–1799)*, exhibition catalogue, Bilbao 1991.

BOCCHI, G. AND U., AND SPIKE, J.T., *Naturalia. Nature morte in collezioni pubbliche e private*, Turin 1992.

BONET CORREA, A. (ed.), *Historia de las artes aplicadas e industriales en España*, Madrid 1982.

BORDEAUX 1955, *L'Age d'or espagnol*, exhibition catalogue, G. Martin-Méry and J. Baticle, Galerie des Beaux-Arts, 1955.

BORDEAUX 1978, *La nature morte de Brueghel à Soutine*, exhibition catalogue, G. Martin-Méry and J. Baticle, Galerie des Beaux-Arts, 1978.

BORDEAUX/PARIS/MADRID 1979–80, *L'Art européen à la cour d'Espagne au XVIIIe siècle*, exhibition catalogue, Bordeaux, Galerie des Beaux-Arts; Paris, Grand Palais; Madrid, Museo del Prado, 1979–80.

BRAHAM, A., 'A second dated *bodegón* by Velázquez', *The Burlington Magazine*, (107) 1965, pp. 362–5.

BROWN, J., *Images and Ideas in Seventeenth-Century Spanish Painting*, Princeton 1978.

BROWN, J., *Velázquez. Painter and Courtier*, New Haven and London 1986.

BROWN, J., *The Golden Age of Painting in Spain*, New Haven and London 1991.

BROWN, J., AND ELLIOTT, J.H., *A Palace for a King. The Buen Retiro and the Court of Philip IV*, New Haven and London 1980.

BROWN, J., AND KAGAN, R.L., 'The Duke of Alcalá: His Collection and its Evolution', *The Art Bulletin*, 69 (1987), pp. 231–55.

BRUÑÉN IBÁÑEZ, A.I., CALVO COMÍN, M.L., AND SENAC RUBIO, M.B., *Las Artes en Zaragoza en el tercer cuarto del siglo XVII (1655–1675)*, Zaragoza 1987.

BRYSON, N., *Looking at the Overlooked. Four Essays on Still Life Painting*, London 1990.

BUENDÍA, J.R., AND GUTIÉRREZ PASTOR, I., *Vida y obra del pintor Mateo Cerezo (1637–1666)*, Burgos 1986.

BUENOS AIRES 1980, *Panorama de la pintura española desde los Reyes Católicos a Goya*, exhibition catalogue, Palacio del Consejo Deliberante, 1980.

BURKE, M., *Private Collections of Italian Art in Seventeenth-century Spain*, doctoral dissertation, 2 vols, New York University, 1984.

BURKE, M., AND CHERRY, P., GILBERT, M.L. (ed.), *Documents for the History of Collecting: Collections of Paintings in Madrid 1601–1755*, Getty Provenance Index, Munich (forthcoming 1995).

CADOGAN, J.K. (ed.), *Wadsworth Atheneum Paintings II: Italy and Spain, Fourteenth through Nineteenth Centuries*, Hartford 1991.

CAEN 1990, *Les Vanités dans la peinture au XVIIe siècle*, exhibition catalogue, ed. Alan Tapié, Musée des Beaux-Arts, 1990.

CALATAYUD, M.A., *Real Gabinete de Historia Natural, 1752–1786*, Madrid 1987.

CALVO SERRALLER, F.J., et al., *El Cuaderno italiano 1770–1786, Los orígines del arte de Goya*, Madrid 1994.

CAMÓN AZNAR, J., *La pintura española del siglo XVIII*, Summa Artis, vol. 25, Madrid 1977.

CARACAS 1981, *400 años de pintura española*, exhibition catalogue, Museo de Bellas Artes, 1981.

CARDUCHO, V., *Diálogos de la pintura*, Madrid 1633, ed. F.J. Calvo Serraller, Madrid 1979.

CARRETE PARRONDO, J., CHECA CREMADES, F., AND BOZAL, V., *El grabado en España (Siglos XV al XVIII)*, Summa Artis, vol. 31, Madrid 1989.

CATURLA, M.L., 'New Facts on Zurbarán', *The Burlington Magazine*, (87) 1945, pp. 302–4.

CATURLA, M.L., 'Don Juan de Zurbarán', *Boletín de la Real Academia de la Historia*, (141) 1957, pp. 269–86.

CAUSA, R., 'Natura morta a Napoli nel Seicento-Settecento', *Storia di Napoli*, vol. V, Naples 1972.

CAVESTANY, J., *Floreros y bodegones en la pintura española*, Madrid 1936–1940.

CEÁN BERMÚDEZ, J.A., *Diccionario histórico de los más ilustres profesores de las bellas artes en España*, 6 vols, Madrid 1800. (Facsimile edn, Madrid 1965.)

CHECA, F., *Felipe II mecenas de las artes*, Madrid 1992.

CHERRY, P., Review of the exhibition 'Pintura española de bodegones y floreros de 1600 a Goya', *The Burlington Magazine*, (126) 1984, p. 60.

CHERRY, P., 'La intervención de Juan Bautista Crescenzi y las pinturas de Antonio de Pereda en un retablo perdido (1634)', *Archivo Español de Arte*, (239) 1987, pp. 299–305.

CHERRY, P., *Still Life and Genre Painting in Spain in the First Half of the Seventeenth Century*, doctoral thesis, Courtauld Institute of Art, University of London, 1991.

CHERRY, P., 'Nuevos datos sobre Bartolomé González', *Archivo Español de Arte*, (261) 1993, pp. 1–9.

CIARDI, R.P., *Giovan Ambrogio Figino*, Florence 1968.

CURTIS, C.B., *Velázquez and Murillo*, London 1883.

DACOS, N., *La découverte de la Domus Aurea et la Formation des Grotesques à la Renaissance*, (Studies of the Warburg Institute, vol. 31), London 1969.

DACOS, N., *Le Logge di Raffaello*, Rome 1977.

DACOS, N., AND FURLAN, C., *Giovanni da Udine, 1487–1561*, Udine 1987.

DACOSTA KAUFMANN, T., *The Mastery of Nature. Aspects of Art, Science and Humanism in the Renaissance*, Princeton 1993.

DALLAS 1985, see Raleigh/Dallas/New York 1985.

DE DOMINICI, B., *Vite de' pittori, scultori, ed architetti napoletani*, 3 vols, Naples 1742–5.

DELGADO, O., *Luis Paret y Alcázar*, Madrid 1957.

DENNY, D., 'Sánchez Cotán "Still Life with Carrots and Cardoon"', *Pantheon*, (30) 1972, pp. 48–53.

DESPARMET FITZGERALD, X., *L'oeuvre peinte de Goya. Catalogue raisonné*, 4 vols, Paris 1928–50.

DÍAZ DEL VALLE, L., *Epílogo y nomenclatura de algunos artífices. Apuntes varios, 1657–9*, in F.J. Sánchez Cantón (ed.), *Fuentes literarias para la historia del arte español*, vol. II, Madrid 1933, pp. 321–93.

DUQUE OLIART, M., 'Pintura de flores: la obra de Juan de Arellano', *Goya*, (191) 1986, pp. 272–9.

EDINBURGH 1989, *El Greco: Mystery and Illumination*, exhibition catalogue, David Davies, National Gallery of Scotland, 1989.

EISLER, C., *Paintings from the Samuel H. Kress Collection: European Schools excluding Italian*, London 1977.

FARÉ, M. AND F., *La vie silencieuse en France: La Nature morte au XVIIIe siècle*, Fribourg 1976.

FERNÁNDEZ BAYTON, G., *Inventarios Reales: Testamentaria del Rey Carlos II, 1701–1703*, 3 vols, Madrid (Museo del Prado) 1975–85.

FERNÁNDEZ DURO, C., *El último Almirante de Castilla Don Juan Tomás Enríquez de Cabrera*, Madrid 1903.

FERRARI, O., AND SCAVIZZI, G., *Luca Giordano*, 2 vols, Naples 1992.

FLORENCE 1988, *Floralia. Florilegio dalle collezioni fiorentine del Sei-Settecento*, exhibition catalogue, Florence 1988.

FREEDBERG, D., 'The Origins and Rise of the Flemish Madonnas in Flower Garlands. Decoration and Devotion', *Müncher Jahrbuch der Bildenden Kunst*, (32) 1981, pp. 115–50.

FORT WORTH 1985, *Spanish Still Life in the Golden Age 1600–1650*, exhibition catalogue, W.B. Jordan, Kimbell Art Museum, 1985.

FROTHINGHAM, A.W., *Spanish Glass*, New York 1963.

GALERA, P.A., AND MAÑAS, F., 'Blas de Ledesma, pintor de frescos', *Archivo Español de Arte*, (236) 1986, pp. 401–7.

GÁLLEGO, J., *Vision et symboles dans la peinture espagnole du siècle d'or*, Paris 1968.

GÁLLEGO, J., *Velázquez en Sevilla*, Seville 1974.

GÁLLEGO, J., *El pintor de artesano a artista*, Granada 1977.

GÁLLEGO, J., *Visión y símbolos en la pintura española del Siglo de Oro*, Madrid 1972 (edn 1984).

GÁLLEGO, J., AND GUDIOL RICART, J., *Zurbarán 1598–1664*, Barcelona 1976.

GARCÍA CHICO, E., *Documentos para el estudio del arte en Castilla*, 2 vols, Universidad de Valladolid, 1946.

GARCÍA SÁIZ, M.C., AND BARRIO MOYA, J.L, 'Presencia de cerámica colonial mexicana en España', *Anales del Instituto de Investigaciones Estéticas*, (Mexico), (58) 1987, pp. 103–10.

GASSIER, P., AND WILSON, J., *The Life and Complete Work of Francisco Goya*, New York 1971.

GAYA NUÑO, J.A., 'Luis Paret y Alcázar', *Boletín de la Sociedad Española de Excursiones*, (56) 1952, pp. 87–153.

GAYA NUÑO, J.A., 'En el centenario de Collantes: escenarios barrocos y paisajes disimulados', *Goya*, (10) 1956, pp. 222–7.

GAYA NUÑO, J.A., AND FRATI, T., *La obra pictórica completa de Zurbarán*, Barcelona 1976.

GENEVA 1989, *Du Greco à Goya: Chefs-d'oeuvres du Prado et de collections espagnoles*, exhibition catalogue, Musée d'Art et d'Histoire, 1989.

GHILAROV, S.A., 'Juan Zurbarán', *The Burlington Magazine*, (72) 1938, p.190.

GIRONA 1987, *L'Epoca dels genis. Renaixement-Barroc*, exhibition catalogue, Museu d'Història de la Ciutat, 1987.

GLENDINNING, N., 'El Soplón y la Fábula de El Greco; Imitaciones de los clásicos, cuadros de género, o pinturas emblemáticas', *Traza y Baza*, (7) 1978, pp. 53–60.

GOMBRICH, E.H., 'Tradition and Expression in Western Still Life', (1959), in *Meditations on a Hobby Horse*, London 1963 (edn 1978), pp. 95–105.

GOODISON, J.W., AND SUTTON, D., *Fitzwilliam Museum: Catalogue of Paintings*, vol. I (French, German, Spanish), Cambridge 1960.

GRELLE, A., 'I Crescenzi e l'Accademia di Via S. Eustachio', *Commentari*, (12) 1961, pp. 120–38.

GUDIOL RICART, J., *Goya. Biografía, estudio analítico y catálogo de sus pinturas*, 4 vols, Barcelona 1970 (English edn, London 1971).

GUDIOL RICART, J., 'Natures mortes de Sánchez Cotán (1561–1627)', *Pantheon*, (35) 1977, pp. 311–18.

GUDIOL RICART, J., ALCOLEA, S., AND CIRLOT, J.E., *Historia de la pintura en Cataluña*, Barcelona, n.d.

GUINARD, P., *Zurbarán et les peintres espagnols de la vie monastique*, Paris 1960.

GUINARD, P., AND BATICLE, J., *Histoire de la Peinture espagnole*, Paris 1950.

GUTIÉRREZ ALONSO, L.C., 'Precisiones a la cerámica de los bodegones de Luis Egidio Meléndez', *Boletín del Museo del Prado*, (12) 1983, pp. 162–6.

GUTIÉRREZ GARCÍA-BRAZALES, M., *Artistas y artífices barrocos en el Arzobispado de Toledo*, (Caja de Ahorros de Toledo), Toledo 1982.

GUTIÉRREZ PASTOR, I., 'Juan de Espinosa y otros pintores homónimos del siglo XVII', *Príncipe de Viana*, (49) 1988, anejo 11, (Comunicaciones del Primer Congreso General de Historia de Navarra, 1988), pp. 209–28.

THE HAGUE/PARIS 1970, *Goya*, exhibition catalogue, The Hague, Mauritshuis; Paris, Orangerie des Tuileries, 1970.

HARASZTI-TAKÁCS, M., *Spanish Genre Painting in the Seventeenth Century*, Budapest 1983.

HARRIS, E., 'Obras españolas de pintores desconocidos', *Revista Española de Arte*, (12) 1935, pp. 258–9.

HARRIS, E., 'Escritura de contrato para realizar varias obras de pintura entre la Santa Hermandad Vieja de Toledo y el pintor Juan Bautista de Espinosa', *Boletín de Arte Toledano*, (1) 1967, pp. 137, 154–5. (Harris 1967a)

HARRIS, E., 'Spanish Painting at the Bowes Museum', *The Burlington Magazine*, (109) 1967, pp. 483–4. (Harris 1967b)

HARRIS, E., 'Cassiano dal Pozzo on Diego Velázquez', *The Burlington Magazine*, (112) 1970, pp. 364–73.

HARRIS, E., 'Las flores de El Labrador Juan Fernández', *Archivo Español de Arte*, (47) 1974, pp. 162–4.

HARRIS, E., 'G.B. Crescenzi, Velázquez and the "Italian" Landscapes for the Buen Retiro', *The Burlington Magazine*, (122) 1980, pp. 562–4.

HARRIS, E., *Velázquez*, London 1982.

HIBBARD, H., *Caravaggio*, New York 1983.

INDIANAPOLIS 1963, *El Greco to Goya*, exhibition catalogue, John Herron Museum of Art, 1963.

IÑIGUEZ ALMECH, F., *Casas reales y jardines de Felipe II*, Madrid 1952.

JONES, P., 'Christian Optimism in Italy ca.1600', *The Art Bulletin*, (80) 1988, pp. 261–72.

JONES, P., *Federico Borromeo and the Ambrosiana. Art Patronage and Reform in Seventeenth-Century Milan*, Cambridge 1993.

JORDAN, W.B., 'Juan van der Hamen y León (1591–1631): A Madrilenian Still-Life Painter', *Marsyas*, (12) 1964–5, pp. 52–69.

JORDAN, W.B., *Juan van der Hamen y León*, doctoral dissertation, 2 vols, New York University, 1967.

JORDAN, W.B., *The Meadows Museum. A Visitor's Guide to the Collections*, Dallas 1974.

JORDAN, W.B., 'A newly-discovered still life by Juan Sánchez Cotán', *The Burlington Magazine*, (132) 1990, pp. 96–9.

KAGAN, R.L., 'Pedro de Salazar de Mendoza as Collector, Scholar and Patron of El Greco', *Studies in the History of Art*, (13) 1984, pp. 85–92.

KAHR, M., *Velázquez. The Art of Painting*, New York 1976.

KAUFFMANN, C.M., *Catalogue of Paintings in the Wellington Museum*, London 1982.

KINKEAD, D., 'An Important Vanitas by Juan de Valdés Leal', in *Hortus Imaginum*, eds R. Enggass and M. Stokstad, Lawrence, Kansas, 1974, pp. 155–63.

KINKEAD, D., *Juan de Valdés Leal (1622–1690): His Life and Work*, doctoral dissertation, University of Michigan, New York (Garland) 1978.

KINKEAD, D., 'Artistic Trade between Seville and the New World in the Mid-Seventeenth Century', *Boletín de Investigaciones Históricas e Estéticas*, (Caracas), (25) 1983, pp. 73–101.

KINKEAD, D., 'Juan de Luzón and the Sevillian Painting Trade with the New World in the Second Half of the Seventeenth Century', *The Art Bulletin*, (66) 1984, pp. 303–12.

KINKEAD, D., 'The picture collection of Don Nicolás Omazur', *The Burlington Magazine*, (128) 1986, pp. 132–44.

KUBLER, G., AND SORIA, M., *Art and Architecture in Spain and Portugal and their American Dominions*, Harmondsworth 1959.

KUSCHE, M., *Juan Pantoja de la Cruz*, Madrid 1964.

LAFUENTE FERRARI, E., 'La peinture de bodegones en Espagne', *Gazette des Beaux-Arts*, 6th series, (14) 1935, pp. 169–83.

LAW, E., *The Royal Gallery of Hampton Court*, London 1898.

LEÓN TELLO, F.J., AND SANZ SANZ, M.M.V., *La estética académica española en el siglo XVIII: Real Academia de Bellas Artes de San Carlos de Valencia*, Valencia 1979.

LEVEY, M., *The National Gallery Collection*, London 1987.

LIPSCHUTZ, I.H., *Spanish Painting and the French Romantics*, Harvard 1972.

LONDON 1938, *From Greco to Goya*, exhibition catalogue, The Spanish Art Gallery, Tomás Harris Ltd., 1938.

LONDON 1963–4, *Goya and His Times*, exhibition catalogue, The Royal Academy, 1963–4.

LONDON 1976, *The Golden Age of Spanish Painting*, exhibition catalogue, X. de Salas, N. Glendinning and A.E. Pérez Sánchez, The Royal Academy, 1976.

LONDON 1981, *El Greco to Goya. The Taste for Spanish Paintings in Britain and Ireland*, exhibition catalogue, A. Braham, The National Gallery, 1981.

LONDON 1986–7, *Director's Choice: Selected Acquisitions 1973–1986*, exhibition catalogue, M. Levey, The National Gallery, 1986–7.

LONDON 1989, *Painting in Spain during the later eighteenth century*, exhibition catalogue, M. Helston, The National Gallery, 1989.

LONGHI, R., 'Un momento importante nella storia della "Natura Morta"', *Paragone*, (1) 1950, pp. 34–9.

LONGHI, R., AND MAYER, A.L., *The Old Spanish Masters from the Contini-Bonacossi Collection*, Rome 1930.

LÓPEZ MARTÍNEZ, C., *Desde Martínez hasta Pedro Roldán*, Seville 1932.

LÓPEZ NAVÍO, J., 'Velázquez tasa los cuadros de su protector Don Juan de Fonseca', *Archivo Español de Arte*, (34) 1961, pp. 53–84.

LÓPEZ NAVÍO, J., 'La gran colección de pinturas del Marqués de Leganés', *Analecta Calasanctiana*, (8) 1962, pp. 261–330.

LÓPEZ TORRIJOS, R., 'La escuela de Rafael y el bodegón español', *Archivo Español de Arte*, (233) 1986, pp. 33–52.

LÓPEZ-REY, J., 'Goya's Still-Lifes', *The Art Quarterly*, (11) 1948, pp. 251–60.

LÓPEZ-REY, J., *Velázquez. A Catalogue Raisonné of His Oeuvre*, London 1963.

LÓPEZ-REY, J., *Velázquez. The Artist as Maker*, Lausanne and Paris 1979.

LOZOYA, MARQUÉS DE, 'Antonio de Pereda en el Patrimonio Nacional y en los Patronatos Reales', *Reales Sitios*, (7) 1966, pp. 13–24.

LUNA, J.J. 'Presencia de Jean Pillement en la España del XVIII', *Archivo Español de Arte*, (218) 1982, pp. 143–9.

LUNA, J.J., 'Miscelánea sobre bodegones', *Goya*, (183) 1984, pp. 151–7.

LUNA, J.J., 'Novedades y cuadros inéditos de Luis Meléndez', in *El arte en tiempo de Carlos III*, IV Jornadas de Arte, Departamento de Historia del Arte 'Diego Velázquez', Madrid 1989, pp. 367–76.

MACLAREN, N., revised by Braham, A., *The National Gallery. Catalogue of the Spanish School*, London 1970.

MADARIAGA, J. de, *Vida del Seráfico Padre San Bruno Patriarca de la Cartuja con el origen y principio y costumbres desta sagrada religión*, Valencia 1596.

MADRID 1960, *Velázquez y lo velazqueño*, exhibition catalogue, Casón del Buen Retiro, 1960.

MADRID 1964–5, *Exposición Zurbarán en el III centenario de su muerte*, exhibition catalogue, Casón del Buen Retiro, 1964–5.

MADRID 1978, *D. Antonio de Pereda (1611–1678) y la pintura madrileña de su tiempo*, exhibition catalogue, A.E. Pérez Sánchez, Palacio de Bibliotecas y Museos, 1978.

MADRID 1982–3, *Luis Meléndez. Bodegonista español del siglo XVIII*, exhibition catalogue, J.J. Luna, Museo del Prado, 1982–3.

MADRID 1983, *Pintura española de bodegones y floreros de 1600 a Goya*, exhibition catalogue, A.E. Pérez Sánchez, Museo del Prado, 1983.

MADRID 1986a, *Carreño, Rizi, Herrera y la pintura madrileña de su tiempo, 1650–1700*, exhibition catalogue, A.E. Pérez Sánchez, Museo del Prado, 1986.

MADRID 1986b, *Juan Gómez de Mora (1586–1648), Arquitecto y Trazador del Rey y Maestro Mayor de Obras de la Villa de Madrid*, exhibition catalogue, V. Tovar Martín, Museo Municipal, 1986.

MADRID 1986c, *Monstruos, enanos y bufones en la Corte de los Austrias. (A propósito del "Retrato de enano" de Juan van der Hamen)*, exhibition catalogue, Museo del Prado, 1986.

MADRID 1988a, *Carlos III y la Ilustración*, exhibition catalogue, Palacio de Velázquez, 1988. (Also shown at Palacio de Pedralbes, Barcelona 1989.)

MADRID 1988b, *Zurbarán*, exhibition catalogue, A. Domínguez Ortiz, et al., Museo del Prado, 1988.

MADRID 1990, *Colección Cambó*, Museo del Prado, 1990.

MADRID 1991, *Valdés Leal*, exhibition catalogue, E. Valdivieso, Museo del Prado, 1991.

MADRID 1992, *La imitación de la naturaleza. Los bodegones de Sánchez Cotán*, exhibition catalogue, W.B. Jordan, Museo del Prado, 1992.

MADRID 1993, *Goya: El Capricho y la Invención. Cuadros de gabinete, bocetos y miniaturas*, exhibition catalogue, J. Wilson-Bareau and M.B. Mena Marqués, Museo del Prado, 1993. (Also shown at The Royal Academy, London; Art Institute of Chicago, 1993–4.)

MADRID 1994 (*El Real Alázar de Madrid*), *El Real Alázar de Madrid*, Madrid, Palacio Real; Museo del Prado; Real Academia de Bellas Artes de San Fernando; Calcografía Nacional; Fundación Carlos de Amberes, 1994.

MADRID 1994, *Obras Maestras de la Real Academia de San Fernando: su primer siglo de historia*, exhibition catalogue, Real Academia de Bellas Artes de San Fernando, 1994.

MALVASIA, C.C., *Felsina pittrice*, Bologna 1678 (edn Bologna 1841).

MANN PHILLIPS, M., *Erasmus on His Times: A Shortened Version of 'The Adages of Erasmus'*, Cambridge 1967.

MARCOS VILLANUEVA, B., S.J., *La ascética de los Jesuitas en los Autos Sacramentales de Calderón*, Bilbao 1973.

MARÍAS, F., 'Nuevos documentos de la pintura toledana de la primera mitad del siglo XVII', *Archivo Español de Arte*, (204) 1978, pp. 409–26.

MARÍAS, F., *El largo siglo XVI*, Madrid 1989.

MARÍAS, F., 'El Greco y los usos de la antigüedad clásica', in *La visión del mundo clásico en el arte español*, VI Jornadas de Arte, Departamento de Historia del Arte 'Diego Velázquez', Madrid 1993, pp. 173–82.

MARÍAS, F., AND BUSTAMANTE, A., *Las ideas artísticas de El Greco*, Madrid 1981.

MARTÍ Y MONSÓ, J., *Estudios históricos-artísticos relativos principalmente a Valladolid*, Valladolid 1898–1901.

MARTÍN GONZÁLEZ, J.J., 'Sobre las relaciones entre Nardi, Carducho y Velázquez', *Archivo Español de Arte*, (31) 1958, pp. 59–66.

MARTÍN MORALES, F.M., 'Aproximación al estudio del mercado de cuadros en la Sevilla Barroca (1600–1670)', *Archivo Hispalense*, (210) 1986, pp. 137–60.

MARTÍNEZ RIPOLL, A., *Francisco de Herrera 'el Viejo': su vida y su obra*, Seville 1978.

MATILLA TASCÓN, A., AND MARTÍN ORTEGA, A., *Referencias a otorgantes (siglos XVI y XVII)*, Ms. in Archivo Histórico de Protocolos de Madrid, 1983.

MAYER, A.L., *Die Sevillaner Malerschule. Beiträge su ihrer Geschichte*, Leipzig 1911.

MAYER, A.L., *Geschichte der Spanischen Malerei*, Leipzig 1913; 1922.

MAYER, A.L., 'Velázquez und die niederländischen Küchenstücke', *Kunstchronik und Kunstmarkt*, (30) 1918–19, pp. 236–7.

MAYER, A.L., *Goya*, Munich 1923.

MAYER, A.L., 'Some recently discovered paintings (A Still-life by Alexandro de Loarte)', *The Burlington Magazine*, (50) 1927, pp. 115–16.

MAYER, A.L., 'Still Lifes by Zurbarán and Van der Hamen', *The Burlington Magazine*, (51) 1927, p. 320.

MAYER, A.L., *Velázquez. A Catalogue Raisonné of the Pictures and Drawings*, London 1936.

MAYER, A.L., *Historia de la pintura española*, Madrid 1947.

MAZÓN DE LA TORRE, M.A., *Jusepe Leonardo y su tiempo*, Zaragoza 1977.

MIEDEMA, H., 'Realism and the Comic Mode: The Peasant', *Simiolus*, (9) 1977, pp. 205–19.

MEIJER, B.W., 'Essempi del comico figurativo nel Rinascimento lombardo', *Arte Lombarda*, (16) 1971, pp. 259–66.

MÉNDEZ CASAL, M., 'El pintor Alejandro de Loarte', *Revista Española de Arte*, (12) 1934, pp. 187–202.

MOFFITT, J.F., 'Image and Meaning in Velázquez's "El Aguador de Sevilla"', *Traza y Baza*, (7) 1978, pp. 5–23.

MORÁN, M., AND CHECA, F., *El coleccionismo en España: De la cámara de maravillas a la galería de pinturas*, Madrid 1985.

MOXEY, K.P.F., 'Erasmus and the Iconography of Pieter Aertsen's *Christ in the House of Martha and Mary* in the Boymans-van Beuningen Museum', *Journal of the Warburg and Courtauld Institutes*, (34) 1971, pp. 335–6.

MULLER, P., *Goya's 'Black' Paintings: Truth and Reason in Light and Liberty*, New York 1984.

MUNICH/VIENNA 1982, *Von Greco bis Goya*, exhibition catalogue, Munich, Haus der Kunst; Vienna, Künstlerhaus, 1982.

MUNICH 1984–5, *Natura morta italiana*, exhibition catalogue, Bayerische Staatsgemäldesammlungen (Alte Pinakothek), 1984–5.

MÜNSTER/BADEN-BADEN 1979, *Stilleben in Europa*, exhibition catalogue, J. Held, C. Klemm, et al., Münster, Westfälisches Landsmuseum für Kunst und Kulturgeschichte, 1979; Baden-Baden, Staatliche Kunsthalle, 1980.

MUSEO DEL PRADO, *Inventario General de Pinturas I. La Colección Real*, Madrid 1990.

MUSEO DEL PRADO, *Inventario General de Pinturas II. El Museo de la Trinidad*, Madrid 1991.

NAPLES 1964, *La natura morta italiana*, exhibition catalogue, Palazzo Reale, 1964.

NEW YORK 1983, *Italian Still Life Painting from Three Centuries*, exhibition catalogue, J.T. Spike, National Academy of Design, 1983.

NEWARK 1964, *The Golden Age of Spanish Still Life Painting*, exhibition catalogue, J. López-Rey, The Newark Museum, 1964.

NORDSTRÖM, F., 'The Crown of Life and Crown of Vanity. Two Companion Pieces by Valdés Leal', *Figura Nova*, series I, Stockholm 1959.

NOTTINGHAM 1981, *The Golden Age of Spanish Art*, exhibition catalogue, E. Harris and P. Troutman, Nottingham University Gallery, 1981.

NOVAL MAS, A., 'Un Alejandro de Loarte inédito: San Bartolomé sana a la hija del Rey Polimio', *Archivo Español de Arte*, (228) 1984, pp. 378–80.

OÑA IRIBARREN, G., *165 firmas de pintores tomadas de cuadros de flores y bodegones*, Madrid 1944.

ORELLANA, M.A., *Biografía pictórica valenciana o Vida de los pintores, arquitectos, escultores y grabadores valencianos*, ed. X. de Salas, 2nd edn, Valencia 1967.

ORIHUELA MAESO, M., 'Dos obras inéditas de Van der Hamen depositadas en la Embajada de Buenos Aires', *Boletín del Museo del Prado*, (3) 1982, pp. 11–14.

OROZCO DÍAZ, E., 'Cotán y Zurbarán', *Goya*, (64–5), 1965, pp. 224–31.

OROZCO DÍAZ, E., 'La partida de bautismo de Sánchez Cotán', *Cuadernos de Arte y Literatura de la Facultad de la Universidad de Granada*, (1) 1966, pp. 133–8.

OROZCO DÍAZ, E., *El pintor Fray Juan Sánchez Cotán*, Granada 1993.

ORSO, S.N., *Velázquez, 'Los Borrachos', and Painting at the Court of Philip IV*, Cambridge 1993.

ORTÍ, M.A., *Libro de Fiestas por la Canonisación de Santo Thomás de Villanueva*, Valencia 1656.

OVIEDO 1988, *Obras maestras de la colección Masaveu*, exhibition catalogue, Museo de Bellas Artes de Asturias, 1988.

PACHECO, F., *Arte de la pintura*, Seville 1649, ed. F.J. Sánchez Cantón, 2 vols, Madrid 1956.

PACHECO, F. *Arte de la pintura*, Seville 1649, ed. B. Bassegoda i Hugas, Madrid 1990.

PALOMINO, A., *El museo pictórico y escala óptica. El Parnaso español pintoresco laureado*, Madrid 1715/24 (edn Madrid 1947).

PALOMINO, A., *Vidas*, Madrid 1724, ed. N. Ayala Mallory, Madrid 1986.

PALOMINO, A., *Lives of the Eminent Spanish Painters and Sculptors*, Madrid 1724, trans. and ed. N. Ayala Mallory, Cambridge 1987.

PARDO CANALÍS, E., 'Una visita a la Galería del Príncipe de la Paz', *Goya*, (148–50) 1979, pp. 330–41.

PARIS 1938, *Peintures de Goya des collections de France*, exhibition catalogue, Musée de l'Orangerie, 1938.

PARIS 1952, *La nature morte de l'antiquitée à nos jours*, exhibition catalogue, C. Sterling, Musée de l'Orangerie, 1952.

PARIS 1987–8, *De Greco à Picasso*, exhibition catalogue, Musée du Petit Palais, 1987–8.

PAZ Y MÉLIA, A., *Papeles de Inquisición. Catálogo y extractos*, Archivo Histórico Nacional, Madrid 1947.

PÉMAN, C., 'Juan de Zurbarán', *Archivo Español de Arte*, (31) 1958, pp. 193–211.

PÉREZ DE MONTALVÁN, J., 'Indice de los ingenios de Madrid', appended to *Para todos, exemplos morales, humanos y divinos*, Huesca 1633.

PÉREZ SÁNCHEZ, A.E., *Borgianni, Cavarozzi y Nardi en España*, Madrid 1964. (Pérez Sánchez 1964a)

PÉREZ SÁNCHEZ, A.E., *Real Academia de Bellas Artes de San Fernando. Inventario de las pinturas*, Madrid 1964. (Pérez Sánchez 1964b)

PÉREZ SÁNCHEZ, A.E., *Pintura italiana del siglo XVII en España*, Madrid 1965.

PÉREZ SÁNCHEZ, A.E., 'Sobre bodegones italianos, napolitanos especialmente', *Archivo Español de Arte*, (40) 1967, pp. 309–23.

PÉREZ SÁNCHEZ, A.E., 'Carlo Saraceni à la cathédrale de Tolède, et les relations hispano-romaines espagnole au début du XVIIe siècle', in *Actes du XXIIe Congrés International d'Histoire de l'Art*, Budapest 1969, in *Évolution Générale et Développements Régionaux en Histoire de l'Art*, Budapest, II, pp. 25–31.

PÉREZ SÁNCHEZ, A.E., 'Las colecciones de pintura del Conde de Monterrey (1653)', *Boletín de la Real Academia de la Historia*, (174) 1977, pp. 417–59.

PÉREZ SÁNCHEZ, A.E., *La nature morte espagnole du XVIIe siècle à Goya*, Paris 1987.

PÉREZ SÁNCHEZ, A.E., 'Don Giuseppe Recco, caballero de calatrava',

Scritti di storia dell'arte in onore di Raffaello Causa, Naples 1988, pp. 239–41.

PÉREZ SÁNCHEZ, A.E., 'Miscelanea Seiscentista', *Cinco siglos de arte en Madrid (XV–XX)*, III Jornadas de arte, Departamento de Historia del Arte 'Diego Velázquez', Madrid 1991, pp. 311–19.

PÉREZ SÁNCHEZ, A.E., *Pintura Barroca en España (1600–1750)*, Madrid 1992.

PLINY THE ELDER, *Natural History*, trans. H. Rackham, London 1984.

PONZ, A., *Viaje de España*, 18 vols, Madrid 1772–94 (edn Madrid 1947).

PRINCETON 1982, *Painting in Spain, 1650–1700, from North American Collections*, exhibition catalogue, E.J. Sullivan and N.A. Mallory, Princeton University, 1982.

PROTA GIURLEO, U., *Pittori napoletani del Seicento*, Naples 1953.

PUERTO SARMIENTO, F.J., 'Botánica, medecina, terapéutica y jardines botánicos', in Madrid 1988a, pp. 295–306.

RALEIGH/DALLAS/NEW YORK 1985, *Luis Meléndez: Spanish Still-Life Painter of the Eighteenth Century*, exhibition catalogue, E. Tufts and J.J. Luna, Raleigh, North Carolina Museum of Art; Dallas, Meadows Museum; New York, National Academy of Design, 1985.

RAMÍREZ-MONTESINOS, E., 'Objetos de vidrio en los bodegones de Velázquez', in *Velázquez y el arte de su tiempo*, V Jornadas de Arte, Departamento de Historia del Arte 'Diego Velázquez', Madrid 1991, pp. 397–404.

ROBELS, H., *Frans Snyders: Stilleben- und Tiermaler, 1579–1657*, Munich 1989.

ROME 1930, *Gil antichi pittori spagnoli della Collezione Contini Bonacossi*, exhibition catalogue, R. Longhi and A.L. Mayer, Galleria d'Arte Moderna, 1930.

ROSE WAGNER, I.J., *Manuel Godoy. Patrón de las artes y coleccionista*, doctoral dissertation, Universidad Complutense, Madrid 1983.

RUÍZ ALCÓN, M.T., 'Colecciones del Patrimonio Nacional. Pintura XXVIII. Juan van der Hamen', *Reales Sitios*, (52) 1977, pp. 29–36.

SAINSBURY, W.N., *Original Unpublished Papers Illustrative of the Life of Sir Peter Paul Rubens*, London 1859.

SALAS, X. de, 'Sobre dos bodegones de Francisco de Palacios', *Archivo Español de Arte*, (2) 1935, pp. 275–7.

SALAS, X. de, 'Sur les tableaux de Goya qui appartenirent à son fils', *Gazette des Beaux-Arts*, 6th series, (63) 1964, pp. 99–110.

SALAS, X. de, *Museo del Prado. Adquisiciones de 1969 a 1977*, Madrid 1978.

SALERNO, L., *Still Life Painting in Italy: 1560–1805*, Rome 1984.

SALTILLO, MARQUÉS DE, *Mr. Fréderic Quilliet, comisario de Bellas Artes del gobierno intruso en Sevilla el año 1810*, Madrid 1933.

SALTILLO, MARQUÉS DE, 'Prevenciones artísticas para acontecimientos regios en el Madrid sexcentista (1646–1680)', *Boletín de la Real Academia de la Historia*, (121) 1947, pp. 365–93. (Saltillo 1947a)

SALTILLO, MARQUÉS DE, 'Efemérides artísticas madrileñas del siglo XVII', *Boletín de la Real Academia de la Historia*, 120, I, 1947, pp. 605–85. (Saltillo 1947b)

SALTILLO, MARQUÉS DE, 'Iniciadores de ferrocarriles y empresas industriales (1845–46)', *Boletín de la Real Academia de la Historia*, (129) 1951, pp. 39–72.

SALTILLO, MARQUÉS DE, *Miscelánea madrileña, histórica y artística. Goya en Madrid, su familia y allegados (1746–1856)*, Madrid 1952.

SALTILLO, MARQUÉS DE, 'Artistas madrileños (1592–1850)', *Boletín de la Sociedad Española de Excursiones*, (57) 1953, pp. 138–243.

SAMBRICIO, V. DE, *Tapices de Goya*, Madrid 1946.

SAMBRICIO, V. DE, *Francisco Bayeu*, Madrid 1955.

SAN ROMÁN, F. DE B., 'Noticias nuevas para la biografía del pintor Luis Tristán', *Boletín de la Real Academia de Bellas Artes y Ciencias Históricas de Toledo*, (VI, nos 20–1) 1924, pp. 113–39.

SÁNCHEZ CANTÓN, F.J., 'Cómo vivía Goya', *Archivo Español de Arte*, (19) 1946, pp. 73–106.

SÁNCHEZ CANTÓN, F.J., *La colección Cambó*, Barcelona 1955.

SÁNCHEZ CANTÓN, F.J., *Escultura y pintura del siglo XVIII. Francisco de Goya, Ars Hispaniae*, vol. 17, Madrid 1965.

SCHROTH, S., 'Early Collectors of Still-Life Painting in Castile', in Fort Worth 1985, pp. 28–39.

SCHROTH, S., *The Private Picture Collection of the Duke of Lerma*, doctoral dissertation, Institute of Fine Arts, New York University, 1990.

SECKEL, H.P., 'Francisco de Zurbarán as a painter of still life', *Gazette des Beaux-Arts*, 6th series, (30) 1946, pp. 279–300; (31) 1947, pp. 61–2.

SERRERA, J.M., 'El viaje a Marruecos de Blas de Prado. Constatación documental', *Boletín del Museo e Instituto 'Camón Aznar'*, (25) 1986, pp. 23–6.

SEVILLE 1973, *Caravaggio y el naturalismo español*, exhibition catalogue, A.E. Pérez Sánchez, Reales Alcazares, 1973.

SHAKESHAFT, P., 'Elsheimer and G.B. Crescenzi', *The Burlington Magazine*, (123) 1981, pp. 550–1.

SORIA, M., 'Sánchez Cotán's "Quince, Cabbage, Melon and Cucumber"', *Art Quarterly*, 1945, pp. 225–30.

SORIA, M., 'Firmas de Luis Egidio Meléndez (Menéndez)', *Archivo Español de Arte*, (83) 1948, pp. 215–17.

SORIA, M., *The Paintings of Zurbarán*, London 1953; 1955.

SORIA, M., 'Notas sobre algunos bodegones españoles del siglo XVII', *Archivo Español de Arte*, (32) 1959, pp. 273–80.

STEINBERG, L., Review of J. López-Rey, *Velázquez: A Catalogue Raisonné of His Oeuvre*, *The Art Bulletin*, (47) 1965, pp. 274–94.

STERLING, C., *La nature morte de l'antiquité à nos jours*, Paris 1952.

STERLING, C., *Still Life Painting from Antiquity to the Present Time*, Paris 1959; New York 1981.

STIRLING-MAXWELL, SIR W., *Annals of the Artists of Spain*, 4 vols, London 1848; 2nd edn 1891.

STIRLING-MAXWELL, SIR W., *Velázquez and His Works*, London 1855.

SULLIVAN, E.J., *North Carolina Museum of Art. Catalogue of Spanish Paintings*, Raleigh 1986.

SULLIVAN, S.A., *The Dutch Gamepiece*, Suffolk (The Boydell Press) 1984.

SYMMONS, S., *Goya. In Pursuit of Patronage*, London 1988.

TAGGARD, M.N., 'Juan Sánchez Cotán and the Depiction of Food in Seventeenth-Century Spanish Still-Life Painting', *Pantheon*, (47) 1990, pp. 76–80.

TOKYO 1992, *Pintura española de bodegones y floreros*, exhibition catalogue, A.E. Pérez Sánchez, The National Museum of Western Art, 1992.

TOLEDO 1982, *El Greco of Toledo*, exhibition catalogue, J. Brown, et al., Toledo Museum of Art (Ohio), 1982.

TOMLINSON, J.A., 'The provenance and patronage of Luis Meléndez's Aranjuez still lifes', *The Burlington Magazine*, (132) 1990, pp. 84–9.

TORMO Y MONZÓ, E., *Un gran pintor vallisoletano: Antonio de Pereda*, Valladolid 1916. Reprinted in *Pintura, escultura y arquitectura en España: Estudios dispersos de Elías Tormo y Monzó*, (Instituto Diego Velázquez), Madrid 1949, pp. 247–336.

TORMO Y MONZÓ, E., 'Visitando lo no-visitable. La clausura de la Encarnación de Madrid', *Boletín de la Sociedad Española de Excursiones*, (25) 1917, pp. 121–34.

TORMO Y MONZÓ, E., *Cartilla Excursionista 'Tormo' VII. La visita a las colecciones artísticas de la Real Academia de San Fernando*, Madrid 1929.

TORRES MARTÍN, R., *La naturaleza muerta en la pintura española*, Barcelona 1971.

TORRES MARTÍN, R., *Blas de Ledesma y el bodegón español*, Madrid 1978.

TRAPIER, E. DU GUÉ, *The Hispanic Society of America. Handbook: Museum and Library Collections*, New York 1938.

TRAPIER, E. DU GUÉ, *Valdés Leal. Spanish Baroque Painter*, New York 1960.

TRAPIER, E. DU GUÉ, 'Sir Arthur Hopton and the Interchange of Paintings between Spain and England in the Seventeenth Century', *Connoisseur*, (164) 1967, pp. 239–43; (165) 1967, pp. 60–3.

TUFTS, E., *A Stylistic Study of the Paintings of Luis Meléndez*, doctoral dissertation, Institute of Fine Arts, New York University, 1971.

TUFTS, E., 'Luis Meléndez, Still-Life Painter *Sans Pareil*', *Gazette des Beaux-Arts*, 6th series, (100) 1982, pp. 143–66.

TUFTS, E., *Luis Meléndez: Eighteenth-Century Master of Spanish Still Life, with a Catalogue Raisonné*, Columbia 1985.

URREA FERNÁNDEZ, J., *La pintura italiana del siglo XVIII en España*, Valladolid 1977.

VALDIVIESO, E., 'Un florero firmado por Juan Fernández "El Labrador"', *Archivo Español de Arte*, (45) 1972, pp. 323–4.

VALDIVIESO, E., 'Un bodegón inédito de Juan van der Hamen', *Archivo Español de Arte*, (48) 1975, pp. 402–3.

VALDIVIESO, E., 'Una Vanitas de Arellano y Camilo', *Boletín del Seminario de Estudios de Arte y Arqueología* (Valladolid), 1979, pp. 479–82.

VALDIVIESO, E., 'Nuevos datos y obras de Pedro de Camprobín', *Revista de Arte Sevillano*, (3) 1983, pp. 72–5.

VALDIVIESO, E., *Historia de la pintura sevillana. Siglos XIII al XX*, Seville 1986.

VALDIVIESO, E., *Juan de Valdés Leal*, Seville 1988.

VALDIVIESO, E., AND SERRERA, J.M., *Catálogo de las pinturas del Palacio Arzobispal de Sevilla*, Seville 1979.

VALDIVIESO, E., AND SERRERA, J.M., *El Hospital de la Caridad de Sevilla*, Seville 1980.

VALDIVIESO, E., AND SERRERA, J.M., *Historia de la pintura española: Escuela sevillana del primer tercio del siglo XVII*, Madrid 1985.

VAN DER DOORT, A., *A catalogue and description of King Charles the First's capital collection of pictures ... now first published from the original manuscript in the Ashmolean Museum at Oxford* (1639), London 1757.

VARIA VELAZQUEÑA. Homenaje a Velázquez en el III centenario de su muerte, 1660–1960, 2 vols, Madrid 1960.

VELÁZQUEZ Y EL ARTE DE SU TIEMPO, V Jornadas de Arte, Departamento de Historia del Arte 'Diego Velázquez', Madrid 1991.

VIENNA, Harrach Collection. Catalogue by Günter Heinz, Vienna 1960.

VILLALÓN, C. DE, *Ingeniosa comparación entre lo antiguo y lo presente*, Valladolid 1539 (edn Madrid 1898).

VISCHER, B., '"La Transformación en Dios". Zu den Stilleben von Juan Sánchez Cotán (1560–1627)', *Zeitschrift für Ästhetik und allgemeine Kunstwissenschaft*, (38/2) 1993, pp. 269–308.

VOLK, M.C., 'Rubens in Madrid and the Decoration of the King's Summer Apartments', *The Burlington Magazine*, (123) 1981, pp. 513–29.

VOLPE, C., 'I Caravaggeschi Francesi alla Mostra di Roma', *Paragone*, (287) 1974, pp. 29–44.

VON LOGA, V., *Die Malerei in Spanien*, Berlin 1923.

WIND, B., '"Pitture ridicole": some comic Cinquecento genre paintings', *Storia dell'Arte*, (20) 1974, pp. 25–35.

WIND, B., *Velázquez' "Bodegones". A Study in Seventeenth-Century Genre Painting*, Fairfax, Virginia, 1987.

YOUNG, E., 'New Perspectives on Spanish Still Life Painting in the Golden Age', *The Burlington Magazine*, (118) 1976, pp. 203–14.

ZARCO CUEVAS, J., *Inventario de las alhajas, relicarios, estatuas, pinturas, tapices y otros objetos de valor y curiosidad donados por el rey don Felipe II al Monasterio de El Escorial. Años de 1571 a 1598*, Madrid 1930.

ZERI, F., AND PORZIO, F. (eds), *La natura morta in Italia*, 2 vols, Milan 1989.

Works in the Exhibition

1 Juan Sánchez Cotán, 1560–1627   (PAGE 27)
Still Life with Quince, Cabbage, Melon and Cucumber

c.1600. Signed lower centre: *Juº Sāchez Cotan F.*
Oil on canvas, 69.2 x 85.1 cm
San Diego Museum of Art. Gift of Anne R. and Amy Putnam. Inv. 45:43

PROVENANCE: Artist's inventory, 1603; possibly Bernardo de Sandoval y Rojas, Toledo, until 1618; possibly Royal Collection (palace of El Pardo) until 1813 (see Madrid 1992, pp. 47–52, for discussion); private collection United States, about 1818 (possibly Joseph Bonaparte, Comte de Survilliers, Bordentown, New Jersey); possibly Mrs Richard Worsam Meade, Washington, about 1847; private collection, Boston; Newhouse Galleries, New York (jointly owned with Mondshein Gallery, New York); bought by the Misses Putnam in 1945 through Jacob Heimann, New York.

REFERENCES: Soria 1945, pp. 225–30, fig. 2; Sterling 1952, pp. 94–5, no. 71, pl. 27; Angulo and Pérez Sánchez 1972, p. 99, no. 213, pl. 71; Gudiol 1977, p. 316, fig. 4; Madrid 1983, pp. 28, 34; Fort Worth 1985, pp. 58–60, no. 3; Pérez Sánchez 1987, pp. 21, 23, pl. 5; Bryson 1990, pp. 63–70, fig. 20; Jordan 1990, pp. 96–9, fig. 20; Madrid 1992, pp. 58–61, no. 1 (with complete bibliography); Orozco Díaz 1993, pp. 213–14, 317, no. 20; Vischer 1993, pp. 269–308, fig. 4.

2 Juan Sánchez Cotán, 1560–1627   (PAGE 30)
Still Life with Game Fowl

c.1600. Oil on canvas, 67.8 x 88.7 cm
The Art Institute of Chicago. Gift of Mr and Mrs Leigh B. Block. Inv. 1955.1203

PROVENANCE: Probably Diego de Valdivieso, Toledo, in 1603; Munich, Hohenthal Sale, 24 November 1933; Frederick Mont and Newhouse Galleries, New York, 1955.

REFERENCES: *A. Inst. of Chicago Bull.*, vol. 50, no. 2, 1956, p. 37; Bergström 1970, pp. 20–1; Angulo and Pérez Sánchez 1972, p. 97, no. 204; Gudiol 1977, pp. 311–18, ill.; Madrid 1983, pp. 28–9; Fort Worth 1985, p. 61, pl. 4; Pérez Sánchez 1987, p. 21, fig. 8; Jordan 1990, p. 97, fig. 19; Madrid 1992, pp. 62–3, no. 2 (with complete bibliography); Orozco Díaz 1993, pp. 368–9, no. 90; Vischer 1993, pp. 269–308, fig. 2.

3 Juan Sánchez Cotán, 1560–1627   (PAGE 31)
Still Life with Game Fowl, Fruit and Vegetables

Signed and dated, lower centre: *Juº sanchez cotan. f./1602*
Oil on canvas, 68 x 89 cm
Madrid, Museo del Prado. Inv. 7612

PROVENANCE: Probably Juan de Salazar, Toledo, 1603; Infante Don Sebastián Gabriel de Borbón y Braganza (1811–75); Museo Nacional de la Trinidad, no. 393 (the Infante's collection was appropriated by the government in 1835 because of his Carlist political affiliations and placed on public view; it was restored to him in 1861); Infante Don Pedro de Borbón y Borbón, Duque de Durcal; Infante Don Alfonso de Borbón, Madrid; Don Manfredo de Borbón, Duque de Hernani y de Ansola, Madrid; his heirs until 1991, when acquired by the Museo del Prado.

REFERENCES: Stirling 1848, II, p. 507; Cavestany 1936–40, pp. 150–1, no. 9, pl. XIV; Angulo and Pérez Sánchez 1972, pp. 58, 60, 97, no. 206, pl. 74; Gudiol 1977, pp. 311–17, fig. 3; Münster/Baden-Baden 1979, pp. 382–90, ill.; Madrid 1983, p. 31, no. 3; Fort Worth 1985, pp. 54–5, pl. 1; Bryson 1990, p. 63, fig. 19; Madrid 1992, pp. 70–3, no. 4 (with full bibliography); Orozco Díaz 1993, pp. 315–16, cat. 18; Vischer 1993, pp. 269–308, fig. 3.

4 Unknown artist   (PAGE 33)
Still Life with Hanging Fish and Baskets of Fruit

c.1615–25. Oil on canvas, 66.3 x 84 cm
Washington, Mrs H. John Heinz III

PROVENANCE: Sir William Stirling-Maxwell of Kier; by descent in the family; Christie's, London, 14 December 1990, lot 43 (as Attributed to Loarte).

REFERENCES: Stirling 1848, III, p. 1410; 2nd edn, 1891, IV, p. 1596 (as Velázquez); Curtis 1883, p. 40, no. 90 (as Velázquez); London 1981, p. 96, no. 55 (as School of Seville).

5 Felipe Ramírez, doc. 1628–31   (PAGE 35)
Still Life with Cardoon, Francolin, Grapes and Irises

Signed and dated in the background, upper right: *Philipe Ramírez/fa. 1628*
Oil on canvas, 71 x 92 cm
Madrid, Museo del Prado. Inv. 2802

PROVENANCE: Confiscated from an unknown owner during the Spanish Civil War; acquired by the Museo del Prado in 1940.

REFERENCES: Ceán Bermúdez 1800, IV, p. 146; Cavestany 1936–40, p. 81; Soria 1945, p. 229; Angulo and Pérez Sánchez 1972, p. 108, no. 2; Gudiol 1977, p. 317, pl. 6; Münster/Baden-Baden 1979, p. 142, no. 134; Madrid 1983, p. 33, no. 7; Madrid 1992, pp. 82–4, no. 7 (with complete bibliography).

6 Diego Velázquez, 1599–1660 (PAGE 39)
Kitchen Scene with Christ in the House of Martha and Mary

Inscribed at right with fragmentary date: *1618*
Oil on canvas, 60 x 103.5 cm
London, The National Gallery. NG 1375

PROVENANCE: Fernando Afán de Rivera y Enríquez, 3rd Duque de Alcalá de los Gazules, Marqués de Tarifa, Seville, 1637; Lt. Col. Packe, Twyford Hall, Norfolk; sale, London, 18 June 1881, lot 18; Sir William H. Gregory, until 1892 (when bequeathed to the National Gallery).

REFERENCES: Beruete 1906, pp. 12, 157, pl. 7; Mayer 1918–19, pp. 236–7; López-Rey 1963, pp. 32–3, 125, no. 8; Steinberg 1965, p. 279; Braham 1965, pp. 362–5; MacLaren/Braham 1970, pp. 121–5; Gállego 1974, pp. 100–1, 135–6; London 1981, p. 57, no. 12,; Harris 1982, pp. 45–6; Fort Worth 1985, pp. 83–6, no. 7 (with extensive bibliography); Brown 1986, pp. 16–21; Brown and Kagan 1987, p. 249, III, no. 12.

7 Diego Velázquez, 1599–1660 (PAGE 41)
An Old Woman cooking Eggs

Inscribed with the date: *1618*
Oil on canvas, 100.5 x 119.5 cm
Edinburgh, The National Gallery of Scotland. Inv. 2180

PROVENANCE: Nicolás Omazur, Seville, by 1690 (described more specifically in 1698); Sir J. Charles Robinson, London; Sir Frederick Lucas Cook, Bart., Richmond; Sir Francis Cook, Bart., Richmond; acquired by the National Gallery of Scotland in 1955.

REFERENCES: Curtis 1883, p. 37, no. 84; Beruete 1906, pp. 9, 157, pl. 5; Mayer 1936, p. 25, no. 111, pl. 37; Soehner in *Varia Velazqueña* 1960, pp. 237–8; López-Rey 1963, p. 159, no. 108; Harris 1982, pp. 37–56, fig. 28; Brown 1986, p. 12; Kinkead 1986, pp. 132–44; Wind 1987, pp. 93–5, Brigstocke 1993, pp. 191–3.

8 Diego Velázquez, 1599–1660 (PAGE 43)
The Waterseller of Seville

c.1620. Oil on canvas, 106.7 x 81 cm (including a 4 cm strip added at the top)
London, Apsley House, The Wellington Museum. The Board of Trustees of the Victoria and Albert Museum. Inv. WM 1600–1948

PROVENANCE: Juan de Fonseca y Figueroa, Madrid, until 1627; bought by Gaspar de Bracamonte, Madrid; Cardinal Infante don Fernando (d. 1641), traditionally; Royal Collection, Madrid: Buen Retiro Palace (1701 inventory, no. 496); Royal Palace (1772 inventory, no. 497), hanging in the passage to the king's pew; 1794 inventory, king's dining room); captured by the Duke of Wellington from Joseph Bonaparte at Vitoria, 1813; presented to the Duke by Ferdinand VII of Spain in 1816; Duke of Wellington Bequest, 1947.

REFERENCES: Palomino 1724 (edn 1947), pp. 892–3; Ceán Bermúdez 1800, V, pp. 158, 178; Stirling 1855, p. 35; Beruete 1906, pp. 10, 151, 157; Mayer 1936, no. 118; López Navío 1961, p. 64; López-Rey 1963, no. 124; Gállego 1974, pp. 99ff.; Moffitt 1978, pp. 5–23; Kauffmann 1982, pp. 140–1 (with extensive bibliography); Brown 1986, pp. 12–15; Wind 1987, pp. 81–114; Ramírez Montesinos 1991, pp. 397–404.

9 Juan van der Hamen y León, 1596–1631 (PAGE 47)
Dessert Still Life with a Vase of Flowers, a Clock and a Dog

c.1625–30. Oil on canvas, 228 x 95 cm

10 *Dessert Still Life with a Vase of Flowers and a Puppy* (PAGE 47)

c.1625–30. Oil on canvas, 228 x 95 cm
Madrid, Museo del Prado. Inv. 6413 and 4158

PROVENANCE: Jean de Croy, Comte de Solre, Baron de Molembais, Madrid, until 1638; acquired from his estate by Philip IV; thence by descent in the Spanish Royal Collection; first catalogued in the Real Museo de Pintura in 1854, nos 354 and 341, respectively; Museo del Prado (from 1922 until 1983 on deposit in the Spanish Embassy in Buenos Aires).

REFERENCES: Orihuela 1982, pp. 11–14; Madrid 1983, p. 57; Fort Worth 1985, pp. 110–11, ill.; Madrid 1986, pp. 44–7; Pérez Sánchez 1987, pp. 52–3, figs 31 and 32; Museo del Prado (La Colección Real) 1990, pp. 343, 352; Cherry 1991, pp. 130–1.

11 Juan van der Hamen y León, 1596–1631 (PAGE 50)
Still Life with Fruit Bowl and Hanging Grapes

Signed and dated, lower left: *Juº Vander Hamen/de Leon a.1622*
Oil on canvas, 59 x 93.3 cm
Spain, Juan Abello collection

PROVENANCE: Christie's, New York, 18 January 1984, lot 15; Stanley Moss, Riverdale-on-Hudson, New York. Christie's, New York, 10 January 1990, lot 224.

REFERENCES: Fort Worth 1985, pp. 109–10, fig. VI.9; Pérez Sánchez 1987, pp. 45, 50, fig. 29.

12 Juan van der Hamen y León, 1596–1631 (PAGE 51)
Still Life with Sweets and Glassware

Signed and dated, lower left: *Juº Vanderhamen/... faᵗ 1622*
Oil on canvas, 52 x 88 cm
Madrid, Museo del Prado. Inv. 1164

PROVENANCE: Buen Retiro Palace, Madrid, by at least 1702; first inventoried in the Museo del Prado 1849, no. 104.

REFERENCES: Cavestany 1936–40, p. 142; Mayer 1947, p. 464; Soria 1959, p. 235; Bergström 1963, pp. 26–7; Jordan 1964–5, p. 65; Jordan 1967, no. 8; Bergström 1970, pp. 31–2; Angulo 1971, p. 29; Madrid 1983, p. 53, no. 20 (with extensive bibliography); Fort Worth 1985, pp. 112–13; Pérez Sánchez 1987, p. 54, fig. 33.

13 Juan van der Hamen y León, 1596–1631 (PAGE 53)
Still Life with Sweets and Pottery

Signed and dated on ledge at right: *Ju vanderHamen i Leon/faᵗ 1627*
Oil on canvas, 84.2 x 112.8 cm
Washington, DC, National Gallery of Art. Samuel H. Kress Collection. Inv. 1961.9.75

PROVENANCE: Diego Mexía Felipez de Guzmán, Marqués de Leganés, 1655; Victor Spark, New York, 1950; David M. Koetser Gallery, New York; Kress Collection, 1955.

REFERENCES: Longhi 1950, p. 39, pl. 16; Sterling 1952, p. 96; López Navío 1962, p. 274, no. 97; Jordan 1967, p. 333, no. 16; Bergström 1970, p. 35; Angulo 1971, p. 29; Eisler 1977, pp. 206–7, no. K2109; Fort Worth 1985, p. 135, pl. 17; Pérez Sánchez 1987, pp. 54–5, fig. 34.

14 **Juan van der Hamen y León,** 1596–1631   (PAGE 54)
Still Life with Artichokes and Vases of Flowers
Signed and dated, lower right: *Ju⁰ vanderHammen faᵗ,/1627*
Oil on canvas, 81.5 x 110.5 cm
Madrid, Naseiro collection

PROVENANCE: Diego Mexía Felipez de Guzmán, Marqués de Leganés, 1655.
Unpublished.

15 **Juan van der Hamen y León,** 1596–1631   (PAGE 55)
Still Life with Flowers and Fruit
Signed and dated, lower right: *Ju⁰ vanderHamen faᵗ, 1629*
Oil on canvas, 84 x 131 cm
Collection of Lila and Herman Shickman

PROVENANCE: Dr Fritz Rosenberg, Boulder, Colorado (auctioned at Parke-Bernet Galleries, New York, 19 March 1969, lot 28).

REFERENCES: Valdivieso 1975, vol. 48, pp. 402–3, fig. 7; Fort Worth 1985, pp. 142–3, no. 21.

16 **Alejandro de Loarte,** *c.*1600–26   (PAGE 60)
Still Life with Game and Fruit
Signed and dated, lower left: *Alexandro de Loarte, fat. 1623*
Oil on canvas, 84 x 105 cm
Madrid, Fundación Asilo de Santamarca

PROVENANCE: Nicolás de Vargas, 1800(?); Duques de Nájera; donated by the Duquesa de Nájera to the Fundación Santamarca, Madrid.

REFERENCES: Ceán Bermúdez 1800, III, p. 43; Mayer 1927, p. 116; Méndez Casal 1934, p. 193; Cavestany 1936–40, p. 40, pl. 10; Angulo and Pérez Sánchez 1972, p. 221, no. 94, pl. 62; Madrid 1983, p. 36, no. 8 (with additional bibliography).

17 **Juan Bautista de Espinosa,** *c.*1585–1640   (PAGE 62)
Still Life with Silver-Gilt Salvers
Signed and dated on shelves above: *Joannes Bapᵗᵃ Despinossa faciebat anno D, 1624*
Oil on canvas, 98 x 118 cm
Spain, Masaveu collection

PROVENANCE: Art market, London, 1920; Sir Anthony Doughty-Tichborne, Hampshire, 1955; Christie's, London, 21 June 1968; A.R. Lunde, New York; the Hilmar Reksten Foundation, Bergen, Norway; Christie's, London, 9 April 1990, lot 58.

REFERENCES: Harris 1935, p. 259, figs. 3, 4; Lafuente Ferrari 1935, p. 176; Cavestany 1936–40, p. 76; Bergström 1970, p. 47; Young 1976, pp. 213–14, fig. 30; Madrid 1983, p. 45, ill; Fort Worth 1985, p. 92, no. 9 (with extensive bibliography); Pérez Sánchez 1987, p. 62, pl. 46.

18 **Francisco Barrera,** 1595–after 1657   (PAGE 64)
Still Life with Meat, Fruit and Vegetables (the Month of April)
*c.*1640s. Fragmentary signature, lower right
Oil on canvas, 101.5 x 156 cm
Private collection

PROVENANCE: Caylus, Galería de Arte, Madrid.

REFERENCES: Caylus, *El gusto español: Antiguos maestros*, Madrid 1992, pp. 90–3.

19 **Antonio Ponce,** 1608–77   (PAGE 66)
Still Life with Artichokes and a Talavera Vase of Flowers
*c.*1650s. Signed, lower left: *A. Ponze fecit*
Oil on canvas, 72 x 94 cm
Spain, Juan Abello collection

PROVENANCE: Sotheby's, Monaco, 22 February 1986, lot 216 (as Joris Ponse); Matthiesen Fine Art Ltd, London, 1986.

REFERENCES: Matthiesen, *Baroque III (1620–1700)*, 12 June–15 August 1986, pp. 101–3.

20 **Juan de Espinosa,** doc. 1628–59   (PAGE 69)
Still Life with Grapes, Fruit and a Terracotta Jar
Signed and dated on ledge at left: *Ju⁰ despinosa/1646*
Oil on canvas, octagonal, 67.5 x 68 cm
Madrid, Naseiro collection

PROVENANCE: Unknown.

REFERENCES: Sotheby's, London, 8 July 1992, lot 11.

21 **Juan Fernández, El Labrador,** doc. 1630s   (PAGE 72)
Still Life with Hanging White Grapes
*c.*1620s. Oil on canvas, 29.5 x 38 cm
Madrid, Naseiro collection

PROVENANCE: Unknown.
Unpublished.

22 **Attributed to Juan Fernández, El Labrador?,**
doc. 1630s   (PAGE 74)
Still Life with Bunches of Hanging Grapes
1630s–40s. Oil on canvas, 44 x 61 cm
Madrid, Naseiro collection

PROVENANCE: D. Manuel Montesinos, Valencia, 1850.

REFERENCES: *Catálogo de pinturas de la propiedad del Coronel de Caballería, Visitador General de los Presidios del Reino y Comandante del de esta ciudad D. Manuel Montesinos*, Valencia 1850, p. 23.

23 **Juan Fernández, El Labrador,** doc. 1630s   (PAGE 75)
Still Life with Apples, Grapes, Chestnuts and Acorns
*c.*1632. Oil on canvas, 83 x 68.4 cm
Hampton Court Palace, Her Majesty The Queen. Inv. 402559

PROVENANCE: Lord Cottington, c.1633–5 (sent by Arthur Hopton from Madrid); King Charles I, by 1639; sold by the Commonwealth for £5 following the execution of Charles I but reacquired by the Crown; King James II; King William III.

REFERENCES: Van der Doort 1639, p. 4; Law 1898, p. 194, no. 539; Lafuente Ferrari 1935, p. 172; Cavestany 1936–40, p. 66, fig. 4; Sterling 1959, p. 70; Trapier 1967, p. 242; Harris 1967, p. 484, fig. 63; Madrid 1983, p. 43; Fort Worth 1985, pp. 155–7, no. 23 (with additional bibliography).

24 Juan Fernández, El Labrador, doc. 1630s (PAGE 77)
Vase of Flowers

1630s. Oil on canvas (fragment), 44 x 34 cm
Madrid, Museo del Prado. Inv. 2888

PROVENANCE: Gaspar Méndez de Haro y Guzmán, Marqués de Eliche, 1651 (?); Antonio Pons, Málaga (on loan to the Museo Provincial de Bellas Artes, Málaga, 1931–40); acquired from Pons by the Ministerio de Educación Nacional in 1946 for the Museo del Prado.

REFERENCES: Cavestany 1936–40, p. 151, no. 13, pl. 21; Seckel 1946, p. 287, fig. 6; Guinard 1960, p. 281, no. 607; Madrid 1978, no. 77; Madrid 1983, p. 58, no. 30; Fort Worth 1985, p. 160 (with extensive bibliography).

25 Antonio de Pereda, 1611–78 (PAGE 80)
Still Life with Walnuts

Signed and dated, bottom right: AP/1634
Oil on panel, 20.7 cm diameter
Spain, Private collection

PROVENANCE: Unknown.

REFERENCES: Angulo and Pérez Sánchez 1983, pp. 152, 223, no. 148; Madrid 1983, p. 107, no. 66; Fort Worth 1985, pp. 212–13, no. 39.

26 Antonio de Pereda, 1611–78 (PAGE 81)
Vanitas

c.1634. Oil on canvas, 139.5 x 174 cm
Vienna, Kunsthistorisches Museum. Inv. 771

PROVENANCE: Juan Alfonso Enríquez de Cabrera, 9th Almirante de Castilla, 5th Duque Medina de Rioseco, until 1647; Juan Gaspar Alonso Enríquez de Cabrera, 10th Almirante de Castilla, 6th Duque de Medina de Rioseco, until 1691; Juan Tomás Enríquez de Cabrera, 11th Almirante de Castilla, 7th Duque de Medina de Rioseco, until 1703; Austrian Imperial collection from before 1733 (when recorded in Stallburg).

REFERENCES: Díaz del Valle 1656–9 (edn 1933), p. 375; Palomino 1724 (edn 1947), p. 958; Fernández Duro 1903, p. 203; Mayer 1911, p. 199; Kubler and Soria 1959, pp. 281–2; Gállego 1968, p. 200 (Spanish edn 1984, p. 207); Vienna, Kunsthistorisches Museum, 1973 cat., p. 133; Madrid 1978, no. 7; Angulo and Pérez Sánchez 1983, pp. 235–6, no. 160; Fort Worth 1985, pp. 214–18, pl. 40; Pérez Sánchez 1987, pp. 116–21; Pérez Sánchez 1992, pp. 245–7; Madrid 1994, pp. 31–7 (with extensive bibliography).

27 Antonio de Pereda?, 1611–78 (PAGE 83)
The Dream of the Knight

c.1650. Oil on canvas, 152 x 217 cm
Madrid, Museo de la Real Academia de Bellas Artes de San Fernando. Inv. 639

PROVENANCE: Unless it should be the painting (El Desengaño del mundo) documented in the testament of the painter Francisco de Palacios in 1651, undocumented until being seen by Pedro González de Sepúlveda in the palace of Manuel Godoy, Príncipe de la Paz, on 12 November 1800 (as Pereda); among the list of fifty paintings selected by Goya, Maella and Napoli to be sent to France, 1810 ('Pereda, La vida es sueño'); Paris, Musée Napoléon, 1810–14 (as Pereda); among the list of fifty-seven paintings returned from France, 1815 ('Pereda, Los placeres de hombre pasando como un sueño'); first catalogued in the Academia collection in 1818, p. 32, no. 270 (as Pereda).

REFERENCES: The seventeenth- and eighteenth-century references usually associated with this painting all refer instead to the painting in Vienna (cat. 26). The following are certain references to the Madrid painting: P.-L. Dubray, Notice des tableaux des écoles primitives de l'Italie, de l'Allemagne et de plusiers autres tableaux de différentes écoles, exposés dans le grand Salon du Musée Royal, ouvert le 25 de juillet, 1814, Paris 1814, no. 90; Stirling 1848, p. 505; Tormo 1916, pp. 60–75; Saltillo 1933, pp. 54–5; Guinard and Baticle 1950, pp. 127, fig. 127; Gállego 1968, p. 200, pl. 25 (Spanish edn 1972, pp. 246–7); Pardo Canalís 1979, p. 300 ff.; Angulo and Pérez Sánchez 1983, pp. 227–9, no. 154; Fort Worth 1985, p. 218, fig. XIV.6; Barrio Moya 1987, pp. 425–35; Pérez Sánchez 1992, p. 246; Madrid 1994, pp. 31–7 (with extensive early bibliography).

28 Unknown Artist (PAGE 85)
Still Life with Books and an Hour-glass

c.1640. Oil on canvas, 35 x 55 cm
Berlin, Staatliche Museen, Gemäldegalerie. Inv. 1667

PROVENANCE: T. Hookham Frere, Roydon Hall, Norfolk (as Velázquez); M. Langton Douglas, who donated it to the Kaiser Friedrich Museum in 1908.

REFERENCES: Von Loga 1923, p. 260 (as Pereda); Gaya Nuño 1956, p. 228, no. 18 (as Collantes); López-Rey 1963, p. 180, no. 168 (as not by Velázquez); Catalogue, Berlin 1975, p. 407 (as Pereda; discussion of previous attributions); Madrid 1978, no. 86 (as anonymous); Madrid 1983, p. 67; Fort Worth 1985, pp. 20, 22 (as anonymous); Tokyo 1992, no. 30 (as possibly by Murillo).

29 Antonio de Pereda, 1611–78 (PAGE 86)
Still Life with Vegetables

Signed and dated on ledge at left: PEREDA. F./1651
Oil on canvas, 74.5 x 143 cm
Lisbon, Museu Nacional de Arte Antiga. Inv. 470

PROVENANCE: Collection of Queen Carlota Joaquina of Portugal; incorporated into the museum in 1859.

REFERENCES: Cavestany 1936–40, p. 78; Mayer 1947, p. 457; Kubler and Soria 1959, p. 282; Bergström 1970, p. 69; Madrid 1983, p. 109, no. 69; Angulo and Pérez Sánchez 1983, pp. 225–6; Fort Worth 1985, pp. 219–21 (with more extensive bibliography).

30 **Antonio de Pereda,** 1611–78 (PAGE 88)
Still Life with Sweets, Vessels and an Ebony Chest

c.1652. Signed on round wooden box: *pereda f.*
Oil on canvas, 80 x 94 cm
St Petersburg, State Hermitage Museum. Inv. 327

PROVENANCE: W. Coeswelt, Amsterdam; acquired by Czar Alexander I in 1815.

REFERENCES: Mayer 1913, p. 194; X. Malitzkaya, 'Los dos cuadros de Antonio Pereda en el Museo del Bellas Artes de Moskú', *Archivo Español de Arte y Arqueología*, VIII, 1932, pp. 201–2; Kubler and Soria 1959, p. 282; Bergström 1970, p. 69, fig. 7; Bordeaux 1978, pp. 5, 9; Angulo and Pérez Sánchez 1983, pp. 158, 225, no. 151 (with extensive bibliography); Fort Worth 1985, p. 209; Pérez Sánchez 1987, p. 114, fig. 102.

31 **Antonio de Pereda,** 1611–78 (PAGE 91)
Kitchen Scene (Allegory of Lost Virtue)

c.1650–5. Oil on canvas, 179.2 x 226 cm
Penrhyn Castle, The Douglas-Pennant collection (The National Trust). Inv. PEN/P/54

PROVENANCE: Frank Hall Standish; bequeathed to King Louis Philippe of France in 1841; exhibited in the Galerie Espagnole of the Louvre from 1842 until 1848; returned to Louis Philippe in 1850; sold Christie's, London, 27 and 28 May 1853, lot 220 (bought by Hickman); Col. Edward Gordon Douglas Pennant, 1st Lord Penrhyn (d. 1886); thence by descent.

REFERENCES: *Catalogue des tableaux, dessins et gravures de la collection Standish, légués au Roi par M. Frank Hall Standish*, Paris 1842, no. 154; Alice Douglas Pennant, *Catalogue of the Pictures at Penrhyn Castle and Mortimer House in 1901*, Bangor 1902, no. 54; Lipschutz 1972, p. 227.

32 **Francisco de Burgos Mantilla,** 1609/12–1672 (PAGE 92)
Still Life with Dried Fruit

Signed and dated, lower right: *frº. Burgensis Mantilla fᵗ 1631*
Oil on canvas, 29.1 x 58.9 cm
New Haven, Yale University Art Gallery, Stephen Carlton Clark, B.A. 1903, Fund. Inv. 1972.43

PROVENANCE: Frederick Mont, Inc., New York, c.1970; acquired from Mont by Yale University Art Gallery in 1972.

REFERENCES: Volpe 1974, p. 34, fig. 20; Young 1976, p. 211, fig. 18; López-Rey 1979, p. 123, pl. 35; Agulló and Pérez Sánchez 1981, pp. 359, 361, 368, ill.; Sterling 1981, p. 19; Madrid 1983, pp. 46–7, 66, no. 46; Cherry 1984, p. 60; Fort Worth 1985, p. 200, no. 36; Pérez Sánchez 1987, p. 70, fig. 61.

33 **Francisco de Palacios,** 1622/5–1652 (PAGE 94)
Still Life with Fruit and a Wine Cooler

Signed and dated, lower right: *Fᶜᵒ. DE PALACIOS. Fᵀ./1648*
Oil on canvas, 59 x 78 cm

34 *Still Life with Braided Bread* (PAGE 95)

Signed and dated, lower left: *F. DE PALACIOS. Fᵀ./1648*
Oil on canvas, 60 x 80 cm
Schloss Rohrau, Austria, Graf Harrach'sche Familiensammlung

PROVENANCE: Count Ferdinand Bonaventura Harrach; thence by descent in the Harrach family.

REFERENCES: Mayer 1922, pp. 427–8; Salas 1935, pp. 275–7, pl. 1; Cavestany 1936–40, pp. 39, 80; Vienna, Harrach, 1960 cat., pp. 55–6, no. 152; Bergström 1970, p. 206; Munich/Vienna 1982, nos 60 and 61; Angulo and Pérez Sánchez 1983, pp. 136–7, nos 4 and 5; Madrid 1983, p. 47; Fort Worth 1985, pp. 203–5 (with extensive bibliography); Pérez Sánchez 1987, pp. 76–7, figs 62 and 63.

35 **Attributed to Mateo Cerezo,** 1637–66 (PAGE 96)
Kitchen Still Life

c.1660–75. Oil on canvas, 100 x 127 cm
Madrid, Museo del Prado. Inv. 3159

PROVENANCE: Unknown.

REFERENCES: *Inventario del Prado, Nuevas adquisiciones*, no. 1922; Madrid, Prado, 1972 cat., p. 908; London 1976, no. 78; Paris 1976, no. 76; Young 1976, p. 212; Salas 1978, pp. 13–14; Madrid 1978, no. 110; Caracas 1981, no. 57; Madrid 1983, p. 115, no. 76; Pérez Sánchez 1987, pp. 121 and 124; Buendía and Gutiérrez Pastor 1986, pp. 100 and 160, no. 69.

36 **José Antolínez,** 1635–75 (PAGE 98)
Still Life with Papillon

Signed and dated lower right: *Joseph Antolinez F./70*
Oil on canvas, 55.9 x 41.3 cm
Spain, Private collection

PROVENANCE: General John Meade, Consul General at Madrid; Christie's, London, 7 March 1851, lot 250; purchased by Graves on behalf of William Stirling, later Sir William Stirling-Maxwell, 9th Bt. (1818–78); thence by descent at Keir; Christie's, London, 14 December 1990, lot 44.

REFERENCES: Angulo 1954, pp. 231–2; Angulo 1957, pp. 33 and 43, pl. 48; Camón Aznar 1977, p. 416; Haraszti-Takács 1983, pp. 108 and 163, no. 2; Geneva 1989, p. 112.

37 **Andrés Deleito, active** 1680 (PAGE 99)
Vanitas

c.1680. Signed on cartellino: *ANDRES DE/LEITO F.*
Oil on canvas, 73 x 93 cm
Madrid, María Begoña García-Diego y Ortiz

PROVENANCE: Unknown.

REFERENCES: Oña Iribarren 1944, pp. 49, 95, no. 52; Madrid 1960, pp. 119–20; Madrid 1978, no. 56; Madrid 1983, p. 113, no. 73; Pérez Sánchez 1987, p. 128; Paris 1987, p. 268, no. 77; Tokyo 1992, p. 107, no. 33.

38 **Francisco de Zurbarán,** 1598–1664 (PAGE 105)
Still Life with Four Vessels

c.1658–64. Oil on canvas, 46 x 84 cm
Madrid, Museo del Prado. Inv. 2803

PROVENANCE: Francisco Cambó, Barcelona; donated to the Museo del Prado in 1940.

REFERENCES: Mayer 1927, p. 320; Caturla 1945, p. 303; Seckel

1946, pp. 287–8; Soria 1953, no. 73; Sánchez Cantón 1955, p. 82; Pemán 1958, pp. 193–211; Guinard 1960, no. 609; Gaya Nuño-Frati 1976, no. 103; Gállego-Gudiol 1976, no. 541; Madrid 1983, p. 86, no. 57; Fort Worth 1985, pp. 222, 227; Valdivieso 1986, p. 177; Madrid 1988, no. 117; Madrid 1990, pp. 374–80. no. 40 (with extensive bibliography).

39 Juan de Zurbarán, 1620–49   (PAGE 106)
Plate of Grapes
Signed and dated, l.l.: *Juan deZurbaran façie.../·1639*
Oil on copper, 28 x 36 cm
Bordeaux, Private collection

PROVENANCE: Unknown.

REFERENCES: Bordeaux 1955, no. 93bis; Pemán 1958, pp. 193–211; Soria 1959, p. 275; Guinard 1960, p. 282, no. 613; Madrid 1964–5, p. 85; Gállego-Gudiol 1976, p. 69; Madrid 1983, p. 77; Fort Worth 1985, pp. 224–5; Pérez Sánchez 1987, pp. 95, 98.

40 Juan de Zurbarán, 1620–49   (PAGE 106)
Plate of Fruit with a Linnet
c.1639–40. Oil on canvas, 40 x 57cm
Barcelona, Museu Nacional d'Art de Catalunya. Inv. MAC 5671

PROVENANCE: Unknown. Acquired by the Museu Nacional d'Art de Catalunya in 1904.

REFERENCES: Girona 1987, no. 27 (as Camprobín).

41 Juan de Zurbarán, 1620–49   (PAGE 106)
Still Life with Chocolate Service
Signed and dated, l.l.: *Juan deZurbaran fati.../1640*
Oil on canvas, 48 x 75 cm
Kiev, Museum of Western and Oriental Art.

PROVENANCE: Khanenko collection, St Petersburg.

REFERENCES: V. Voinov, in *Apollon* (Institut d'Art e d'Archéologie de l'Université de Paris), 1916, p. 1; letter from Sir Robert Witt to *The Burlington Magazine*, vol. 45, 1924, p. 52; Ghilarov 1938, p. 190; Cavestany 1936–40, p. 77; Seckel 1946, pp. 289–90, and Appendix 1947, p. 62, no. 8; Soria 1955, p. 177; Pemán 1958, p. 193–211; Guinard 1960, p. 282; Fort Worth 1985, pp. 225–7; Pérez Sánchez 1987, pp. 94, 98.

42 Juan de Zurbarán, 1620–49   (PAGE 109)
Plate of Quinces, Grapes, Figs and Plums
c.1645. Oil on canvas, 33.5 x 47 cm
Private collection

PROVENANCE: Unknown.
Unpublished.

43 Pedro de Camprobín, 1605–74   (PAGE 112)
Still Life with Sweets
Signed and dated on table at right: *Pº de Camprouin passano fᵗ. 1663*
Oil on canvas, 42.5 x 62.5 cm

44 *Still Life with Chestnuts, Olives and Wine*   (PAGE 113)
1663. Oil on canvas, 42 x 62 cm
Private collection

PROVENANCE: López Cepero y Cañaveral, Seville; Marqués de Casa Torres, Madrid; with Edward Speelman & Son, London, 1983. Unpublished.

45 Juan de Valdés Leal, 1622–90   (PAGE 116)
Allegory of Vanity
Signed and dated on the engraving in the open book to the right of the skull: *1660 Juº de baldes Leal FA.*
Oil on canvas, 130.4 x 99.3 cm
Hartford, Connecticut, Wadsworth Atheneum. The Ella Gallup Sumner and Mary Catlin Sumner Collection Fund. Inv. 1939.270

PROVENANCE: The Spanish Art Gallery (Tomás Harris), London, 1938; Durlacher Brothers, New York, 1939; there acquired in 1939 by Wadsworth Atheneum.

REFERENCES: London 1938, pp. 16, 56; Nordström 1959, pp. 135–7; Trapier 1960, pp. 14, 30–2, 34, 54; Gállego 1968, pp. 201–2 (Spanish edn 1984, pp. 208–9); Angulo 1971, p. 374; Kinkead 1974, pp. 156–61; Kinkead 1978, pp. 155–8; Princeton 1982, p. 108; Valdivieso 1988, pp. 117–20, 243 (with extensive bibliography); Cadogan 1991, pp. 324–7.

46 Juan de Valdés Leal, 1622–90   (PAGE 117)
Allegory of Salvation
1660. Oil on canvas, 130 x 99 cm
York City Art Gallery (presented by F.D. Lycett Green through the National Art-Collections Fund). Inv. 810

PROVENANCE: Spanish Art Gallery, London, 1938; F.D. Lycett Green, Constantia, South Africa (bequeathed to the York City Art Gallery in 1955).

REFERENCES: London 1938, p. 56; Nordström 1959, pp. 127–37; Trapier 1960, pp. 14, 32–4; 54; *York Art Gallery Catalogue*, Vol. I, 1961, p. 98; Gállego 1968, pp. 201–2 (Spanish edn 1984, pp. 208–9); Angulo 1971, p. 374; Kinkead 1978, pp. 152–5, 401–2; Madrid 1983, pp. 130–1, no. 108; Valdivieso 1986, p. 270; Valdivieso 1988, pp. 117–20, 243 (with extensive bibliography); Madrid 1991, no. 50.

47 Tomás Hiepes, c.1610–74   (PAGE 122)
Still Life with Grapevine, Marigolds and Fruit
Signed and dated on pot in foreground: *ORIGINAL DE THOMAS HIEPES, EN Vᶜ. 1654...*
Oil on canvas, 110.5 x 134.6 cm
Madrid, Plácido Arango collection

PROVENANCE: Unknown.

REFERENCE: Christie's, New York, 12 January 1994, lot 95.

48 Pseudo-Hiepes   (PAGE 126)
Still Life with Honeycomb, Fruit and a Vase of Flowers
c.1650–75. Oil on canvas, 77 x 115 cm
Madrid, Private collection

PROVENANCE: Manuel Salvador López, Madrid, 1870; thence by descent.
Unpublished.

49 Juan de Arellano, 1614–76 (PAGE 132)
Festoon of Flowers with Cartouche Surrounding a Landscape

Signed and dated: *Juan de Arellano, 1652*
Oil on canvas, 58 x 73 cm
Madrid, Museo del Prado. Inv. 2508

PROVENANCE: Xavier Lafitte, Madrid (donated to the Prado in 1930).

REFERENCES: Cavestany 1936–40, p. 82; Bergström 1970, p. 62; Madrid 1983, no. 84; Duque Oliart 1986, pp. 274–5, fig. 4; Pérez Sánchez 1987, 133–4, fig. 123.

50 Juan de Arellano, 1614–76 (PAGE 135)
Still Life with Flowers and Fruit

*c.*1665–70. Signed on plinth at left: *Juan. deArellano*
Oil on canvas, 98.5 x 63 cm
Spain, Masaveu collection

PROVENANCE: Bernardo de Iriarte, Madrid; José de Madrazo, Madrid, in 1856; José de Salamanca, Marqués de Salamanca, Madrid; his sale Paris, Hotel Drouot, 25 and 26 January 1875, lot 3 (as coming from the Madrazo collection); private collection, United States; Edmund Peel y Asociados, Madrid, 28 February 1991, lot 5.

REFERENCES: P. Madoz, *Madrid. Audiencia, provincia, intendencia, vicaría, partido y villa*, Madrid 1848, p. 350; *Catálogo de la galería de cuadros del Excmo. Sr. D. José de Madrazo...*, Madrid 1856, p. 81, no. 328 (as coming from the collection of 'G. [*sic*] Iriarte'); Tokyo 1992, no. 37.

51 Juan de Arellano, 1614–76 (PAGE 136)
Basket of Flowers

*c.*1670–5. Signed on plinth at right: *Juan de Arellano*
Oil on canvas, 84 x 105 cm
Madrid, Museo del Prado. Inv. 3138

PROVENANCE: Condesa Viuda de Moriles, Madrid (donated to the Prado in 1969).

REFERENCES: Salas 1978, p. 9; Buenos Aires 1980, p. 98; Munich/Vienna 1982, no. 3; Madrid 1983, p. 121, no. 87; Pérez Sánchez 1987, pp. 134, 138, fig. 131.

52 Bartolomé Pérez, 1634–98 (PAGE 138)
Flowers in a Sculptured Vase

Signed and dated on plinth: *Bme Perez Facieb/..66*
Oil on canvas, 82.6 x 62.2 cm
Cambridge, Fitzwilliam Museum. Inv. PD.43–1954

PROVENANCE: Galleria San Giorgio, Venice, 1913; bequeathed to the museum by Sir Robert Hyde, K.C.M.G., 1953.

REFERENCES: Goodison and Sutton 1960, I, p. 215; Bergström 1970, p. 64, fig. 47; Münster/Baden-Baden 1979, p. 336, no. 191; Madrid 1983, p. 99; Pérez Sánchez 1987, p. 142, fig. 139.

53 Bartolomé Pérez, 1634–98 (PAGE 140)
Garland of Flowers with Saint Anthony and the Christ Child

After 1689. Signed: *Bme. Pérez RP* (*Regis Pictor*) interlaced and crowned
Oil on canvas, 65 x 84 cm
Madrid, Museo del Prado. Inv. 3655

PROVENANCE: Duques de Pastrana (donated to the Prado in 1889).

REFERENCES: Buenos Aires 1980, p. 96; Madrid 1983, p. 124, no. 96; Pérez Sánchez 1987, p. 143, fig. 144; Tokyo 1992, no. 42.

54 Bartolomé Pérez, 1634–98 (PAGE 141)
Garland of Flowers on a Gold Ground

*c.*1689–91. Oil and gold on panel, 63.5 x 54 cm
Madrid, Private collection

PROVENANCE: Probably Alcázar of Madrid, inventories of 1734 and 1747; Palacio del Buen Retiro, 1772.

REFERENCES: Unpublished. Related documentation can be found in Cavestany 1936–40, pp. 143–4; Fernández Bayton 1975, pp. 287–8; Barbieto 1992, pp. 195–6; Madrid 1994 (*El Real Alcázar de Madrid*), p. 170.

55 Attributed to Gabriel de la Corte, 1648–94 (PAGE 144)
Flowerpiece

*c.*1670s. Oil on canvas, 62 x 84 cm
Madrid, Museo del Prado. Inv. 1055

PROVENANCE: Museo de la Trinidad, no. 594.

REFERENCES: Madrid 1983, cat. 93 (as Bartolomé Pérez); Tokyo 1992, cat. 43 (as Bartolomé Pérez).

56 Luis Meléndez, 1716–80 (PAGE 158)
Still Life with Fruit, Cheese and Containers

Signed and dated on box at right: *Ls. Mz./1771*
Oil on canvas, 40 x 62 cm
Madrid, Museo del Prado. Inv. 909

PROVENANCE: Spanish royal collections: Casita del Príncipe, El Escorial, 1778; palace of Aranjuéz, 1818.

REFERENCES: Soria 1948, p. 216; Tufts 1971, p. 167, fig. 8; Bordeaux/Paris/Madrid 1979–80 (Spanish edn, no. 39); Belgrade 1981, no. 28; Munich/Vienna 1982, no. 46; Tufts 1982, p. 150, no. 8; Madrid 1982–3, pp. 108–9; no. 32; Gutiérrez Alonso 1983, p. 166; Tufts 1985, pp. 73–4 (cat. 27), 163, pl. 27; Pérez Sánchez 1987, pp. 186, 189, fig. 194; Tomlinson 1990, pp. 86–7, fig. 2.

57 Luis Meléndez, 1716–80 (PAGE 159)
Still Life with Sea Bream and Oranges

Signed and dated: *Ls Eo Mes Dra Dzo ISto pe/Ano 1772*
Oil on canvas, 41 x 62.8 cm
Spain, Masaveu collection

PROVENANCE: Bonhams, London, 8 December 1992, lot 108.

REFERENCES: *De la Edad Media al Romanticismo*, Madrid (Galería Caylus) 1993–4 , pp. 164–7.

58 Luis Meléndez, 1716–80   (PAGE 160)
Still Life with Oranges and Walnuts

Signed and dated on wooden box at right: *Lˢ. Eᵒ. Mᶻ. D.N (?)/ANO 1772.*
Oil on canvas, 61 x 81.3 cm
London, The National Gallery. NG 6505

PROVENANCE: Matthiesen Fine Art Ltd, London; acquired by the National Gallery in 1986.

REFERENCES: London 1986–7, no. 27; Levey 1987, p. 192; London 1989, pp. 9, 82, no. 23; Luna 1989, pp. 370–2, fig. 1.

59 Luis Meléndez, 1716–80   (PAGE 162)
Still Life with Artichokes and Tomatoes in a Landscape

*c.*1771. Signed on small stone at right: *L. Mz*
Oil on canvas, 61.6 x 81.9 cm
Collection of Lila and Herman Shickman

PROVENANCE: Lord Sackville; Sotheby's, London, 16 March 1966, lot 71; Hallsborough Gallery, London.

REFERENCES: Tufts 1971, p. 183; Madrid 1982, p. 31; Tufts 1982, p. 163, no. 82; Tufts 1985, p. 103 (cat. 81), 185, pl. 81; Raleigh/Dallas/New York 1985, no. 24.

60 and 61 Luis Paret, 1746–99   (PAGE 164)
Pair of Floral Bouquets

*c.*1780. Each signed, lower right: *L. Paret fecᵗ*
Oil on canvas, 39 x 37 cm
Madrid, Museo del Prado. Inv. 1042 and 1043

PROVENANCE: Spanish royal collections: Casita del Príncipe, El Escorial; palace of Aranjuéz.

REFERENCES: Cavestany 1936–40, p. 98; Aguilera 1946, p. 18, pl. XVIII; Gaya Nuño 1952, pp. 126 and 144, no. 70, fig. 31; Delgado 1957, pp. 132 and 245, no. 27, fig. 34; Sánchez Cantón 1965, p. 238; Madrid 1983, pp. 172–3, nos 158–9; Luna 1984, p. 103; Pérez Sánchez 1987, pp. 191–2, figs 200 and 201; Bilbao 1991, p. 187; Tokyo 1992, no. 57 (Prado Inv. 1042 only).

62 Benito Espinós, 1748–1818   (PAGE 167)
Sprig of Orange Blossom

*c.*1783. Signed, lower right: *Benito Espinós, f.ᵗ*
Oil on canvas, 43 x 29.5 cm
Barcelona, Reial Acadèmia Catalana de Belles Arts de Sant Jordi. Inv. 115

PROVENANCE: Unknown.

REFERENCES: Madrid 1983, p. 182, no. 170; Pérez Sánchez 1987, p. 211; Tokyo 1992, no. 58.

63 Juan Bautista Romero, 1756–after 1802   (PAGE 169)
Vase of Flowers

1796. Signed, lower centre: *Juan bauta romero*
Oil on panel, 55 x 37 cm
Madrid, Museo de La Real Academia de Bellas Artes de San Fernando. Inv. 97

PROVENANCE: Manuel Godoy, Príncipe de la Paz; confiscated by the Spanish state in 1808 and deposited in the Academia de San Fernando.

REFERENCES: Tormo 1929, p. 18; Cavestany 1936–40, pp. 100 and 168, no. 147 (the description of the flowers pertains to the painting exhibited as no. 149); Pérez Sánchez 1964b, p. 19, no. 97; Sánchez Cantón 1965, p. 326; Madrid 1983, p. 174, no. 160 (by a cataloguer's inadvertent error, the entry continues to confuse this work with its pendant); Rose Wagner 1983, II, p. 399; Pérez Sánchez 1987, p. 193, fig. 205, p. 200.

64 José López Enguídanos, 1760–1812   (PAGE 172)
Still Life with Melon, Birds and a Glass of Water

1807. Signed on table edge, at right: *Josef Lopez Enguídanos f.*
Oil on canvas, 51 x 68 cm
Madrid, Museo de la Real Academia de Bellas Artes de San Fernando. Inv. 52

PROVENANCE: Manuel Godoy, Príncipe de la Paz; confiscated by the Spanish state in 1808 and deposited in the Academia de San Fernando in 1816.

REFERENCES: Tormo 1929, p. 45; Pérez Sánchez 1964b, no. 52; Madrid 1983, p. 175, no. 163; Rose Wagner 1983, II, p. 256, no. 329; Pérez Sánchez 1987, p. 200, fig. 212; Tokyo 1992, no. 59.

65 Francisco Lacoma y Fontanet, 1784–1849   (PAGE 173)
Vase of Flowers with Lute and Lyre

Oil on canvas, 116 x 90 cm
Barcelona, Museu Nacional d'Art de Catalunya. On permanent loan from the Reial Acadèmia de Belles Arts de Sant Jordi, Barcelona, since 1906. Inv. MNAC/MAM 10440

PROVENANCE: Given by the artist to the Real Academia de Bellas Artes de San Jorge, Barcelona.

REFERENCES: Gudiol Ricart, et al., n.d., p. 202, fig. 98; Madrid 1983, p. 187, no. 180; Pérez Sánchez 1987, p. 218, fig. 280; Tokyo 1992, no. 61.

66 Francisco de Goya, 1746–1828   (PAGE 178)
Still Life with Golden Bream

*c.*1808–12. Signed, right foreground (almost vertically): *Goya*
Oil on canvas, 44.1 x 61.6 cm
Houston, Museum of Fine Arts. Museum purchase with funds provided by the Alice Pratt Brown Museum Fund and the Brown Foundation Accessions Endowment Fund. Inv. 94.245

PROVENANCE: Javier de Goya y Bayeu, Madrid, 1812; Mariano de Goya y Goicoechea, Madrid, until 1846; Francisco de Narváez, Conde de Yumuri, Carabanchel Alto, until *c.*1865; Zacharie Astruc, Paris; Madame Thévenot, Paris; David Weill collection, Paris, since 1926; acquired by the Museum of Fine Arts, Houston, in 1994.

REFERENCES: López-Rey 1948, pp. 251–60, fig. 6; Desparmet Fitzgerald 1928–50, I, no. 178; Gassier and Wilson 1970 (edn 1971), pp. 254, 263, no. 907; Gudiol 1971, I, pp. 156, 323, no. 592, IV, fig. 946; The Hague/Paris 1970, no. 36.

67 Francisco de Goya, 1746–1828   (PAGE 179)
Still Life with Woodcocks

c.1808–12. Oil on canvas, 45.2 x 62.6 cm
Dallas, Texas, Southern Methodist University, Meadows Museum,
Algur H. Meadows Collection. Inv. MM71.01

PROVENANCE: Javier Goya y Bayeu, Madrid, 1812; Mariano Goya y
Goicoechea, Madrid, until 1846; Francisco de Narváez, Conde de
Yumuri, Carabanchel Alto, until c.1865; Terbek de Compiègne,
Paris, until 1877, private collection, Paris; private collection, New
York, 1948; acquired by the Meadows Museum in 1971.

REFERENCES: López-Rey 1948, pp. 251–60, fig. 8;
Indianapolis/Providence 1963, no. 29; London 1963–4, no. 125;
Newark 1964–5, pp. 5, 15, no. 11; Gassier and Wilson 1970 (edn
1971), pp. 254, 263, no. 910; Gudiol 1971, I, pp. 156, 323, no. 587,
II, fig. 941; Jordan 1974, pp. 64–5, 114–15, no. 27; Madrid 1983,
p. 197, no. 189; Pérez Sánchez 1987, p. 223.

68 Francisco de Goya, 1746–1828   (PAGE 182)
Still Life with Dead Turkey

c.1808–12. Signed, bottom centre (almost vertically): *Goya*
Oil on canvas, 45 x 63 cm
Madrid, Museo del Prado. Inv. 751

PROVENANCE: Javier de Goya y Bayeu, Madrid, 1812; Mariano de
Goya y Goicoechea, Madrid, until 1846; Francisco de Narváez,

Conde de Yumuri, Carabanchel Alto, until c.1865; art market,
Madrid; acquired by the Museo del Prado in 1900.

REFERENCES: Mayer 1923, no. 731; Beruete 1917, p. 174; López-Rey
1948, pp. 251–60, fig. 1; Desparmet Fitzgerald 1928–50, I, no. 177;
Gassier and Wilson 1970 (edn 1971), pp. 254, 262, no. 904; Gudiol
1970 (English edn 1971), I, p. 323, no. 589, IV, fig. 943; Madrid
1983, p. 194, no. 186; Pérez Sánchez 1987, pp. 227, 229, fig. 239;
Paris 1987–8, no. 107.

69 Francisco de Goya, 1746–1828   (PAGE 183)
*Still Life with Pieces of Rib, Loin and a Head
of Mutton*

c.1808–12. Signed in red in the shadow underneath the head: *Goya*
Oil on canvas, 45 x 62 cm
Paris, Musée du Louvre. Inv. R.F.1937.120

PROVENANCE: Javier de Goya y Bayeu, Madrid, 1812; Mariano de
Goya y Goicoechea, Madrid, until 1846; Francisco de Narváez,
Conde de Yumuri, Carabanchel Alto, until c.1865; private collection,
Paris (?); acquired by the Musée du Louvre in 1937.

REFERENCES: Paris 1938, no. 24; López-Rey 1948, pp. 251–60; Paris
1952, pp. 111–12, no. 86; The Hague/Paris 1970, no. 35; Gassier
and Wilson 1970 (edn 1971), pp. 254, 262, no. 903; Gudiol 1970
(English edn 1971), I, p. 232, no. 596, IV, fig. 950; Pérez Sánchez
1987, p. 229, fig. 238.

Lenders to the Exhibition

Lent by Her Majesty The Queen (cat. 23)
Juan Abello Collection, Spain (cats 11, 19)
Plácido Arango Collection, Madrid (cat. 47)
The Art Institute of Chicago. Gift of Mr and Mrs Leigh B. Block (cat. 2)
Lent by the Syndics of the Fitzwilliam Museum, Cambridge (cat. 52)
Fundación Asilo de Santamarca, Madrid (cat. 16)
María Begoña García-Diego y Ortiz, Madrid (cat. 37)
Graf Harrach'sche Familiensammlung Schloss Rohrau (cats 33, 34)
Collection of Mrs H. John Heinz III, Washington (cat. 4)
Kunsthistorisches Museum, Vienna (cat. 26)
Masaveu Collection, Spain (cats 17, 50, 57)
Algur H. Meadows Collection, Meadows Museum, Southern Methodist University, Dallas, Texas (cat. 67)
Musée du Louvre, Département des Peintures, Paris (cat. 69)
Museo del Prado, Madrid (cats 3, 5, 9, 10, 12, 24, 35, 38, 49, 51, 53, 55, 56, 60, 61, 68)
Museo de la Real Academia de Bellas Artes de San Fernando, Madrid (cats 27, 63, 64)
Museu Nacional de Arte Antiga, Lisbon (cat. 29)
Museu Nacional d'Art de Catalunya, Barcelona (cats 40, 65)
The Museum of Fine Arts, Houston. Museum Purchase with Funds provided by the Alice Pratt Brown Museum Fund and the Brown Foundation Accessions Endowment Fund (cat. 66)
Museum of Western and Oriental Art, Kiev (cat. 41)

Naseiro Collection, Madrid (cats 14, 20, 21, 22)
National Gallery of Art, Washington. Samuel H. Kress Collection (cat. 13)
National Gallery of Scotland, Edinburgh (cat. 7)
Penrhyn Castle, The Douglas-Pennant Collection (The National Trust) (cat. 31)
Private Collection (cat. 18)
Private Collection (cat. 42)
Private Collection (cats 43, 44)
Private Collection, Bordeaux (cat. 39)
Private Collection, Madrid (cat. 48)
Private Collection, Madrid (cat. 54)
Private Collection, Spain (cat. 25)
Private Collection, Spain (cat. 36)
Reial Acadèmia Catalana de Belles Arts de Sant Jordi, Barcelona (cat. 62)
San Diego Museum of Art. Gift of Misses Anne R. and Amy Putnam (cat. 1)
Collection of Lila and Herman Shickman (cats 15, 59)
Staatliche Museen zu Berlin, Gemäldegalerie (cat. 28)
State Hermitage Museum, St Petersburg (cat. 30)
The Board of Trustees of the Victoria and Albert Museum, London (cat. 8)
Wadsworth Atheneum, Hartford, CT. The Ella Gallup Sumner and Mary Catlin Sumner Collection Fund (cat. 45)
Yale University Art Gallery. Stephen Carlton Clark, B.A. 1903, Fund (cat. 32)
York City Art Gallery (presented by F.D. Lycett Green through the National Art-Collections Fund) (cat. 46)

Picture Credits

Many of the photographs were supplied from Dr Jordan's photographic archive. Full credit lines are given in the illustration captions, except as follows:

The Royal Collection © 1994 Her Majesty Queen Elizabeth II: cat. 23
Barcelona, Ampliaciones y Reproducciones MAS: figs 71, 72, 143
Barcelona, Photograph © Museu Nacional d'Art de Catalunya. MNAC Photographic Service
   (Calveras/Sagristà): cats 40, 65
Berlin, Staatliche Museen Zu Berlin, Gemäldegalerie. Photos Jörg P. Anders: cat. 28; fig. 26
Chicago, Photograph © 1994, The Art Institute of Chicago. All rights reserved: cat. 2
Cologne, Wallraf-Richartz-Museum. Photo Rheinisches Bildarchiv: fig. 24
Granada, Javier Algarra: fig. 6
Lisbon, Museu Nacional de Arte Antiga. Arquivo Nacional de Fotografia – Instituto Português de
   Museus: cat. 29; fig. 62
London, The Trustees of the British Museum: figs 23, 151, 152
London, Rafael Valls: fig. 145
London, The Board of Trustees of the Victoria and Albert Museum: cat. 8
Los Angeles County Museum of Art Conservation Center: fig. 77
Madrid, Galeria Caylus: cat. 18; fig. 83
Madrid, © Museo del Prado. All rights reserved: cats 3, 5, 9, 10, 12, 24, 35, 38, 49, 51, 53, 55, 56,
   60, 61, 68; figs 17, 29, 30, 36, 51, 54, 58, 76, 103, 121, 127, 129, 130, 132, 135, 141, 147, 154
Madrid, Fotografía cedida y autorizada por el Patrimonio Nacional: figs 32, 125
Madrid, Sotheby's: fig. 39
Mexico, Museo de San Carlos, INBA: fig. 69
Moscow, © Photo – Pushkin State Museum of Fine Arts: fig. 64
Munich, Bayerische Staatsgemäldesammlungen, Fotoarchiv: fig. 150
New York, Courtesy of the Hispanic Society of America: fig. 123
Paris, Galerie Gismondi. Photo Claude Germain: fig. 33
Paris, Musée du Louvre. © Photo R.M.N.: cat. 69; fig. 124
Riverdale-on-Hudson, Stanley Moss & Company, Inc.: fig. 75
Schloss Rohrau, Graf Harrach'sche Familiensammlung. Photos Ali Meyer: cats 33, 34
Santa Monica, Getty Center Photo Study Collection: fig. 111
Seville, Arenas Fotografía Artistica, S.C.: figs 10, 14, 15
Seville, Junta de Andalucia, Consejería de Cultura y Medio Ambiente. Photo Pedro Feria Fernandez:
   fig. 46
Washington, © 1994 Board of Trustees, National Gallery of Art, Washington, Samuel H. Kress
   Collection: cat. 13

Index